OFFENSE TO OTHERS

The MORAL LIMITS

VOLUME TWO

NEW YORK　OXFORD

of the CRIMINAL LAW

Offense to Others

JOEL FEINBERG

OXFORD UNIVERSITY PRESS ♕ 1985

Oxford University Press

Oxford   New York   Toronto
Delhi   Bombay   Calcutta   Madras   Karachi
Petaling Jaya   Singapore   Hong Kong   Tokyo
Nairobi   Dar es Salaam   Cape Town
Melbourne   Auckland

and associated companies in
Beirut   Berlin   Ibadan   Nicosia

Library of Congress Cataloging in Publication Data
Feinberg, Joel, 1926–
The moral limits of the criminal law.
Includes index.
Contents: v. 1. Harm to others—
v. 2. Offense to others. 1. Criminal law—Philosophy.
2. Criminal law—Moral and religious aspects. I. Title.
K5018.F44   1985   345h.001   83-13431
ISBN 0-19-503449-X   342.5001
ISBN 0-19-505215-3 (PPBK)

2   4   6   8   10   9   7   5   3   1
Printed in the United States of America

For Betty again

About the Longer Work

Offense to Others is the second volume in a four-volume work, *The Moral Limits of the Criminal Law*. The subsequent volumes will be published separately at short intervals, each with a brief synopsis of the earlier volumes. Volume one, *Harm to Others*, discusses the concept of harm, its relation to interests, wants, hurts, offenses, rights, and consent; hard cases for the application of the concept of harm, like "moral harm," "vicarious harm," and "posthumous harm"; the status of failures to prevent harm; and problems involved in assessing, comparing, and imputing harms. Volume three, *Harm to Self*, will discuss the problems of legal paternalism, the nature of personal autonomy, and the concept of voluntariness. Volume four, *Harmless Wrongdoing*, will discuss critically various positions often lumped indiscriminately under the heading "legal moralism," including the claims that criminal prohibitions can be justified by their role in preserving a way of life, enforcing true morality, preventing wrongful gain from exploitation even when it has no proper "victim," and elevating taste and perfecting character.

Synopsis of Volume One

The basic question of the longer work that volume one introduces is a deceptively simple one: What sorts of conduct may the state rightly make criminal? Philosophers have attempted to answer this question by proposing what I call "liberty-limiting principles" (or equivalently, "coercion-legitimizing principles") which state that a given type of consideration is always a morally relevant reason in support of penal legislation even if other reasons may in the circumstances outweigh it. Each volume of *The Moral Limits of the Criminal Law* corresponds to a leading liberty-limiting principle (but see the longer list, with definitions, of ten such principles at the end of this synopsis). The principle that the need to prevent harm to persons other than the actor is always a morally relevant reason in support of proposed state coercion I call *the harm to others principle* ("the harm principle" for short). At least in that vague formulation it is accepted as valid by nearly all writers. Controversy arises when we consider whether it is the *only* valid liberty-limiting principle, as John Stuart Mill declared.

Three other coercion-legitimizing principles, in particular, have won widespread support. It has been held (but not always by the same person) that it is always a good and relevant reason in support of penal legislation that (1) it is necessary to prevent hurt or offense (as opposed to injury or harm) to others (*the offense principle*); (2) it is necessary to prevent harm to the very person it prohibits from acting, as opposed to "others" (*legal paternalism*); (3) it is necessary to prevent inherently immoral conduct whether or not such conduct is harmful or offensive to anyone (*legal moralism*). I defined "liberalism" in respect to the subject matter of this book as the view that the harm and offense principles, duly clarified and qualified, between them exhaust the class of morally relevant reasons for criminal prohibitions. ("Extreme liberalism" rejects the offense principle too, holding that only the harm principle states an acceptable reason.) I then candidly expressed my own liberal predilections.

The liberal program of this work is twofold. Volumes one and two propose interpretations and qualifications of the liberal liberty-limiting principles that are necessary if those two principles are to warrant our endorsement (assuming from the start that they do warrant endorsement). Assuming that the harm and offense principles are correct, we ask, how must those principles be understood? What are we to mean by the key terms "harm" and "offense", and how are these vague principles to be applied to the complex problems that actually arise in legislatures? Volumes one and two attempt to define, interpret, qualify, and buttress liberalism in such ways that in the end we can say that the refined product is what liberalism must be to have its strongest claim to plausibility, and to do this without departing *drastically* from the traditional usage of the liberal label or from the motivating spirit of past liberal writers, notably John Stuart Mill. The second part of the liberal program, to which Volumes three and four are devoted, is to argue against the non-liberal principles (especially paternalism and moralism) that many writers claim must supplement the liberal principles in any adequate theory.

Volume one then proceeds to ask what is the sense of "harm" in the harm principle as we shall understand it in this work. I distinguish at the outset a non-normative sense of "harm" as setback to interest, and a normative sense of "harm" as a *wrong*, that is a violation of a person's rights. Examples are given of rare "non-harmful wrongs," that is wrongs that do not set back the wronged party's interests, and more common "non-wrongful harms," that is setbacks to interest, like those to which the "harmed party" consented, that do not violate his rights. Neither of these will count as "harms" in the sense of the harm principle. Rather, that sense will represent the overlap of the other two senses, and apply only to setbacks of interests that are also wrongs, and only to wrongs that are also setbacks to interests. Chapters 1 and 2 are devoted to problems about harm that stem from its character as a setback to interest, while Chapter 3 discusses in more detail the features of harmful acts that stem from their character as violations of rights.

Chapter 2 discusses hard cases for the application of the concept of harm: Does it make sense to speak of "moral harm," "vicarious harm," "posthumous harm," or "prenatal harm"? First, can we harm a person by making him a worse person than he was before? Plato insisted that "moral harm" *is* harm (and severe harm) even when it does not set back interests. But our analysis of harm denies Platonism. A person does not necessarily become "worse off" when he becomes "worse"; he is "morally harmed" only if he had an antecedent interest in having a good character. Second, can we harm one person by harming another? This question I answer in the affirmative. *A* causes "vicarious harm" to *B* when *B* has an interest in *C*'s welfare or in *C*'s character, and *A* then directly harms or corrupts *C*. Third, can a person be harmed by his own death or by events that occur after his death? These questions raise extremely subtle problems that defy brief summary. My conclusion, however, is that death can be a harm to the person who dies, in virtue of the interests he had ante-mortem that are totally and irrevocably defeated by his death. Posthumous harm too can occur, when a "surviving interest" of the deceased is thwarted after his death. The subject of a surviving interest, and of the harm or benefit that can accrue to it after a person's death, is the living person ante-mortem whose interest it was. Events after death do not retroactively produce effects at an earlier time (as this account may at first suggest), but their occurrence can lead us to revise our estimates of an earlier person's well-being, and correct the record before closing the book on his life.

As for prenatal harms, I argue that fetuses (even if they are not yet persons) can be harmed in the womb, but only on the assumption that they will eventually be born to suffer the harmful consequences of their prenatal injuries. People can also be harmed by wrongful actions that occurred before they were even conceived, when the wrongdoer deliberately or negligently initiated a causal sequence that he might have known would injure a real person months or years later. I even conceded that in certain unusual circumstances a person might be harmed by the act of being given birth when that was avoidable. I denied, however, that a person can be harmed by the very act of sexual congress that brings him into existence unless he is doomed thereby to be born in a handicapped condition so severe that he would be "better off dead." If a child was wrongfully conceived by parents who knew or ought to have known that he would be born in a handicapped condition less severe than *that*, then he cannot later complain that he was wronged, for the only alternative to the wrongful conception was for him never to have come into existence at all, and he would not have preferred that. If parents are to be legally punished for wrongfully bringing other persons into existence in an initially handicapped condition, but one that is preferable to nonexistence, it will have to be under the principle of legal moralism. The harm principle won't stretch that far.

Another difficult analytic question, discussed in Chapter 4, is whether the harm principle will stretch to cover blamable failures to prevent harm. I consider the standard arguments in the common law tradition against so-called "bad samaritan statutes" that require persons to undertake "easy rescues" under threat of legal punishment for failure to do so. I reject all of these arguments on the grounds either that they systematically confuse active aid with gratuitous benefit, or that they take far too seriously the problem of drawing a non-arbitrary line between reasonably easy and unreasonably difficult rescues. (Similar line-drawing problems exist throughout the law, and most have been found manageable.) I conclude then that requiring people to help prevent harms is sometimes as reasonable a legal policy as preventing people, by threat of punishment, from actively causing harms. The more difficult question is whether this conclusion marks a departure from the harm principle as previously defined. I argued that it does not, partly on the ground that omissions, under some circumstances, can themselves be the cause of harms. To defend *that* contention, I must rebut powerful arguments on the other side, and in the final section of Chapter 4 I attempt to do so.

The final two chapters (5 and 6) of Volume one attempt to formulate "mediating maxims" to guide the legislature in applying the harm principle to certain especially complicated kinds of factual situations. Its formulation, up to that point, is so vague that without further guidance there may be no way in principle to determine how it applies to merely minor harms, moderately probable harms, harms to some interests preventable only at the cost of harms to other interests irreconcilable with them, structured competitive harms, imitative harms, aggregative harms, accumulative harms, and so on. I argue for various supplementary criteria to govern the application of the harm principle to these difficult problems, thus giving its bare bones some normative flesh and blood. These supplementary guides take a variety of forms. Some are themselves independent moral principles or rules of fairness. Others apply rules of probability or risk assessment. Others are common-sense maxims such as the legal *de minimis* rule for minor harms. Others distinguish dimensions of interests to be used in comparing the relative "importance" of conflicting harms in interest-balancing, or for putting the "interest in liberty" itself on the scales. Others are practical rules of institutional regulation to avoid the extremes of blanket permission and blanket prohibition in the case of aggregative and accumulative harms. As a consequence of these and other mediating maxims, the harm principle begins to lose its character as a merely vacuous ideal, but it also loses all semblance of factual simplicity and normative neutrality.

Definitions of Liberty-limiting Principles

1. *The Harm Principle:* It is always a good reason in support of penal legislation that it would probably be effective in preventing (eliminating, reducing) harm to persons other than the actor (the one prohibited from acting) *and* there is probably no other means that is equally effective at no greater cost to other values.*

2. *The Offense Principle:* It is always a good reason in support of a proposed criminal prohibition that it is probably necessary to prevent serious offense to persons other than the actor and would probably be an effective means to that end if enacted.†

3. *The Liberal Position* (on the moral limits of the criminal law): The harm and offense principles, duly clarified and qualified, between them exhaust the class of good reasons for criminal prohibitions. ("The extreme liberal position" is that only the harm principle states a good reason . . .)

4. *Legal Paternalism* (a view excluded by the liberal position): It is always a good reason in support of a prohibition that it is probably necessary to prevent harm (physical, psychological, or economic) to the actor himself.

5. *Legal Moralism* (in the usual narrow sense): It can be morally legitimate to prohibit conduct on the ground that it is inherently immoral, even though it causes neither harm nor offense to the actor or to others.

6. *Moralistic Legal Paternalism* (where paternalism and moralism overlap *via* the dubious notion of a "moral harm"): It is always a good reason in support of a proposed prohibition that it is probably necessary to prevent *moral harm* (as opposed to physical, psychological, or economic harm) to the actor himself. (Moral harm is "harm to one's character," "becoming a worse person," as opposed to harm to one's body, psyche, or purse.)

7. *Legal Moralism* (in the broad sense): It can be morally legitimate for the state to prohibit certain types of action that cause neither harm nor offense to anyone, on the grounds that such actions constitute or cause evils of other ("free-floating") kinds.

---

*The clause following "and" is abbreviated in the subsequent definitions as "it is probably necessary for . . . ," or "the need to . . ." Note also that part of a conjunctive reason ("effective *and* necessary") is itself a "reason," that is, itself has some relevance in support of the legislation.

†The clause following "and" goes without saying in the subsequent definitions, but it is understood. All of the definitions have a common form: X is probably necessary to achieve Y (as spelled out in definition 1) and is probably an effective means for producing Y (as stated explicitly in definitions 1 and 2).

8. *The Benefit-to-Others Principle:* It is always a morally relevant reason in support of a proposed prohibition that it is probably necessary for the production of some *benefit* for persons other than the person who is prohibited.

9. *Benefit-Conferring Legal Paternalism:* It is always a morally relevant reason in support of a criminal prohibition that it is probably necessary to *benefit* the very person who is prohibited.

10. *Perfectionism* (Moral Benefit Theories): It is always a good reason in support of a proposed prohibition that it is probably necessary for the improvement (elevation, perfection) of the character—
    a. of citizens generally, or certain citizens other than the person whose liberty is limited (*The Moralistic Benefit-to-Others Principle*), *or*
    b. of the very person whose liberty is limited (*Moralistic Benefit-Conferring Legal Paternalism*).

Principles 8, 9, and 10b are the strong analogues of the harm principle, legal paternalism, and moralistic legal paternalism, respectively, that result when "production of benefit" is substituted for "prevention of harm."

Acknowledgments

Various parts of this volume, from small passages to the major sections of whole chapters, have already been published in independent articles. I am grateful to their publishers for permission to republish these materials here. Several paragraphs in Chapters 7 and 8 originally appeared in my "Reply" (to Michael Bayles) in *Issues in Law and Morality*, edited by Norman S. Care and Thomas K. Trelogan (Cleveland: Case Western Reserve University Press, 1973), pp. 111–26. Most of sections 5 and 6 of Chapter 9 was first published in my "Sentiment and Sentimentality in Practical Ethics," in *Proceedings and Addresses of the American Philosophical Association*, vol. 56, no. 1 (September, 1982). An earlier version of Chapter 10 was given as the Lindley Lecture at the University of Kansas in 1979. It was published by the University of Kansas Department of Philosophy in 1980, as "The Idea of the Obscene." Chapter 11, §§1–6, was published as "Obscenity, Pornography, and the Arts: Sorting Things Out," in *Contemporary Value Conflicts*, edited by Burton M. Leiser (New York: Macmillan, 1981), pp. 237–54. The bulk of Chapter 12 was published in an article entitled "Pornography and the Criminal Law," in *The University of Pittsburgh Law Review*, vol. 40 (1979). Chapter 16 appeared under the title "Obscene Words and the Law" in *Philosophy and Law*, vol. 2 (1983).

Contents

OFFENSE TO OTHERS

7

Offensive Nuisances

1. Disclaimers: the relative triviality of mere offense

Passing annoyance, disappointment, disgust, embarrassment, and various other disliked conditions such as fear, anxiety, and minor ("harmless") aches and pains, are not in themselves necessarily harmful. Consequently, no matter how the harm principle is mediated, it will not certify as legitimate those interferences with the liberty of some citizens that are made for the sole purpose of preventing such unpleasant states in others. For convenience I will use the word "offense" to cover the whole miscellany of universally disliked mental states (see Vol. I, Chap. 1, §4) and not merely that species of the wider genus that are offensive in a strict and proper sense. If the law is justified, then, in using its coercive methods to protect people from mere offense, it must be by virtue of a separate and distinct legitimizing principle, which we can label "the offense principle" and formulate as follows: *It is always a good reason in support of a proposed criminal prohibition that it would probably be an effective way of preventing serious offense (as opposed to injury or harm) to persons other than the actor, and that it is probably a necessary means to that end* (i.e., there is probably no other means that is equally effective at no greater cost to other values). The principle asserts, in effect, that the prevention of offensive conduct *is* properly the state's business.

Like the word "harm", the word "offense" has both a general and a specifically normative sense, the former including in its reference any or all of a miscellany of disliked mental states (disgust, shame, hurt, anxiety, etc.), and the latter referring to those states only when caused by the wrongful (right-violating) conduct of others. Only the latter sense—wrongful offense—is intended in the offense principle as we shall understand it. In this respect there is a parallel with the harm principle. We can also use the verb "to offend" meaning "to cause another to experience a mental state of a universally disliked kind (e.g., disgust, shame). The offense principle then cites the need to prevent some people from *wrongfully offending* (offending and wronging) others as a reason for coercive legislation. Finally, the word "offense" in the strict and proper sense it bears in ordinary language is specific in a different way. Whereas "offense" in the sense of the offense principle specifies an objective condition—the unpleasant mental state must be caused by conduct that really is wrongful—"offense" in the strict sense of ordinary language specifies a subjective condition—the offending act must be taken by the offended person to wrong him whether in fact it does or not. In the strict and narrow sense, I am offended (or "take offense") when (a) I suffer a disliked state, and (b) I attribute that state to the wrongful conduct of another, and (c) I *resent* the other for his role in causing me to be in the state. The sense of grievance against the other or resentment of him for wronging me in this way is a phenomenological component of the unpleasant experience itself, an element that actually reenforces and magnifies its unpleasantness. If I am disgusted by the sight of a hospital patient's bloody wounds, the experience is one of that miscellany of disliked states I call "offended states of mind in the broad sense," but I can hardly resent the poor fellow for his innocent role in causing me to suffer that state of mind, and indeed there may be nobody to resent, in which case I do not "take offense," which is to say I am not offended in the strict and narrow sense.

The offense principle requires that the disliked state of mind (offense in the broad sense) be produced wrongfully by another party, but not that it be an offense in the strict sense of ordinary language. The victim may not know, or may not care, that another has wrongfully caused his unease, and therefore his unpleasant state of mind will not contain the element of resentment, and thus will not be offense in the strict sense. The offense principle as we shall interpret it then applies to offended states in either the broad or the strict sense—that is either with or without resentment—when these states are in fact wrongfully produced in violation of the offended party's rights. It is necessary that there *be* a wrong, but not that the victim *feel* wronged. And there will always be a wrong whenever an offended state (in the generic sense) is produced in another without justification or excuse.

Since I shall be defending a highly restricted version of the offense principle in this chapter, I should begin with some important disclaimers. To begin with, *offense is surely a less serious thing than harm*. That comparative value judgment seems to me self-evident, yet not simply true by definition. It is possible to deny it without contradiction if only because offense is not strictly commensurable with harm. It is a misconception to think of offenses as occupying the lower part of the same scale as harms; rather offenses are a different sort of thing altogether, with a scale all of their own. Yet most people after reflection will probably acknowledge that a person is not treated as badly, other things being equal, when he is merely offended as when he is harmed. We may (at most) be inclined to rank extreme offenses as greater wrongs to their victims than trifling harms, but perhaps that is because they may become so offensive as to be actually harmful, in a minor sort of way. (At any rate the comparison of extreme offense with minor harm is the only place controversy could reasonably arise over the relative seriousness of offenses and harms.) Continued extreme offense, as we have seen (Vol. I, Chap. 1, §4), can *cause* harm to a person who becomes emotionally upset over the offense, to the neglect of his real interests. But the offended mental state in itself is not a condition of harm. From the moral point of view, considered in its own nature (apart from possible causal linkages to harmful consequences), it is a relatively trivial thing.

It follows from this evident but unprovable truth that the law should not treat offenses as if they were as serious, by and large, as harms. It should not, for example, attempt to control offensiveness by the criminal law when other modes of regulation can do the job as efficiently and economically. For the control of uncommon and transitory forms of offensiveness, for example, reliance can be placed on individual suits for injunctions, or by court orders initiated by police to cease and desist on pain of penalty, or by licensing procedures that depend on administrative suspension of license as a sanction. These alternatives would not entirely dispense with the need for punishment (which is almost always a disproportionately greater evil to the offender than offended mental states are to his "victims"), but punishment would be reserved as a back-up threat, not inflicted for offending others so much as for defying authority by persisting in prohibited conduct (see Vol. I, Introduction, §7). It may well be that the ordinary criminal law need not concern itself at all with defining crimes of offensiveness, even though offensiveness is the sort of evil it could in principle be used legitimately to combat. It is more likely, however, that for various practical reasons, reliance on injunctions, administrative orders, and license withdrawals would be insufficient to control *all* properly prohibitable offensive conduct. In some cases, we can know very well in advance that conduct of a certain kind will offend; that is, we don't have to wait for the particular circumstances to decide the question. Moreover, in some cases there will not be time to get an injunction or administrative hearing. By the time that sort of relief is forthcoming, the annoyance has come and gone, and the offense, such as it is, already committed.

Even if there must be defined crimes with specified penalties for purely offensive conduct, however, the penalties should be light ones: more often fines than imprisonment, but when imprisonment, it should be measured in days rather than months or years. Where crimes are divided into the categories of misdemeanor and felony, purely offensive crimes should always be misdemeanors, never felonies. Where penal codes follow the American Law Institute model[1] in dividing offenses into felonies, misdemeanors, petty misdemeanors, and "violations,"[2] harmlessly offensive conduct at its worst should be a petty misdemeanor, but typically only a violation—a status it would share with traffic and parking violations, various illegal sales, and unintentional violations of health or safety codes. When a given crime is both harmful and offensive the punishment can properly be severe, but legislators and judges should make it clear that the severity of the punishment is primarily a function of the harmfulness (or dangerousness) of the criminal act, not a reaction to its offensiveness. The state should punish a very harmful or dangerous but only routinely offensive crime much more severely than a crime that is greatly offensive but harmful or dangerous only to a minor degree.

These strictures would seem too obvious to mention were it not for the fact that they have been traditionally flouted by legislatures. Indeed, it hardly overstates the case to say that until very recently, at least, legislatures have tended to go haywire and treat offensiveness as *more* serious than harm![3] In 1961, Herbert Wechsler[4] made a survey of state penal codes and reported, among other things, that the New York Penal Law provided a maximum sentence of ten years for first degree assault and twenty years for sodomy; that Pennsylvania's Penal Code specified a maximum of seven years' imprisonment for assault with intent to kill, but ten years for pandering; that California provided a maximum of two years for corporal injury to wife or child but fifteen years for "perversion." Mayhem and assault with intent to commit a serious felony got fourteen and twenty years respectively in California, but statutory rape and incest got fifty years each. (Is incest two and half times as great an evil as mayhem?) From colonial times until 1869 North Carolina, following English precedents, punished "the unmentionable crime against nature," even when perpetrated with a willing partner, by the death penalty,[5] a punishment much more severe than that for aggravated battery or grand larceny. But Zechariah Chafee gives the best example I know of perverse judicial zeal to avenge mere offense: "The white slave traffic was first exposed by W.T. Stead in a magazine article, 'The Maiden Tribute'. The English law did absolutely nothing to the profiteers in vice, but put Stead in prison for a year for writing about an indecent subject."⁶[!]

Because of legislators' tendency to overreact to offensiveness we should approach the subject with the greatest caution. Any legislator who votes to punish open lewdness or disrespect to the flag with prison terms *far* greater than those provided for genuinely and deliberately harmful acts of battery or burglary must be simply registering his hatred, revulsion, or personal anxiety rather than rationally applying some legislative principle to the facts. No one in his right mind could claim that lewd indecencies or even privately performed sexual deviations that are shocking merely to think about are some sort of menace to individual or collective interests, a threat from which we all urgently need protection at any cost to the offenders. Offensive behavior as such is no kind of menace, but at its worst only severely irritating nuisance.

2. The model of nuisance law

There are "mere nuisances," however, with which the law in England and America has long been engaged, a concern which has not hitherto disturbed libertarian reformers. The word "nuisance," which is derived from the French *nuisance*, was sometimes spelled "*anoysance*" in early legal English,⁷ which shows its early connection with the idea of annoyance, irritation, or inconvenience. Extreme nuisances can actually reach the threshold of harm, as when building noises in the house next door prevent a student from studying at all on the evening before an examination, or when an obstructed road causes a person to be late for an important appointment. But we are not very happy with nuisances even when they do not cause harm to our interests, but only irritations to our senses or inconvenient detours from our normal course. The offending conduct produces unpleasant or uncomfortable experiences—affronts to sense or sensibility, disgust, shock, shame, embarrassment, annoyance, boredom, anger, fear, or humiliation—from which one cannot escape without unreasonable inconvenience or even harm. We demand protection from nuisances when we think of ourselves as *trapped* by them, and we think it unfair that we should pay the cost in inconvenience that is required to escape them.

In the Anglo-American Law the term "nuisance" refers to two quite different sorts of wrongs: a miscellany of minor criminal offenses bearing the label "public nuisance" or "common nuisance," and a tort called "private nuisance" which consists in an interference with a landowner's use or enjoyment of his land. Private nuisances inconvenience specific individuals in the possession of their land, whereas public nuisances inconvenience

random assortments of people ("the public") in the exercise of rights common to all citizens. Thus, a landowner can sue his neighbor for private
nuisance when the latter keeps a howling dog (irritating others) or a malarial
pond (alarming others), whereas an intentional or negligent wrongdoer can
be convicted of "public nuisance" in a criminal court for unreasonably
obstructing a public highway, (inconveniencing others), letting odors from
his fertilizer plant escape over half the town (discomfiting others), keeping
diseased animals (threatening others), storing explosives (alarming others),
holding indecent public exhibitions (shocking others), conducting cock
fights or dog fights (offending the sensibilities of others), or causing large
noisy crowds to gather (disquieting others). Public and private nuisances, of
course, have different kinds of legal remedies. Moreover, they have little in
common, according to Prosser, except that "each causes inconveniences to
someone."[8] But that common element is sufficient to justify both the law's
traditional concern, and our own present theoretical interest.

The most interesting aspect of the law of nuisance is its own version of
the unavoidable legal balancing act. Both legislators formulating statutes
that define public nuisances and courts adjudicating conflicts between
neighboring landowners must weigh opposing considerations. We have already seen (Vol. I, Chap. 5, §6) how interest-balancing is required in cases
of those conflicts that make some harms unavoidable. Similar considerations
apply in the law of nuisance when private and public interests of diverse
sorts must be weighed against one another and against such non-interests as
inconveniences, annoyances, and "offended mental states." The law of nuisance, in its full complexity, provides a model for the legislative application
of an offense principle to the tangled problems of urban civilization. In the
case of private nuisances, things may seem somewhat simpler than in criminal nuisance, since there are only two parties whose convenience and interests are directly involved, namely, the inconvenienced or offended plaintiff
and the defendant whose conduct occasioned the suit, but even in this case
public interests are indirectly involved, and the balancing tests are no easier
to apply than in the criminal analogue. Balancing tests are at the very heart
of judicial deliberations in tort cases, as they often are in legislative deliberations over the wording of criminal statutes. One influential legal manual
explains why that is so:

> Practically all human activities, unless carried on in a wilderness, interfere to
> some extent with others or involve some risk of interference, and these interfer-
> ences range from mere trifling annoyances to serious harms. It is an obvious
> truth that each individual in a community must put up with a certain amount
> of risk in order that all may get on together. The very existence of organized
> society depends upon the principle of give and take, live and let live, and

therefore the law of torts does not attempt to impose liability or shift the loss in every case where one person's conduct has some detrimental effect on another. Liability is imposed only in those cases where the harm and risk [or inconvenience or offense] to one is greater than he ought to be required to bear under the circumstances, at least without compensation.[9]

Establishing that one person's conduct is a nuisance to someone else, then, is not yet sufficient to warrant legal interference. We must first compare carefully the magnitude of the nuisance to the one against the reasonableness of the conduct of the other, and the necessity "that all may get on together."

In his philosophically rewarding text on the law of torts,[10] William L. Prosser shows us how complicated the comparison of plaintiff and defendant can be, and how, inevitably, consideration of public interests must enter into the measurements. Describing the various factors that weigh on each side of the scale, Prosser tells us that the magnitude of the nuisance (or "seriousness of the inconvenience") to the plaintiff in a private nuisance action depends upon (1) the extent, duration, and character of the interference, (2) the social value of the use the plaintiff makes of his land, and (3) the extent to which the plaintiff can, without undue burden or hardship, avoid the offense by taking precautions against it.[11] These three factors yield the weight to be assigned to the seriousness of the inconvenience. They must be weighed against the reasonableness of the defendant's conduct, which is determined by (1) "the social value of its ultimate purpose, (2) the motive of the defendant [in particular its character as innocent or spiteful], and (3) whether the defendant by taking reasonable steps can avoid or reduce the inconvenience to the plaintiff without undue burden or inconvenience to himself."[12] Finally Prosser would have us throw on to the scale the interests of the "public at large," in particular its interest in "the nature of the locality" where the nuisance occurred—to "what particular use it is already devoted"—and given that background, "the suitability of the use made of the land by both plaintiff and defendant."[13]

On both sides of the comparison then, a variety of factors must be considered.

1. *The seriousness of the inconvenience* depends on
   a. *The extent, duration, and character of the interference.* "The law does not concern itself with trifles," Prosser writes, "or seek to remedy all the petty annoyances and disturbances or everyday life . . . Thus it has been held that there is no nuisance arising from the mere unsightliness of the defendant's premises . . . or from the temporary muddying of a well, or from an occasional unpleasant odor or whiff of smoke."[14] Constant and unrelieved stench or smoke, on the other

hand, and a residence reeking of offal and overrun with vermin, would be "substantial interferences" with a neighbor's enjoyment of his land, and hence genuine nuisances. The law of nuisance treats special susceptibility to annoyance in the same way that the law in general treats abnormal vulnerability to harm (see Vol I, Chap. 5, § 3.) Hence, "so long as the interference is substantial and unreasonable, and such as would be offensive or inconvenient to the normal person, virtually any disturbance of the enjoyment of the property may amount to a nuisance."[15]

b. *The social value of the use the plaintiff makes of his land.* Some balance must be struck by the courts, other things being equal, between the uses to which the plaintiff and the defendant put their property when the uses are incompatible. If the plaintiff's "use" during the night hours is to sleep, and the defendant's is to enjoy large and raucous parties, then even though both have claims based on their property rights to those uses, the incompatibility of the uses may compel the court to declare the plaintiff's employment of greater "value". The court's judgment might be different, however, if the plaintiff's "use" were to throw raucous parties, and the defendant's to operate a blast furnace, or a hospital frequently subject to emergency nocturnal visits by ambulances with noisy sirens.

c. *The extent to which the plaintiff can, without undue burden or hardship, avoid the offense by taking precautions against it.* The plaintiff cannot plausibly complain, for example, that occasional smoke from his neighbor's land has entered his own home, when he has neglected to close the windows through which the smoke enters.

2. *The reasonableness of the defendant's conduct* depends on

a. *The social value of its ultimate purpose.* "The world must have factories, smelters, oil refineries, noisy machinery, and blasting, even at the expense of some inconvenience to those in the vicinity, and the plaintiff may be required to accept and tolerate some not unreasonable discomfort for the general good . . . On the other hand, a foul pond, or a vicious or noisy dog will have little if any social value, and relatively slight annoyance from it may justify relief."[16]

b. *The motive of the defendant*, in particular its character as innocent or spiteful: ". . . where the defendant acts out of pure malice or spite, as by erecting a fence for the sole purpose of shutting off the plaintiff's view . . . or leaving the kitchen door open in order to give the plaintiff the benefit of the aroma of cooking onions,[17] his conduct is indefensible from the social point of view, and he is liable for the nuisance."[18]

c. *Whether the defendant, by taking reasonable steps, can avoid or reduce the inconvenience to the plaintiff without undue burden or inconvenience to himself.* This is the counterpart on the defendant's side of the scales of factor 3 in the plaintiff's list. A socially useful factory may be forgiven for emitting moderate amounts of smoke when emission control equipment would cost the owner hundreds of thousands of dollars, but not when the emissions are substantial and unpleasant to others, and can be prevented by minor inexpensive adjustments.

3. *The interest of the community or the public at large* includes not only the social utility of the defendant's conduct and the interest in supporting the resale of the plaintiff's property, but also, as "a decisive consideration in many cases",[19] the nature of the neighborhood, and the uses to which it has hitherto been devoted. Both for reasons of their physical characteristics and for accidental reasons, various localities have come to be devoted primarily to one specific sort of activity—commerce, industry, agriculture, or residence. Some of these activities are mutually incompatible so that uses of land come to be more or less segregated to prevent conflicts. Sometimes courts are called upon, in effect, "to determine the paramount use to which a locality is [already] devoted."[20] Thus a householder who takes up residence in a manufacturing district cannot complain, as a plaintiff in a private nuisance suit, of the noise, dust, or vibration. On the other hand, the very same amount of noise, dust, or vibration, caused by a factory located in a primarily residential district, will be declared a nuisance to the landowners in its vicinity.

Social philosophers very rarely argue about the role of law in the control of noise, dust, smoke, barking dogs, obstructed roads, and the like. They prefer instead to enter the ancient controversies about the role of law in the control of shocking or unsettling indecencies, obscene utterances, pornography, blasphemy, nudity, and similar affronts to sensibilities. But the offended and otherwise unpleasant states caused by these more interesting activities are objectionable for roughly the same kind of reason as the evils combatted by nuisance law. Even when they are not harms, they are annoying distractions, unwelcome demands on one's attention, a bother that must be coped with however inconvenient it may be at the time to do so. They are, in short, themselves nuisances in a perfectly ordinary sense. When they inconvenience home owners (or tenants) in their own residences, they are already covered by tort law, and can be remedied by civil suits for damages or injunctive relief. (In that way a householder can protect himself from regular indecent behavior on his neighbor's lawn or obscene signs or pornographic displays on the external walls of his neighbor's

house.) If they are to be the concern of the criminal law at all, it should be
only when they occur in open places and thereby inconvenience elements of
the general public, in the manner of "public" or "common" nuisances. In
neither case will the law be justified in interfering with the offending conduct on the sole ground that it *does* annoy or inconvenience someone or
other, for the consequences of such massive interference with liberty would
be chaotic and paralyzing. Instead, the offense principle will have to be
mediated by balancing tests similar to those already employed in the law of
nuisance.

3. A ride on the bus

There is a limit to the power of abstract reasoning to settle questions of
moral legitimacy. The question raised by this chapter is whether there are
any human experiences that are harmless in themselves yet so unpleasant
that we can rightly demand legal protection from them even at the cost of
other persons' liberties. The best way to deal with that question at the start
is to engage our imaginations in the inquiry, consider hypothetically the
most offensive experiences we can imagine, and then sort them into groups
in an effort to isolate the kernel of the offense in each category. Accordingly, this section will consist of a number of vividly sketched imaginary
tales, and the reader is asked to project himself into each story and determine as best he can what his reaction would be. In each story the reader
should think of himself as a passenger on a normally crowded public bus on
his way to work or to some important appointment in circumstances such
that if he is forced to leave the bus prematurely, he will not only have to
pay another fare to get where he is going, but he will probably be late, to
his own disadvantage. If he is not exactly a captive on the bus, then, he
would nevertheless be greatly inconvenienced if he had to leave the bus
before it reached his destination. In each story, another passenger, or group
of passengers, gets on the bus, and proceeds to cause, by their characteristics or their conduct, great offense to *you*. The stories form six clusters
corresponding to the kind of offense caused.

A. *Affronts to the senses*

    Story 1. A passenger who obviously hasn't bathed in more than a
    month sits down next to you. He reeks of a barely tolerable stench.
    There is hardly room to stand elsewhere on the bus and all other
    seats are occupied.

    Story 2. A passenger wearing a shirt of violently clashing orange and
    crimson sits down directly in your forward line of vision. You must
    keep your eyes down to avoid looking at him.

Story 3. A passenger sits down next to you, pulls a slate tablet from his brief case, and proceeds to scratch his fingernails loudly across the slate, sending a chill up your spine and making your teeth clench. You politely ask him to stop, but he refuses.

Story 4. A passenger elsewhere in the bus turns on a portable radio to maximum volume. The sounds it emits are mostly screeches, whistles, and static, but occasionally some electronically amplified rock and roll music blares through.

B. *Disgust and revulsion*

Story 5. This is much like story 1 except that the malodorous passenger in the neighboring seat continually scratches, drools, coughs, farts, and belches.

Story 6. A group of passengers enters the bus and shares a seating compartment with you. They spread a table cloth over their laps and proceed to eat a picnic lunch that consists of live insects, fish heads, and pickled sex organs of lamb, veal, and pork, smothered in garlic and onions. Their table manners leave almost everything to be desired.

Story 7. Things get worse and worse. The itinerant picnickers practice gluttony in the ancient Roman manner, gorging until satiation and then vomiting on to their table cloth. Their practice, however, is a novel departure from the ancient custom in that they eat their own and one another's vomit along with the remaining food.

Story 8. A coprophagic sequel to story 7.

Story 9. At some point during the trip the passenger at one's side quite openly and nonchalantly changes her sanitary napkin and drops the old one into the aisle.

C. *Shock to moral, religious, or patriotic sensibilities*

Story 10. A group of mourners carrying a coffin enter the bus and share a seating compartment with you. Although they are all dressed in black their demeanor is by no means funereal. In fact they seem more angry than sorrowful, and refer to the deceased as "the old bastard," and "the bloody corpse." At one point they rip open the coffin with hammers and proceed to smash the corpse's face with a series of hard hammer blows.

Story 11. A strapping youth enters the bus and takes a seat directly in your line of vision. He is wearing a T-shirt with a cartoon across his chest of Christ on the cross. Underneath the picture appear the words "Hang in there, baby!"

Story 12. After taking the seat next to you a passenger produces a bundle wrapped in a large American flag. The bundle contains, among other things, his lunch, which he proceeds to eat. Then he spits into the star-spangled corner of the flag and uses it first to clean his mouth and then to blow his nose. Then he uses the main striped part of the flag to shine his shoes.

D. *Shame, embarrassment (including vicarious embarrassment), and anxiety*

Story 13. The passenger who takes the seat directly across from you is entirely naked. On one version of the story, he or she is the same sex as you; on the other version of the story, he or she is the opposite sex.

Story 14. The passenger in the previous story proceeds to masturbate quietly in his or her seat.

Story 15. A man and woman, more or less fully clothed to start, take two seats directly in front of you, and then begin to kiss, hug, pet, and fondle one another to the accompaniment of loud sighs and groans of pleasure. They continue these activities throughout the trip.

Story 16. The couple of the previous story, shortly before the bus reaches their destination, engage in acts of mutual masturbation, with quite audible instructions to each other and other sound effects.

Story 17. A variant of the previous story which climaxes in an act of coitus, somewhat acrobatically performed as required by the crowded circumstances.

Story 18. The seat directly in front of you is occupied by a youth (of either sex) wearing a T-shirt with a lurid picture of a copulating couple across his or her chest.

Story 19. A variant of the previous story in which the couple depicted is recognizable (in virtue of conventional representations) as Jesus and Mary.

Story 20. The couple in stories 15–17 perform a variety of sadomasochistic sex acts with appropriate verbal communications ("Oh, that hurts so sweet! Hit me again! Scratch me! Publicly humiliate me!").

Story 21. The two seats in front of you are occupied by male homosexuals. They flirt and tease at first, then kiss and hug, and finally perform mutual fellatio to climax.

Story 22. This time the homosexuals are both female and they perform cunnilingus.

Story 23. A passenger with a dog takes an aisle seat at your side. He or she keeps the dog calm at first by petting it in a familiar and normal way, but then petting gives way to hugging, and gradually goes beyond the merely affectionate to the unmistakably erotic, culminating finally with oral contact with the canine genitals.

E. *Annoyance, boredom, frustration*

Story 24. A neighboring passenger keeps a portable radio at a reasonably low volume, and the sounds it emits are by no means offensive to the senses. Nor is the content of the program offensive to the sensibilities. It is, however, a low quality "talk show" which you find intensely boring, and there is no possible way for you to disengage your attention.

Story 25. The two seats to your left are occupied by two persons who put on a boring "talk show" of their own. There is no way you can avoid hearing every animated word of their inane conversation, no way your mind can roam to its own thoughts, problems, and reveries.

Story 26. The passenger at your side is a friendly bloke, garrulous and officious. You quickly tire of his conversation and beg leave to read your newspaper, but he persists in his chatter despite repeated requests to desist. The bus is crowded and there are no other empty seats.

F. *Fear, resentment, humiliation, anger* (from empty threats, insults, mockery, flaunting, or taunting)

Story 27. A passenger seated next to you reaches into a military kit and pulls out a "hand grenade" (actually only a realistic toy), and fondles and juggles it throughout the trip to the accompaniment of menacing leers and snorts. Then he pulls out a (rubber) knife and "stabs" himself and others repeatedly to peals of maniacal laughter. He turns out to be harmless enough. His whole intent was to put others in apprehension of harm.

Story 28. A passenger sits next to you wearing a black arm band with a large white swastika on it.

Story 29. A passenger enters the bus straight from a dispersed street rally. He carries a banner with a large and abusive caricature of the Pope and an anti-Catholic slogan. (You are a loyal and pious Catholic.)

Story 30. Variants of the above. The banner displays a picture of a black according to some standard offensive stereotype (Step 'n Fetchit, Uncle Tom, etc.) with an insulting caption, or a picture of a sneering, sniveling, hook-nosed Fagin or Shylock, with a scurrilous anti-Jewish caption, or a similar offensive denunciation or lampooning of groups called "Spicks," "Dagos," "Polacks", etc.

Story 31. Still another variant. A counter-demonstrator leaves a feminist rally to enter the bus. He carries a banner with an offensive caricature of a female and the message, in large red letters: "Keep the bitches barefoot and pregnant."

4. The modes and meaning of "offense"

I have tried to make a number of different points by telling these bloodcur-
dling tales: that there are at least six distinguishable classes of offended
states that can be caused by the blamable conduct of others; that to suffer
such experiences, at least in their extreme forms, is an evil; but that to the
normal person (like the reader) such experiences, unpleasant as they are, do
not cause or constitute harm. It is very important that the reader put
himself on the bus and imagine his own reactions, for no amount of abstract
argument can convince him otherwise that the represented experiences are
in principle of a kind that the state can legitimately make its business to
prevent.

When I imagine myself on the bus in these various stories, I find that one
of the least unsettling experiences is that of the otherwise well-behaved
nude passenger (story 13). Needless to say, I have never seen a nude person
on a public bus, so I cannot be certain what my reaction would be. But I
know that the sight of a nude body as such never did a normal person any
harm, and as for the "unsettling experience" itself, one might escape it, I
suppose, by turning one's eyes elsewhere, or escaping into one's private
reveries. For all that, however, I suspect that I would be made at least
vaguely ill at ease by the nude body (for reasons that urgently require
examination—see below, pp. 17ff.), and perhaps less stable persons in such
a situation would be thrown into the kind of inner turmoil to which even
the reader and I would be subject in most of the other situations.

The examples of "affronts to the senses" are all cases where the gratingly
unpleasant experience derives entirely from its sound, color, or odor, and
not at all from any symbolic representation, or recognized object. The shirt
in story 2 "offends the eye" not because it is recognized as a shirt or because
it symbolically asserts or suggests any proposition about shirts or any other
subject. It is the sensuous garb of the experience rather than any cognitively
mediated content that directly assails the eye, and that is the very feature
that distinguishes affronts to the *senses* from shock to the *sensibilities*. That
most of us are more disturbed emotionally by assaults on our sensibilities
than by direct affronts to our senses is a contingent fact about our psyches
and our common culture that could well have been other than it is without
violating any law of nature. Story 3 (fingernails scratching slate) is designed
to show, moreover, that affronts to senses can be so intensely unpleasant as
to be nearly unbearable, even when they do not involve the cognitive
faculties (and hence the sensibilities) in the offense. On the other hand, it is
likely that the offense in story 1 (a passenger's odor) is influenced to some
extent by one's awareness of its source as an unwashed human being, and

the revulsion attendant upon that recognition. Precisely the same odor, if it were recognized as one's own, for example, would not be quite an equal offense, presumably, in one's own nostrils. Indeed, the unpleasantness of smells (perhaps more than that of other senses) is very difficult to separate from associated beliefs and sensibilities. The smell of freshly baked macaroni and cheese smells very little different from that of much human vomit, yet the latter but not the former, when mediated by recognition, is offensive. A carton of rotten eggs, however, would smell no worse for being recognized as such, or as some particular person's property, and it may well be a transcultural truth that no one finds sulphurous oxide or the smell of skunk in high concentration very pleasant. These examples suggest that some affronts to the olfactory sense may be less dependent on cognition than others.

Another fact suggested by the stories in group A is that offensive sounds and smells can reach much greater extremes of intensity than directly offensive shapes and colors. Quite apart from the point that visual affronts are more easily avoided (we can shut our eyes more easily than our noses and ears), the visual sense seems less vulnerable to affront than the others, a purely neurological fact that has certain obvious implications for the legislator who employs an offense principle mediated by the kind of balancing tests used in the law of nuisance. Eyesores, so called, are for the most part not as great nuisances as noisome stenches and loud or grating sounds.

Disgust and revulsion, as illustrated by the stories in group B, differ from mere sensuous assaults in two important respects. In the first place, their impact on the offended person, while not *always* more intense, is less localized and more profound. Indeed, the etymology of the word "disgust" (from the Latin for "bad taste") suggests that the condition it designates is more likely to involve the digestive tract than the organs of perception. The first definition of the word in *Webster's New International Dictionary* (Third Edition, 1961) presumably captures something like its original sense: "marked aversion or repugnance toward food or toward a particular dish or kind of food . . ." In a second, more generalized definition, disgust is an extremely disagreeable emotional reaction "excited by exposure to something [anything] highly distasteful or loathesome," for example, the sight of a patient's festering wounds. Whatever the object of the disgust, the term is distinguished only in degree from its near synonyms "sicken" ("a disgust so strong that one is affected physically as by a turning of the stomach") and "nausea" ("stronger still, suggesting a loathesomeness that provokes vomiting"). To be acutely disgusted is to suffer as disagreeable a state of mind and body as is possible below the threshold of actual harm, since to be sickened or nauseated is, in most cases, to cross that threshold.

In the second place, disgust—unlike sensuous affront—is always mediated by recognition or belief. What turns the spectator's stomach when he sees the itinerent picnickers in stories 6–8 consume their unusual "food" is not the color, shape, touch, sound—not even the smell—of the objects of their appetite (although these may be independently offensive to the senses), but rather the recognition of those things as objects of a certain kind—live insects, slugs, sex organs, feces, vomit, etc. If the spectator mistakenly believed that the picnickers were eating eggplant, macaroni and cheese, and sweetbreads, he might still experience some aversion in the circumstances, but it would not amount to disgust or revulsion of the near-sickening kind. Disgust then is an offense not merely to sense but rather to *sensibility*, that susceptibility to offense from witnessing objects or events which, because of the observer's recognition of them as objects of a certain kind, are painful for him to behold.

The sensibilities offended in the stories of group B might be called "lower order sensibilities," and as such they can be contrasted with the moral, religious, and patriotic sensibilities in group C. We are disgusted at the sight of a person eating a dripping, wriggling, live sea slug, simply because we recognize it to be such, and given the character of our gastronomic sensibility, that recognition is quite sufficient to induce disgust. It is not necessary to the process that we hold a moral principle, or even a specific moral conviction, that eating sea slugs is cruel, sinful, or wicked. It is simply disgusting in some pre-rational, nondiscursive way, and that is an end to the matter. An additional step is involved in the production of disgust by offense to higher level sensibilities. When we see a strapping young man arrogantly push aside an aged lady in his haste to occupy the only remaining seat on the bus, we recognize the items in our experience as *young man*, *aged lady*, *push*, and *seat*, and that brings to mind a moral principle prescribing the proper conduct of persons of the type perceived. Then, in virtue of the perceived gross violation of that principle, we are disgusted. Similarly, the sight of a person wantonly desecrating a crucifix offends the religious sensibility not simply because the abused object is recognized as a wooden object in the shape of a cross, but because of the conventional symbolism of such shapes, and a whole complex of religious convictions, commitments, and emotions directed to the objects symbolized.[21]

The examples of indecorous sexual conduct in group D include some extreme deviations from prevailing standards of "normalcy" (stories 20–23), but they also include examples of perfectly ordinary and acceptable ways of deriving sexual pleasure when done in private (stories 14–17) and at least one commonplace state of being in which almost everyone in the world participates daily in private (story 13). Why should examples of the latter kinds be so upsetting? Why should conduct perfectly acceptable in itself become "indecent" when performed in public? These examples are not like the instances of disgusting eating in group B. Rather they would seem analogous to examples of "normal eating" in a public place, for example, munching peanuts or eating sandwiches, alone or with a friend, on a bus, activities which are not generally thought shameful, embarrassing, or indecent, but are at the very most, minor violations of etiquette.

Our culture, of course, is far more uptight about sexual pleasures than about "harmless" pleasures of any other kind, which is easy enough to understand given the danger in, and harmful consequences of, sexual behavior in the past—disease, personal exploitation, unwanted pregnancy, etc.—and the intricate association of sexual taboos with rules of property transfer, legitimacy, marriage, and the like. Perhaps our abundant anxieties and our susceptibilities to shock will all fade away in the future, as improved contraceptive techniques reduce dangers of disease and unwanted pregnancy, and candid treatments of sexual themes in public forums and private conversations become more common still. But that day, despite recent relaxations of attitudes, still seems far off.

The disquietude caused in captive observers by public nudity and sexual behavior is a complicated psychological phenomenon, difficult to explain not only because of wide individual differences, but also because so many psychic elements are involved, and combine in so many possible ways. To begin with, nude bodies and copulating couples, like all forms of nuisance, have the power of preempting the attention and absorbing the reluctant viewer, whatever his preferences in the matter. The presence of such things in one's field of perception commands one's notice; they are distractions that must be attended to and coped with whatever one might prefer to be doing or thinking. Moreover, the problem of coping, for many persons at least, is a bit of a difficult one, not insurmountable, but something of an unpleasant strain. Part, but only part, of the explanation of that displeasure, no doubt rests on the fact that nudity and sex acts have an irresistible power to draw the eye and focus the thoughts on matters that are normally repressed. Indeed, most of us spend an inordinate amount of time and energy, even without provocation, in sexual fantasies and the repression of lust. The unresolved conflict between instinctual desires and cultural taboos leaves many people in a state of unstable equilibrium and a readiness to be wholly fascinated, in an ambivalent sort of way, by any suggestion of sexuality in their perceptual fields. There is a temptation to see and savour all, and to permit oneself to become sexually stimulated, as by a pornographic film, but instantly the temptations of voyeurism trigger the familiar mechanism of inhibition and punishment in the form of feelings of shame.

The primary basis of one's "offended state" then is this tension between attracting and repressing forces, against a psychic background of total fascination, a combination which can be at once exciting, upsetting, and anxiety-producing. When the precipitating experience is not mere nudity, but actual sexual activity, even of a "normal" kind, it will create a kind of inner agitation at best, and at worst that experience of exposure to oneself of one's "peculiarly sensitive, intimate, vulnerable aspects" which is called *shame*.[22] When one has not been able to prepare one's defenses, "one's feeling is involuntarily exposed openly in one's face. . . . We are . . . caught unawares, made a fool of."[23] For some relatively unenlightened persons the result will be a severe psychic jolt; those of us who are better able to cope with our feelings might well resent the necessity to do so and regard it as an irritating distraction and a bore, much the same as any other nuisance.

Understandable doubt has been expressed by some writers over the contention that the public nudity or sexual behavior of others can produce something called "shameful embarrassment" in oneself. Michael Bayles has effectively entered a challenge to that way of describing matters:

> It is difficult to understand how the public nudity of others invades one's privacy or causes one embarrassment. Surely the privacy involved is the nude's, but one has not invaded it. For one to be ashamed of something, it must have a relation to oneself, be something for which one takes responsibility. One can be ashamed of the conduct of one's friends, for one may take vicarious responsibility for their conduct or consider oneself responsible for who one's friends are . . .[24]

Shame, in the relevant sense, is "a painful emotion caused by consciousness of guilt, shortcoming, or impropriety in one's own behavior or position, or in the behavior or position of a closely associated person or group."[25] It is, therefore, difficult to understand how the painful emotion felt by the captive observer of nudity or sex play on the bus could possibly be shame, for *he* is not the one who is behaving improperly or indecorously. If the nude passenger or lewd lovers were his fellow countrymen in a foreign country, his children, friends, or business partners, he might well feel ashamed of *them*, but in our hypothetical story, the offending persons are total strangers and the offended observer is in his own country.

Still, for all of that, it does seem natural to describe the offended reaction of the observer as "shame." After all, the unexpected apprehension of nudity or "indecency" can be expected to bring a blush to the face of the observer, which is a recognized symptom both of intense self-consciousness and "shame, modesty, or confusion."[26] How then could the reaction to another's misconduct be shameful embarrassment? There are at least two answers to this question. First, the "guilt, shortcoming, or impropriety of one's own" that is the object of the shame may well be the instantaneous reaction of one's own to the offending experience, a sudden loss of control, soon recovered, over impulses normally restrained by the firmest reins. One reacts in a certain way and then is immediately ashamed of that reaction. Second, one can feel shame or embarrassment vicariously in a way other than that which Bayles acknowledges. Bayles accounts for those cases where one person is ashamed of or *because of* another person with whom he is closely associated or for whom he is responsible. In those cases some of the other's shame "rubs off" on him, so to speak. But there are other cases in which the improper or inept actions of a total stranger can induce shame or embarrassment in an observer. In these cases, the observer, by a kind of sympathetic identification with the other party that comes naturally to sensitive and imaginative people, feels ashamed or embarrassed *for* the other party. In these cases the observer feels the shame he would feel were he in the other's place. In many cases, an observer's painful emotion is complex and contains elements of shame of both the personal and vicarious kinds.

And sometimes the offended mental state is still more complex. When the observer can perceive the whole embarrassing situation not only from his own vantage point, but also imaginatively from the point of view of the offenders, he comes to feel that whatever *they* may think about it, his own presence is a jarring foreign element in their privacy. His own witness then seems a part of their humiliation, and since they neither know nor care about their own public disgrace, their human dignity is further diminished in his eye, to his further distress. Still another quite independent element in the unwilling observer's painful emotion may be the feeling that he is threatened by what is happening, that either the unrestrained public performers or his own stirred up feelings may surge out of control. Thus one becomes anxiously apprehensive, and concerned lest unwilling revelations of one's own feeling discredit or embarrass one at any moment. Another element may be a response to the whole spectacle, performance *and* audience, not merely the performers themselves. What may seem obscene to the observer is not simply that the offenders are there nude or tumescent in his eye, but that they stand (or lie) revealed to many other eyes. (See Chap. 9, §5 on "obscene spectacles.") The obscenity consists not in the object of observation but in the fact that many people are looking and 'collectively' experiencing their own inadmissible feelings. The observer might thus feel embarrassed to be part of the spectacle perceived by the other members of the observing audience and also vicariously embarrassed on *their* behalf. And so, a final element steals into the complex mental state of the offended observer: a near total confusion and disarray of feeling.

The stories of abnormal sexual acts (numbers 20–23) provide examples of public behavior that would be even more disagreeable to witness. Two elements are present in the painful feelings induced in these stories that are rarely present to the same degree in mere nudity and ordinary sex: (1) The witnessed incidents are taken to be immediately and powerfully *threatening*, and (2) "lower-level sensibilities" are shocked so that a spontaneous *disgust* arises to mingle with the other painful elements in the experience. The point about threats is best illustrated by the example of male homosexuality. The general nervousness about this subject is even reflected in the way it is treated in the most iconoclastic pornographic films. The celebrated film *Emmanuelle*, for example, included numerous scenes of female homosexuality (not very graphically displayed) presumably because such scenes are thought to be especially titillating to the males who constitute the bulk of the audience for those films. But there was not so much as a suggestion of male homosexuality, a practice which many males loathe and execrate, and hold in considerable terror. Not only do homosexual acts violate powerful taboos in our culture; they also threaten the "ego ideals" of heterosexual men. Homosexuals are the objects of near universal contempt and ridicule, and their peculiar practice is held inconsistent with the ideals of genuine manhood. Hatred of homosexuality, therefore is a part of the psychic fortress many men build around their self-esteem. The point about disgust is best illustrated by the story about bestiality (number 23). Not even the story of the feces-and-vomit-eating picnickers in group B is more disgusting to most of us than that.

After considering such jolts to sensibility, it may seem altogether anticlimactic to turn to the offenses in group E, for the boredom of radio shows and dull conversation are of such a common type that we suffer from it to some degree almost every day of our lives. At their extremes, however, the mental states they induce can be almost as intensely disliked and difficult to tolerate as fingernails on a slate board or unavoidable witness to homosexual couplings. Boredom is sometimes conceived as mere listless aimlessness or ennui, the state of a solitary person who cannot think of anything to do. That condition is unhappy enough, but there is nothing acute or piercing about it, and it is not necessarily an "offense" directly caused by another person. When one is button-holed by a "cocktail party bore," or a "discussion-period bore," on the other hand, the displeasure can be so sharp and penetrating as to suggest the pointed revolving tool that "bores" holes in firmly held objects. The bore is persistent and undivertable; he *will* command your attention; there is no escape. The offended state he produces results from another kind of tense inner conflict: one is trying desperately to escape by thinking up stratagems, excuses, and diversions, but clear thinking is impossible in the face of the bore's peremptory demands on one's attention. Often there is no escape possible without unacceptable rudeness, so one resigns oneself in depressed and weary annoyance. At that point one is "crushed with irksome tediousness." The boring people on the bus are surely not that bad, however, if only because (stories 24 and 25) they do not attempt to exact responses from you, whereas in story 26, the officious talker can in the end be requested, without rudeness, to be quiet. But insofar as the boring passengers commandeer one's attention irresistibly, they are nuisances in the same manner, even if to a lesser degree, as their disgusting, shocking, embarrassing, and threatening counterparts in the other stories.

The group insults issued by passengers in the stories in group F, the contemptuous mockery, the deliberate baiting and taunting through the display of offensive signs and symbols, can be the most disturbing behavior of all in its effects on members of the insulted groups, and even on others to whom such conduct is odious. In these cases, as in the others, disagreeable emotions are aroused that have to be coped with, but it is distinctive of these cases that the emotion is the most difficult of all to handle, namely sudden violent anger, conjoined with anxious fear, and a feeling of humiliation and impugned "honor." Again, as soon as the emotion flares it is likely to be followed by a feeling of shame and worry over its presence and a desperate effort at repression. But the offending symbols are still there in one's visual field, still mocking and threatening, nagging and tugging at one's attention, like another kind of efficient boring tool. And attendant upon one's shame is a new anxiety: fear of making a fool of oneself by losing control. These conflicting elements pull a person in all directions and throw him into confusion. Despite the legal doctrine of "fighting words" which permits states to ban "personally abusive epithets . . . that are inherently likely to provoke violent reaction,"[27] it is unlikely that present laws would permit one who is personally insulted to accept what he takes to be a challenge and vent his anger in retaliatory aggression, any more than it would permit the sexually excited witness of nudity or indecency on the bus to force his lust on the provoking person. But again, having to cope with one's rage is as burdensome a bore as having to suffer shame, or disgust, or noisome stenches, something unpleasant to experience and inconvenient to accommodate, even when it causes one no harm. (See Chap. 9, §7.)

It should be clear at this point that despite the miscellaneous character of "offended states" they have some important characteristics in common. They are at the very least unpleasant to the one who suffers them, though the mode of displeasure varies from case to case. With the exception of irritations to the senses, and only some of these, they are complex states whose unpleasantness is in part a function of the tension between conflicting elements. And, most importantly from the legislative point of view, they are nuisances, making it difficult for one to enjoy one's work or leisure in a locality which one cannot reasonably be expected to leave in the circumstances. In extreme cases, the offending conduct commandeers one's attention from the outside, forcing one to relinquish control of one's inner state, and drop what one was doing in order to cope, when it is greatly inconvenient to do so.

5. The relation between offense and privacy

In what manner, if any, do the offensive people on the bus violate the privacy of their fellow passengers? The word "privacy" may seem clear enough in ordinary discourse, but its ever more frequent use in law courts and legislatures has caused increasing bewilderment and controversy. Privacy as a legal category came into American law less than a century ago. Its first appearance was in the law of torts, where it served to protect persons from misappropriation of their names or pictures for commercial purposes, and then was gradually extended to include protection of persons from embarrassing publicity, from being put in a false light by the public attribution of beliefs they do not hold, and most importantly, from unwarranted intrusion into their personal affairs by such means as wire tapping, electronic surveillance, shadowing, and peeping. The moral rights to be free of these various evils are certainly genuine ones, and the evils themselves, genuine evils. These rights, moreover, had not been adequately protected by the common law before the "right to privacy" was invented or discovered. But they have an irreducibly heterogeneous character summarizable in a unitary way only by such an imprecise phrase as "the right to be let alone."

Soon it became popular to designate still other legal protections under the same flexible rubric. The old privilege of confidentiality protecting certain special relationships is now considered a special case of privacy.[28] In torts, the right to privacy came to encompass not only the right not to be known about in certain ways by others, but also the right to avoid "seeing and hearing what others say,"[29] apparently on the ground that "it may be as distasteful to suffer the intrusions of a garrulous and unwelcome guest as to discover an eavesdropper or peeper."[30] In constitutional law, the Supreme Court has come to discover a miscellany of "penumbral rights" of privacy against governmental action that impose limits even on otherwise valid legislation, including a right to marital privacy which is violated by a state statute prohibiting the sale of contraceptives even to married couples.[31] (See *infra*, Vol. III, Chap. 19, §8.) The tendency to apply the one concept "privacy" to such a motley collection of rights has alarmed many commentators who fear that so plastic and expansive a concept will obfuscate legal analysis. "Given this disparity of central issues," wrote Paul Freund, "privacy becomes too greedy a legal concept."[32]

Many or most of the disparate legal uses of the idea of privacy, however, can be grouped in one or the other of two families of sense. Elizabeth Beardsley has put the distinction well: "Alleged violations [of privacy] seem to fall into two major categories: conduct by which one person A restricts the power of another person B to determine for himself whether or not he will perform an act X or undergo an experience E, and conduct by which one person A acquires or discloses information about B which A does not wish to have known or disclosed."[33] Beardsley labels the right to privacy violated in the former case, the right to *autonomy*, and that violated in the latter case, the right to *selective disclosure*. Window peeping, secret shadowing or photographing, wire tapping, publishing of intimate conversation, intercepted correspondence, candid photographs, and the like, all violate a person's privacy in the sense that they invade his right not to be observed or known about in certain ways without his consent. Nothing like that kind of wrong is committed by the offensive passengers on the bus against their fellow travelers, so we can put that notion of privacy aside. A typical violation of privacy in the sense of autonomy occurs when unwanted noises obtrude upon one's experience restricting one's power to determine for oneself "whether one will do X, or undergo E, or not." "Noise removes [one's] power to choose effectively between sound and silence, or between one sound and another, as features of [one's] immediate experience."[34] The offensive passengers clearly *do* violate their neighbors' privacy in this sense (autonomy) not only when they are noisy, but also when they are disgusting, shocking, embarrassing, boring, threatening, and enraging, for in each case, they deprive the unwilling spectators of the power to determine for themselves whether or not to undergo a certain experience. No passenger, moreover, would decide, if the choice were left to him, to undergo experiences of these offensively unpleasant kinds. Each must spend the whole bus trip coping with feelings induced in himself from the outside when he would much prefer, presumably, to be doing something else. In being made to experience and be occupied in certain ways by outsiders, and having had no choice in the matter whatever, the captive passengers suffer a violation of their autonomy (assuming that the "boundaries" of the autonomous realm do not shrink to the vanishing point when they enter the public world.)

We can agree with Beardsley that "selective disclosure" and "autonomy" are two different kinds of things commonly called "privacy," while insisting that they are not without a common element that explains why the word "privacy" is commonly applied to both. They are, in short, two species of the genus "privacy" rather than two distinct senses of the word "privacy." The root idea in the generic concept of privacy is that of a privileged territory or domain in which an individual person has the exclusive authority of determining whether another may enter, and if so, when and for how long, and under what conditions. (See Vol. III, Chap. 19, §§1 and 8.) Within this area, the individual person is—pick your metaphor—boss, sovereign, owner. The area includes not only the land and buildings he owns and occupies, but his special relationships with spouse, attorney, or priest, and his own mental states or "inner sanctum." His rightful control over his "inner property" is violated when another learns and/or reveals its secret contents without his consent, for he should be the one who decides what is to be known of them and by whom. His will alone reigns supreme over them. But his sovereignty or ownership is also violated when others obtrude their own sounds, and shapes, and affairs upon his "territory" without his consent, for within the privileged area, he has the sole right to determine what he is to experience, insofar as these matters are rightfully subject to his control.[35] When he is forced to experience loud or grating sensations, disgusting or enraging activities while on his privileged ground, something like a property right has been violated,[36] and violated in a manner similar to that of "private nuisance." The legislative problem of determining when offensive conduct is a public or criminal nuisance could with equal accuracy be expressed as a problem about determining the extent of personal privacy or autonomy. The former way of describing the matter (in terms of "nuisance") lends itself naturally to talk of *balancing* (the independent value or reasonableness of the offending conduct against the degree of seriousness of the offense caused) whereas the latter way (in terms of "privacy") lends itself naturally to talk of drawing *boundaries* between the various private domains of persons, and between the private domain of any given person and the public world. The metaphors are different; the actual modes of reasoning are the same.

8

Mediating the Offense Principle

1. On the scales: the seriousness of the offense

The case for the legitimacy of the criminal law's concern with "mere" offensiveness even in the absence of harm or danger, must in the end rest on the intuitive force of the examples given, most of which have been made as extreme as possible and depicted with uncompromising vividness. Offensiveness produces unpleasant experiences and causes annoying inconveniences, both of which are surely evils, though not as great evils as actual harms. Unlike certain other evils, however, offenses and harms are done to persons. They have determinate victims with genuine grievances and a right to complain against determinate wrongdoers about the way in which they have been treated. (Contrast the "free-floating evils" discussed in Vol. IV, Chap. 28.) Those facts, it seems to me, constitute as good reasons as one could expect to find for the legitimacy in principle of legal interference, even though in a given case, or even in all given cases, there are stronger countervailing reasons of a practical kind.

There are abundant reasons, however, for being extremely cautious in applying the offense principle. People take offense—perfectly genuine offense—at many socially useful or even necessary activities, from commercial advertisement to inane chatter. Moreover, bigoted prejudices of a very widespread kind (e.g., against interracial couples strolling hand in hand down the main street of a town in the deep South) can lead onlookers to be disgusted and shocked, even "morally" repelled, by perfectly innocent activities, and we should be loath to permit their groundless repugnance to outweigh the innocence of the offending conduct. For these and similar reasons, the offense principle must be formulated in a very precise way, and supplemented by appropriate standards or mediating maxims, so as not to open the door to wholesale and intuitively unwarranted legal interference.

As formulated so far, the offense principle commits us only to the view that when public conduct causes offense to someone, the fact of that offense is relevant to the permissibility of the conduct in question. A relevant consideration, of course, can be outweighed by relevant reasons on the other side, and there always is another side, namely that of the offending actor's own interests. Hence conscientious legislators can no more escape the necessity of balancing conflicting considerations when they consider prohibiting offensive conduct than they can escape interest-balancing in the application of the harm principle. Following the model of nuisance law, they will have to weigh, in each main category and context of offensiveness, the seriousness of the offense caused to unwilling witnesses against the reasonableness of the offender's conduct. The seriousness of the offensiveness would be determined by (1) the intensity and durability of the repugnance produced, and the extent to which repugnance could be anticipated to be the general reaction of strangers to the conduct displayed or represented (conduct offensive only to persons with an abnormal susceptibility to offense would not count as *very* offensive); (2) the ease with which unwilling witnesses can avoid the offensive displays; and (3) whether or not the witnesses have willingly assumed the risk of being offended either through curiosity or the anticipation of pleasure. (The maxim *Volenti non fit injuria* applies to offense as well as to harm.) We can refer to these norms, in order, as "the extent of offense standard," "the reasonable avoidability standard," and "the *Volenti* standard."

These factors would be weighed as a group against the reasonableness of the offending party's conduct as determined by (1) its personal importance to the actors themselves and its social value generally, remembering always the enormous social utility of unhampered expression (in those cases where expression is involved); (2) the availability of alternative times and places where the conduct in question would cause less offense; (3) the extent, if any, to which the offense is caused with spiteful motives. In addition, the legislature would examine the prior established character of various neighborhoods, and consider establishing licensed zones in areas where the conduct in question is known to be already prevalent, so that people inclined to be offended are not likely to stumble on it to their surprise.

The metaphor of the balancing scales is especially fortunate since it leads us to expect that most of the factors under consideration are of a kind that can vary in degree (of "weight"). We are not then tempted to speak of the variable factors as if they were absolutes whose presence in some specified degree is necessary or sufficient for some indicated legislative decision. Rather, all we should say is that the more widespread the offense (for example), the stronger the case for prohibition of the conduct that produces it, that is, the weightier must be the considerations on the other side to counterbalance it. What we cannot say is that conduct is properly prohibitable under the offense principle *if and only if* offense is the anticipated reaction of more than 50% of all potential observers, or 75%, or 99%, or 100%. Again, all we are warranted in saying is that the higher the projected percentage, the stronger the case for prohibition.[1]

The seriousness of the offense, of course, varies directly with the intensity of the offended states induced, or those that could reasonably be expected to be induced, in the mind of a standard observer. A mere weak annoyance has very little weight of its own. Hence minor eccentricities of fashion or taste, for example long hair on men or crewcuts on women, could probably never be banned by a reasonably mediated offense principle. Similarly, the seriousness of the offense varies directly with its actual or "standard" duration. A mere exiguous irritation, even if momentarily intense, would have hardly any weight in the scale and would probably be outweighed, therefore, if caused by any conduct that had the slightest bit of redeeming value, either to the actor himself or to society in general.

When we come to the number of persons who could reasonably be expected to be offended by the kind of conduct in question, we come to our first problem. Many kinds of public behavior cause extreme and durable offense to some observers, but little or no offense to others. Perhaps there is no kind of conduct that would not cause offense to someone or other. The more people we can expect to be offended, *other things being equal*, the stronger the case for legal prohibition. "Other things," however, are rarely equal. It is important to remember that certain kinds of valuable, or at least innocent actions, can be expected to offend large numbers of people, perhaps even a majority of the nation's population, certainly an overwhelming majority in particular regions. The interracial couple strolling hand in hand down the streets of a deep southern town might still cause shock, even shame and disgust, perhaps to the majority of white pedestrians who happen to observe them, but we surely don't want our offense principle applied to justify preventive coercion on that ground.

In my previous writings on this subject,[2] I fell into a trap at just this point by forgetting the useful scales analogy, and resorting too quickly to an absolutist mediating maxim which I called, rather grandly, the "standard of universality." If I wanted a reason against *ever* criminalizing interracial hand-holding and the like, all I had to do was cite the reasonableness of the conduct it would forbid, its intimate personal importance, its independent social value (despite its offensiveness to most observers), its status as expression, the unavailability of reasonable alternatives, the easy avoidability of the offense, and other decisively heavy factors on the weighing scales. Insofar as the conduct intensely offends most witnesses, I could have conceded, that is a reason for banning it, but a reason that is decisively outweighed by the other factors on the scales. Instead, I recommended a stringent standard to be met before the "extent of offense" could be put on the scales at all, namely that "in order for the offense (repugnance, embarrassment, shame, etc.) to be sufficient to warrant coercion, it should be the reaction that could reasonably be expected from almost any person chosen at random, taking the nation as a whole, and not because the individual selected belongs to some faction, clique or party."[3] I pointed out with some complacency that this "standard of universality" would probably not prevent a legislature from outlawing coprophagy, abuse of corpses, masturbation, and coitus, among other things, when done on public buses, though mere nudity would be a closer case. But the standard would certainly prevent outlawing interracial strolling in public in all conceivable circumstances except those in which virtually everybody could be expected to find such a sight profoundly offensive; and such a reaction would equally be that of young and old, male and female, liberal and conservative, northerner and southerner, even white and black. The chance of these conditions being satisfied, I assumed, should not cost the liberal any sleep.

My own dogmatic slumber, however, was quickly interrupted by another kind of liberal nightmare, caused by application of the universality standard to examples like the stories in category F—abusive, mocking, insulting speech attacking specific subgroups of the population, especially ethnic, racial, or religious groups. Public cross-burnings, displays of swastikas (with their symbolic suggestions of barbarity and genocide), "jokes" that ridicule Americans of a certain ethnic descent told on public media, public displays of banners with large and abusive caricatures of the Pope,[4] and so on. Such behavior is extremely offensive to the groups so insulted, and no doubt also offensive to large numbers of sympathetic outsiders. But still there are many millions of people who would not respond emotionally at all, and many millions more who might secretly approve. Thus, the offense principle as mediated by the standard of universality would not warrant the prohibition of such speech or conduct. To prevent this unhappy consequence (as I thought of it), I proposed an *ad hoc* amendment to the standard of universality itself, so that for the special class of offensiveness that consists of abusive, mocking, insulting behavior of a sort bound to upset, alarm, anger, or irritate those it insults, the offense principle could be applied, even though the behavior would *not* offend the entire population. Legislatures then could protect those who are vulnerable to abuse, even though they are—indeed, precisely because they are—a minority.[5]

Like most hasty *ad hoc* patch-up jobs, this one put the theory in even worse trouble. What I had set out to do in the first place was to find a ground for distinguishing some of the more lurid gross activities of the people on the bus from conduct such as that of the affectionate interracial couple, even when the latter causes acute distress to witnesses. I thought I had found the difference in the extent and distribution of the offense that could be anticipated. Indeed that is *a* difference. Surely, one can anticipate finding disgusted reactions to vomit-eating (say) to be far more universal (in our culture) than to interracial love affairs, to which offense is *not* taken at all by whole groups of people, even though it may be the reaction of a large majority among other groups. I was not looking in the wrong quarter, but there was no need to look exclusively in that corner, for I could just as well have looked, on the other side of the scale, at the reasonableness of the offending conduct as at the magnitude of the offense. The behavior of the interracial couple has much to be said for it: it is reasonable, personally valuable, expressive and affectionate, spontaneous, natural, and irreplaceable, and the offense it causes easily avoidable. The behavior of the people on the bus, on the other hand, has nothing to be said for it at all! So even if the extent of the offense were the same in the two kinds of cases (which it is not), the balancing scales would tip in sharply different directions anyway.

My other problem had been to explain how there ever could be much of a case for prohibiting racial affronts, and the like, in those examples where the *extent* of the offense is not great, in fact far less than "universal," even less than a majority. Two complementary solutions were available, both preferable to the hasty *ad hoc* solution I adopted. First, I could have looked at the other factors in the weighing scales for compensatory increases in weight when the extent of offense factor diminishes, and second, I could have reinterpreted the extent of offense standard to show that insults to single individuals and to minority groups are much more generally offensive than we might have supposed. Let us take the first tack first. Consider the plight of the innocent black on the bus who is deeply offended by racist banners, or the Jew who is insulted by swastikas that mock the memory of his murdered kinsmen. Even though the interpersonal *extent* of the offense caused might not be great (not as great as that caused by public defacation, eating vomit, etc., etc.), the other weighable factors could make up for that. The sharply pointed, threatening edge of the offense could make up in intensity, for example, for what is lacking in extent. Indeed, the intensity of

the offense, within certain limits, may tend to vary inversely with the
number of those likely to share it. Thus, a banner saying that "All Americans are Pigs" would tend to offend most Americans to some extent, but
few very intensely, whereas "All American blacks are pigs" might offend
fewer but those much more intensely. If John Smith, the only black on the
bus, sees it, he will be shocked and outraged. If the sign says simply "John
Smith is a pig," or "John Smith's wife [or mother] is a pig," Smith may be
no more offended on balance than he would be by the insult to his race, but
the sign will be even more ominously personal and threatening, and his
evoked feelings appropriately more intense. Clearly, the pointed and personal character of the offense tends to make up in "weight" for its lack of
widespreadedness. Finally, it should be pointed out (as it will be in detail in
Chap. 9, §5) that when banners are *purely* abusive, meant only to offend,
incite, or insult, without any other form of expressiveness, they lack the
redeeming social importance of genuine communications of opinion, or of
attempts, no matter how crude, at art or wit. Moreover, whatever "value"
they have to those who display them would be severely discounted for their
malice and spite.[6]

The second tack, while hardly necessary given the effectiveness of the
first, would still have a point. There is a sense, and a relevant one, in which
the susceptibility to deep offense at individual and group insults *is* very
widespread, in fact nearly universal, after all. When blacks or Jews are
insulted, the extent of the offense caused to white or non-Jewish observers
may not be as great as it is or would be to black or Jewish ones, and when
John Smith or his wife or mother are insulted, very few spectators who do
not know them will be offended to anywhere near the same degree as John
Smith himself. On the other hand, a much higher number of people would
be deeply offended by a gross insult to *their own* race, religion, or ethnic
group, or by a banner calling *their own* wife or mother a pig. These responses may be somewhat short of "universal," but they are widespread
enough to add substantial weight to the "extent of offense" factor, when it
is measured by a test of hypothetical universalizability. In this sense then,
the propensity to take deep offense at pointed insults is very widespread
indeed.

We can abandon the absolutist "standard of universality" and its unbend-
ing requirement of near unanimity, so long as we continue to attach substantial weight to the *extent of offense* as one among several important factors
governing the application of the offense principle. When the offense caused
by a contemplated action is predictably likely to offend virtually any person
who might happen to behold it (or would offend nearly any person who
found himself the target of a similar affront, when the offense is aimed

MEDIATING THE OFFENSE PRINCIPLE

more narrowly), then there is a very powerful case for forbidding it, even though the universality of the response is neither necessary nor, taken by itself, sufficient for legitimate prohibition. This point has an interesting consequence for "the people on the bus." When conduct is so extremely offensive that it is likely to offend nearly everyone, there is hardly anyone who would be willing to engage in it! Seriously offending everyone is no normal person's idea of a good time. It is a tautology to say that people don't like to be offended. They have a tendency to strike back and one way or another make life miserable for the people they find revolting, disgusting, embarrassing, and annoying. That is why most of the bizarre examples of offense in the stories about the bus are so very contrived. I dare say that the reader of these lines has never seen a nude person enter a bus, much less public vomit-eating, desecration of crucifixes, mutilation of corpses, public sexual intercourse, and the like. Our social taboos, enforced by the powerful sanction of "public opinion," are more than powerful enough to protect us from such conduct without the assistance of the law. We hardly need specific legislation directed at evils that are so rare that they occur only once a decade in a country of two hundred million citizens. And so there is a benign sort of paradox pointed up by the "extent of offense" standard: the more universal and severe a form of offensiveness, the less danger there is that it will occur, and the less we need rely on criminal sanctions to deter it.

Some of the conduct in our stories about the bus is not so bizarre, and in fact occurs commonly to the great irritation of observers. Some of these activities, like playing portable radios (or cigar smoking), fail to offend near-universally only because there are large numbers of people, cutting across boundaries of age, race, and the like, who are prepared to engage in the activities themselves. Thus radio players don't resent other radio players and certainly aren't offended by their own radio playing, and cigar smokers do not offend themselves, and are more ready than others to tolerate the smoke and stench of other smokers' cigars. But if it should be true that radio players on buses tend to offend virtually all the passengers who are not themselves actual or potential traveling radio players, and cigar smokers tend to offend virtually all passengers who are not themselves actual or potential cigar smokers, then radio playing and cigar smoking might well be prohibited on buses. The "extent of offense" standard, therefore, must be interpreted as not giving as much weight to the tolerance of those who engage in an offensive activity themselves as would be given to the tolerance of others. But the larger the number of those who engage in the activity in question and therefore tolerate it, the more weight their tolerance should be given, so that at the point where more than half of the population engages in it and tolerates it, their tolerance should be given as much weight as anyone else's. In the latter case, the offensiveness would be *far* from "universal," and the case for suppression proportionately weak.

The second mediating maxim for the application of the offense principle is the *standard of reasonable avoidability*. The easier it is to avoid a particular offense, or to terminate it once it occurs, without inconvenience to oneself, the less serious the offense is. The people on the bus in the offensive stories cannot escape the various offenses inflicted on them without leaving the bus, waiting for the next bus, paying a new fare, and arriving at their destinations later than they had wished. Even if these inconveniences did not amount to enough harm to mention, it would be unreasonable to require the passengers to incur them to avoid the offensive conduct of others. Similarly, obscene remarks over a loudspeaker, pornographic handbills thrust into the hands of passing pedestrians, and lurid billboards in Times Square graphically advertising the joys of pederasty would all fail to be reasonably avoidable.[7]

On the other hand, no one has a right to protection from the state against offensive experiences if he can easily and effectively avoid them without unreasonable effort or inconvenience. In particular, the offense principle, properly qualified, can give no warrant to the suppression of *books* on the grounds of obscenity. When printed words hide decorously behind covers of books sitting passively on the shelves of a bookstore, their offensiveness is easily avoided. The opposite position is no doubt encouraged by the common comparison of obscenity with "smut," "filth," or "dirt." This in turn suggests an analogy to nuisance law, which governs cases where certain activities create ugly messes and terrible odors offensive to neighbors. There is, however, one vitiating difference. In the case of "dirty books," the offense is easily avoidable. Nothing comparable to the smell of rancid garbage oozes out through the covers of a book whether one looks at it or not. When an "obscene" book sits on a shelf, who is there to be offended? Those who want to read it for the sake of erotic stimulation presumably will not be offended (else they wouldn't read it), and those who choose not to read it will have no experience of it to be offended by. If its covers are too decorous, some unsuspecting readers might browse through it by mistake and then be offended by what they find, but they need only close the book again to escape the offense.

Still another mediating maxim for the application of the offense principle is our old friend, *Volenti non fit injuria*. One can in fact be offended by conduct to which one has consented. A businessman Doe may know that Roe is filthy, smelly, and vulgar, yet quite deliberately choose to put up with his offensive presence at a business luncheon for the sake of future profits. On another occasion Doe may quite voluntarily enter a pornographic cinema quite confident that the film he is about to see will disgust, embarrass, and annoy him, yet he will be willing to suffer that offense for the sake of curiosity, or for some other good reason of his own. The offended states induced by such voluntarily undertaken experiences are perfectly real, just as the broken bones incurred by the stunt motorcyclist are perfectly real harms, but in neither case can the victim complain of a grievance. Insofar as they undertook the dangerous activity or the offensive experience voluntarily, they were not *wronged* by anyone. For the purpose of a plausible offense principle, voluntarily suffered offenses are not to count as offenses at all, and voluntarily assumed risks of offense render inadmissible subsequent complaints that the risked offense has materialized.

One further restriction on the offense principle is necessary. This qualification, though implicit in the extent of offense standard, is important enough to be made fully explicit and emphatic. This is the requirement, parallel to a mediating maxim for the harm principle, that the seriousness of the offense be discounted to the extent that it is the product of abnormal susceptibilities. As we have already seen, the law of nuisance has for centuries downgraded the inconveniences that stem from rare and special susceptibilities in unfortunate plaintiffs; a criminal law of nuisance, protecting the senses and sensibilities of the general public, would have no choice but to do the same.[8] "The standard," writes Prosser, "must necessarily be that of definite offensiveness, inconvenience, or annoyance to the normal person in the community".[9] It is not a public nuisance to ring church bells (Vol. I, Chap. 5, §3) or to "run a factory where the smoke aggravates the plaintiff's bronchitis [provided it would not affect the health of a normal person] . . . Neither is a keg of spikes by the side of the road a public nuisance because it frightens an unduly skittish horse."[10]

Human beings who take offense at remarkably little provocation should have the same standing in law courts as the owners of skittish horses. The most "skittish" imaginable person is he who suffers acute disgust and revulsion, shock to sensibilities, shameful embarrassment, annoyance, frustration, resentment or humiliation *not* from something he sees, feels, smells, or hears, but rather from unseen activities he knows or fears may be happening beyond his ken. If the law permits some form of harmless activity that he regards as odious and disgusting, but permits it only when done discreetly between consenting adults behind locked doors and drawn blinds, he fears as he walks down the street that such activities may be going on in any of the darkened houses he passes, and the "bare knowledge" fills him with dread, anxiety, and shame. It will be even worse if he has strong evidence that the revolting activities are occuring in a given house on the street, for the "bare thought" in this case is more likely to get an obsessive grip on his consciousness. As David Conway points out: "In fact it may be more difficult to avoid the offense resulting from merely being aware of private immorality. For instance, the person greatly offended by the mere fact that homosexuals inhabit the house three doors away and there nightly indulge in their 'abominable practices' may be virtually incapable of ridding himself of such thoughts. There is no equivalent here to shutting one's eyes or looking the other way."[11]

It seems clear, however, that the more fragile our sensitive sufferer's psyche, the less protection he can expect from the criminal law. Provided that the conduct the very thought of which upsets him has any redeeming value at all, personal or social, his own claim to protection is likely to be overridden. If a mere sneeze causes a glass window to break, we should blame the weakness or brittleness of the glass and not the sneeze. Similarly, if "bare knowledge" that discreet and harmless "immoralities" are occurring in private leads to severe mental distress, we should attribute the distress to abnormal susceptibilities rather than to the precipitating cause. We don't punish persons when their normally harmless and independently valuable (at least to themselves) activities happen to startle a skittish horse whose presence was unsuspected. Rather we expect the owners of skittish horses to keep them away from "startling" activities and to take steps to cure them of their skittishness.

We can make two further assumptions about the extremely susceptible person. The repugnance he feels might itself be "normal," "natural," and "reasonable," indeed it may be shared, though not to the same degree, by most members of the community. At the very least, there is no necessity that it be contrary to reason, simply for being more intensely felt and suffered. Secondly, we assume that excessive susceptibility to extreme offense is, in most cases, something subject to the control of the susceptible person himself, something mitigable, if not totally curable. In all but pathological cases, we assume that there is something almost self-indulgent about cultivating feelings of loathing, disgust, or rage (like Bobby Burns's sulky, "sullen dame", who "nurses her wrath to keep it warm"), and that one can learn not to let the object of one's feelings bother one so. In this respect, human "skittishness" is more corrigible than the equine variety, and more of a character flaw than an illness. Surely it commands less compassion and less accommodation then allergies, epilepsy, or blindness, and there is a limit to how much accommodation even these genuine maladies can command. (For further discussion of the "bare knowledge problem," see *infra*, Chap. 9, §§3, 4.)

In summary, the seriousness of an offense is determined by the following standards:

1. *The magnitude of the offense*, which is a function of its intensity, duration, and extent.
   a. *Intensity*. The more intense a typical offense taken at the type of conduct in question, the more serious is an actual instance of such an offense.
   b. *Duration*. The more durable a typical offense taken at the type of conduct in question, the more serious is an actual instance of such offense.
   c. *Extent*. The more widespread the susceptibility to a given kind of offense, the more serious is a given instance of that kind of offense.
2. *The standard of reasonable avoidability*. The more difficult it is to avoid a given offense without serious inconvenience to oneself the more serious is that offense.
3. *The Volenti maxim*. Offended states that were voluntarily incurred, or the risk of which was voluntarily assumed by the person who experienced them, are not to count as "offenses" at all in the application of a legislative "offense principle."
4. *The discounting of abnormal susceptibilities*. (This can be thought of as a kind of corollary of 1.) Insofar as offended states occur because of a person's abnormal susceptibility to offense, their seriousness is to be discounted in the application of a legislative "offense principle."

It should be noted that no mention has been made of the *reasonableness* of the offense. There are a number of reasons for *not requiring* that offenses be taken reasonably in order to qualify for legal intervention, and even for not including the degree of reasonableness of an offense among the determinants of its seriousness. A reasonableness requirement, in the first place, would be in large degree redundant and unnecessary, given our endorsement of the extent of offense standard. It is possible, I suppose, but extremely unlikely, that *virtually everyone* would have an unreasonable disposition to be offended by a certain kind of experience. Insofar as balancing tests tend to justify prohibitions of actions only of the most widespread offensive kind, chances are effectively minimized that actions which cause only unreasonable offense will be prohibited. Secondly, by relying on the extent of offense standard rather than a reasonableness standard, legislators need not themselves assume the prerogative of determining the reasonableness of emotional reactions, a dangerous power indeed in a democracy.

The cost we pay for failing to include the reasonableness of offenses in determining their "seriousness" is that persons in some rare cases might be prevented by law from acting in ways that offend, even though the offense is not taken reasonably. But for the most part, these cases will be examples

of types of offense that in their very nature have nothing to do with reasonableness. It is neither reasonable nor unreasonable but simply "nonreason-
able" to be bothered by the sight of nude bodies, public defecation, disgusting "food," and the like. One can no more give "reasons" for these culturally determined reactions than one can for the offensiveness of "evil smells."
Yet the offended states are real, predictable, unpleasant, and unmodifiable
by argument; and these characteristics seem to me clearly to ground *prima
facie* claims against the state for protection, claims that *can* be outweighed
by stronger claims in the opposing balance pan, but which nevertheless do
have some weight of their own.

Other offended states, I must concede, *are* subject to rational appraisal
and criticism. It is perfectly reasonable to be offended by the word "nigger," and profoundly contrary to reason to be offended by the sight of an
interracial couple. The principles defended here would protect people, in
certain circumstances, from offense that happens to be reasonable, so that
category raises no problem. As for *most* forms of *unreasonable* offense, the
very unreasonableness of the reaction will tend to keep it from being sufficiently widespread to warrant preventive coercion. As for the handful of
remaining cases of unreasonable offense, there is still a claim for protection
of those who suffer them, it seems to me, even though offense is taken
unreasonably. Provided that very real and intense offense is taken predictably by virtually everyone, and the offending conduct has hardly any countervailing personal or social value of its own, prohibition seems reasonable
even when the protected sensibilities themselves are not. There may be
parallel cases here for the harm principle. We can at least imagine that
because of some widespread superstitious (and thus "irrational") belief, virtually all persons in a given community react with such horror to a given
type of otherwise innocent conduct that they suffer real physical damage,
say to their hearts, whenever confronted with such conduct. Harm, of
course, is a more serious thing than mere offense, but the point at issue
applies in the same way to both harm and offense. The claim of superstitious people to protection from foreseeable harm is in no way weakened by
the objective unreasonableness of their response to the offending conduct.
Nor does the unreasonableness of the response count against the description
of the resultant harm (heart attacks) *as* harm. The same point, I should
think, would apply to foreseeable and universal offense when it too is
partially the product of unreason.[12]

Perhaps the greatest source of my reluctance to restrict the offense principle to "reasonable offense," however, is that it would require agencies of the
state to make official judgments of the reasonableness and unreasonableness
of emotional states and sensibilities, in effect closing these questions to

dissent and putting the stamp of state approval on answers to questions which, like issues of ideology and belief, should be left open to unimpeded discussion and practice. Much offense, for example, is caused by the obnoxious or aggressive expression of disrespect, scorn, or mockery of things that are loved, esteemed, or venerated. (See Chap. 9, §3.) To take offense at expressed scorn for something that is not worthy of respect in the first place is, I suppose, to take offense unreasonably. But when is something truly worthy of love or respect or loyalty? To make *those* questions subject to administrative or judicial determination, I should think, would be dangerous and distinctly contrary to liberal principles.[13]

2. On the scales: the reasonableness of the offending conduct

Having determined the seriousness of a given category of offense by the application of four standards to it, the careful legislator will proceed to balance that seriousness against the reasonableness of the various kinds of conduct that can produce it. For the reasons already cited he will not concern himself with whether or not the offense is taken reasonably, but the reasonableness of the conduct to which the offense is taken is quite another matter. Conduct that is ordinary, useful, or necessary cannot properly be interfered with except for the most urgent reasons; whereas conduct that is trivial or frivolous will have less weight on the balancing scales.

The "reasonableness" of a type of conduct that may cause offense is determined first of all by its importance to the actor himself. If the conduct in question is part of the activity by which the actor earns his living so that its curtailment would harm his economic interest, then obviously it is important to him, whatever others may think of it. Similarly, it will be a matter of great personal importance if it contributes significantly to his health, talent, knowledge, or virtue, and even more so if it is necessary for the promotion of those goals. Similarly, the conduct has importance to its actor if it contributes to his pleasure, or is an integral part of a pattern of activities central to his love life, family life, or social life. Even if the conduct is not necessary to the promotion of any of his interests, it may have some value to him in that alternatives to it, while equally effective means to his goals, would be inconvenient. After all, if the convenience of offended parties has weight on the legislative scales, there is no reason to discount the convenience of the persons whose conduct offends. On the other hand, utterly frivolous, wanton, perverse, or gratuitous behavior; easily avoidable actions done impulsively on a passing whim; self-defeating actions that have no more value for the actor than for those he offends; and trivial, mindless, arbitrary actions, all fail to satisfy the standard of personal importance and can be discounted accordingly.

A second standard for judging the "reasonableness" of the offending conduct is its social utility, or as Prosser puts it, "the social value which the law attaches to its ultimate purpose."[14] If the conduct that annoys or inconveniences others is part of the activity of moving or demolishing buildings, repairing ruptured gas or water lines, investigating a crime, pursuing an escaped felon, or reporting a news story, it has a great deal of public value, as part of a kind of activity that is socially useful, but if it is valuable only to the person who engages in it, as for example, hawking a product for sale, loitering in or near a public place for the purpose of soliciting deviate sexual relations, purveying offensive materials for the purpose of making a personal profit, and so on, then it contributes little but nuisance to the rest of the community. Playing a portable radio on a public bus may have some value to the person who does it and to that extent at least deserves a legislator's respect, but it is hardly the sort of activity that contributes to the public good. Conversing freely, easily, and naturally with an acquaintance, on the other hand, whether in a public bus (story 25) or elsewhere, is a type of activity that is not only vitally important to individuals, but also productive of far more good than harm to the community on the whole. Unregulated impromptu communication between individuals is in general a necessary condition for efficient social functioning.

It is at least partly by virtue of the high social value attached to it that unfettered *expression of opinion* has such a privileged position in American law.[15] To be sure, expressing opinions openly in spontaneous conversation, writing, or through more powerful media of communication is also of great importance to private individuals themselves, since self-expression is valued both as an end in itself and as a means of effecting desired changes. But it is also a necessary condition for the satisfactory functioning of any government that relies heavily on enlightened public opinion in its decision making. It is important to each individual to voice his own opinion about matters of public policy, but it is also important to him that he have fair access to the opinions and arguments of all his fellows, and important to the whole community that all possible roads to truth be left open lest our leaders become committed to insufficiently examined policies, with disastrous social consequences. It is necessary to emphasize here, as Mill did in *On Liberty*,[16] that unpopular, unorthodox, and extreme opinions, no less than any others, need their spokesmen, in order that our chances of discovering truths and making wise decisions be increased. There is a social gain then from constantly reexamining public policies, probing for difficulties and soft spots, bringing to light new and relevant facts, and subjecting to doubt hitherto unquestioned first premises. Without these challenges, nations have a natural tendency to drift complacently into dead ends and quagmires. For that reason, no amount of offensiveness in an expressed opinion can counterbalance the vital social value of allowing unfettered personal expression.

There are two ways, however, in which an expression of opinion can be offensive. An audience can be offended by the opinion expressed or implied in an utterance, as, for example, a devout Christian might be offended by the bare assertion of atheism; or the audience might be offended instead by the manner in which the opinion itself is expressed, for example as a caption to an obscene poster of Jesus and Mary (see stories 11 and 19). Something other than an opinion itself offends when offending conduct does not involve language or symbolism, or when it offends by means of an utterance with no clear propositional content at all (for example, obscene epithets), or when an opinion is expressed but is only incidental to the cause of offense, which is the manner or context of expression.[17] Utterances that give offense in the latter ways may have some value to the person who makes them, and have some weight for that reason, but they derive very little weight from the standard of social utility, and consequently can be rightly restricted by law when the offense they cause is sufficiently serious. In contrast, the offensiveness of the opinion itself is never serious enough to outweigh the heavy public interest in open discussion and free expression of opinion. One should be free to shout to a crowd, or carry a sign or words on one's back, to the effect that we should abandon democracy for Nazism or Communism, that our troops should invade Cuba or bomb China, that churches should be nationalized, that homosexual intercourse in public should be encouraged—offensive as these opinions may be to many people. A non-offensive utterance of an opinion, even of an offensive opinion, is a kind of trump card in the application of the offense principle. The standards of personal importance and social utility confer on it an absolute immunity; no amount of offensiveness can enable it to be overriden.

It should be clear then how the qualified offense principle would apply to so-called "thematic obscenity." It would permit public *advocacy*, whether in hand bills or magazines, on billboards, or from soap boxes, of *any* policies or values whatever, pertaining to sex, religion, politics, or anything else; but it would not necessarily permit graphic portrayals of seriously offensive scenes to unwilling captive audiences, for example lurid paintings of sexual couplings on billboards in a crowded urban center. So precious is free speech on questions of public policy, however, that public *advocacy* of laws permitting graphically obscene billboards should be permitted. Indeed, public advocacy even of the legalization of homicide should be permitted provided the manner of advocacy itself is not offensive in one of the ways recognized by the qualified offense principle.

Another factor to be considered in any determination of the reasonableness of conduct that causes offense to others is the degree to which non-offensive alternatives that are equally satisfactory to the actor are available. If the offending person, by doing his thing at another place or time, can avoid causing offense to a captive audience without loss or unreasonable inconvenience to himself, then his offending conduct is unreasonable if done in circumstances that permit offense. Very often offensive conduct is quite unobjectionable in itself and could be performed quite legally in the privacy of the actor's own abode or some other private place, in which case he can have no complaint if the law prevents him from doing it right under the noses of unwilling observers. One can, however, make too much of this point, for as David Conway points out, "it very often is not true that if an action is prohibited in public, one is left 'at liberty to do the same thing in private. . . .' For in many cases it is highly inconvenient or virtually impossible to perform the same action in private, and more importantly, in other cases, the very point or rationale of the action disappears if one is restricted to privacy."[18] As examples of possibly offensive conduct that would be unreasonably inconvenient or even impossible to restrict to private areas, Conway cites wearing long hair or a beard. But the point about inconvenience is secondary:

> Not only is there inconvenience involved in such cases, but presumably the very point of having long hair or a beard is to "go about looking that way." The same is true of a woman wearing a mini-skirt, or a very brief bikini, or only the bottom half of the bikini, or no bikini at all. One can be nude in private, but again, the point of so doing (a feeling of freedom in the supermarket, or whatever) may be lost, just as it is if it is demanded that one wear a beard-cover in public.[19]

The point, then, of behaving or dressing or undressing in a certain way may be totally lost if the behavior in question is done only in private. In such cases, it is not unreasonable, by the standard of available alternatives at least, to perform the offensive conduct in public. But whether this factor is to carry much weight in the final analysis depends very much on what the "point" of the conduct is. If the point of being nude is to facilitate one's movements, get a suntan, keep cool, or "feel free in the supermarket," then the conduct has a certain amount of reasonableness, *despite* its tendency to offend (shock, embarrass, inconvenience) others. But if the whole point of nudity is to offend others, if one goes bare in the supermarket not despite but *because* of the known tendency of nudity to offend, then the legislature must, at the very least, discount the reasonableness of the offending conduct.

This brings us to the next maxim for determining the reasonableness of offensive conduct. By and large the offending person's motives are his own business, and the law should respect them whatever they are. But when the motive is merely malicious or spiteful it deserves no respect at all. Offending the senses or sensibilities of others simply for the sake of doing so is hardly less unreasonable than harming the interests of others simply for the sake of doing so. Conduct cannot be reasonable in the eyes of the law (or on the scales of the legislator) if its entire motive is malice or spite. Even abnormal vulnerabilities and super-sensitive, "skittish" sensibilities, which, as we have seen, have little claim to protection against even minimally reasonable behavior, can make some claim at least to protection against persecuting harassment and wholly spiteful flaunting that has no purpose whatever except to cause offense. Unlike special vulnerabilities to harm, however, abnormal susceptibilities to offense find more appropriate legal protection against malicious exploitation through means other than the criminal law, for example, through injunctions, civil suits, or permitted private "abatement."

In practice, however, malice and spite may be very hard to distinguish from another motive that is surely more reasonable, however it must be treated by the law. The nude housewife in the supermarket may fancy herself a kind of moral reformer, trying to exercise a modifying influence on prevailing attitudes that she regards as benighted. She may be trying to do her share (her *duty* as she conceives it) to habituate the public to the sight of nude bodies so that what she takes to be the unreasonable susceptibility to offense at the sight of nudity may diminish and eventually disappear along with various unwholesome attitudes towards sex to which it may be connected. She may be aware that her nudity will cause some observers to experience painful embarrassment, but she acts despite that awareness, not because of it. Her case is surely to be distinguished from that of the mischievous troublemaker and the spiteful misanthrope. One would hope that she would not be seriously punished by a court. The question of whether her conduct could pass the tests of reasonableness required by an enlightened application of the offense principle, however, is more difficult.

Donald VanDeVeer argues persuasively that it is possible in principle to distinguish malicious from what he calls "conscientious" offensive conduct. As an example of the former, he has us consider the following: "Smith, an eccentric liberal Democrat, paints a swastika on his roof to irritate his Jewish neighbor, but not with the intention of winning converts to Neo-Nazism or achieving any further purpose."[20] We already have an example of "conscientious offensiveness" in the dutiful nudist in the supermarket. An example more parallel to VanDeVeer's eccentric liberal would be a Nazi who wishes to persuade others to consider the Nazi ideology with less prejudice by painting a swastika on his roof (assuming that Nazis can have genuine convictions and hold them conscientiously). VanDeVeer also points out that political dissidents often cannot "get a hearing" without media attention, and "cannot achieve that without offensive behavior" like guerilla theatre performances and shocking symbolic acts. VanDeVeer would discount purely spiteful motivation, as we too have suggested, while permitting offensive conduct when conscientious. I am sympathetic with his view, although I draw back from an absolutist principle that would make conscientiousness an automatically sufficient condition for permissibility. What conscientiousness in VanDeVeer's sense shows is that the conduct is genuine political expression and not mere malicious insult without advocacy, or some use of symbolism other than defending a thesis or making a point. It therefore brings the full weight of free expression as an important social value down on the side of the scale weighing the reasonableness of the offending conduct. There would be considerably less political value in using a symbol simply to shock a neighbor, or exposing oneself in the supermarket for sexual self-stimulation, or to solicit sexual relations, or simply to upset the excessively prudish as an end in itself.

The final consideration relevant to the reasonableness of conduct that tends to offend has to do with the nature of the neighborhood in which the offending conduct takes place. The maxim that offensive conduct performed in *de facto* restricted areas where it is known to be common is more reasonable than it would be were it performed in locales where it is uncommon is a corollary of the "available alternatives" standard that deserves some separate discussion. Homosexual lovers petting and kissing on a public bus are unreasonably offensive, by the present standard, if there is an area of their city, not unreasonably distant, that is known to be frequented regularly and primarily by homosexuals who commonly engage in the same sort of activity on the street corners, in the taverns and night clubs, even in the local buses. Similarly, sex shops, pornographic cinemas, and dirty book stores, all with neon identifying signs and lurid advertising posters, create an irritating and unwanted ambience in residential and most commercial areas of a city, but can cause very little offense in neighborhoods already abandoned to them, like 42nd Street and Charing Cross Road. Large cities might very well tolerate such free zones (while carefully monitoring them for genuinely harmful effects) as a means of providing "available alternatives" for persons whose deviant practices have some personal value, but are likely to cause serious offense if engaged in elsewhere. As Prosser reminds us in his account of the law of private nuisance, "courts are frequently called on to determine the paramount use to which a locality is devoted."²¹ Legislatures might very well permit courts a similar discretion in the process of determining the reasonableness of offensive conduct when this calls for assessing the paramount character of a neighborhood.

Very likely the balancing tests on the whole would still tell against prohibitions of such natural and spontaneous practices as gestures of affection even among "deviant" groups. We could not plausibly require any kind of licensing for the kind of private communications and expressions that we think of as natural rights in our own cases. Walking hand in hand down the main street of a town is just as much a right of homosexual as of interracial couples. On the other hand, residential restrictions might more plausibly be applied to more overtly erotic behavior, and to acts of solicitation, places of assignation, houses of prostitution, adult book stores and sex shops, pornographic movie theatres, and the like. In fact, American cities have tried two different techniques to control such offensive activities short of outright criminal prohibition. What might be called the Boston technique did not work well in that New England metropolis. Licenses for adult book stores, massage parlors, and porno theatres were issued as revocable privileges (most of which were later revoked in fact) provided the merchants located their businesses in a narrow strip of blocks in downtown Boston. This area, which had already largely deteriorated, soon became known to wagsters as "the combat zone," as it quickly filled up with harlots, pimps, protection racketeers, gangsters, pickpockets, bullies, runaway children, criminals in hiding, armed and nervous policemen both in uniform and plain clothes, and other human landmines. Violence and fraud flourished, the most common victims being high school and college students. The city soon tired of the experiment and reverted to the *status quo ante*. By segregating offensiveness the authorities had so increased its magnitude, not to mention danger and harm, that it had become an intolerable blight on the city.

Detroit took the opposite approach. The city was divided into geographic areas of roughly equal size and shape, and a very small number of revocable licenses for "offensive" commercial establishments (hiding behind reasonably decorous fronts) were issued for each district. This number was treated as an absolute maximum, so that unsavory elements would not tend to locate in any one place, creating higher concentrations of ugliness and sordid corruption for the city as a whole. There are obvious difficulties and dangers in the Detroit system too, but it at least spared the city (in theory) the presence of any one neighborhood of quite intolerable degeneracy. Whether the diffusion or concentration of offensiveness works best depends on many variables that differ from city to city, especially the supply and demand for "offensive services" already present. In the right circumstances, however, either is likely to be a more efficient control than outright prohibition, and both are greater respecters of individual liberty.

In summary, the reasonableness of conduct that happens to cause offense to others is determined by the following standards, each of which can be understood to be a kind of mediating maxim governing the application of the offense principle to legislative or judicial deliberations:

1. *Personal importance.* The more important the offending conduct is to the actor, as measured by his own preferences and the vitality of those of the actor's own interests it is meant to advance, the more reasonable that conduct is.
2. *Social value.* The greater the social utility of the kind of conduct of which the actor's is an instance, the more reasonable is the actor's conduct.
3. *Free expression.* (A corollary of 1 and 2.) Expressions of opinion, especially about matters of public policy, but also about matters of empirical fact, and about historical, scientific, theological, philosophical, political, and moral questions, must be presumed to have the highest social importance in virtue of the great social utility of free expression and discussion generally, as well as the vital personal interest most people have in being able to speak their minds fearlessly. No degree of offensiveness in the expressed opinion itself is sufficient to override the case for free expression, although the offensiveness of the manner of expression, as opposed to its substance, may have sufficient weight in some contexts.
4. *Alternative opportunities.* The greater the availability of alternative times or places that would be equally satisfactory to the actor and his partners (if any) but inoffensive to others, the less reasonable is conduct done in circumstances that render it offensive to others.
5. *Malice and spite.* Offensive conduct is unreasonable to the extent that its impelling motive is spiteful or malicious. Wholly spiteful conduct, done with the intention of offending and for no other reason, is wholly unreasonable. Especial care is required in the application of this standard, for spiteful motives are easily confused with conscientious ones.
6. *Nature of the locality.* (A corollary of 4.) Offensive conduct performed in neighborhoods where it is common, and widely known to be common, is less unreasonable than it would be in neighborhoods where it is rare and unexpected.

3. Reading the balance

Having assessed the reasonableness of the offender's conduct by the application of the above standards, the legislator or judge (when the legislature has permitted him discretion) must "balance" it against the seriousness of the offense caused, as determined by the four standards mentioned earlier. A legislature does not, of course, concern itself with specific actions and specific offended states. Rather it must weigh against one another generalized *types* of conduct and offense. In hard cases this balancing procedure can be very complex and uncertain, but there are some cases that fall clearly under one or another standard in such a way as to leave no doubt how they must be decided. Thus, for example, the *Volenti* standard preempts all the rest when it clearly applies. Film exhibitors, for example, cannot reasonably be charged with criminally offensive conduct when the only people who witness their films are those who voluntarily purchased tickets to do so, knowing full well what sort of film they were about to see.[22] One cannot be *wrongly* offended by that to which one fully consents. Similarly, *books* cannot be legitimately banned on the grounds of offensiveness, by virtue of the standard of reasonable avoidability, nor can inoffensive expressions of offensive political or theological opinions, by virtue of their personal and social importance. On the other side, purely spiteful motives in the offender can be a preemptive consideration weighting the balance scale decisively on the side of unreasonableness.

In some cases, no one standard is preemptive, but nevertheless all applicable standards pull together towards one inevitable decision. The public eating of feces (coprophagia) fully and unambiguously satisfies the extent of offense standard. One doesn't have to be abnormally squeamish to be offended by the very sight of it. If it is done (say) on a public bus, it definitely fails to win the support of the reasonable avoidability and *Volenti* standards, which is to say that it causes intense disgust to captive observers. Hence, by *all* the relevant criteria, it is seriously offensive. By all the criteria for weighing reasonableness, public coprophagia does poorly too. It cannot be very important to the neurotic person who does it (not as important, for example, as earning a living, or eating fresh food); it has a definitely limited social utility; it is not the expression in language of an opinion, nor does it fall into a recognized genre of aesthetic expression; and it could as well be done in private. Hence it is both seriously offensive and unredeemed by independent "reasonableness." Proscription by means of the criminal law then would be in principle legitimate, even though in practice it might be unwise, uneconomical, or unnecessary.

In hard cases, however, when standards conflict and none apply in a preemptive way, where for example a given kind of conduct is offensive to a moderate degree, and only moderately unreasonable, there will be no automatic mathematical way of coming to a clearly correct decision. The theorist can identify the factors that must be considered and compared, but, in the end, there is no substitute for *judgment*. When the facts are all in, and the standards all duly applied to them, there is no more need for a philosopher; the judge or legislator is entirely on his own. The scales used in the legislative and judicial balancing act have no dials and pointing arrows like those on ordinary bathroom scales (which suggests another interpretation of the saying that justice is blind). When the case is close, and all the relevant principles have been applied to it by means of all the proper standards, the legislative or judicial decision may yet be unwise, or properly criticized as "wrong," but it cannot be "illegitimate," in the sense of applying an inadmissible kind of reason.

Many criminal statutes that have long been part of the penal codes of American states would not pass the test of our rigorously qualified offense principle. Laws forbidding mistreatment of a corpse even in the privacy of one's home fail to pass; so do laws against private sexual conduct of all kinds, consensual adultery, prostitution (except for rules regulating commerce), private showings of pornographic films, obscene books, and blasphemy, among others. Some statutes, however, do receive a warrant even from our highly restricted version of the offense principle. Some of these are worded in such a general and imprecise way that they leave it to the courts, in effect, to apply the offense principle in their own way, as for example, Section 415 of the California Penal Code which prohibits "maliciously and willfully disturbing the peace or quiet of any neighborhood or person . . . by tumultuous or offensive conduct." The statute proceeds to list various examples including loud and unusual noise, challenging to a fight, running a horse race for wager or amusement on a public street, firing a gun, and using "any vulgar language within the presence or hearing of women or children in a loud and boisterous manner." (The clause about "women and children" would not do well by the extent of offense standard, however. See Chap. 16, §1.) Similarly, the *Model Penal Code* forbids "open lewdness" defined as "any lewd act which [the actor] . . . knows is likely to be observed by others who would be affronted or alarmed,"[23] leaving it to the courts to judge which acts are "lewd" and likely to affront. Other sections of the Code, applying the offense principle directly to a given type of conduct, are more precise. A model "indecent exposure" statute penalizes "exposure of the genitals for the purpose of arousing or gratifying sexual desire in circumstances likely to cause affront or alarm."[24] Solicitation of deviant sexual relations is made a crime by the Code when the actor "loiters in or near any public place" for the purpose of such solicitation.[25] As Louis Schwartz points out, the comments attached to the final draft of the Code "make it clear that the target of this legislation is not private immorality but

a kind of public 'nuisance' caused by congregation of homosexuals offensively flaunting their deviance . . ."²⁶ Even something like "blasphemy" is
prohibited by the Code, not when it occurs before *any* public audience, or
even *any* captive audience, but only when it takes the form of a mischievous
disruption of a "religious meeting or procession with utterances designed to
outrage the sensibilities of the group . . ."²⁷ A final example is closer to the
borderline of illegitimacy, namely, the Code's prohibition of "desecration of
the national flag or other object of public veneration" but only when "others
are likely to observe or discover."²⁸

4. Cultural change and the martyrdom of the premature

Even the most cursory survey of cultural variations reveals how diverse are
the things thought to be offensive, how steady are the changes even within
a culture in prevailing sensibility, and how different are the reactions of
different persons to the same stimuli. The offense principle, therefore, is
dependent on cultural standards that vary greatly from place to place, and
within our own nation "constantly and rapidly change."²⁹ Even public defacation is common and inoffensive in many parts of the world, and there are
many examples of conduct that was once universally offensive in our country but is now commonplace. One of the more dramatic of these was the
not-so-gradual evolution of the ankle-length bathing suit into the bikini, and
the development now occurring before our very eyes of the bikini into the
topless suit. There is little doubt that nude bathing will be common on
many beaches before many more years. None of these facts, considered
simply as facts, need embarrass the "reluctant" defender of the legitimacy
of the offense principle. One can imagine similar changes in the conditions
for the application of the harm principle, but they don't weaken anyone's
confidence in that principle. Conduct that is banned at a given time because
it spreads disease ought not to be banned at a subsequent time when that
disease is rendered harmless by universal vaccination. Similarly, conduct
that causes universal offense at a given time ought not to be banned at a
later time when many people no longer are offended, whatever the cause of
the change. The two cases seem to me to be precisely on the same footing
in this respect.

Cultural change, however, causes a problem for the defender of an offense principle more serious than any caused for the harm principle by
technological change. The principle as mediated by the extent of offense
standard seems to permit punishment of offenders in the transitional stage
that is unfair and morally unsettling. It is true by definition that the vast

majority of people are "not the first by whom the new is tried, nor yet the last to cast the old aside." The vast majority, then, have little to fear from laws derived from the restricted offense principles. Reformers and trend-setters, on the other hand, those in each generation who are responsible for the movement and direction of the prevailing sensibility, may not be so fortunate. How do the sensibilities of people (as opposed to their moral judgments and opinions) come to change? Surely one of the more common causes of such change is a steady increase in the number of offending cases. What once caused spontaneous horror, revulsion, shame, or wrath, becomes less horrifying and revolting as it becomes more common. We become accustomed to it, and hardened against it, and then invulnerable to it, and finally (even) tolerant of it. But what of those offending persons who have the misfortune to engage in a given type of behavior during the transitional period between the time when the qualified offense principle clearly applies and when it clearly no longer can apply? Some of them, no doubt, will be punished for what may be done a year later with impunity—and according to my principle, rightly so. These unfortunate chaps are in a way like the last soldiers to be killed in a war. They are treated no worse than their predecessors were in an earlier period, who were punished in the same way for the same thing, but coming near the end of an earlier stage of cultural history their punishment is somehow more poignant. To a later tolerant age, they will appear to be martyrs punished for exercising their rightful liberties a trifle prematurely. More to the point, their conduct had a direct causal influence on the attitudes and sensibilities they were punished for offending. Their punishment was for conduct that helped destroy the very conditions that rendered that kind of conduct legitimately criminal in the first place.

Thus, I could be in the uncomfortable position of making a case for the punishment of anti-war demonstrators in 1965 for parading a Viet-Cong flag (shocking!) while denouncing the punishment of other protestors in 1970 for doing the same thing (yawn). Rapid cultural change will always claim some victims in this way, and perhaps I should sadly conclude that some unfair martyrdom in the transitional stages is simply inevitable, a tragic fact of life. My discomfort in this position is at least mitigated by the thought that martyrs to the cause of cultural change, in my view, should never be subject to more than very minor penalties or coercive pressure. So the "tragedy" of their punishment is not at all that lamentable. Moreover, those who are penalized for anticipating rapid changes already in progress will soon enough be vindicated by the very changes they helped to produce, which should be ample reward and compensation for most of them.

5. Conclusion

To be forced to suffer an offense, be it an affront to the senses, disgust, shock, shame, annoyance, or humiliation, is an unpleasant inconvenience, and hence an evil, even when it is by no means harmful. Offense, moreover, belongs to that class of evils (which also includes harms as another species) that are directly suffered by specific persons, who then voice real grievances. (We must leave open for the present whether there are genuine evils that are not in this general category, but see *infra*, Book IV, Chap. 28.) Their victims are wronged even though they are not harmed. For that reason alone, it is morally legitimate for the criminal law to be concerned with their regulation. The offense principle then is hereby endorsed as one of the legislative legitimizing principles which we have been seeking. That endorsement, however, does not directly imply approval of criminal prohibitions of any or all types of offensive conduct, for if the legislature is to avoid wholesale invasions of liberty that are contrary to common sense and liberal conviction, it must mediate its application of the offense principle by the various restrictive standards listed above, and balance in each type of case the seriousness of the offense caused against the independent reasonableness of the offender's conduct.

The final emphasis of this chapter should lie in the same place as the initial emphasis of the preceding chapter. Offensive nuisance is a complex and difficult subject that well deserves extended treatment in any work on the moral limits of the criminal law. But when we recall (1) the relative triviality of offenses (when compared with harms) that renders them unsuitable occasions for severe punishment and (2) the effective power of custom and public opinion to prevent altogether their more egregious instances without the assistance of law, we can conclude that the theoretical fascination of this subject is equalled only by its practical unimportance.

9

Profound Offense

1. Limits to the nuisance model

If the full gravamen of the wrong in all offensive conduct is mere nuisance—harmless annoyance, unpleasantness, and inconvenience—then it is quite impossible to understand why the criminal law, rightly or wrongly, has taken offensiveness so seriously in the past. The very word "nuisance" suggests something relatively trivial, hardly a term to do justice to the profound feelings of righteous abhorrence that certain practices evoke in persons of ordinary sensitivity, even when those practices are believed to be, by and large, harmless and unobtrusive. Nuisance may be a matter of small importance for the criminal law, but there are some forms of offensiveness that are taken so seriously that some have advocated severe punishment for them even when they are not, strictly speaking, nuisances.

It will be useful to reserve the term "nuisance" for the miscellany of unpleasant states discussed in Chapters 7 and 8 when they are imposed upon someone in circumstances that make them difficult to avoid or escape. Nuisances so conceived are annoyances or inconveniences, and when they are believed to be caused wrongfully, they are resented ("taken offense at"), and thus become offenses in a strict and narrow sense. When they are in fact unjustified, as determined by the balancing tests of Chapter 8, that is a reason for legally prohibiting the conduct that produces them. Some of the offended states of mind in the broad miscellany have a felt character that seems to mark them off from all the others and for which the term "nuisance" seems too pallid even when they are not difficult to avoid or escape without annoying inconvenience. Sometimes, to be sure, these *profound offenses* are produced in circumstances (like those of the bus ride in Chapter 7) that make them impossible to avoid witnessing and add an extra dimension of annoyance and inconvenience to them. But unlike the other offensive nuisances, these profound ones would continue to rankle even when unwitnessed, and they would thus be offensive even when they are not, strictly speaking, nuisances at all. On the other side, those inescapable unpleasant experiences that are contrasted with the "profound" ones we can call *offensive nuisances merely*. Lacking the felt "profound" character of the others, they can be called "mere nuisances" without trivializing understatement, and we can plausibly claim legal protection from them only in circumstances in which they *are* indefensible intrusions (difficult to escape and unjustified by the balancing tests), and then only because they are such nuisances. Not all of the offensive actions on the bus ride in Chapter 7 are "offensive nuisances merely," though surely most are. The affronts to the senses clearly are of this kind, as are the disgusting indulgences and embarrassing indecencies. The religious caricatures and ethnic insults, however, while also "nuisances" in the situation (that is, they are annoying and inescapable), are somehow *that and more*, so that "nuisance" seems an understatement, and their evil seems independent of its unavoidability (in the strict sense that word bears in the balancing tests). Some might wish to criminalize the acts that knowingly produce these "profound offenses" even when they do not fully satisfy the balancing tests that are modelled after nuisance law. I think I understand the motives of these people, but I will try to rebut their arguments here.

Before listing the defining characteristics of "offensive nuisances merely" and "profound offenses," it would be wise to examine some putative examples of the latter. Profound offenses are disconcertingly diverse, but perhaps the following are representative.

1. *Voyeurism.* In 1983 the CBS television news show "Sixty Minutes" told the story of some women employees of a Kentucky coal mining company. The women had won employment as miners, a job hitherto reserved for men, and for several years they had discharged their duties competently and faithfully. But they had never been fully accepted by many of the male miners. One day they discovered to their horror that there were peepholes bored through a wall that separated a supply room to which the men had access from the womens' shower room and lavatory. To say that the women "took offense" at this discovery or "suffered annoyance" is grossly inadequate. Both the women and their lawyer spoke passionately of the victims' embarrassment, mortification, humiliation, and of the affront to their dig-

nity. Their chagrin was so severe that it probably had genuinely harmful effects on most of them, perhaps setbacks to a genuine "interest in personal privacy," or a permanent damaging of their relations with their fellow workers, or debilitating depression, sleeplessness, and anguish; but even in the possible cases where the threshold of actual harm had not been reached, a serious wrong was surely done them. The feelings of mortification and the like were no less powerful for being retroactive, and the description that characterizes the evil they suffered as "unpleasant states of mind" even of great intensity and durability (the language of nuisance) seems to miss a qualitative difference from ordinary offensive nuisances. The example is an impressive and pertinent one even though criminal prohibitions of the offending behavior would probably be legitimized anyway by both the harm principle and the offense principle as mediated by the balancing tests proposed in Chapter 8. (The women chose to sue for civil damages, and settled out of court for an undisclosed payment and a public apology.)

2. *Nazis and klansmen.* The feelings of an aged Jewish survivor of a Nazi death camp as a small band of American Nazis strut in full regalia down the main street of his or her town, or those of some American blacks as robed Ku Klux Klan members hold a demonstration in the public square of their town, have several relevant components that help to mark them off from ordinary offensive nuisances. First, the feelings cannot be wholly escaped merely by withdrawing one's attention, by locking one's door, pulling the window blinds, and putting plugs in one's ears. The offended state of mind is at least to some degree independent of what is directly perceived. Second, there is an element of direct personal danger and threat to others whom one holds dear. The demonstrators, after all, are affiliated by their own design with the very groups that have murdered millions of Jews and tormented and lynched countless blacks in the past. Third, and more importantly, the hated symbols of the demonstrators are affronts to something the offended parties hold dear and, like the memory of their dead kinsmen, even sacred.

3. *Execrated but "harmless" deviant religious and moral practices.* A religious practice or moral conviction may be just as "dear" or "sacred" to a totally committed person as the memory of murdered kinsmen is to the Jew or the black, and cults or practices thought to be heretical or deviant judged to be as abominable and loathsome as the Nazi parades and Klan demonstrations. Thus Robert Paul Wolff claims that to a devout Calvinist or a principled vegetarian "the very presence in his community of a Catholic or a meat-eater may cause him fully as much pain as a blow to the face or a theft of

his purse" and speaks of "the presence of ungodly persons in [the] community" as "torturing [one's] soul" and "destroying [one's] sleep."[1] Note that
Wolff refers only to the "presence in the community" of religiously or
morally deviant persons even when they are withdrawn, private, and discreet, unlike the arrogant demonstrators of the previous example. Lest this
hypothetical example seem too extreme, the reader should be reminded that
for centuries Protestant churches were illegal in Catholic Spain, that the
"private" slaughtering of beef cattle is illegal in India, raising hogs commercially is forbidden to Israelis, and the celebration of the mass and the
wearing of Christian clerical garb even by foreigners and in private are
criminal offenses in Saudi Arabia, where they are thought to be stenches in
the nostrils of God. Of course such criminal prohibitions cannot be legitimized either by the harm principle, or the offense principle as applied to
ordinary offensive nuisances through the balancing tests. If religious rites
and private dining customs were prohibited on such grounds, no one could
ever feel secure in his liberty so long as "devout and principled persons" are
filled with loathing at the very thought of what he does in private. (Where
different devout and principled groups loathe one another equally, a situation not unknown to history, a prohibitive criminal law aimed at the practices of either could only lead to civil strife.) But if we advocate relaxing the
balancing tests for the application of the offense principle in the case of
profound offenses like those of the Jews and the blacks in the earlier example, we shall have to find a way of distinguishing that kind of case from
the present one. The profoundly offended states of mind in the two kinds
of example may *feel* very much alike.

4. *Venerated symbols.* Traditionally, criminal codes have contained provisions
outlawing defacing the national flag or other objects of public veneration,
and mistreating corpses. Since flags, crucifixes, and dead bodies are not the
sorts of objects that have interests of their own, they cannot be "harmed" in
the sense of the harm principle. (See Vol. I, Chap. 1, §1.) When these
profoundly offensive acts are done in public they can be considered public
nuisances and punished accordingly, though when they are interpreted as
expressions of dissent, or "private expression of political disaffection,"[2] it is
doubtful that they would be certified as wrongful by any balancing test that
gives great importance to the value of political expression. But when these
acts are done discreetly in private they are more surely unreachable by any
plausible balancing test that gives preemptive weight to reasonable avoidability. Indeed, since they are easily avoidable by everyone, they are not
even properly called "nuisances" in the first place. And yet state penal
codes have commonly prohibited such acts in the past, no doubt because of

the qualitatively unique, "profound" character of the offense they produce in the bare contemplation. In Pennsylvania, for example, a 1945 statute provides punishment for anyone who "publicly *or privately* mutilates, defaces, defiles, or tramples upon, or casts contempt either by words or acts upon any such flag."[3]

There is no doubt that widespread and profound offense would be taken at an atheist group that held regular private, but open-to-the-public meetings, in its own anti-church building, at which they defaced prints of religious paintings, obscenely decorated religious icons, set fire to sacred texts, and so on. Modern blasphemy and sacrilege statutes penalize, for the most part, only "the mischievous or zealous blasphemer who purposely disrupts a religious meeting or procession with utterances designed to outrage the sensibilities of the group and thus provoke a riot."[4] But in other times and places, the privately meeting atheists would not have been so fortunate, and the penalties of the law would have been imposed on them if only because of the peculiarly deep character of the offense they produced to the religious sensibility. It is worth noting that a sense of fairness has never impelled a legislature to penalize clergymen and their congregations for savage denunciations in their churches of law-abiding atheists. The point is not, or is not simply, that the lawmaker's sense of reciprocity was deficient, but rather that the resentment of the atheists at the mockery of their beliefs does not constitute *profound* offense, since nothing they hold sacred is impugned by it.

There is also widespread and profound offense taken at the defilement of the ultimate symbol of love of country, the national flag under whose banners generations of heroes have fought and died. And even more profound feelings are aroused by the mistreatment of dead bodies. The authors of the *Model Penal Code* struggled with the question of whether offenses of these two kinds are profound enough to warrant punishment even of the private performance of the acts that cause them. The outcome was a compromise. "Section 250.10 penalizes mistreatment of a corpse 'in a way that [the actor] . . . knows would outrage ordinary family sensibilities', although the actor may have taken every precaution for secrecy . . . On the other hand, desecration of the national flag or other object of public veneration, an offense under Section 250.9, is not committed unless others are likely to 'observe or discover'."[5] Why should there be this difference? One of the chief authors of the Code, Louis Schwartz, explains it as follows:

> As I search for the principle of discrimination between the morals offenses made punishable only when committed openly and those punishable even when committed in secrecy, I find nothing but differences in the intensity of the aversion with which the different kinds of behavior are regarded. It was the

intuition of the draftsman and his fellow lawmakers at the Institute that disrespectful behavior to a corpse [is a] more intolerable affront to ordinary feelings
than disrespectful behavior to a flag. Therefore, in the former case but not the
latter, we overcame our general reluctance to extend penal controls . . . to
private behavior that disquiets people solely because they learn that things of
this sort are going on.[6]

It accords with my "intuition" too that most people would find mistreatment of dead bodies a "more intolerable affront" to their feelings than
desecration of a flag, but this does not imply necessarily that the "intensity
of their aversion" in the dead body case is greater than in the flag case. If
intensity were the relevant criterion of comparison, then deferring to "ordinary feelings" of the public at large, we might well criminalize coprophagia,
the eating of live worms, anal intercourse, even scratching fingernails on
slate and going bathless for weeks at a time, "although the actors may have
taken every precaution for secrecy". The more likely explanation is that
though the offended reactions in both the flag and dead body cases are
qualitatively different from other kinds of offense, in that they are both
affronts to the higher-order sensibilities (See Chap. 7, §4), they also differ
from one another in that the moral principle affronted symbolically by
mistreatment of corpses—respect for humanity—is more fundamental than
the moral principle symbolically affronted by flag desecration, namely fidelity to country. The offense taken at the mistreatment of corpses then
might be still more "profound," questions of intensity and duration of
aversion aside.

There is another difference between dead bodies and flags that may have
some bearing on the difference in our reactions to their respective mutilations. A flag is an arbitrary or conventional symbol of an abstraction, which
bears no striking similarity to what it symbolizes. Rather it comes to represent a country only by virtue of a conventional understanding. If someone
designed an entirely different flag, say one that featured green geometrical
abstractions on a field of gold and black stripes, and we all agreed to adopt
the new emblem, then it would come to represent the United States,
though its colors and shapes are no less arbitrary than those of the symbol it
replaced. A dead body, on the other hand, is a natural symbol of a living
person, and needless to say has a striking similarity to the real thing. When
one mutilates a corpse one is doing something that *looks* very much like
mutilating a real person, and the spontaneous horror of the real crime spills
over on the symbolic one. Schwartz makes a different but closely related
point when he writes: "I submit that legislative tolerance for private flag
desecration is explicable by the greater difficulty an ordinary [person] has in
identifying with a country and all else that a flag symbolizes as compared

with the ease in identifying with a corpse . . ."[7] There is a point to this observation. If I saw a stranger on the bus open a coffin and pound the face of the newly dead person inside of it with a hammer (Chap. 7, §3), my reaction would be to move my hand to my own face, and wince as if I were the one who had been struck. My reaction to the desecration of a flag would be nothing like that. Imaginative projection of self into the mistreated object, however, while significant, only helps to explain the greater intensity of the aversion, not the degree of impact on moral sensibility, the factor that makes an offense "profound".

5. *Abortion and the mistreatment of corpses.* Some opponents of abortion think of the human fetus from the moment of conception as a living person with interests and rights, chief of which are the interest in staying alive and the corresponding "right to life". According to this view, when one deliberately kills the fetus at any stage of its development one violates that right and defeats the corresponding interest, thus wronging and harming (in the sense of the harm principle) the "victim". Many other persons, including some who are opposed to abortion for other reasons, find it insurmountably difficult to think of a fetus, especially in its earlier stages (and *a fortiori* when it is a mere fertilized egg) as an actual person, since it lacks many of the characteristics that a person has: more than rudimentary consciousness, understanding, possession of a concept and awareness of oneself.[8] The fetus possesses these characteristics *potentially*, of course, but that shows only that the fetus is a potential person, not that it is an actual one already possessed of interests and rights.

Still, from as early as the tenth week the fetus has a recognizably human face and chubby little human hands. If only we could see it then, we would be struck by its physical resemblance to a little baby. Zealous opponents of legalized abortion take advantage of that resemblance to push their case. Many of them carry photographs of cute and lovable ten-week-old "unborn babies", and descriptions of the violence normal methods of surgical abortion impose on them. It is hard not to recoil at the very thought of their forceful destruction. Yet that does not prove that ten-week-old fetuses are right-bearing persons. One can still deny with unshaken confidence that they have a right to life, since having recognizably human features and the capacity to evoke tender responses from observers are not plausible criteria of personhood. The strongest inference we can make from the impact of the photograph on our sentiments is that there may be morally relevant properties of fetuses other than rights and personhood that have a bearing on how we ought to treat them (though not necessarily on any question of the propriety of legal coercion.) In particular, what is suggested to me is that ten-week-old fetuses, by virtue of their recognizably human features, are natural symbols, themselves only prepersons, yet as such sacred symbols of the real thing. As symbols they become the objects of transferred tender sentiments, and their destruction might understandably shock some persons in the manner of a violent desecration of any cherished icon, causing profound offense indeed.

The question of the relevance of profound offense arises even more clearly in a class of issues to be treated below (§5) involving the treatment of corpses. A newly dead human body is even more natural a symbol of a human person than is a developing fetus. Both postpersons and prepersons are naturally associated with actual persons, and thus become natural repositories for the sentiments real persons evoke in us, but our sentiments are even more sharply focused on the neomort because it is not only a symbol of human beings generally, but unlike the fetus, it is the symbolic remains of a particular person and his specific traits and history. Moreover, we are not even tempted in rhetoric to ascribe rights and interests to the neomort (with the possible exception of those stemming from testimonial directions he left before he died), and surely not "the right to life." One cannot murder a corpse, or commit assault or battery or rape on it; but one can violate it symbolically, and few societies are prepared to tolerate its public mutilation. Hacking it up and throwing its limbs about would be, as we say, a shock to decent human sentiment.

If any *rights* at all are violated by such treatment, it must be the rights of captive spectators not to suffer offense, and of other third parties not to suffer profound offense even at what they do not witness. But the conduct might be wrong without violating anyone's rights at all.

2. The distinctive characteristics of profound offense

Now that we have some examples of profound offenses in mind, how can we summarize their differences from what we have called "offensive nuisances merely"? Let us begin by enumerating the features generally characteristic of the offended states in mere offensive nuisance. These experiences are, first of all, relatively trivial or shallow, not only compared to harms but also compared to some other mental states, for example those that result from offense to higher-order sensibilities. Second, the wrong in mere offensive nuisance coincides with the perceptual experience that is imposed on the victim and its caused aftereffects, and is inseparable from those experiences. Without the direct perception of the offending conduct, there would be no offense, even if the person learned secondhand that the offending conduct would occur or had occurred. It is experiencing the conduct, not merely knowing about it, that offends. In respect to a mere offensive nuisance, its *esse est percipii* (its being consists in its being perceived). Third, the offense in ordinary offensive nuisance is experienced in all cases as at least partly *personal*, and in most cases as wholly personal. The offended party thinks of *himself* as the wronged victim of the conduct that causes him to have certain unpleasant and inescapable states of mind. Being disgusted, revolted, shocked, frightened, angered, bored, embarrassed, shamed, or made anxious, are like being hurt in that one has a grievance in one's own name, on one's own behalf, against the offender for making one undergo the experience. And if one had not been present, one could have had no such complaint. Fourth, it is generally characteristic of the wrong in mere offensive nuisances that it derives from an affront to one's senses, or to one's lower order sensibilities (see Chap. 7, §4.) One does not think of the offending conduct as the sort that would be wrong (in contravention of one's own standards) wherever it might occur, but wrong only because it occurs here and now, thus victimizing its reluctant witnesses. In language suggested by Kurt Baier,[9] the conduct affronts our sensibility without necessarily violating any of our *standards* of sensibility or propriety. It can therefore "offend our senses" (or lower order sensibilities) without offending *us*. Fifth and finally, in ordinary offensive nuisances the offending behavior is thought wrong (and hence resented, and hence an "offense" in the strict and narrow sense) because it produces unpleasant states in the captive witnesses, not the other way around. It does not produce unpleasant states because it is thought wrong on independent grounds.[10]

The characteristics of profound offense contrast with those of the ordinary nuisances in all five respects. First, they have an inexpressibly different felt "tone", best approximated by saying that they are deep, profound, shattering, serious, even more likely to cause harm by their obsessiveness to those who experience them. That is why the word "nuisance", with its unavoidable suggestions of triviality, is inadequate. Second, even when one does not perceive the offending conduct directly, one can be offended "at the very idea" of that sort of thing happening even in private. A nude person on the public bus may be an offense in my sight, but I am not offended at the very idea of that person being nude in the privacy of his or her own rooms, which is to say that my offense is not of the profound kind. Some of the examples of disgusting conduct (mere offensive nuisance) may seem different in this respect. I am disgusted by the sight of the bus passengers eating vomit, and at first it might seem that I am almost as offended by the very thought of them doing so in the privacy of their own dining rooms. But in fact my offense at what is not present seems to grow only as I succeed in forming a precise image—visual, auditory, and olfactory—in my imagination, in which case it is not that a standard of propriety is violated by the very idea of certain conduct; rather an offense is produced by my own energetic image-making. *I* am the party in that case who produces an offensive experience in myself, and I can have a grievance only against myself. It is as if by intense concentration I form a precise image of the bus passenger naked in his or her own bedroom, focus all of my attention on it, and then complain that that person "profoundly offends" me by his or her habitual unwitnessed nudity. My offense at the very idea of certain conduct is not profound because I *would* be offended by that conduct if I were to witness it; rather it is profound because I am offended by its taking place at all whether I witness it or not. On the other hand, if it were possible for a person to have the strange basic moral conviction that even private nudity is sinful because (say) it is an embarrassment to God," then the offense such a person feels at others being naked in their own homes every night would indeed be of the "profound" variety.

Third, in the case of profound offense, even when the evil *is* in the perceiving, something offends *us* and not merely our senses or lower order sensibilities. Our reaction is not like that of the man in the proverbial tale who, unable to bear the sight of a lady standing in the bus, always averted his eyes (rather than offer his seat) when confronted with the prospect. Profound offense cannot be avoided by averting one's eyes. Fourth, because profound offense results from an affront to the standards of propriety that determine one's higher-order sensibilities, it offends because it is believed wrong, not the other way round. It is not believed to be wrong simply and entirely because it causes offense.

Finally, profound offenses in all cases are experienced as at least partly *impersonal*, and in most cases as entirely impersonal. The offended party does not think of *himself* as the victim in unwitnessed flag defacings, corpse mutilations, religious icon desecrations, or abortions, and he does not therefore feel aggrieved (wronged) on his own behalf. The peeping-Tom and racial insult cases are, of course, exceptions to this. Here we should say that there is a merging of the two kinds of offense. The victim's outrage is profound because it is caused by a shocking affront to his or her deepest moral sensibilities, but he or she also happens to be the violated or threatened victim of the affronting behavior. In contrast, in the flag, icon, dead body, and abortion cases, there is no person at all in whose name to voice a complaint, except the profoundly offended party, and the only thing he could complain about in his own behalf is his offended state of mind. But *that* is not what he is offended at.

Still, in the confusion of strong feelings of different kinds, people are likely to mistake what it is they are indignant about. Mill reminds us that

"There are many who consider as an injury to themselves any conduct which they have a distaste for [witnessed or not], and resent it as an outrage to their feelings . . ."[12] These people might be those whose profound offense at the reported private conduct of others is taken on behalf of an impersonal principle, or sacred symbol, or the like. Then coming to resent their own unpleasant state of mind as a nuisance (even though its character as felt annoyance was originally an insignificant component in what was experienced), they refocus their grievance, putting themselves in the forefront as "injured" parties. When they take this further step, however, their grievance—originally impersonal but now voiced in their own behalf— loses almost all its moral force. Mill's response to them is devastating:

> . . . as a religious bigot, when charged with disregarding the religious feelings of others, has been known to retort that they disregard his feelings by persisting in their abominable worship or creed. But there is no parity between the feeling of a person for his own opinion and the feeling of another who is offended at his holding it, no more than between the desire of a thief to take a purse and the desire of the right owner to keep it. And a person's taste is as much his own peculiar concern as his opinion or his purse.[13]

Takers of profound offense at unwitnessed conduct are better advised to rest their claim for "protection" on impersonal grounds.

In the voyeurism and racial insult cases the primary offended parties are the direct intended targets of the behavior that does the offending, and their offense is profound because what they feel to be violated or affronted is something they hold precious (human dignity, solidarity with martyred kinsmen). Their reaction *of course* is more than mere "annoyance," and for that reason, among others, we call it "profound". In the other cases, the offense is taken on behalf of something external to oneself, and the offense is profound because of its powerful impact on one's moral sensibilities, even in the absense of any strong feeling of personal involvement. Indeed, as the feeling of aggrieved personal nuisance becomes stronger, the impersonal shock and outrage necessarily becomes weaker, and the whole experience begins to lose its profound character. When the offended reaction to a reported private mutilation of a dead body (say) is genuinely profound in the sense developed here, the offended party is not thinking of himself at all. He is involved in the offended state simply as its subject, not as part of its subject matter.

3. The bare knowledge problem again

The notion of profound offense leads us to take more seriously a question we earlier treated somewhat dismissively (see Chap. 8, §1). The "bare knowledge" problem calls for a decision about how the offense principle is to be applied. When it is the prevention of offense to which legislators appeal for the legitimization of a proposed statute, *whose* offense may appropriately be considered? (1) That of all observers? Clearly not, for those who voluntarily assumed the risk of offense have no complaint, and those who can escape it easily have hardly any more complaint. Shall we say then that (2) all and only *captive* observers should be considered? Or should we weigh also (3) the offense of non-observers who are affected by the "bare knowledge" that the offending acts are taking place in a known location beyond their observations? Perhaps we should go even further and consider (4) the offense of anyone with the very bare knowledge that when such acts are legal they *might* be taking place somewhere—almost anywhere at all— for all one knows, and with perfect impunity at that? If we draw the line to include (3) and exclude (4), then those who practice their profoundly offensive vices silently and discreetly behind locked doors and drawn blinds would escape the clutches of the law because they do not offend any *observers* and, since no non-observer can *know* what takes place in their rooms, no one can be offended by the bare thought that flag-defacing, homosexual lovemaking, or the like is going on there. But those who behave in unobserved privacy but make no effort to conceal from others what they are doing, may indeed offend some non-observers who suffer from their bare knowledge, and these offenders could even incur criminal liability if the sensibilities of the people in group (3) are included.

Kurt Baier has made this point with his usual clarity:

> . . . where there are standards that are widely and deeply embedded, witnessing is not necessary to cause offense. Of course, if I draw the blinds whenever I eat human flesh for dinner or have sexual intercourse with my goat or with my devoted sister, then no one's sensibilities can be affronted by witnessing what I am doing. But if I tell others or invite them to parties and ask them to bring their own favorite corpse or goat or relative, the case is different. The fact that they need not come or participate is not necessarily sufficient to make my behavior inoffensive . . . A neon sign on my house proclaiming "*Cannibalism, Bestiality, Incest*. Tickets $5.00. Meals $25. Close relatives half price" would be even more offensive to those who accept the relevant standards of sensibility.[14]

If we permit the activities in Baier's examples, but prohibit the participants from describing their activities to others, inviting others to join them, or soliciting through public announcement or advertising, then we have respected their liberty to act as they wish in private at the cost of their liberties to speak, write, communicate, or express themselves as they wish (one of their basic rights). On the balancing scales, by virtue of the great weight of free expression as both a personal and public good, the case against forbidding the expressive behavior might be even stronger than the case against criminalizing the primary offensive conduct.

The American Law Institute was indeed tempted to recommend, in its *Model Penal Code*, that profoundly offensive but harmless conduct be permitted in private but only when the participants have made reasonable efforts to be discreet and preserve the secrecy of their activities. Those who recommended this approach suggested the use of a familiar phrase in Anglo-American criminal statutes for the sort of behavior they would penalize: *open and notorious* illicit relations, as opposed to discreet and unflaunted ones, would be made criminal. Louis B. Schwartz tells us that the Institute finally rejected this suggestion on the ground that it is unwise to establish a penal offense in which "guilt would depend on the level of gossip to which the moral transgression gave rise."[5] I am not sure exactly what this means, but I can imagine that the code-makers had in mind such a scenario as the following. Two "profound offenders" (homosexual lovers, flag defacers, corpse mutilators, whatever) rent a flat for the purpose of secretly engaging in their odious practice at regular times and intervals. At first, no one in the neighborhood knows or cares. After a time, however, their landlady, overcome with curiosity, peeps in the keyhole, and is duly scandalized. Being a compulsive gossiper, she quickly spreads the word all over the neighborhood. In time groups of children form the habit of waiting for the couple to arrive and following them, jeering and taunting, all the way to their door, while grown-ups stand on the fringes of the excitement, gathered in animated gossiping groups. Inevitably the comings and goings of the scandalous couple become a kind of public spectacle, and everyone knows exactly what they are doing, and where and when they do it, despite their best efforts at concealment. In time their activities, even though unwitnessed, become a "flagrant affront" to the whole community, and the offense principle, extended to protect the sensibilities of those in group (3), justifies their arrest and criminal conviction. Surely criminal liability, the code-makers seem to be saying, ought not to rest on one's bad luck in finding a gossipy landlady. Either those who are lucky in keeping their secret ought *also* to be punished [in virtue of their offense to those with "very bare knowledge" in group (4)] or neither the lucky nor the unlucky ones should be punished despite the offense to those in group (3). To treat the two groups differently would be to let their guilt "depend on the level of gossip" reached through causes beyond their control. But that would still leave a third group—Baier's unrepentent indiscreet offenders, whose offending actions are done in private, but who take no steps to keep their existence unknown to others. The argument against penalizing *them*, as we have seen, is that interference with free expression can be justified by the balancing tests only when there is an enormous weight on the opposite side of the scale. The highly diluted "very bare knowledge" of the offended in these cases can hardly have very great weight.

Traditionally, liberals have categorically rejected statutes penalizing harmless unwitnessed private conduct no matter how profoundly upset *anyone* may become at the bare knowledge that such conduct is or might be occurring. Mill had deep and well-justified suspicions of the good faith of the parties who claim to need protection of their own sensibilities from the self-regarding conduct of others,[16] and he offered many examples of liberties unfairly withdrawn from minorities on the disingenuous ground that the prohibited conduct, even when harmless and unwitnessed, was a deep affront to the others: the liberty to eat pork (in Moslem countries), to worship God as a Protestant or Jew (in Spain), to perform music, dance, play games, or attend theatres on the Sabbath (in Puritan Great Britain and New England), to drink beer in one's own home (during Prohibition in the United States).

H. L. A. Hart is even more emphatic:

> The fundamental objection surely is that a right to be protected from the distress which is inseparable from the bare knowledge that others are acting in ways you think wrong, cannot be acknowledged by anyone who recognizes individual liberty as a value. For the . . . principle that coercion may be used to protect [persons] . . . from this form of distress cannot stop there. If distress incident to the belief that others are doing wrong is harm [better "preventable offense"], so also is the distress incident to the belief that others are doing what you do not want them to do; and the only liberty that could coexist with this extension of . . . the principle is liberty to do those things to which no one seriously objects. Such liberty is clearly nugatory.[17]

Hart overstates his case here somewhat. If the prohibition of unwitnessed acts were limited to profound offenses, and balancing tests were scrupulously observed, there would be little danger that the offense principle so mediated could commit legislatures to banning private conduct by some parties on the ground that other parties don't *want* them acting that way *simpliciter*. And provided balancing tests are assumed, it is a *non sequitur* to say that the only permitted liberty would be "the liberty to do those things to which *no one* seriously objects;" rather the sole liberty would be to do those things to which *not everybody* (or nearly everybody) seriously objects. Nevertheless, Hart's point is a sobering one that should take away the appetite of any liberal for criminalizing harmless and unobserved behavior or any kind:

> Recognition of individual liberty as a value involves, as a minimum, acceptance of the principle that the individual may do as he wants, even if others are

distressed when they learn what it is that he does—unless of course there are other good grounds for forbidding it. No social order which accords to individual liberty any value could also accord the right to be protected from distress thus occasioned.[18]

Again, there is some overstatement. One could hold that liberty has *some* value and that prevention of distress at bare knowledge has some value too, so that the two must sometimes be balanced against one another. But Hart's point does seem to apply to the view that defines the *liberal's* values (see Vol. I, Introduction, §5), namely that liberty has very great value indeed, and not simply "a value" or "any value". It is impossible that liberty should at once have great value and be properly sacrificed to prevent "mere distress" to others caused by their bare or very bare knowledge. And even though the protection of moral sensibility from profound offense does not logically imply the protection of persons from *any* kind of distress, it is true as a matter of empirical fact (and this was Mill's major emphasis) that legislatures are prone to slide in that direction once they start down the slope.

The endorsement of the offense principle by the liberal theorist thus creates tensions for him in two directions. Those who are impressed with the unique character of profound offense urge a relaxing of the normal balancing tests derived from nuisance law for determining when offenses are serious enough to warrant criminal prohibition, so that even unwitnessed offensive conduct might be prohibited in some circumstances. Those who are impressed by the great value of liberty, on the other hand, urge the liberal theorist to stand more resolutely against any acceptance of criminal statutes that ban harmless and unwitnessed conduct. These liberals often argue that the balancing tests are not protection enough, since in some cases the tests might themselves warrant punishment of unobserved and harmless actions, so that they should be replaced by more categorical protection. My position up until this point in the book has been to resist the pressure to grant an exemption to "profound offense" from the requirements of the normal mediating standards for the application of the offense principle, while reassuring my fellow liberals that the balancing tests are not likely ever to permit offense at bare knowledge to outweigh any private and harmless offending conduct, and certainly not any that has the slightest hint of redeeming value. But perhaps I was too sanguine.

4. Solution of the bare knowledge problem

My argument for the adequacy of the balancing tests rested on the assumption that secret and private activity is never the object of *serious* offense, because the offense it causes cannot be as intense or widespread as that caused by directly observed conduct, and such as it is, it is always "reasonably avoidable." Where there are exceptions to these generalizations, I assumed that they were the consequence of an excessive, even pathological, susceptibility to offense that can hardly warrant interference with any wholly self-regarding actions of others that are minimally reasonable, that is, either individually or socially valuable, discreet as can be expected without forfeiting the right of free expression, and not maliciously or spitefully *intended* to offend those who are excessively susceptible to offense. The key assumption, of course, is that only the excessively "skittish" would bolt at the mere idea of harmless but repugnant unobserved conduct, and *their* reactions, like that of rare skittish horses, cannot be the ground for interfering with otherwise innocent or valuable activity that cannot conveniently be done in a way to avoid upsetting the skittish.

The argument from moral skittishness, however, does not give the nervous liberal all the protection he needs, and no doubt both Mill and Hart would feel insecure with it. It is no doubt true, as a matter of fact, of the western democracies in the twentieth century that extreme, widespread, and inescapable offense at unobserved but disapproved harmless conduct is possible only for the morally skittish. But there is no necessity that this connection hold universally, for all societies in all ages. What if this kind of susceptibility to offense ceased to be rare and exceptional? What if it spread through the whole community and became a new norm of susceptibility? Then clearly it would no longer be, in the same sense, excessive or "skittish." We can ask the same questions about *literal* skittishness. What if 90% of all domestic horses, and hence the statistically "average" horse, came to have just the characteristics we have in mind *now* when we call a given horse "skittish"? We don't call the average horse skittish, because "skittish" means abnormally or exceptionally nervous, and the normal horse cannot, in the statistical sense, be abnormal. We would have to raise our standards of skittishness so that only those horses who were more nervous even than the new average would be properly called "skittish." It would still be true that people should not be liable for starting skittish horses through their otherwise routine and useful behavior, but people could rightly be required to be more careful than they are now in the way they act before the normal horses.

The analogy is plain. In Saudi Arabia, it may well be that 90% of the population is morally skittish by our standards even though "normal" of course by their own. In the United States almost everyone would be put into intensely disagreeable offended states by the repulsive conduct on the bus of Chapter 7, but hardly anyone would be put into equally disagreeable and unavoidable states by the bare idea of such conduct occurring at a known place in private, or simply occurring somewhere or other (for all one knows) because it is legal. But it is at least conceivable (barely) that almost all Saudis are put in precisely the same intensely unpleasant state of mind by the thought that wine or pork is being consumed somewhere or Christian rites conducted somewhere in their country beyond their perception as they would be by their direct witnessing of such odious conduct. For at least some of these examples, our balancing tests would pose no barrier to legitimate criminal prohibition. In particular, where the private conduct is neither expressive (because there is no audience with which to communicate) nor religious, and without other redeeming social importance or personal value (it consists, say, of the casual defacing and smashing of religious icons or patriotic emblems), then its value might not outbalance the inescapably intense offense suffered by all "normal" outsiders at the bare knowledge of what is going on. And so the liberal's argument concludes that although the balancing tests work well to render illegitimate the criminalization here and now of private harmless acts, they could be used, unfortunately, to legitimize criminal statutes in more homogenous and authoritarian societies where minorities, actual and potential, are even more in need of protection.

It must be conceded in response, that the offense principle mediated by the balancing tests does not give the liberal all the reassurance he needs. That is not to say that it fails to give him any substantial reassurance, but only that it falls short of a guarantee against misapplication. It cannot be used in any society to punish, on grounds of offensiveness merely, acts of expression (to non-captive audiences) or of private religious rituals, or of voluntary sexual conduct in private (with its great personal value to the participants). But it can be used to protect persons from "profound offense" when it is almost equally unpleasant as the worst of the public nuisances, and is so to almost everyone, and the offending private conduct has little redeeming value. These are conditions not likely to be satisfied in our own society, but conceivably would be satisfied elsewhere. The liberal can be further reassured, however, that even where the offense principle legitimizes in principle a prohibition, it is not likely that a legislature would find justifying reasons on balance for enacting the legislation. Either the offending conduct would be so eccentric and infrequent that it would not be cost-efficient to bother with it, or else for other practical reasons enforcement would have unacceptable side effects. The statute itself would encourage busybodies, eavesdroppers, and informers, require police to engage in unsavory detection practices, or else put the privacy of everyone in jeopardy, lead to arbitrarily selective enforcement, increase the leverage of blackmailers, and, in general, use expensive police resources in unproductive or counterproductive ways. Finally, even if there were such prohibitive statutes, since they are based only on the offense principle, they could rightly impose only minor penalties (see Chap. 7, §1) and would therefore have little deterrent value. So the liberal need not fear that legislative acceptance of the offense principle would pose an immediate threat to our liberties here and now. But that is not strong enough assurance. What he needs is a way of demonstrating that punishment of wholly private and harmless conduct for the purpose of preventing offended reactions occasioned by the bare knowledge that such conduct is or could be occurring is *illegitimate in principle*, and thus always wrong, here or elsewhere. To reach that conclusion, a different and supplementary liberal strategy is needed.

Let me return to the concept of "profound offense". If governmental invasions of liberty to protect others from bare knowledge are *ever* legitimate, it must surely be when the resultant offense is of the "profound" variety. If mere offense to the senses or the lower-order sensibilities (e.g. by "disgusting" activities) could be protected even from unwitnessed conduct, then as we have seen, the offendable party would be protected from conduct to which he has no objection except that it is unpleasant to witness, and then even when he is not made to witness it! In that case what he is actually protected against is his own vivid imaginings, which should be subject to his own control unless they are, because of neurosis, irresistibly obsessive. In the case of genuinely profound offenses, however, the offended party has a powerful objection to the unwitnessed conduct quite apart from the effects on his own state of mind that come from thinking about it when it is unobserved. Indeed, these derivative unpleasant effects are the consequence of the behavior's affront to his moral sensibilities and would not exist but for that affront. It would put the cart before the horse to say that the moral sensibilities are shocked because of the unpleasant states produced in the offended party's mind. These states have nothing to do with his complaint. His grievance is not a personal one made in his own behalf. It is therefore odd to ground a prohibition of the offending conduct on a fancied need to protect *him*.[19] When an unwitnessed person defaces flags and mutilates corpses in the privacy of his own rooms, the outsider is outraged, but *he* would not claim to be the *victim* of the offensive behavior. He thinks that the behavior is wrong whether it has a true victim or not, and *that* is what outrages him. As soon as he shifts his attention to his own discomfiture, the whole nature of his complaint will change, and his moral fervor will seep out like air through a punctured inner tube.

But if it is not the offended party himself who needs "protection" from unobserved harmless conduct, who can it possibly be that can make claim to "protection"? Whose rights are violated when an impersonal object is smashed in the privacy of the descecrator's rooms? Surely not the object itself; it is not the kind of thing that can have rights in the first place. Surely not the desecrator. He is acting voluntarily and doing exactly what he wants. Perhaps it is an evil that sacred symbols, artificial or natural, should be defaced, whether observed or not. But it doesn't seem to be the kind of evil that can be the basis of anyone's grievance.

The advocate of punishment for those whose unwitnessed and unharmful activities offend in their very description can now be confronted with a dilemma. Either he bases his argument on an application of the offense principle or else on a (tacit) appeal to the illiberal principle of legal moralism. The former would be a claim to protection from their own unpleasant mental states by those who are offended by a "bare thought" or by "bare knowledge" of the occurence of the loathesome behavior. The latter would be an application of the liberty-limiting principle that all liberals (by definition) reject: that it is a good reason for a criminal prohibition that it is necessary to prevent inherently immoral conduct whether or not that conduct causes harm or offense to anyone. If it is the liberal offense principle to which ultimate appeal is made, the argument has a fatal flaw. According to that principle as we have interpreted it (Chap. 7, §1) criminal law may be used to protect persons from *wrongful offense*, that is, from their own unpleasant mental states when wrongfully imposed on them by other parties in a manner that violates their rights. On the plausible assumption that desecration of sacred symbols even in private is wrong (even without a victim), there is a sense then in which it produces "wrongful offense" in the mind of any disapproving person who learns about it: The conduct is wrongful *and* it is a cause of a severely offended mental state. But that is not yet sufficient for it to be a "wrongful offense" in the sense intended in a truly liberal offense principle. The offense-causing action must be more than wrong; it must be *a wrong* to the offended party, in short a violation of *his* rights.[20] But as we have seen, even the offended party himself will not claim that his own rights have been necessarily violated by any unobserved conduct that he thinks of as morally odious. If he does make that further personal claim he becomes vulnerable to Mill's withering charges of moral egotism and bad faith. (See footnotes 12, 13, and 16 *supra*.) His profoundly offended condition then is not a wrong to him, and thus not a "wrongful offense" in the sense of the liberal offense principle.

The offended party experiences moral shock, revulsion, and indignation, not on his own behalf of course, but on behalf of his moral principles or his moral regard for precious symbols. If those moral reactions are to be the ground for legal coercion and punishment of the offending conduct, it must be by virtue of the principle of legal moralism which enforces moral conviction and gives effect to moral outrage even when there are no violated rights, and in general no persons to "protect". The liberal, however, is adamantly opposed to the principle of legal moralism, and he sees no reason to let into the criminal law on offense-principle grounds what he insists on excluding when candidly presented on moralistic grounds. In summary, the argument for criminalization of private conduct to prevent bare-knowledge offense rests either on the offense principle or on legal moralism. If it appeals to the liberal's offense principle it fails, since bare-knowledge offense is not "wrongful offense" in the sense employed by that principle. But if it appeals to legal moralism, it may be valid on those grounds, but it cannot commit the liberal, since the liberal rejects legal moralism. It follows that there is no argument open to a liberal that legitimizes punishment of private harmless behavior in order to prevent bare-knowledge offense. Moreover, the liberal can continue to endorse the offense principle without fear of embarrassment. John Stuart Mill can rest secure.

There is, however, a complication to add of this solution to the bare-knowledge problem. There may be some cases of unwitnessed bare-knowledge offense where the case for banning the conduct that causes it does not require legal moralism. I refer to those *personal* deep affronts, whose victims claim that a personal grievance remains even after the moralistic case is severed from their argument. That is because the offending conduct is somehow addressed to them in an unmistakably direct way, even when not observed by them. For example, it should be illegal to acquire a corpse and conduct violent accident research on it (see *infra*, §5) without the next of kin's consent. If that were not so, a widow, for example, might learn that her dear late husband's face is being smashed to bits in a scientific experiment, whether she likes it or not. She does not have to witness it (fortunately) but she suffers at the bare thought, which she cannot keep out of her mind. Even when she is thinking of other things she is generally depressed. She has a grievance in this case that she does not share with every stranger who may know of the experiments and conscientiously disapprove of them. Her grievance is personal (voiced on her own behalf) not simply because her moral sensibility is affronted (she has no personal *right* not to have her moral sensibility affronted) and she cannot keep *that* out of her mind, but rather because it is *her* husband, and not someone else. In this quite exceptional kind of case, the personally related party is the only one whose rights are violated, though many others may suffer profound offense at the bare knowledge. (Racist mockery and abusive pornography received "in private" by willing audiences can also cause acutely *personal* offense to members of the insulted groups who have bare knowledge of it, and must therefore be treated as exceptional cases. See the discussions below in §§ 7 and 8, and especially in chapter 11, §9.) Her rights therefore would be more economically protected by injunctive orders or civil actions than by the criminal law.

One hard question remains. What of the bare-knowledge offender (say a human flesh-eater who receives his dead bodies through donations or other legal means) who engages in his profoundly offensive activity in private, and who not only makes no effort to conceal the fact, but "openly and notoriously" flaunts his tastes, invites others to join in his activities, openly advertises for others to join him, even with garish neon signs (as in Kurt Baier's example)? Those to whom the human body is a sacred icon are not only morally shocked at the very idea of cannibalism; they are prevented by the advertisement from ridding their minds of the shocking idea whose offensiveness is revitalized by every encounter with the intrusive sign. I think the liberal principles can warrant interference with excessive displays of this character, though not with the basic rights of privacy, communication, and expression. But the balance of conflicting values is delicate, and the risk of erroneous judgment great.

Consider a spectrum of cases. In the first, the lonely cannibal solicits collaborators by phone calls to his friends, letters, and private conversation only. If it is his right to engage in the primary offensive behavior in private (and in the absence of harm to others, the liberal cannot deny that right), then surely it is his right to talk about it with others and invite them to join him. If he solicits strangers on the street, however, and does so aggressively and tenaciously, he becomes a public nuisance, even a harasser. (See Chap. 16, §2.) Suppose now a second example, in which discreet and dignified advertisements are placed on his building, and notices put in newspapers. Still the liberal has no objection. The third example is our original one, in which the advertisement is by means of a garish neon sign. In the fourth example, the advertisements are on large billboards throughout the city and on huge neon signs on an elevated platform dominating the downtown center of the city. Finally, in the fifth example, the conspicuous signs are now illustrated graphically with paintings (say) of attractive men and women carving rump roasts out of a recognizably human corpse.

The liberal could approve banning the graphic signs on ordinary nuisance grounds. The public streets are for many as inescapable as the public bus was for the unfortunate passengers in Chapter 7, and vivid depictions of conduct can be as disgusting, nauseating, grating, embarrassing, or irritating as the actual behavior depicted. The fourth example is more difficult. If the conspicuous and unavoidable non-graphic signs are to be prohibited, it must be because they alter the public environment in a way that misrepresents the public intention. Every part of a city might belong to someone or other, but the city as a whole represents all its citizens. They might wish to have trees planted along all the public thoroughfares, or build monuments to public heroes, or decorate public spaces with sculpture, works of art, and plaques with lines of classic poetry. Even the great dominating neon signs illuminating the night on Broadway or Piccadilly Circus, though they are on private land and communicate private messages to the public, create a unique city ambience that becomes a kind of distinctive public possession and a symbol of the city to outsiders. When the more visible "monuments" include invitations to cannibalism, sodomy, symbol desecration, flag burning, and corpse mutilating, among other harmless eccentricities, then the public ambience of the city has been quite unsubtly altered, to the detriment of a public interest. "Is this really what we want the symbol of our city to be?", the citizens might ask, and provided less destructive modes of communication and advertisement are left open, the liberal might not object if the citizens answer "No!", and take appropriate regulative action.

The example with which we began, the single neon sign, is a borderline case, just because it is an isolated instance and not likely to affect the visual environment of the city as a whole. It could offend, however, as a kind of eyesore, indeed even as a neon sign advertising beer, or church worship, or philosophy books, might be an eyesore in some neighborhoods. But even its written message itself, being an affront to what is held by many to be sacred, when aggressively obtruded upon the attention of passersby, is a kind of public nuisance. It is not an illiberal response to say: "I don't care what you do in private; that is your business. But stop making me a party to it, by rubbing my nose in it." The private unobserved eating of human flesh is like the private unobserved desecrating of a holy symbol. The neon sign advertising it, on the other hand, is like the *public* desecrating of a holy symbol, like displaying on one's house an illuminated cross defaced with obscene figures and messages to scandalize the pious. There is a sense in which desecration cannot truly *be* desecration unless it is public. When it is public, and more than is necessary for some legitimate purpose, it crosses the line of offensive nuisance. Words, of course, are not the same as pictures, and pictures are not the same as real conduct right out in public. Perhaps then "desecration" is too strong a word for mere words that call attention to desecration, itself unobserved. The lonely cannibal could receive the benefit of that doubt if he ceased using garish neon, and advertised less aggressively.

5. The mistreatment of dead bodies

The reader should not infer from the nature of the examples employed thus far that I take all forms of profound offense lightly. It is a very good thing that people have higher-level sensibilities, that some things are dear to them, even sacred to them, and that the symbols of these things too are taken with comparable seriousness and held to be beyond legitimate mockery. It gives one pause to think of what life would be like if no one ever held anything to be precious or dear or worthy of profound respect and veneration. If most people held nothing to be sacred, then I suspect that the rest of us would be less secure even from personal harm, and social stability would have a soggy and uncertain foundation. It is natural then for persons to tacitly invoke the (public) harm principle when profound offenses are at issue, just as other persons tacitly assume legal moralism. The effect is to squeeze the offense principle out of the discussion, or (quite rightly) assign it a minor derivative role.

The remainder of this chapter will take a closer look at the controversies that actually arise (and not merely in the ingenious hypothetical examples of philosophers and lawyers) in cases of symbolic disrespect to the dead, insults to ethnic and racial minorities, and to a lesser extent, abortion. In particular, we shall note that even when these controversies abandon the offense principle for liberty-limiting principles of other kinds, they must employ something like balancing tests, otherwise they will be biased and one-sided. Granted that it is important that we respect certain symbols, it is even more important that we do not respect them too much. Otherwise we shall respect them at the expense of the very values they symbolize, and fall into the moral traps of sentimentality and squeamishness.

Contrary to what might have been suggested by our examples thus far, few people subject dead human bodies to harsh treatment out of personal taste (cannibalism, necrophilia, misanthropy, personal rage). Moral disagreements in the real world arise when bodies are harshly treated out of at least a fancied necessity. The motive is invariably to help individual living human beings even at an acknowledged cost to a precious natural symbol of humanity. In their characteristic modern form, ethical controversies about the treatment of corpses began when scientists discovered how useful the careful study of human bodies could be. A Benthamite Member of Parliament in 1828 introduced what became known as the Dead Body Bill to permit the use of corpses for scientific purposes when the death occurred in a poor house, hospital, or charitable institution maintained at public expense, and the body was not claimed within a specified time by next of kin. This bill was eventually passed but not before it was emphatically denounced by its opponents as unfair to poor people. So powerful was the dread of posthumous dissection it was predicted that the aged poor would be led by this bill to "avoid the hospitals and die unattended in the streets"![21]

Similar political battles, with similar results, occurred later in the nineteenth century over proposals to make autopsies mandatory when needed for crime detection or public health. These controversies died down until the recent spurt in medical technology but now they are coming back. One recent example was the controversy in 1978 between a California Congressman and the Department of Transportation. The government had contracted with several university laboratories to test designs for automobile air bags in actual crashes of cars at varying velocities. Dummies had proved unsatisfactory for measuring the degree of protection for living passengers, so some researchers had substituted, with the consent of next of kin, human cadavers. Congressman Moss addressed an angry letter to the Secretary of Transportation charging that "the use of human cadavers for vehicle safety research violates fundamental notions of morality and human dignity, and must therefore permanently be stopped."[22] And stopped it was, despite the Department's feeble protest that prohibition of the use of cadavers would "set back progress" on safety protection for "many years."[23]

Moral philosophers might well ponder the question why the use of cadavers for trauma research would seem to violate "morality" and "decency" more than their use in pathological examinations and autopsies. The answer probably has something to do with the perceived symbolism of these different uses. In the air-bag experiments cadavers were violently smashed to bits, whereas dissections are done in laboratories by white-robed medical technicians in spotless antiseptic rooms, radiating the newly acquired symbolic respectability of professional medicine. One might protest that there is no "real difference" between these two uses of cadavers, only symbolic ones, but symbolism is the whole point of the discussion, the sole focus of concern and misgiving. The decision in the collision experiments to exclude cadavers did not involve the criminal law, so it is not quite germane to our purpose here. But if the decision had been up to legislators considering whether to pass a criminal statute forbidding this kind of research on cadavers, the offense principle would not have warranted their interference with the experimenters' liberty. No workers were made to participate without their consent, and there is no record of subtle coercion employed against them. Next of kin, the group most vulnerable to deeply wounded feelings, were consulted, and all voluntarily agreed. The experiments were in a relevant sense done in private. That is, they were not held in a place open to widespread and random public observation like the city streets or a public park, though the superintending officials did not exclude members of the public from witnessing if they wished. Still, no effort was made to keep the fact of the experiments a secret, and the work was done on such a large scale, that in effect the experiments were "open and notorious". Therefore, a great many people had bare knowledge of them to be offended by. Very likely then the experiments produced a large amount of profound offense among the members of this knowledgable group. But that offense would register on each offended psyche in an impersonal way, not in the manner of an offensive nuisance merely which is a wholly personal grievance. As we have seen, the normal argument for legal protection from the profound kind of offense is based on the principle of legal moralism, not on the offense principle, and the liberal will not accept legal moralism. But the harm principle too can be invoked and that principle *is* endorsed by the liberal. The harm principle would underlie the argument, for example, of the person who speaks of the social utility of there being widespread respect for certain natural symbols (see *infra*, §6). That real but diffuse value would be outweighed, however, in the present case (if the Department of Transportation was to be believed) by the clear and present prospect of saving lives and preventing injuries.

The most widespread and persistent current controversies over treatment of dead bodies are probably those concerning procedures for transplantating organs from the newly dead to ailing patients who desperately need them. We are familiar, from the ingenious work of recent philosophers,[24] with the hypothetical moral problems raised by the new possibility of taking organs for transplant from *living* persons, thus setting back their interests or taking their lives with or without their consent. But the problems to which I call attention here involve possible conflicts not between interest and interest, or life and life, but between interest or life on one side and symbolism and sentiment on the other.

Should a dying person or his next of kin have the legal right to deny another the use of his organs *after* he has died a natural death? Few writers, even among those of marked utilitarian bent, would make the salvaging of organs compulsory over the protests of dying patients or their next of kin. In many cases this would override deep religious convictions, and in this country, probably violate the freedom of religion guaranteed by the first amendment. A more frequently joined issue is whether organs should be taken from the newly dead only if they have previously registered their consent, or whether organs should be salvaged routinely unless the deceased had registered his objection while alive or his next of kin objects after his death. The routine method would produce more organs for transplant and experimentation, thus leading both directly and indirectly to saving more lives in the long run. On the other side, writers have objected that since a person's body is essential to his identity while alive, it becomes a "sacred possession" whose fate after his death he must actively control, and that these facts are properly recognized only by a system that renders a body's transfer to others into a freely given *gift*. Failing to make objection to the posthumous use of one's organs is not the same thing, the argument continues, as "real giving." "The routine taking of organs," Paul Ramsey protests, "would deprive individuals of the exercise of the virtue of generosity."[25] On the one side of the scale is the saving of human lives; on the other is the right of a person—not simply to grant or withhold his consent to the uses of his body after his death (that right is protected under either scheme)—but his power by the use of a symbolic ritual to convert his consent into a genuine "gift." Even in this extreme confrontation of interest with symbol, Ramsey gives the symbol more weight. If the subject were not itself so grim I might be tempted to charge him with sentimentality.

Sentimental actions very often are excessive responses to mere symbols at great cost to genuine interests, one's own or others'. In the more egregious cases, the cherished symbol is an emblem of the very class of interests that are harmed, so that there is a kind of hypocritical inconsistency in the sentimental behavior. William James's famous example of the Russian lady who weeps over the fictitious characters in a play while her coachman is freezing to death on his seat outside the theatre is an instance of sentimentality of this kind. The error consists of attaching a value to a symbol, and then absorbing oneself in the sentiments evoked by the symbol at the expense of real interests, including the very interests the symbol represents. The process is not consciously fraudulent, for the devotion to sentiment may be sincere enough. Nor does it consist simply in a conflict between avowal and practice. Rather the faulty practice is partly *caused* by the nature of one's commitment to the ideal. Sentimental absorption in symbols distracts one from the interests that are symbolized.

Even honest and true, profoundly worthwhile sentiments then can fail as decisive reasons for legislative actions when the restrictions they support invade legitimate interest of others. If acting out of sentiment against interest is one of the things called "sentimentality" in the pejorative sense, then many of the appeals to sentiment in practical ethics are in fact appeals to sentimentality. A fetus is a natural symbol of a human being and as such should be respected, but to respect it by forbidding abortion to the twelve-year-old girl who becomes pregnant and contracts a life-threatening venereal disease because of a gang rape is to protect the symbol of humanity at the expense of the vital human interests of a real person. Similarly, a newly dead human body is a sacred symbol of a real person, but to respect the symbol by banning autopsies and research on cadavers is to deprive living human beings of the benefits of medical knowledge and condemn unknown thousands to illnesses and deaths that might have been prevented. That is a poor sort of "respect" to show a sacred symbol.

The balancing tests that mediate application of the offense principle dictate that appeals to interest, both of the "offensive actor" and those he might be helping, have greater weight and cogency than appeals to offended sentiment, and should take precedence when conflict between the two is unavoidable. The point applies more obviously when the sentiment itself is flawed in some way (contrived, artificial, false, or inhuman), but it applies in any case, no matter how noble or pure the sentiment. Justice Cardozo once wrote, in a civil case involving the reburial of a body, that "sentiments and usages devoutly held as sacred, may not be flouted for caprice."[26] I would agree but qualify the judgment in the obvious way: lifesaving, medical research, criminal detection, and the like are not capricious.

The most dramatic confrontation between interest and sentiment in connection with newly dead bodies probably lies in the future. It has been clearly anticipated in Willard Gaylin's remarkable article "Harvesting the Dead."[27] Gaylin has us imagine some consequences of the new medical technology combined with new definitions of death as irrevocable loss of brain function or loss of higher cortical function. Under these new definitions a body may be pronounced dead even though its heart continues to beat, its lungs breathe, and all other visceral functions are maintained. If there is total brain death then these physiological functions depend on the external support of respirators, but if only the cortex is dead, then the irrevocably comatose bodies might function on their own. As Gaylin puts it "they would be warm, respiring, pulsating, evacuating, and excreting bodies requiring nursing, dietary, and general grooming attention, and could probably be maintained so for a period of years."[28]

Gaylin then has us imagine institutions of the future—he calls them "bioemporiums"—where brain-dead bodies, now euphemistically called "neomorts," are maintained and put to various important medical uses. The bioemporiums would resemble a cross between a pharmaceutical laboratory and a hospital ward. Perhaps there will be hospital beds lined up in neat rows, each with a freshly scrubbed neomort under the clean white sheets. The neomorts will have the same recognizably human faces they had before they died, the same features, even the same complexions. Each would be a perfect natural symbol not only of humanity in general but of the particular person who once animated the body and had his life in it. One might not even notice at first that the person was dead, his body lives on so efficiently.

But now along comes a team of medical students being taught the tech-

niques of rectal or vaginal examination without fear of disturbing or embarrassing real patients with their amateur clumsiness. Later an experiment is
scheduled to test the efficacy or toxicity of certain drugs in a perfectly
reliable way—by judging their effects on real human bodies without en-
dangering anyone's health or life. Elsewhere in the ward other neomorts are
proving much better experimental subjects than live animals like dogs and
mice would be, and they feel no pain, unlike living animals who would be
tortured if treated in the same way. Other neomorts serve as living organ
banks or living storage receptacles for blood antigens and platelets that
cannot survive freezing. From others are harvested at regular intervals
blood, bone marrow, corneas, and cartilage, as needed for transfusion or
transplant by patients in an adjacent hospital. Still others are used to manu-
facture hormones, antitoxins, and antibodies to be marketed commercially
for the prevention or cure of other medical ailments.

Even if we use the whole-brain death criterion, Gaylin estimates that our
population could produce at least 70,000 suitable neomorts a year from
cerebrovascular attacks, accidents, homicides, and suicides. Some of the
uses of these bodies would be commercially profitable, thereby supporting
the uses that were not, and the net benefit in the struggle against pain,
sickness, and death would be incalculable. Yet when I asked my class of
philosophy and third year law students for a show of hands, at least half of
them voted that the whole scheme, despite its benefits, was too repugnant
to take seriously. Gaylin himself poses my question eloquently. After describing all the benefits of bioemporiums, he writes—

> And yet, after all the benefits are outlined, with life-saving potential clear,
> the humanitarian purposes obvious, the technology ready, the motives pure,
> the material costs justified—how are we to reconcile our emotions? Where in
> this debit-credit ledger of limbs and livers and kidneys and costs are we to
> weigh and enter the repugnance generated by the entire philanthropic
> endeavor?[29]

Repugnance alone will not outweigh the humanitarian benefits Gaylin
describes. There is a possibility, however, that where the offense principle
falters, other liberty-limiting principles, including the liberal harm principle, can pick up the justificatory load on behalf of prohibition. That is the
possibility to which we now turn.

6. Moral sensibility, sentimentality, and squeamishness

Three types of argument designed to bolster or supplement the appeal to
profound offense come to mind. The first tacitly appeals to the liberty-limiting principle we shall call "perfectionism" (see Vol. IV, Chap. 33) that

criminal prohibitions can be supported by their expected effect in improv-
ing, elevating, or "perfecting" human character. The second applies the
offense principle but in a sophisticated manner designed to take account of
the subtle but serious offenses that come from inappropriate "institutional
symbolism". The third is an appeal to the public harm that comes indirectly from the widespread weakening of respect for certain natural symbols. That argument, of course, contains an appeal to the harm principle.
All three arguments are deployed in a very useful article by William May
supporting the deliverances of offended sentiment against utilitarian calcula-
tions of public gain in order to oppose the routine salvaging of organs and
the "harvesting of the dead."[30] May's arguments support moral conclusions
about what ought and ought not to be done, not political-moral conclusions
about what prohibitive legislation it would or would not be legitimate to
enact (our present concern). Nevertheless, his arguments can be easily recast as political-moral ones simply by adding the appropriate liberty-limiting principle as a premise. (There is no reason to think that May would
approve of this recasting of his arguments, and I attribute no views to him
at all about the legitimacy of criminal legislation.) I shall now attempt to
reconstruct, adapt to the legal-legislative context, and criticize three arguments derived from May.

1. *The argument that the offended sentiment is essential to our humanity.* May
recalls the Grimm brothers' folk tale about the young man who was incapable of experiencing horror:

> He does not shrink back from the dead—neither a hanged man he en-
> counters nor a corpse with which he attempts to play. From one point of view,
> his behavior seems pleasantly childish, but from another angle, inhuman. His
> father is ashamed of him, and so the young man is sent away "to learn how to
> shudder." Not until he learns how to shudder will he be brought out of his
> nameless, undifferentiated state and become human.[31]

May plausibly suggests that this story testifies to "our deep-going sense of
the connection between human dignity and a capacity for horror."[32] The
practice of routinely salvaging the re-usable organs of the newly dead, he
contends, is to be rejected for its "refusal to acknowledge the fact of human
horror." "There is a tinge of the inhuman," he writes, "in the humanitarianism of those who believe that the perception of social need easily overrides
all other considerations and reduces the acts of implementation to the everyday, routine, and casual."[33] We can acknowledge the second-level horror,
implied in May's remarks, that consists of the perception that the primary
horror has been rubbed off a practice to which it naturally belongs, so that
what was formerly a morally shocking occurrence now becomes routine and

normal. Recall the daily television news during the Vietnam War when deliberate shootings, mangled babies, and regular "body counts" became mere routine occurrences portrayed in a humdrum fashion as if they were commonplace sporting events.

We can reconstruct May's argument so that it fits what can be called "one standard form of the argument from sentiment." The argument runs as follows:

1. Whatever leads to the weakening or vanishing of a natural, honest, human sentiment thereby degrades ("dehumanizes") human character and is in that way a bad thing.
2. There are natural, honest, human sentiments toward dead human bodies.
3. Routine salvaging of organs and harvesting of the brain-dead would lead to the weakening and eventual vanishing of these sentiments.
4. Therefore, these practices would degrade human character, and in that way be a bad thing.

Now we can add—

5. It is always a good and relevant reason in support of a proposed criminal prohibition that it is necessary to improve (or prevent the degrading of) human character. (Legal Perfectionism)
6. Therefore there is good and relevant reason to prohibit routine salvaging of organs and harvesting of the brain-dead.

I have several comments about this argument. First, it is to be distinguished from the moral use of the offense principle, with which it might otherwise be confused. The offense principle argument takes as its first premise the proposition that whatever causes most people, or normal people, deep revulsion is for that reason a bad thing. (It is unpleasant to experience revulsion, and wrong to cause others unpleasantness.) Professor May's argument, in contrast, is that whatever weakens the tendency of most people, or normal people, to experience revulsion in certain circumstances is a bad thing. He is less concerned to protect people from revulsion than to protect their "humanity" to which the capacity for spontaneous revulsion is essential.

Similarly, Professor May's argument should be contrasted with the "causal argument," which assumes natural causal connections between watching and shrinking from, and between shrinking from and judgments of disapproval. This technique for producing conviction would be a kind of *argumentum ad hominem*. The person in whom the appropriate sort of repugnance is naturally induced needs no further argument; one can simply appeal to the disapproval he feels already. Obviously that tactic will not do for Professor May since the thought of routine salvaging and the like does not cause his opponents to shrink away and disapprove, and Professor May does not want to impugn *their* humanity (although he does discern a "tinge of the inhuman" in their proposals).

My first objection to May's argument is that it proceeds in a kind of vacuum, abstracted from the practical world to which it is directed. There is no qualifying clause in premise or conclusion to acknowledge even the bare relevance of benefits gained and harms prevented, as if "the promise of cures for leukemia and other diseases, the reduction of suffering, and the maintenance of life"[34] were of no account at all. Indeed both May and Ramsey, whose earlier argument against routine salvaging rested on a subtle preference for symbolic gift-giving and guaranteed consciousness of generosity, approach these urgent questions more in the manner of literary critics debating the appropriateness of symbols than as moralists. One wants to remind them forcibly that while they distinguish among symbols and sentiments, there are people out there suffering and dying. William James's sentimental Russian countess too may have been experiencing genuine human feelings toward the characters on the stage, but the point of the story is not *that*, but the death of her coachman.

To be properly appreciated May's argument should be further recast. At most, the data from which he draws his premises show that insofar as a practice weakens natural human sentiment, it is a bad thing, so that unless there is some countervailing consideration on the other side, that practice is bad on balance and should not be implemented. Very well, one can accept that proposition, while pointing to the prevention of deaths and suffering as a countervailing reason to weigh against the preference for untarnished symbols.

Why do May and like-minded writers seem so dismissive of appeals to the reduction of suffering and the saving of lives? I suspect it is because they assimilate all such consequentialist considerations to the most vulnerable kind of utilitarianism, as if weighting life-saving over sentiment were a moral misjudgment of the same category as sacrificing an unwilling individual to use his organs to save the lives of others. It simply won't bear rational scrutiny to claim that there is a right not to be horrified, or not to have one's capacity to be horrified weakened, of the same order of priority as a right not to be killed and "disorganized."[35] May speaks dismissively of those who let mere "social needs" override all other considerations, as if a desperate patient's need for an organ transplant were a mere social need like a city's call for an additional public library or improved public transportation. In another place he uses in a similar way the phrase "the social order," adding the suggestion of disreputable ideology. There he writes of the routine salvaging scheme that "One's very vitals must be inventoried, extracted, and distributed by the state on behalf of the social order."[36] The moral conflict, as May sees it, is between honest human sentiment and an inferior kind of value, often called "merely utilitarian". What is overlooked is that the so-called "social utility" amassed on one side of the controversy is itself partly composed of individual *rights* to be rescued or cured. If, opposed to these, there are rights derived from sentiment, one would think that they are less weighty than the right to life and to the relief of suffering. Jesse Dukeminier makes the point well. He objects to labeling one of the conflicting interests "the need of society of organs." "Organs," he protests, "are not transplanted into society, organs are transplanted into people!"[37]

To give substance to this point, let us consider the following scenarios: Patient *A* dies in his hospital room, not having said anything, one way or the other, about the disposition of his cadaver. *B*, in the next room, needs his organ immediately to survive. *A*'s next of kin refuses to grant permission for the transplantation of his kin's organ, so *B* dies. Were *B*'s rights violated? Was an injustice done or was mere "social utility" withheld? Perhaps we would call this not merely an inutility but an injustice because *B* is a specific known person, a victim, and not a mere unknown possibility or abstraction. But consider a second scenario. Patient *C* dies in his hospital room not having said anything, one way or the other, about the disposition of his cadaver. *D*, at just that moment, is in an automobile crash. Five minutes later he arrives in an ambulance at the hospital in desperate need, as it turns out, of one of *C*'s organs to survive. At the time of *C*'s death no one knew anything about *D* who was a total stranger to all involved parties. At that moment *C*'s next of kin gives his blanket refusal to let anyone use *C*'s organs, so *D*, ten minutes later, dies. Were *D*'s rights violated or mere social utility diminished? To argue for the latter, it would not be relevant to point out that no one knew who *D* was; no one knew his name; no one had any personal intention in respect to him. That would be to treat him as if he *had* no name, no identity, and no rights, as if his unknown and indeterminate status at the time of *C*'s death deprived him of personhood, converting him into a mere impersonal component of "social utility."

Even in its fully recast form with its more tentative conclusion ("insofar as . . ."), May's first argument causes misgivings. I have no problem with premise 2, that there are natural human sentiments toward newly dead bodies that are in no way flawed when considered in their own right. But I have reservations about premises 1 and 3. Premise 1 needs qualifying. It states that whatever leads to the weakening or vanishing of such a sentiment is a bad thing. What is important, I think, is not only our capacity to have such sentiments but our ability to monitor and control them. To be sure persons sometimes need to "learn how to shudder," but it is even more commonly the case that people have to learn how *not* to shudder. Newly dead bodies cannot be made live again, nor can they be made to vanish forever in a puff of smoke. Some of us can shudder and avert our eyes, but others must dispose of them. Pathologists often must examine and test them, surgeons in autopsies skin them open like game, cutting, slicing, and mutilating them; undertakers embalm them; cremators burn them. These professionals cannot afford to shudder. If they cultivate rather than repress their natural feelings in order to "preserve their humanness," then their actions will suffer and useful work will not be done. There is an opposite danger, of course, that these persons' work will be done at the expense of their own humanity and the extinction of their capacity for essential feeling. What is needed is neither repression nor artificial cultivation, the one leading to inhumanity, the other to sentimentality. Instead what is called for is a careful rational superintendency of the sentiments, an "education and discipline of the feelings."[38]

I must take stronger exception to the partially empirical premise number 3, that routine salvaging of organs (and *a fortiori* "harvesting the dead") would lead to the general weakening or vanishing of essential human sentiments. These medically useful practices need not be done crudely, indiscreetly, or disrespectfully. They are the work of professionals and can be done with dignity. As for the professionals themselves, their work is no more dehumanizing than that of pathologists and embalmers today. Other professionals must steel their feelings to work on the bodies of *living* persons. I wonder if Professor May would characterize abdominal surgeons as "inhuman," as various writers in the 19th century did? Does their attitude of the everyday, routine, casual acceptance of blood, gore, and pain lead them inevitably to beat their wives, kick their dogs, and respond with dry-eyed indifference to the loss of their dear ones? That of course *would* render them inhuman.

This is the point where I should concede to Professor May that complete loss of the capacity for revulsion *is* dehumanizing. To be incapable of revulsion is as bad a thing as the paralysis of succumbing to it, and for the same kind of reason. The perfect virtue is to have the sensibility but have it under control, as an Aristotelian man of courage has natural fear in situations of danger (otherwise *he* would be "inhuman") but acts appropriately anyway.

2. *The argument from institutional symbolism.* Hospitals traditionally have been places where the sick and wounded are healed and nursed. The modern

hospital mixes this therapeutic function with a variety of ancillary ones, leading in the public mind to a conflict of images and an obscuring of symbolism. Hospitals now are training facilities, places of medical research and experiment, warehouses for the permanently incapacitated and terminally ill and so on. Now, Professor May warns us, "The development of a system of routine salvaging of organs would tend to fix on the hospital a second association with death . . . the hospital itself becomes the arch-symbol of a world that devours."[39] Perhaps it is fair to say that all institutions are in their distinctive ways symbols, and that the mixing of functions within the institution obscures the symbolism, but it is hard for me to see how this is necessarily a bad thing, much less an evil great enough to counter-balance such benefits as lifesaving and relief of suffering. Schools are traditionally places of book-learning. Now they host such diverse activities as driver-training and football teams. Prisons are traditionally places of punishment and penitence; now they also are manufacturing units and occupational therapy centers. Churches, which are essentially places of worship, now host dances and bingo games. One might regret the addition of new functions on the ground that they interfere with the older more important ones, but that is not the nub of Professor May's argument. He does not suggest that the healing function of the hospital will be hurt somehow by the introduction of routine organ salvaging. Rather his concern is focused sharply on the institutional symbolism itself. Like a skilled and subtle literary critic, he argues for the superiority of one kind of symbolism to another, just as if such benefits as lifesaving were not involved at all.

Of course May's fear for the hospital's benign image is not for a symbol valued as an end in itself. With the change he fears, hospitals will come to be regarded in new ways by the patients. The prospect of an eventual death in a hospital is bad enough; now the patient has to think also of the hospital as a place where dead bodies are "devoured". It is just as if we landscaped hospital grounds with cemeteries and interspersed "crematorium wards" among the therapeutic ones. That would be rubbing it in, and as prospective hospital patients we might all register our protest. These examples show that May does have a point. But the disanalogies are striking. It is not necessary that burial and cremation be added to the functions of a hospital. There would be hardly any gain, and probably a net loss, in efficiency, and a very powerful change for the worse in ambience. Organ transplanting, however, *requires* hospital facilities; its beneficiaries are sick people already hospitalized and its procedures are surgical, requiring apparatus peculiar to hospitals. The most we can say for the argument is that if the change in symbolism is for the worse, that is a reason against the new functions, so that if the change is capricious—not required for some tangible benefit—then it ought not be allowed. But greater lifesaving effectiveness is not a capricious purpose.

Professor May's ultimate concern in this argument, however, may not be so much with symbolic ambience as with the morale of patients who are depressed by the bare knowledge that organ salvaging occurs routinely in their hospital, even though it will not occur in their case because they have registered their refusal to permit it. But it is difficult to understand how the thought of bodies having their organs removed before burial can be more depressing than the thought of them festering in the cold ground or going up in flames. Only the morale of a patient with a bizarre "sentimental belief," or an independently superstitious belief about corpses similar to one once analyzed by Adam Smith[40], would be hurt by such bare knowledge, and such beliefs are nearly extinct.

3. *The argument that the threatened sensibility has great social utility.* The argument I have in mind is the familiar "rule-utilitarian" one. It is only suggested in Professor May's article but it has been spelled out in detail by other writers discussing other topics in practical ethics, notably abortion and infanticide. The argument I have in mind differs from May's first argument from sentiment in that it appeals in its major premise not to the intrinsic value of a threatened sentiment, its status as the "best" or "most human" feeling, but to the high social utility of this sentiment being widespread. Formulated in a way that brings out a structure parallel to May's first argument, it goes as follows:

1. Whatever leads to the weakening or vanishing of a socially beneficial (harm-preventing) human sentiment is socially harmful and in that way a bad thing.
2. There are sentiments toward dead bodies which when applied to things other than dead bodies promote actions that have highly beneficial consequences and whose absence would lead to harmful consequences.
3. Routine salvaging of organs and harvesting of brain-dead bodies would lead to the weakening or vanishing of these sentiments.
4. Therefore, these practices would lead to widespread harm and in that way would be a bad thing.

Now we can add—

5. It is always a good and relevant reason in support of a proposed criminal prohibition that it is necessary to prevent harm. (The Harm Principle)
6. Therefore, there is good and relevant reason to prohibit routine salvaging of organs and harvesting of the brain-dead.

Stanley Benn has a similar but more plausible argument about infanticide and abortion.[41] Benn concedes that fetuses and even newborn infants may not be actual persons with a right to life, but points out that their physical resemblance to the undoubted human persons in our everyday experience evokes from us a natural tenderness that is highly useful to the species. If we had a system of "infanticide on demand," that natural tenderness toward the infants we did preserve and raise to adulthood might be weakened, and the consequences both for them and the persons they later come in contact with could be highly destructive. If as infants they would be emotionally stunted, then as adults they would be, in consequence, both unhappy and dangerous to others. The argument, in short, is an appeal to the social disadvantages of a practice that allegedly coarsens or brutalizes those who engage in it and even those who passively acquiesce to it. Benn cites the analogy to the similar argument often used against hunting animals for sport. Overcoming the sentiment of tenderness toward animals, according to this argument, may or may not be harmful on balance to the animals; but the sentiment's disappearance would be indirectly threatening to other human beings who have in the past been transferred beneficiaries of it. The advantage of this kind of argument is that it permits rational discussion among those who disagree, in which careful comparisons are made between the alleged disadvantages of a proposed new practice and the acknowledged benefits of its introduction.

The weakness of the argument consists in the difficulty of showing that the alleged coarsening effects really do transfer from primary to secondary objects. So far as I know, doctors who perform abortions do not tend to be cruel to their own children; the millions of people who kill animals for sport are not markedly more brutal even to their own pets than others are; and transplant surgeons are not notably inclined to emulate Jack the Ripper in their off hours. I think that the factual premise in arguments of this form usually underestimates human emotional flexibility. We can deliberately inhibit a sentiment toward one class of objects when we believe it might otherwise motivate inappropriate conduct, yet give it free rein toward another class of objects where there is no such danger.[42] That is precisely what it means to monitor the intensity of one's sentiments and render them more discriminating motives for conduct. Those who have not educated their sentiments in these respects tend to give in to them by acting in ways that are inadvisable on independent grounds, and then cite the "humanness," "honesty," or "naturalness" of the sentiment as a reason for their action. This pattern is one of the things meant by "sentimentality" in the pejorative sense. Fortunately, it does not seem to be as widespread as some have feared, and in any event, the way to counter it is to promote the education of the feelings, not to abandon the fruits of lifesaving technology.

In summary, I find no unmanagable conflict between effective humanitarianism and the maintenance, under flexible control, of the essential human sentiments. I hope that conclusion is not too optimistic.

7. The Nazis in Skokie

Profound offense is never more worthy of respect than when it results from brandishing the symbols of race hatred and genocide. The attempt of an American Nazi Party to demonstrate in the 60% Jewish community of Skokie, Illinois in 1977 was a rare pure case of symbolic conduct of just that kind, and has since become a kind of symbol of the category ("Skokie-type cases"). The case became legally complex and difficult, ironically, because of its very purity. Political expression is almost categorically defended by the First Amendment, and no one can validly prevent the public advocacy (in appropriate time, place, and manner) of any political opinions no matter how odious. But the small group of American Nazis planned no political advocacy in Skokie. Their avowed purpose was to march in the Village parks without giving speeches and without distributing literature, but dressed in authentic stormtroopers' uniforms, wearing swastikas, and carrying taunting signs. Free expression of opinion, a preemptive constitutional value, was not obviously involved. Rather the point was deliberately and maliciously to affront the sensibilities of the Jews in Skokie (including from 5,000 to 7,000 aged survivors of Nazi death camps), to insult them, lacerate their feelings, and indirectly threaten them. Surely if they had carried banners emblazoned only with the words "Jews are scum," they could not have been described as advocating a political program or entering an "opinion" in "the marketplace of ideas." Only some speech acts are acts of advocacy, or assertions of belief; others are pure menacing insult, no less and no more.[43] The Nazi demonstration was to have been very close to the pure insult extreme.[44]

One of the holocaust survivors in Skokie had witnessed the death of his mother during the Second World War, when fifty German troopers, presumably attired in brown shirts, boots, and swastika armbands, threw her and fifty other women down a well and buried them alive in gravel. The other survivors had all suffered similar experiences. Now their village was to be the scene of a celebration of Hitler's birthday by jack-booted youths in the same Nazi uniforms. The American Nazis had deliberately sought them out; their "message" was not primarily for non-Jews. Who could blame the anxious residents of Skokie for interpreting that "message" thus:

"You escaped us before, you dirty Jew, but we are coming and we will get you"?[45] This seems a much more natural interpretation of the "symbolic behavior" of the uniformed demonstrators than that of the Illinois Supreme Court in 1978, when it struck down the prohibitive injunction of a lower court. Addressing only the somewhat narrower question of whether an injunction against display of the swastika violated First Amendment rights, it wrote: "The display of the swastika, as offensive to the principles of a free nation as the memories it recalls may be, is symbolic political speech intended to convey to the public the beliefs of those who display it." That is almost as absurd as saying that a nose thumbing, or a giving of "the finger," or a raspberry jeer is a form of "political speech," or that "Death to the Niggers!" is the expression of a political opinion.

The Nazi demonstration without question would have produced "offended states of mind" of great intensity in almost any Skokie resident forced to witness it. Equally clearly, the offense would be of the profound variety since the planned affront was to values held sacred by those singled out as targets. But since the Nazis announced the demonstration well in advance, it could be easily avoided by all who wished to avoid it, in most cases with but minimal inconvenience. Even those who would have to endure some inconvenience to escape witnessing the spectacle, for example a mother who could not take her children to the park that afternoon, could complain only of a minor nuisance, since with so much notice, nearly as satisfactory alternative arrangements could be made. The main complainants then would be those who stayed at home or at work, and found that physical separation from the witnessed event was no bar to their experiencing intolerably severe emotions. The offense derived from bare knowledge that the demonstration was taking place in Skokie was an experience that could have been shared at the time equally intensely and equally profoundly by a Jew in New York, Los Angeles, or Tel Aviv. That offense would be a complex mental state, compounded of moral indignation and disapproval, resentment (offense in the strict sense), and perhaps some rage or despair. But insofar as the moral elements predominate, there will be little sense of *personal* grievance involved, and even less of a case, objectively speaking, that the person in question was himself wronged. It is not a necessary truth that we are personally wronged by everything at which we are morally outraged. Insofar as there is a sense of personal grievance in the non-witnessing Skokie Jew, it would no doubt be directed at the nuisance he suffered in having to avoid the area of the Village Hall and adjacent public parks. That element in the experience, however, is not "profound".

Despite the intense aversion felt by the offended parties, there was not an exceptionally weighty case for legal interference with the Nazis, given the relative ease by which their malicious and spiteful insults could be avoided. But the scales would tip the other way if their behavior became more frequent, for the constant need to avoid public places at certain times can become a major nuisance quickly. Even more to the point, if the Nazis, at unpredictable intervals, freely mingled with the throngs in shopping malls or in public sidewalks while wearing swastika armbands and stormtrooper uniforms, then they would clearly cross the line of public nuisance. Practically speaking, the best remedies for those nuisances that consist of group affronts are administrative—cease and desist orders, withheld permits, and injunctions, with criminal penalties reserved only as back-up sanctions. But without such measures, the whole public world would become as unpleasant for some as the revolting public bus of Chapter 7, and equally inescapable.

The controversy that raged over the Skokie case was about the proper interpretation of American Constitutional law, a topic beyond the scope of this book. But many of the arguments given both by deniers and affirmers of the Nazis' right to demonstrate are of more general relevance to our concern with what the law, both statutory and constitutional, ideally ought to be. We have applied the offense principle to the case as mediated by the balancing tests of Chapter 8, and concluded that the insults in question cause intense, profound, and widespread offense to persons of normal susceptibility, but that the seriousness of the offense in the actual Skokie case had to be discounted by its relatively easy avoidability. On the other side of the scale, the offending conduct carried even less weight, in view of the fact that the "social value" of free expression for pure insults is much less than that of genuine political advocacy and debate (which were not involved), and that the offensive conduct was clearly motivated by malice and spite. If the value of these diverse variables were subtly changed, however, the scales would have tipped decisively in the direction of tolerance. The Nazis might have added ideology to insult by distributing campaign documents containing only their stands on public issues—advocacy of greater vigilance against Communist spies, arguments that affirmative action programs for disadvantaged minorities violate the rights of white men, advocacy of a constitutional amendment forbidding racial intermarriage, etc. In that case their behavior would have had greater claim to protection, both under the first amendment as interpreted by the courts, and under our offense principle as mediated by the free expression standard. But the gratuitous Nazi symbolism would still have been present to lacerate the feelings of the Jewish audience, and these symbols were in no obvious way necessary to the content of the advocacy. The manner of expression, surely, rather than its ideological content, would be the basis of the case against tolerance. Had the Nazis worn street clothes instead of uniforms, and not displayed swastikas at all, there would be no case left for prohibiting their conduct. On the other side of the balance, as we have seen, had the flagrant affronts of military uniform and genocidal symbols been less easily avoidable, the case for prohibition would have been proportionately strengthened.

Those who opposed giving permission for the Nazi demonstration in the actual historic Skokie case, however, rarely rested their arguments on such bland notions as "nuisance," "offense," "affront," "insult," and the like, and argued instead that the planned demonstration must be forbidden in order to prevent various kinds of *harms*. These arguments rarely carried much conviction, and were often demolished by spokesmen for the American Civil Liberties Union who favored tolerance.[46] It was sometimes said, for example, that the Nazi presence in Skokie would "cause a panic," on the analogy of a false shout of fire in a theatre, a rather stretched analogy at best. Only slightly more plausible is the argument that the Nazis' uniformed demonstration would be an "incitement to riot." No one meant by this allegation, of course, that the Nazis would inflame a mob of sympathizers and incite them through explicit exhortation, or rhetorical manipulation, to attack groups of Jews, blacks, or police. Rather, the complaint filed by the Village of Skokie with the Illinois appellate court claimed that the Nazis' silent demonstration would naturally infuriate Skokie Jews who would inevitably attack their symbolic tormentors with physical violence. The court heard testimony from a number of witnesses supporting this prediction:

> A resident of Skokie, an officer in several Jewish organizations, testified that he learned of the planned demonstrations from the newspapers. As a result, meetings of some 15 to 18 Jewish organizations within Skokie and surrounding areas were called, and a counterdemonstration was scheduled for the same day as the demonstration . . . The witnesses estimated that some 12,000 to 15,000 people were expected to participate. In the opinion of the witness, this counterdemonstration would be peaceful if the [Nazi] defendants did not appear. However, if they did appear, the outrage of the participants might not be controllable . . . Plaintiff also called as a witness a Jewish resident who was a survivor of Nazi concentration camps. He testified as to the effect the swastika has on him and other survivors. According to his testimony, the swastika is a symbol that his closest family was killed by the Nazis, and that the lives of him and his children are not presently safe. He further stated that he does not presently intend to use violence against defendants should they appear in Skokie, but that when he sees the swastika, he does not know if he can control himself . . .[47]

These reactions of course are understandable, and if, in a given case, an outraged person were to attack a demonstrator, we should judge the provocation to be a mitigation of the assailant's guilt. But we can hardly allow the possibility of retaliatory violence by enraged audiences to be a ground for prohibiting demonstrations if the demonstrators have otherwise a right to do what they are doing. That would be to recognize "the heckler's veto" not only of offensive demonstrations but of unpopular speakers and political advocates of all stripes. If the law suppresses public speech or symbolic conduct, either by withholding permits in advance or punishing afterwards, simply on the ground that the expressed views or symbols are so unpopular that some auditors can be expected to launch physical assaults, then the law punishes some for the criminal proclivities of others. "A man does not become a criminal because someone else assaults him . . ." writes Zechariah Chafee. Moreover, he continues, on any such theory, "a small number of intolerant men . . . can prevent *any kind* of meeting . . . A gathering which expressed the sentiment of a majority of law abiding citizens would become illegal because a small gang of hoodlums threatened to invade the hall."[48] When violent response to speech threatens, the obvious remedy is not suppression, but rather increased police protection.

If Nazis have a right to demonstrate quietly on public property while wearing Nazi uniforms and swastikas, then, that right cannot be denied in a given case because of the expectation of violent response. That would make a mockery of the whole system of free expression. The crucial question before us, however, is whether the Nazis do have a right to the public display of those emblems before audiences that have little opportunity to avoid them without inconvenience. The Illinois appelate court agreed that this was the issue, and upheld that part of the original injunctive order by a county court which (as modified) enjoined the Nazis from "intentionally displaying the swastika on or off their persons, in the course of a demonstration, march, or parade within the Village of Skokie". The ground of this prohibition should not have been that it was necessary to prevent the violent harms that would otherwise be provoked from outraged citizens, but rather that

> The swastika is a personal affront to every member of the Jewish faith, in remembering the nearly consummated genocide of their people committed within memory by those who used the swastika as their symbol . . . and the brutal destruction of their families and communities by those then wearing the swastika. So too, the tens of thousands of Skokie's Jewish residents must feel gross revulsion for the swastika and would immediately respond to the personally abusive epithets flung their way in the form of the defendant's chosen symbol, the swastika.[49]

In short, the inherent nature of this profoundly offended mental state is itself ground, quite apart from harm, for the prohibition of certain symbols, provided of course that "reasonable avoidability" requirements are violated, that free expression values are not centrally involved, and the other balancing tests are scrupulously applied.

The appellate court also gave some respectful consideration to the "fighting words" doctrine in its defense of the prohibition against displaying the swastika.[50] (See *infra*, Chap. 14, §3) The judges suggested plausibly enough that the displays of that hated symbol be treated just like "those personally abusive epithets which, when addressed to the ordinary citizen, are, as a matter of common knowledge, inherently likely to provoke violent reaction."[51] We should note immediately that violent response to an abusive epithet may be known in advance to be "inherently likely" and still not be legally justified. If a stranger walks up to me on the street and gratuitously insults me or something I hold dear, his provocation may mitigate my guilt if I respond by breaking his jaw, and may even be independently penalizable, but my violent response to mere words, when I was not threatened with physical danger nor subjected to further harassment, can hardly be legally justified. It will surely not be treated, like self-defense, as a totally exculpating defense to a charge of criminal battery. The "reasonable person" in a democracy must be presumed to have enough self-control to refrain from violent responses to odious words and doctrines. If he is followed, insulted, taunted, and challenged, he can get injunctive relief or bring charges against his tormentor for harassment; if there is no time for this and he is backed to the wall he may perhaps be justified in using "reasonable force" in abatement of the nuisance; or if he is followed to his own home, he can use the police to remove the nuisance. But if he is not personally harassed in these ways, he can turn on his heels and leave the provocation behind, and this is what the law should require of him, if he can do it without loss or hardship.

The Jewish residents of Skokie then would be put in a very difficult position by the entry into their town and into their everyday experience of swastika-brandishing Nazis. Their feelings would be so deeply lacerated that they would be powerfully motivated to lash out at their tormentors, and even though this violent response would be natural and predictable, it cannot be permitted by the law. Thus, frustration of natural impulse, confusion over what would be right, and the clash of profound loyalties commingle with other elements in the offended party's turbulent mental states—hatred, felt desecration of venerated memories, moral outrage, fear and revived despair. If there is no plausible way for him to escape or prevent the experience, and no legal way to give vent to his barely controllable impulses, and no social value in the malicious conduct that torments him, then he is forced by his own legal system to suffer for no respectable purpose. The alternatives are either to permit him his violence, or to prevent (or remove) the provocation. The prohibition of the swastika is not justified by the "inherent likelihood of violence" in response to its display, but rather by the intolerable frustrations that would be imposed on offended parties by the joint permission of the symbolic affront and prohibition of violent response to it. Yet violent response must be prohibited.

The injunctive order of the appellate court forbidding displays of swastikas in Skokie was overturned, however, by the Illinois Supreme Court. Much of the higher court's reasoning I have already rejected, in particular the claim that swastikas are "symbolic political speech" instead of symbolic abusive affronts. Some of it I have accepted, in particular the claim that on the particular facts of the case, the affronts were reasonably avoidable, even though on only slightly different facts, they would not be. There is another argument, only sketched in the Court's opinion, that is the most forceful. That is the difficulty of distinguishing the swastika from other odious symbols that we would be less inclined to prohibit in other contexts. If a particular court judgment is not to be arbitrary it must invoke a more general rule that does not have unacceptable applications to other cases. To the Arab-American community of Dearborn, Michigan, the star of David might be as repellant as the Swastika in Skokie. Would a different Supreme Court decision in the Skokie case have warranted an injunction against a Zionist rally in Dearborn? What of a pro-Castro rally in Miami? If the difference is merely in degree of aversion, how do we draw a workable line? Would banning the Nazi demonstration in Skokie entail enjoining a militant black group from parading with "Black Power" signs in white neighborhoods that have excluded them?

This form of argument is very common when public policy issues are debated. It has two quite distinct forms, each of which bears a number of names. The first is the argument from the *logical* impossibility of holding a given judgment without commitment to other judgments that one wishes to reject. This is often called the "line-drawing argument," "the wedge argument," the "*reductio ad absurdum* argument," or the logical form of the "slippery slope argument." The second form is the argument from the political danger of adopting a certain position given that interested parties might then be encouraged to foist other judgments on us which are not logically entailed by the first one, but to which we might be driven by political forces. This is often called the "falling dominoes argument," or the "foot in the door argument," or the empirical (or political) form of the "slippery slope argument." The first, or logical, form of the argument is one that courts must take seriously insofar as their assigned mission is *principled* decision-making. The second, or political form of the argument, is one that policy-makers and legislators must take seriously if they don't wish their efforts to be self-defeating.

Does banning the swastika, at least in certain localities, on the grounds of its peculiar offensiveness *logically* commit us to banning other conventional symbols on the same grounds?[52] I should think that the white robes and hoods, ropes, and burning crosses of the Ku Klux Klan would fall into the same category as the swastika, but I am hard put to think of any others. Black power emblems are defensively oriented. They say in effect "Don't tread on us; we will defend our rights." The main distinguishing features of the swastika and K. K. K. emblems is their deliberate association with actual historic atrocities—lynchings, tortures, mass killings committed to vindicate the alleged prerogatives of a master race. We are hardly committed to banning a civil rights demonstration in a Mississippi town by our banning of a K. K. K. parade in Harlem, because the two classes of symbols can be distinguished. The civil rights marchers make no threat of violence; they do not issue gratuitous affronts to what is held sacred or precious; they do not associate themselves with historic instances of torture and genocide.

The real force of the argument from the difficulty of drawing a line is practical, not logical. Civil libertarians in particular are nervous about letting a repressive judicial foot in the door. Courts may well have logical grounds for making distinctions between cases, and yet fail to do so because of the subtleties of discrimination required or because of political pressures. Thus, if the swastika and burning crosses are banned today on good grounds, relatively innocuous symbols may be banned tomorrow on not so good grounds. I think that is the true motivation behind much of the A.C.L.U. opposition to legal action against Nazis. One can only have sympathy for the motive even while disagreeing with the stand.

8. Summary

"Profound offenses" are misleadingly characterized as simply "offensive nuisances" both because of their felt qualitative difference from mere nuisances and because of their independence of actual perception. The nub of the offensiveness in the "profound" cases is not personal resentment that a disagreeable experience has been imposed on one that would be inconvenient to avoid. Rather one is outraged at the offending conduct on grounds quite independent of its effect on oneself. The offense principle, however, does not warrant legal interference with a person's private (unwitnessed) conduct on the grounds that those who know that the conduct is (or might be) taking place need protection from the profound offensiveness of their own bare knowledge. The profoundly offended states stemming from bare knowledge are not "wrongful offenses" in the sense required by the offense principle, since they are not personal wrongs to the offended party, not a violation of *his* rights, and indeed, if the conduct is reasonably discreet it may not be a violation of *anyone's* rights. In that event, if the conduct can rightfully be prohibited anyway, the legitimacy of the prohibition would have to be certified by the principle of legal moralism. The offense principle will not stretch that far.

The argument against extending the offense principle to cover bare-knowledge offense has the form of a dilemma:

1. Either the offense in question is "profound" or it is a nuisance merely.
2. If it is profound, then it is not the basis of a *personal* grievance, i.e., not a "wrongful offense."
3. If it is an offensive nuisance merely, then it would be a wholly personal grievance, but it could not exist apart from actual witnessing. Therefore, the bare knowledge, on either interpretation, cannot be a wrongful offense.

This argument clearly applies to such bare-knowledge offenses as those caused by private deviant sexual conduct, unwitnessed descecrations of sacred symbols, mistreatment of corpses, and the like. But there are two classes of apparent exceptions. When bare-knowledge offense is pointedly personal, the offended party might well think of himself as its victim, as when the shock at the knowledge that a newly dead body is being subjected to indignities is not simply "How could such a thing be done?" but also "How could such a thing be done to the body of *my* late beloved husband or child?" "How can they do this to *me?*" More commonly, however, when a person thinks of himself as the victim of learned-about but unwitnessed conduct that he believes to be morally outrageous, he has become confused about the grounds of his own moral feelings through the kind of moral egotism that Mill so frequently criticized. (Offenses that are both profound and personal are discussed more thoroughly in Chapter 11, §9.) Another possible exception to the rule against criminalizing unwitnessed offensive but harmless behavior would be the case of privately performed activities brazenly and aggressively advertised by pictures as offensive as the conduct they depict, or by overly obtrusive words (e.g., in huge neon signs) calling attention to what is happening in private. Notices, advertisements and solicitations cannot be totally banned, however, without violating the offending parties' rights to free expression which are more fundamental than the right of others to be free of offended states. Lines will often be hard to draw, but we should probably be justified, for example, in barring the neon sign advertising private cannibalism, necrophilia, and bestiality (from Baier's example) or a sign decorated with swastikas advertising "private meetings" of Nazis in room 306 for the purpose of glorying in recollections of past mass murders and torture. The offense principle could not be applied to that conduct, however, if there were no public sign at all, and surely not on the grounds that the mere hypothetical possibility that such shocking goings-on might be occurring with impunity behind *someone's* locked door is offensive to think about. Mere possibilities can be reasonably avoided even by the most skittish of moralists.

Because a dead human body is a natural symbol of something precious, namely the real person whose body it once was, and more generally, of all human beings, the moral sensibility that is offended by violent or disrespectful treatment of bodies deserves respect. But where we are faced with a choice between symbol and sentiment, on one side, and the interests of threatened real persons on the other, it could only be moral sentimentality or squeamishness that would lead us to neglect the interests from fear of offending the sentiments. Given the usual balancing tests that govern application of the offense principle, even futuristic schemes to "harvest" the brain-dead (despite the profound offense they cause in our imaginations) cannot be legitimately prohibited on offense-principle grounds.

Certain merely conventional symbols can have as powerful a grip on the moral sentiments as the natural ones. The public desecration of religious and patriotic icons, for example, can powerfully upset the unwilling pious observer. "Unobserved desecration," on the other hand, is not exactly desecration at all, in a strict sense, since that form of symbolic abuse essentially requires display. Conventional symbols of an evil kind are also forms of sacrilege to the moral sensibility. The deep offense they cause by their very display is not a consequence of positive symbols defaced, but rather of precious values directly inpugned by negative symbols. Such symbols as the swastika and the K.K.K. robes have no other function but to affront, insult, and threaten. Because of their association with actual historic instances of barbarity, they are enormously effective. Their actual use at "political rallies" is not to advocate policies, enter political debates, and persuade audiences, but rather to shock, insult, terrorize, and intimidate. They are also "inherently likely" to incite violent response. But that is not why they should be banned where they cannot be reasonably avoided. It is rather because (in addition to the profound offense they cause in other ways) they are "fighting words" to which the law cannot permit fighting response, thus further mortifying and frustrating those who suffer from them. Where genuine free expression is not involved, the balancing tests of Chapter 8 will almost always tell against permitting their use in taunting affronts. They do almost as poorly as possible on the "Reasonableness of the Offending Conduct" test, being flagrantly spiteful and malicious, not genuine political "speech", and not otherwise socially useful. When the conduct purports to be genuine political advocacy, its social value or "reasonableness" goes up, but where the advocacy is (say) of a program to strip blacks of their rights, and is accompanied by the symbols of K.K.K. terror, and takes place in the heart of Harlem, it is clear that threat and insult are its real purpose, not persuasion, and the conduct does poorly by the "Alternative opportunities" and "Nature of the locality" criteria as well.

10

The Idea of the Obscene

1. The judgmental sense of "obscene"

The word "obscene" as used in contemporary English has at least three senses. In its predominant, and presumably original usage, it expresses a judgment about the capacity of its object to produce certain kinds of offended states of mind in observers. When we say "*X* is obscene," we are normally giving *X* very low grades indeed. As we shall see, "the judgmental sense of 'obscene' " is really a family of senses all having to do in one way or another with offensiveness. When the speaker judges *X* to be obscene, he may be expressing his own offended reaction to *X*, or endorsing that reaction as a fitting and proper one, recommending it (so to speak) to others, and defending its reasonableness. In either case the speaker is not saying something very favorable about *X*; he is rather condemning *X* in a very special way. The speaker might be doing something more impartial toward *X*, however, if he is merely predicting that offense would be the reaction of most people toward *X*, but even that purely predictive judgment will fall short of perfect neutrality toward *X* if made by a judge or legislator applying the offense principle. In most living contexts, when a speaker says "*X* is obscene," he will be expressing, endorsing, and predicting offense toward *X*, all three; but there are special contexts in which he may be doing only one or some of these things. Hence, the point of referring to the judgmental "family" of senses.

The judgmental family can be contrasted, right from the start, with two other senses of "obscene". The second sense is an artificial one created by the United States Supreme Court in a series of official legal definitions (see Chap. 12). All of these legal definitions are approximate renderings of the sense of "pornographic" as applied to materials and displays deliberately intended to provoke erotic response. But as renditions of the more general judgmental senses, they are wholly inadequate, being at once too broad and too narrow (see Chapter 11, §1). The third use of "obscene' is as a conventional label, or classifying term, for a certain class of impolite words. This third use neither predicts, expresses, nor endorses any particular response to the words it labels; it simply classifies them. I can describe a person's remarks as "sprinkled with obscene words" without taking, endorsing, or predicting any particular attitude toward those words. In order to defeat the association with judgmentalness derived from the other senses of "obscene", a speaker using the word in this third way will qualify it with the words "so-called," as when he refers to "a so-called obscene epithet," or to "so-called dirty words."

In this chapter I shall attempt an analysis of the basic idea of judgmental obscenity. Obscenity in the sense of "pornography" (the artificial Supreme Court sense) will be treated in Chapters 11 and 12, and so-called "obscene words" in Chapters 13 through 16. We shall try to keep the senses segregated here, though both in ordinary parlance and in legal discourse they are constantly confused. The effects of this ambiguity have been especially unfortunate in courts and legislatures where the fallacy of equivocation has sometimes seemed the prevailing mode of reasoning.

2. Two apparently conflicting rationales for the prohibition of obscenity

To paraphrase a learned judge,[1] it is much easier to recognize obscenity than to say what it is. For a century and a half American appellate courts had little occasion to do either, since the constitutionality of statutes making obscenity a crime was rarely challenged. Indeed, until the post-Civil War period there was very little legislation pertaining to obscenity at all, and even after the proliferation of state laws inspired by the zealous Anthony Comstock, it was not until the twentieth century that official misgivings began to be expressed over either the propriety or the constitutionality of anti-obscenity laws. For the most part, laws prohibiting obscenity were no more questioned than those forbidding other public nuisances—indecent exposure, graffiti, public fornication and excretion.[2] The distinguishing feature of obscenity regulation, however, is that it applies explicitly to forms of expression—oral utterances, written messages, publications, pictures, photographs, exhibitions, dramatic performances, and films—that are normally protected by the free speech guarantee of the first amendment, and the due process clause of the fourteenth amendment. Until the detailed development of free speech doctrine in the period from 1918 to 1958,[3] it was routinely assumed that "obscenity" was the name of one of those large categories of exceptions to the constitutional protection of free expression, along with defamation, incitement to violence, counseling crime, fradulent advertising, and so on. But as free speech protections were steadily tightened during the period in question, pressure mounted on the courts to spell out the obscenity exception with greater clarity and precision. "Thus, the law of obscenity regulation seems to have a kind of 'sleeper' development, outside the main stream of decisions dealing with problems of freedom of speech, until . . . judges were met with the dilemma of reconciling the theories underlying the free-speech cases with the decisions sustaining obscenity regulations."[4] This in turn led to efforts to formulate the underlying rationale for making obscene expressions an exception in the first place.

From the beginning of these efforts there has been a strange divergence of justifications for prohibiting obscenity, stemming in turn, perhaps, from the oddly heterogeneous character of the materials most frequently condemned and prosecuted as obscene. The latter include hardly anything not encompassed in the Unholy Trio: Nudity, Sex, and Excretion. The restriction of the term "obscene" to appropriately offensive materials of these three kinds is so striking that the authors of the Model Penal Code were led to *define* obscene material (in part) as that which appeals to a "shameful or morbid interest in nudity, sex, or excretion."[5] One leading rationale for the obscenity prohibition apparently results from a judicial concentration on nudity and sex to the total neglect of excretion. The normal person finds (some) sex and nudity alluring. Attractive exhibitions, descriptions, or depictions of nude bodies and sex acts can cause people to experience agitative palpitations accompanied by lustful, lecherous, salacious thoughts and images. (It is extraordinary how many ordinary, technical, and slang words we have for precisely the same state of mind.) According to some traditional moral views, now fortunately out of vogue, the very existence of such sexy states of mind is an inherent evil. If a judge or legislator makes this judgment and also holds the legitimizing principle I called "legal moralism," namely that the prevention of sin or immorality as such, quite apart from harm, is a valid ground for prohibitive legislation, he need search no further for a rationale for prohibiting obscenity.

Very quickly, however, such a person is likely to stumble on a related, but distinct, rationale. Not only are sinful thoughts inherent evils, he is likely to hold; they also tend to have dreadful consequences on the character of the person who harbors them. Seductively alluring depictions of sex, according to a traditional legal formula, tend to "deprave and corrupt." Sexy and indecent thoughts turn the thinker into a sexy and indecent person. According to the legitimizing principle called "moralistic paternalism," it is bad (harmful) for a person to have impure thoughts and a depraved character whatever he may think about the matter, and the state has a right to protect him from his own folly by banning the corrupting materials. If a judge or legislator is sufficiently impressed by the allure of sexy materials and the general weakness of the flesh, he may even invoke the harm principle to justify prohibition of obscenity, to prevent his more impressionable neighbors from committing rapes and other anti-social sexual acts.

The rationales based on the aphrodisiac effect of ordinary sexual activity on the normal person are wildly implausible, however, when applied to so-called "emetic"[6] depictions of excretion and other sorts of scatological obscenity, or for that matter to normally disgusting perversions of sexual activity, for example, buggery, bestiality, and sado-masochism, or to grotesquely unattractive nudes. Such materials are also standardly denominated "obscene," yet far from being dangerously tempting, they are disgusting and revolting to the average person. It is in application to these forms of obscenity that the words "filth," "smut," and "dirt" seem most natural. To most of us, they are more like rotten fruit than like lucious, tempting, forbidden fruit. The most obvious ground for prohibiting them, one would think, is the need to prevent offensive nuisances to unwilling observers.

It has proved difficult for the moralist to have it both ways in his case against sexual obscenity. One can rest a case on too many grounds. Sometimes separate reasons may each be plausible considered in its own right, but contradictory or otherwise paradoxical when considered together, as when one child defends himself from the charge of striking another by saying "I didn't hit him and besides he hit me first."[7] Judge Jerome Frank pointed out the difficulty in his concurring opinion in *United States v. Roth* when that case was decided by the Second Circuit Appeals Court in 1956:

> If the argument be sound that the legislature may constitutionally provide punishment for the obscene because, antisocially, it arouses sexual desires by making sex attractive, then it follows that whatever makes sex disgusting is socially beneficial—and thus not the subject of valid legislation which punishes the mailing of 'filthy' matter.[8]

The implacable opponent of obscenity has only one way out of Frank's dilemma. He can treat "alluring" and "disgusting" not as contradictory predicates that exhaust all the possibilities between them, but rather as mere contraries, that is, mutually exclusive alternatives that are not jointly exhaustive. Sex can be discussed or depicted in a way which is *neither* alluring nor repellent, as for example in scientific treatises, medical texts, and clinical analyses. The opponent of sexual obscenity then could urge that any treatment of sex that makes it especially attractive *or* repellent to the ordinary person should be banned. Alluring descriptions and depictions would be prohibited for the usual moralistic and paternalistic reasons (such as they are); repellent descriptions and depictions would be acknowledged to have some value in keeping lascivious thoughts and lewd actions at bay, but would be forbidden nevertheless because of their overriding disvalue as nuisances causing such unpleasant "offended states" of mind as disgust and repugnance. Such a position is at least consistent, though it has little else to recommend it.

While Judge Frank overlooked the possibility that treatments of sex can be *neither* alluring *nor* revolting, Harry Kalven neglected the more subtle possibility that treatments of sex can be *both* alluring *and* revolting: "Since it [obscenity] cannot be both at the same time for the same audience, it would be well to have more explicit guidance as to which objection controls".[9] Kalven here misses one of the most important and elusive points about sexual obscenity: it *can* be both alluring and revolting in the same respect, at the same time, to the same person. This can happen in either of two ways, and here again is an elusive distinction. The experience of simultaneous allure and repugnance can be *shameful*, and hence on balance, profoundly offensive, or it can be what is called *thrilling*, and hence in some complex and qualified way, pleasurable.[10] And to further stagger our already over-burdened conceptual categories, it can be in some proportion or other both shameful *and* thrilling!

Attraction and disgust are both involved in the complex mechanism of shameful embarrassment, perhaps the most distinctive mode of offensive-ness produced by sexual obscenity. Even a prude is vulnerable to the charms of sex. He sees; he momentarily experiences lascivious longings and impure thoughts; he blushes with shame at his own impulses. That may end the battle with conscience restored to its throne, or it may continue for an extended period with lust and shame contending like gladiators. In the most extreme and destructive case, the upshot may be prolonged self-hatred, with prurience curdled into disgust and loathing.

Thrill-seeking is quite another matter, equally complex, and if anything, more mysterious psychologically. Strange as it may seem to the prude, there are those who apparently *enjoy* the tension between allure and disgust, who find its inner turmoil and excitement "thrilling" and actively seek it out, very much as youngsters seek out roller-coasters and other exciting rides at amusement parks for the thrill of sensations that are normally alarming and generally taken to be disagreeable. The analogy is also close (though not perfect) to the thrills of watching horror shows and spooky, scary films. (In New York thousands queued up for hours in 1974 for the opportunity of being frightened nearly out of their wits by the film *The Exorcist*, and dozens of these vomited or fainted during the showings.)[11] There is also an analogy to so-called "tear-jerkers" and even to the genuine danger and discomfort of motorcycle racing or mountain climbing. Most of these thrills (excepting cases of voluntarily incurred genuine danger) function psychologically as vicarious sublimations of genuine human drives for exciting activity and adventure, or as substitute objects for the working out of genuine emotional problems, while knowledge of one's real safety is "temporarily suspended." Similarly, it is exciting to the point of thrilling (for some) to be sexually "naughty" while really safe, to indulge one's lascivious thoughts and images and even to approach and playfully transgress the limits of imagination imposed by the inner censor, when one is no more likely to abandon oneself totally than one is likely in the analogous case to fall out of the roller-coaster.

In such ways as these, sexual pictures, films, and literary descriptions may cause and exploit inner tensions, ambivalence, and conflicts. Precisely the same materials may cause other viewers unalloyed pleasure, and still others may be "left cold," altogether unaffected emotionally. Those whose pleasure is unmixed and those who are unaffected one way or another are not likely to use the word "obscene" to describe what they see, except perhaps with "scare-quotes" around the word and the meaning "what is generally called obscene." When the materials are not thought to be truly offensive, neither are they thought to be *truly obscene* (said with feeling and without scare-quotes). Therein lies the first clue to the analysis of the concept of the obscene.

3. The analysis of obscenity

Obscene materials then, whatever else they may be, are offensive materials. A good start, but it doesn't take us far. A full analysis would specify the sorts of objects that can be obscene, characterize the mode or modes of offensiveness peculiar to the obscene, and tell whom, as well as how, obscenity offends. We can begin with the latter question. One and the same item can offend one person and not another; moreover, given the great diversity of mankind, there may be hardly anything that doesn't offend someone or other. Yet surely the word "obscene" will have very little utility if it can both apply and not apply to the same thing or if it applies near-universally to everything. A better beginning would be to say that "X is obscene" means "X is apt to offend almost anyone." This is to interpret "obscene" as what P. H. Nowell-Smith has called an "aptness word," one which "indicates that an object has certain properties which are apt to arouse a certain emotion or range of emotions."[12] Nowell-Smith contrasted aptness words with purely descriptive words such as "red," "square," "tall," and "wet." Not that aptness words can't suggest that the objects to which they apply have certain properties, at least within a range, but rather that they do more than merely "describe" their objects in this limited way. To say that the view from a certain location is sublime is perhaps to *imply* that it is extensive and panoramic, but it is also to say, according to Nowell-Smith, that it is apt to arouse an emotion of awe or a stirring, breathtaking reaction, in one (anyone) who experiences it. And to say that it is apt to arouse that emotion in anyone is to say that it *will* arouse that emotion in a typical or "average" person in typical circumstances. If John Doe experiences the view from that location but is unmoved by it, that does not prove that the view is not sublime, but only that John Doe is not in certain ways a typical observer. Nowell-Smith's list of typical aptness words includes the following: "terrifying, hair-raising, disappointing, disgusting, ridiculous, funny, amusing, sublime."[13] ("Disappointing" means "apt to disappoint"; "disgusting" means "apt to disgust"; "amusing" means "apt to amuse"; and so on.) The presence of "disgusting" on this list suggests that "obscene" might belong there too.

Aptness words, as Nowell-Smith conceives them, *can* be used simply to predict the reactions of other people to the objects of which they are predicated, with no expression of the speaker's own attitude. John Doe in the previous example, if asked to describe the view at the location in question, might reply, "It is sublime, although I was unmoved by it." But this is artificial and exceptional. For the most part, when a speaker uses an aptness word he wishes to imply that he himself has the reaction most people are apt to have, and further, that the reaction is the *appropriate* one to have in the circumstances. If a person who was in fact bored by a book tells you, in response to your query, that it is amusing, he may not be exactly lying, but he certainly misleads inexcusably, even if in fact the book is apt to amuse you and most other people. That is because when he said the book was amusing he implied, without exactly saying so, that he himself had been amused by it. Nowell-Smith understands this point well:

> In default of other evidence the use of an A-sentence [one applying an aptness word] usually implies that the speaker has the appropriate reaction. It would be odd to say that a book was enlightening or amusing and then go on to say that one was not enlightened or amused by it. Odd but not impossible. 'It was a terrifying ordeal but I wasn't frightened'. 'It may be very funny but I am not inclined to laugh.'. . . . in these cases the 'subjective element' is expressly

withdrawn; and since these statements are not self-contradictory, we cannot say that 'X is terrifying' either means or [logically] entails 'I am frightened by X.' Nevertheless, in default of an express withdrawal, we should always be entitled to infer that the speaker has the appropriate reaction.[14]

In typical usage, however, the speaker does more than imply that he has (has had, or would have) the emotion or feeling in question; he can be understood, in addition, to be *endorsing* that emotion or feeling as the correct or appropriate reaction in the circumstances. When Jones says that X is amusing, in the typical case, he can be understood to be (1) asserting that X would amuse the average person, (2) implying (subject to explicit withdrawal) that it amuses him as well, and (3) endorsing amusement as the correct or appropriate reaction to X. If there is any doubt about his intention to endorse, he can underline it by saying that X is "truly" or "really" amusing. The point applies (with occasional deviant variations) to the other aptness words such as "frightening," and "disgusting." This three-pronged analysis (predicting, expressing, endorsing) defines what we can call the "standard use" of aptness words.

Language is seldom so simple and rigid a thing, however, as to be summarized in such neat formulas, and wherever there is a standard use, there are likely to be various intelligible non-standard uses as well. In particular, aptness words may sometimes be used in a non-endorsing way. A highly disciplined, courageous person might admit that certain circumstances are frightening because he knows that they are apt to frighten his auditors and other typical persons, and yet deny both that they frighten him and that fear is a natural, inevitable, or appropriate reaction to them. A moralist might concede that certain "ethnic jokes" are amusing while not only denying that amusement is the appropriate reaction to them, but also urging people *not* to be amused by them. A nutrition expert might admit that eating insects is disgusting, but deny that disgust is appropriate given the high protein content of broiled grasshoppers.

Sometimes aptness words are applied so constantly to a given class of objects that they acquire almost the force of fixed convention, so that it would seem perverse and even self-contradictory to deny that they properly apply to those classes. Those who would, nevertheless, deny the appropriateness of the conventional response in these cases are forced to do it in other ways, while conceding that the aptness term applies in a *non-endorsing* way. To make that concession would be to use the aptness term in scare-quotes or in an "inverted comma" sense.[15] When an aptness word A is applied to some object X in this way it means roughly "what is called A by most people, but not necessarily by me." A familiar tip-off that a speaker is using A in this non-endorsing fashion is his use of the qualifying phrase "so-called," as in "a so-called dirty joke," or a "so-called nice girl." Even if he thinks that there is nothing dirty about risqué anecdotes, he may use the phrase "dirty jokes" as a conventional label for them, just as he uses (without endorsement of the appropriateness of offense) the conventional label "obscene words" for certain impolite epithets.

Another nonstandard use of such words as "amusing," "frightening," and "disgusting" is to keep the endorsing function while dropping the predictive element. Normally, this is thought to be linguistically odd. If I learn that a situation that amuses me fails to amuse others, I will reluctantly admit that it is not really amusing while insisting that it amused me anyway. If I am frightened of closed doors, I will have to concede that they are not really frightening; they only frighten me. If I am disgusted by the sight of boiled potatoes, I will admit that they are not really disgusting while confessing that nevertheless they disgust me. (I may not know what is bad, but I know what I dislike.) It would indeed seem odd in these cases to insist that amusement, fear, or disgust are appropriate reactions while admitting that their objects are not apt to cause others to have those feelings. But there are times when we have enough self-confidence to stick by our guns and, whether "odd" or not, say: "I don't care whether anyone else in the whole world is amused (frightened, disgusted) by X, X is truly amusing (frightening, disgusting) all the same." When we get to this point our convictions are on the line and our arguments and reasons in readiness, so that we are not likely to have much patience for linguistic quibbles. "I am amused (frightened, disgusted) by X and I can present reasons why anyone in my circumstances *ought* to be amused (frightened, disgusted) by it," we might say. "The important question is whether X has characteristics that make it *worthy* of, or *properly* the object of, amusement (fear, disgust), not whether linguistic conventions permit the application of the word "amusing" ("frightening," "disgusting") to it when no one else is apt to be amused (frightened, disgusted)."

A speaker's use of a word in this way to endorse an emotional response while wholly unconcerned about the extent to which that response is shared, is not so much a "nonstandard use of an aptness word," as the conversion of an aptness word into a word of another kind altogether. Nowell-Smith calls such words as "desirable," "praiseworthy", and "lamentable", whose whole function is to endorse a particular type of response, "gerundive words,"[16] since they say, in effect, that a given responsive attitude "is to be" felt. Sometimes the conversion of an aptness word into a gerundive word creates a linguistic strain that is too great to sustain and the result is intolerable "oddness." Fortunately, there is usually another gerundive word, or endorsing word (as I prefer to call it) at hand to relieve the strain and permit the argument to proceed. Am I the only one who is amused by *X?* Very well then, perhaps *X* is not amusing. (I give up the aptness word.) But it is *funny* anyway, and exquisitely and subtly *comic.* Fully informed and genuinely sensitive people will be amused by it, whatever the general run of people may think. Am I the only one who is frightened by *Y?* Very well then, perhaps *Y* is not frightening, but it is objectively *threatening* and *dangerous* nevertheless, and any sensible prudent person will be frightened of it. Am I the only one who is disgusted by *Z?* Very well then perhaps *Z* is not disgusting, but whether it disgusts others or not, the disgust it arouses in me is fully justified and appropriate. Perhaps more useful words for these notions would be "amuseworthy," "fearworthy," and "disgustworthy." They would *clearly* take the strain off the nonstandardly used aptness words.

How, if at all, can one person rationally defend his judgment that disgust or repugnance is a "worthy," proper, or appropriate response to some object or behavior, and how can one convince another, using rational means of persuasion, to share his emotional reaction? It may be impossible conclusively to support such judgments of appropriateness with reasons, just as it is impossible to *prove* (say) to an unamused person that some joke is truly amusing. The only way to convince the latter person may be to get him *somehow* (perhaps by reiteration, different inflection, background explanation, or contagious laughter) to share one's amusement. On this model for obscenity, the only way to convince a person that *X* is truly offensive is to get him somehow to share one's own shock or disgust, perhaps by exposing him more vividly or thoroughly to *X,* by presenting *X* in a different light, by describing *X* in a new but accurate way, by background explanation, or contagious revulsion. These methods are not very similar to those used by mathematicians when they state the premises from which theorems follow deductively, nor to those used by scientists, historians and lawyers when they muster evidence that gives support to their factual claims, nor even to those used by moralists when they cite the authority for their moral judgments and principles. In contrast to these other modes of reason-giving, the methods for supporting judgments of the appropriateness of certain feelings (including judgments of disgustworthiness) are "nonrational." But there need be nothing sinister involved in using so-called nonrational methods when the "reasons" offered are relevant to the case at hand. Reiteration, background explanation, and the contagion of example are surely "relevant" in a way in which arm-twisting, threats, and the use of drugs or hypnosis are not. And surely there is nothing sinister in the use of the best reasons one can find, even when they fall far short of rational demonstration. Perhaps that is what Aristotle meant when he wrote that in any given branch of discourse, "we should not expect more precision than the subject matter, by its very nature, admits of."[17]

Usage of terms like "obscene," of course, is far from clear-cut. It would be absurd for philosophers to waste time disputing over it. But it is possible to characterize in a general way at least some of its more important uses. Beyond that, further precision is both difficult and unnecessary. The word "obscene" then is commonly used as:

1. A standard aptness word, with predictive, expressive, and endorsing elements, meaning roughly "disgusting," "shocking," or "revolting."
2. A standard gerundive word used only to endorse a certain kind of emotional reaction as appropriate, and having roughly the meaning that "disgustworthy," "shockworthy,", or "repugnanceworthy" would have if there were such words.
3. A nonstandard aptness word used primarily or exclusively to predict the response of other people, actual or hypothetical, to the materials or conduct in question.

In addition, it is commonly used in two, or even in all three of these "judgmental" ways at once. And, of course, the word "obscene" also bears the quite independent senses of "pornographic" and "linguistically tabooed," in which it is used to describe without judgment, or to classify.

4. The genesis of obscenity: vulgarity

Our next task is to characterize more exactly the distinctive sort of offensiveness peculiar to the things that are obscene. In general, there are two sorts of models for the offendedness that inclines us to use the word "obscene", namely our reactions to filth and our reactions to vulgarity, and there is some reason to think that each of these has contributed to the historical development of the concept of the obscene. Beginning with vulgarity, I shall draw on an astute but little known article by Peter Glassen.[18] In this article, Glassen coins the term "charientic"[19] to refer to a class of evaluative judgments which he thinks are quite distinct and different from moral and aesthetic judgments. Statements ascribing *vulgarity* are typical of the judgments in this category:

> It seems to me that they [charientic judgments] are not moral judgments. The things thought to be vulgar—like chewing gum, making scenes, picking one's nose, etc.—are not commonly thought to be morally wrong or immoral. Moreover, a man may be thought to be of the highest moral character, and yet be held to be vulgar in greater or lesser degree . . . Conduct can be judged from more than one perspective at the same time . . . It seems to me to be pretty

clear also that judgments in terms of 'vulgar' are not aesthetic judgments, being~
made mostly about persons and their acts, and not about things and expe.. ·
ences. 'Vulgar' applied to works of art is a transferred epithet; 'beautiful' and
'ugly,' however, are not.[20]

The class of "charientic terms," positive and negative, includes not only
"vulgar," but "uncouth," "boorish," "tasteless," "philistine," "refined,"
"sensitive," "cultivated," "civilized," "tasteful," "classy," and "cool." These
terms as a class clearly seem distinguished from "righteous," "wicked,"
"honest," and "cruel," and also from "beautiful," "ugly," "dainty," and
"dumpy."

Glassen goes on to distinguish moral from charientic approval; the former
is akin to respect, the latter closer to admiration. Moral disapproval is,
among other things, a resentful reaction, leading to indignation and settled
hostility, whereas charientic disapproval is more akin to contempt, a "looking down one's nose reaction," and (when felt at a safe distance where
strong personal offense is not taken) derision and ridicule. "We want to
laugh at the vulgar; we want to punish the wicked."[21] But vulgarity at close
quarters is no laughing matter. Its irritations can be severe, even if short of
harmfulness, and provoke snarling denunciations rather than derisive
laughter or snobbish hauteur:

> But sometimes we hear tirades against vulgarity. They can have the fervor and
> virulence of the outraged moralist, but they do not express a moral point of
> view. They proceed from irritation at having to put up with the unpleasantness
> or frustrations of living in an uncongenial milieu.[22]

The charientic vocabulary runs separately but parallel to the moral vocabulary in various other respects too. Since most vulgarity is unintentional
(done in ignorance) there is no charientic counterpart to guilt, Glassen tells
us, but we do feel a kind of embarrassment analogous to moral shame when
we suddenly realize that we have committed, however inadvertently, a
"charientic *faux pas*."[23] Similarly, moral hypocrisy has its counterpart in
charientic affectation, self-righteousness in snobbishness. People to whom
charientic virtues are supremely important may refrain from immoral conduct not so much because it is immoral as because it is vulgar, "beneath
them," "cheap," "bad form," or "bush league." Acts of dishonesty, rudeness, cruelty, and the like, are very often *also* crude and gross, not the sorts
of things a person of refined sensibility or good upbringing would do. Here
charientic judgments reenforce moral ones and apply with equal relevance
to immoral conduct. Still, the charientic and moral standards, even in
combination, retain their separate identities.[24]

Ascriptions of obscenity to persons, their actions, or as "transferred epithets" to their creations, are the charientic judgments *par excellence*. That is not to say that judgments of obscenity are the most typical or representative charientic judgments, but rather that they are charientic judgments of the most extreme kind. Obscenity is the outer limit of vulgarity. To the question "How vulgar can one get?", the answer is "vulgar to the point of obscenity." Obscene conduct is not merely in "bad form," ungracious and unseemly; it is conduct in the worst possible form, *utterly* crude, coarse, and gross. The adjectives that regularly consort with the noun "obscenity" fully reveal its extreme and unqualified character: the obscene is pure and unmixed, sheer, crass, bare, unveiled, bald, naked, rank, coarse, raw, shocking, blunt, and stark. It hits one in the face; it is shoved under one's nose; shocks the eye. The obscene excludes subtlety or indirection, and can never be merely veiled, implied, hinted, or suggested. The idea of a "subtle obscenity" is a contradiction in terms.[25]

An obscene person, then, is one whose character or conduct is so extremely deficient in the charientic graces as to be downright repulsive, a person who is apt to offend anyone, and in response to whom offense is an appropriate (or at least an understandable) response. The obscene person is *coarse*—and then some. The *Webster's Third New International Dictionary* contains a revealing discussion of the word "coarse," comparing and contrasting it with its near synonyms, among which it includes *vulgar, gross, obscene,* and *ribald*. Coarseness itself when applied to character and conduct is a paradigm of a charientic term referring to one who is "crude or unrefined in taste, manners, or sensibilities; without cultivation of taste, politeness or civility of manner, or delicacy of feeling," often "crude and indelicate of language or idea, especially with violation of social taboos on language." "Vulgar" is much the same in meaning, but is an even stronger term, one which "may suggest boorishness." "Gross" is clearly a close relation, but one which "stresses crude animal inclinations and lack of refinement." "Obscene," of course, "is the strongest of this group in stressing impropriety, indecency, or nastiness. . . ." Finally "ribald" suggests "rough merriment or crude humor at the irreverent, scurrilous, or vulgar." Ribald behavior, I should think, is merely "naughty," though perhaps extremely so, but the other terms in this negative charientic family apply to the repulsively offensive, and of those, "obscene" is by far the strongest, unless we include in this group, as *Webster's* did not, the word "indecent."

The terms "decent" and "indecent" are more confusing than the others we have considered, probably because there are two concepts of decency and indecency, one of which is moral and the other charientic. There is no doubt that the charientic sense is etymologically prior to the moral one, and that "indecent" does belong in the same charientic family that includes "coarse", "gross", "vulgar," and "obscene." The positive term "decent" came into English no later than 1539 from the French *decent*, which was derived in turn from the Latin *decere*, to be fitting or becoming, which is related to the Greek *dokein* to seem good (with emphasis on the seeming) and the Sanskrit verb for seeking to please, or being gracious. It is closely related to such other English words as "decor" and "decorate," "decorous" and "indecorous," and "dignity" and "indignation." The *Oxford English Dictionary* lists among its primary senses "becoming, suitable, or proper to the circumstances . . . seemly," and "in accordance with propriety or good taste, especially free from immodesty or obscenity." *Webster's* defines it as "fitting in words, behavior, dress, or ceremony, especially in relation to an accepted standard: decorous, proper, seemly, as in 'decent conduct', or 'decent language'." Indecency on the other hand, is an "offense against delicacy" or "against decorum." An indecent act is one that is "unbecoming, unseemly, or indecorous," as, for example, one done in "indecent haste," and indecent language is "unfit to be seen or heard, as offensive to modesty and delicacy."

The purely charientic concept of indecency that is captured in these dictionary definitions applies to offensive or unfitting ways of appearing, to "how things look" to observers. Conduct is indecent in this sense because it has characteristics that make it extremely unpleasant to witness. For one reason or another it makes observers uncomfortable; it can make them squirm with embarassment. The wholly charientic sort of indecency has such effects on us even when we have no objection in principle to the category of behavior it exemplifies. There are many kinds of charientically indecent conduct that are not inherently immoral by any one's standards and would be utterly unobjectionable if done unobserved, in private. H. L. A. Hart cites sexual intercourse performed in public by a married couple as behavior that is indecent (in its context) but not immoral, since it would be wholly innocent if done in private.[26] More subtle examples concern areas of life that have nothing to do with sex. Indeed any conspicuous display of behavior that makes observers uncomfortable, any bold flaunting of taste-lessness, can appear "indecent" in the purely charientic sense. Robertson Davies in his novel *Fifth Business* uses the word "indecent" to describe the behavior of an overly ardent clergyman who embarrasses his congregation with excessive public displays of piety, though hardly *any* amount of religious ardor in private could be "excessive" in one who has chosen the religious vocation:

> A few of his flock said that he walked very closely with God, and it made him spooky. *We* had family prayers at home, a respectful salute to Providence

before breakfast, enough for anybody. But he was likely to drop on his knees at any time and pray with a fervor that seemed indecent. Because I was often around their house, I sometimes stumbled in on one of these occasions, and he would motion me to kneel with him until he was finished—which could be as long as ten or fifteen minutes later.[27]

A second class of examples portray conduct that is "indecent" in a hybrid sense, partly charientic and partly moral. Such conduct offends observers not because it is the sort of activity that is generally unpleasant to observe, but rather because it betrays attitudes in the actor that the observer finds morally inappropriate, and the very existence of the attitudes is an affront to moral sensibility. But the offense is also partly charientic because the objectionable attitudes, when publicly flaunted, are symbolic gestures of disrespect and *therefore* unseemly, unbecoming, indecorous. A motley of examples involving "indecent haste" illustrate well this hybrid class. There is nothing inherently immoral in attending a joyous songfest in a tavern, but it is unbecoming (at the very least) when done in indecent haste after the funeral of one's parent or closest friend. And there is nothing immoral as such in seeking to court a lady, but it is unseemly (at the very least) when done in indecent haste after the death of her husband or of one's own wife. The disrespectful attitudes manifested in these examples may or may not be morally objectionable, but when they are morally flawed they are so whether publicly exhibited or not. In these cases, however, their *display* in the circumstances adds a new dimension of offensiveness to them. We are made acutely uncomfortable by the naked exhibition of private feelings and moral flaws which (like their physical analogues) are best kept out of public view. It is bad enough to *be* morally objectionable in a certain way, but it is wrong on an additional ground to let oneself *appear* as one in fact is. It is extremely bad taste to flaunt one's moral flaws. And in the examples, above, the *revelation* of the flaws is itself an insult to the memory of the departed.

Indecency of the third, or purely moral kind is a very special way of being immoral whether one's objectionable behavior occurs in public or in private. The Victorian husband who always keeps up appearances in public but bullies his helpless wife mercilessly in the privacy of their home is not a "decent fellow." His cruelty is so beastly it is "positively indecent," as we say, whether or not there are observers to be offended by it. If he loses his temper in public and shamelessly humiliates his wife in front of his friends and associates, then his behavior is indecent in both senses: shamelessly immoral and tastelessly exhibited. It is only in the latter instance that it is obscene, for in private there are no observers to be disgusted. When it does offend it does so by being a blatant violation of the observer's moral principles, a shock to his moral sensibility, not merely an affront to his senses, his taste, or his dignity, as the sight of a person defecating, for example, might be.

A "thoroughly decent man," in the wholly moral sense, is not simply a person who refrains from unseemly or indecorous public behavior. If that is all the phrase meant it would be faint praise indeed. Rather it is a person of unquestioned integrity and rectitude. It is this same, familiar, wholly moral sense that explains why we sometimes "appeal to a person's decency" when we implore him to help someone in serious need. " In all decency," we may ourselves say, "I could not stand by and watch him suffer." This use has nothing to do with charientic graces, no more than *being* good (in the most basic and important ways) has to do with merely *seeming* good, or more to the point, with merely not seeming outrageously bad.

5. The genesis of obscenity: yukkiness

Extremely coarse and indecent acts are models of obscenity, but they are certainly not the only things, and possibly not even the original sorts of things to which the word has been applied. Etymologically the word is said to derive from the Latin *ob* (to, before, against) plus *caenum* (filth). Presumably, the Romans used a similar term in their language to mean "of or pertaining to filth." The word is still applied in English to natural objects that may in no way be the product of human design. Anything in nature that is rank and raw is likely to strike us as obscene when we think of it as filthy, foul, slimy, snotty, and generally loathsome to the senses. One of the standard uses of the word is to refer to things that are "obscene to the touch." *Webster's* quotes an unnamed writer who reports that "obscene fungi clothed the wall of that dank cavern."[28] An "unnaturally" dank and musty toadstool is hardly surpassed in obscenity unless by a wriggly slug in the black mud under a rock. Obscene objects send shudders up our spines and set our teeth on edge.[29]

It is not unlikely that the psychological origin of the idea of the obscene (quite apart from the derivation of the word) is located in what may be called the "Yuk reaction" implanted in children by their parents in the crawling stage of infancy. Imagine a typical scene in a city park on a spring day. Mother watches from a bench as her child reels or crawls on the grass. Soon an object catches the infant's eye. He moves into its range and by a sudden instinctive motion the object is in his hand, and the hand is moving towards his mouth. The object might be a discarded cigarette package, a thoroughly used wad of chewing gum, a bit of dried animal dung, some unidentifiable slimy thing, a worm, or an ice cream carton with an oozy residue compounded of melted chocolate, saliva, and mud. The mother, of course, springs to her feet in horror. "No, no!" she cries; "Dirty! Nasty! YUK!" These and similar admonitory locutions are uttered with the expression of one who is so ill she is about to regurgitate, and a characteristic tone and inflection that marks this type of prohibition off from various other kinds. Eating strange objects is not morally wrong like eating brother's candy; it is not selfish, mean, unfair, or cruel. It is simply (what better word is there?) *Yukky*.

The child usually learns all too well. The grasping-tasting reflex is brought under control soon enough, but is then followed by a period of excessive fastidiousness (common between the ages of seven and twelve but extending even into adulthood among the childish) during which the child distrusts all strange dishes and reacts to the likes of an unfamiliar Lobster Newburg or Moules Marinières (no doubt imitating mother's original manner) with an emphatic "Yuk!" or a disdainful "How gross!" From then on, education of the tastes is an uphill struggle.

There is little doubt that the yuk reaction serves the cause of hygiene and health, even of infant survival. It is apparently a learned reaction for the most part, the infant learning to control his instinctive movements by negative reenforcement. But repugnance is a virtually universal response to some things, even among small children, and it is possible that it has an instinctive basis. Desmond Morris has suggested, for example, that aversive to snakes, beetles, and small crawly things might be instinctive.[30] Inherited aversive responses of that kind might well have had strong survival value leading to their preservation by evolutionary processes, much in the manner of feline "nervousness," or the constant head movements and general skittishness of birds. In any case, learned or not, there is no doubting their utility, within limits, to the species.

Yuk reactions to things perceived as dirty, gross, or unnaturally strange, whether learned or inherited, are natural and universal phenomena. The sorts of things that can trigger the reaction, of course, vary widely among humankind, with varying conceptions of what is filthy, or strange, or "yukky." And various alternative reactions are possible even to acknowledged dirt, starkness, or rawness. Consider such objects as vivid, close-up, highly magnified, color photographs of male and female sex organs in a state of full engorgement and excitation. A person might have any one (or some combination) of four purposes in peering at these unnaturally abstract and depersonalized objects, and with each purpose goes a characteristic attitude or response. First is the reaction almost anyone would be apt to have if caught off guard and suddenly confronted with the photographs or their images projected on to a large screen, namely, a spontaneous shrinking away. The enlarged technicolored organs are "too much!" Too much even of a good thing is coarse and sickening. The second reaction might be that of a diagnostic physician or a medical student: detached, objective, scientific. Looking at vulvas or penises in that spirit is like looking at any other organ, healthy or diseased, or like looking at an X-ray picture. The third possible reaction is one which would tend to be inhibited by either of the first two, but which might emerge nevertheless, and coexist to some degree or another with the others. That would be to find the pictures strangely moving despite their surface repulsion, and to feel the first internal rumblings of a "genital commotion." The detailed enlargements might make the objects a bit too stark and coarse for full comfort, but the thought that what one is looking at is, after all, somebody's sex organ, might be unsettling and yet erotic. Obscenity, in this case, is a barrier to prurience which must be overcome, and not itself a direct inducement. A fourth possible (but not very likely) reaction would be openly to revel in the coarseness of the pictures, to see them as yukky and yet to wallow in them in full and public abandonment.

To which of our hypothetical observers will the pictures seem *obscene?* Clearly they will be thought and experienced as obscene by the first observer, and clearly not by the second. The ambivalent reaction of the third observer, in which repugnance is overlaid with or even overcome by lust, is no doubt what many judges and moralists have thought to be the very model of obscenity, but it is better analyzed as a mixed case, in which the bald and coarse elements properly called obscene fail to suppress an attraction that arouses and goads withal. The fourth case raises special conceptual problems that will be dealt with below. The open reveler clearly does not regard the pictures as obscene. His is not a yuk reaction. But another person taking in the whole scene that includes (say) the pictures projected on a screen and the observer lewdly reveling in them, is likely to regard the composite spectacle as obscene, just as he might similarly react to a person's joyous reveling at the death of an enemy at the latter's funeral. In both cases, a second party might locate the obscenity not in the stimulus (the pictures, the death) but in a grossly inappropriate response to it. In a similar way, a Moslem or an orthodox Jew might not think that the bare existence of a roast of pork is obscene, but he may behold a coreligionist savoring every bite of the forbidden food, and take that *response* to the roast pork to be obscene.

Tabooed behavior and other conduct that grossly violates an observer's "higher order sensibilities" mark a third category of obscenity, to go with things that are directly offensive to the senses and to the "lower order sensibilities." Almost anyone would be offended by odd and alien creatures who looked as if they were covered with mucus, phlegm, or congealed wound products, all of which are vaguely associated with the unhealthy, the dirty, the excretal. These objects may directly offend the senses, or they may be *seen as* (say) slugs and *therefore* found disgusting. But the roast pork example shows that objects and activities can also be *seen as* tabooed and *therefore* disgusting, and extreme instances of this sort too are called "obscene." Moreover, examples of so-called indecencies show that gross and naked violations of moral principle (e.g., an observed act of torturing a prisoner) are also disgusting to the point of obscenity.[31]

6. The scope of the obscene: clues in extended applications

Instances of crassly repugnant violations of standards of appropriate and decent conduct, or of violations of ideals and principles, are likely to include many things other than the sexual and scatological. It may well be true that the word "obscene" gets stretched in its application to some of these things. To those who follow the Model Penal Code definition that restricts obscenity to offensive treatments of Sex, Nudity, or Excretion, other uses of the word may seem secondary and derivative, or even metaphorical. No discussion of obscenity can be complete, however, that fails to examine some of these "extended applications," for they are common, clear, and unpuzzling uses of the English language, which present clues to what is essential and easily overlooked in the definition of "obscene." All of the examples of usage are based on analogies to something central in the primary applications of the word (to yukky natural objects, coarse behavior, and created objects.) It is especially useful to examine non-sexual and non-scatological uses if we are to find a hidden key to an essential element of the word's meaning that it possesses even when it is applied in more familiar ways. Consider then the following ten sentences.

1. "Death under the stars is somehow obscene."[32]
2. "The machine gunning of Bonnie and Clyde in the climactic scene of the film may have been morally and dramatically justified, but the blood spurting out of the bullet holes as bullets splattered the bodies was a naturally revolting sight—so offensive and shocking to the senses as to be obscene.
3. "Nothing is more obscene than a public beheading."
4. ". . . the obscene little counter-demonstrations lewdly exulting in the forthcoming deaths."[33]
5. " 'We couldn't have Buddhist bonzes [monks] burning themselves on street corners and Madame Nhu [sister-in-law of Mr. Diem] making

obscene comments about bonze barbecues', Mr. Ball said. 'The coup was inevitable'."[34]

6. "In such cases the sufferer may be reduced to an obscene parody of a human being, a lump of suffering flesh eased only by intervals of drugged stupor."[35]

7. "The portrait of Dorian Grey was unveiled in all its obscene horror in the climax of the film."

8. "The debate . . . was almost obscene in its irresponsibility."[36]

9. "It would seem that Mr. Kraft's premise dictates that the primary effort of the United States should be to control its private oil firms so that they begin to operate in the nation's interest instead of continuing their present tactics of reaping obscene profits while unemployment gains and the domestic economy crumbles."[37]

10. " 'Nigger' is the most obscene word in the English language."[38]

The first five examples all have to do with *death,* a subject so liable to obscene treatment, it is a wonder that it has not broken into the Model Penal Code's Unholy Trio and enlarged it into a quartet. To speak in the bluntest terms of sexual intercourse in the company of young ladies was once thought to be the clearest case of obscene conduct, but in this day and age it is probably thought by most to be no more obscene than to speak of death agonies to an audience of octogenarians, and especially to use such crass terms as "croak," "carcass," and "stiff," or to refer to a cemetery as a "bone orchard." Death is now one of the last unmentionable subjects, at least in the company of the ill and aged. And think how uncomfortable we are all made when a very old person speaks in an open way of his own impending death. Furthermore, there is nothing more obscene in a perfectly literal, hardcore sense, nothing from which we naturally shrink with greater disgust and horror, than a close-up view of a dead human body with it protruding eyes and greenish skin. Nor is there any more obscene conduct imaginable than patently inappropriate responses to a dead body—desecration, savage dismemberment, brutal gestures, cannibalism, or necrophiliac embraces.[39]

The first example in the list is perhaps the hardest to interpret out of context. Very likely, the author thinks of the death of an old or ill person in his own bed or in a sickroom as the paradigm of a proper demise, as natural as birth, or growth, or decay, and not be lamented. To be out in the open air under a starry sky, on the other hand, is the proper province of the young and healthy, the active or the pensive, lovers, loners, and dreamers. When a young man, therefore, is shot down "under the stars," the spectacle seems unnatural and "inappropriate" and hence more repellant than death in more normal circumstances.

The death scene in the film *Bonnie and Clyde* employed new cinematic techniques, later widely imitated, to simulate the impact of lethal objects on human bodies in the most startlingly realistic way. The effect of this shocking close-up realism, in contrast to the happy-go-lucky pace of everything that preceded it in the film, is to shock the viewer in an almost intolerably forceful way and bring home the message of retribution with maximal dramatic impact. Rather than impede the dramatic purposes of the film, this utterly revolting scene enhanced them, showing that even emetic obscenity can have its aesthetic uses. For the most part, however, an excess of blood and guts tends to distract and overwhelm the viewer and thus weaken the impact of the play. Havelock Ellis may have been mistaken on etymological grounds, but he was psychologically insightful nevertheless when he suggested that the obscene is what must be kept "off stage" and only referred to or symbolized on the stage (like the blinding of Oedipus).[40]

To any cultivated and moderately unworldly Englishman at the time of the French Revolution, surely nothing was more obscene than the mass public beheadings of The Terror. And indeed public beheadings were paradigmatic obscenities, being blatantly offensive on several distinct grounds. First, the decapitated bodies and severed heads were *obscene objects par excellence*. Second, the act of beheading is such a blatant violation of the ideal of humanity, so stark and open and defiant a breach of moral principle, as to be an obscene *act*. Third, the performance of an obscene act before an *audience* is so grossly repugnant, so gratuitously violative of the victim's dignity and privacy, that it adds still another dimension of obscenity to what is already richly obscene in its own right.[41] Finally, the blood lust manifested in the "obscene" shrieks of joy from the revolutionary mobs as heads fell was so manifestly inappropriate a *response* to the primary event as to sicken a squeamish observer all by itself. The presence of an audience itself makes the spectacle obscene. The responses of that audience make it doubly so.

One can imagine easily enough a context for the fourth specimen in the list. We can think of demonstrators picketing in front of a darkened prison, or standing in prayerful vigil on behalf of doomed political prisoners, the Rosenbergs say, or Sacco and Vanzetti. Across the street a raucous group of counter-demonstrators carries placards urging that the loathsome traitors be given the hangings they deserve, or claiming that hanging is too good a death for the bastards. Reluctant or righteous advocacy of the death penalty is a perfectly civilized and dignified posture; hatred and blood lust, poorly disguised though indirectly conveyed, is another thing, disgusting perhaps, but not yet obscene. Raw unveiled blood lust, on the other hand, loudly and proudly expressed without subtlety or innuendo, is as obscene as a manifested emotion can be. (Unless the cold supercilious barbarism of Madame Nhu's attitude towards the self-sacrificing monks in specimen number five counts as an "emotion.")

A "lump of suffering flesh" that used to be a fully dignified human being is a sight from which all but the most hardened among us would recoil in horror. Such a "person" is a revolting object from which our senses shrink, but it is also a degraded human being, deprived of hope, privacy, dignity, even self-awareness. A rotting fruit offends our senses; a hopelessly decayed human being breaks our heart as well. The "parodying of humanity" is what is grossly repugnant to our sense of appropriateness, and obscene in its revolting horror.

The portrait of Dorian Grey has certain similarities to the previous example, but some interesting differences as well. The painting, of course, is hideously ugly. We recognize it (just barely) as a man's face covered with scabs, running sores, broken teeth, bloody eyes, and a grotesque and depraved expression. It does not merely offend our senses (although it may do that too). Rather it strikes us as obscene because of its hideous distortion of a human face.

It does not follow from our treatment of this example that obscenity is an "aesthetic category," even on the assumption that ugliness itself is an aesthetic category. The judgment that a work of art is ugly is an aesthetic one, though of course it is not by itself the expression of an overall appraisal. (A painting can be ugly yet full of aesthetic merit on balance.) Extreme ugliness, conceived as a "positive" aesthetic flaw, can spontaneously offend the eye and the sensibilities too, and when it is sufficiently barefaced and stark, it is obscene. But the judgment that the painting is obscene is not itself an aesthetic judgment in the way the judgment of ugliness is, nor is the yuk reaction elicited by obscene objects itself an "aesthetic response." A badly decorated room with clashing colors, mismatched pieces of furniture, and inharmonious and cluttered designs, may be judged ugly by the discerning decorator, rightly confident of his professional judgment. Its arrangements conspicuously fail to satisfy certain conventional criteria, and unless some further effect (e.g. amusing campiness) has been deliberately attempted and successfully achieved by means of the contrived ugliness, the overall aesthetic evaluation will be decisively negative too. But if the furniture is all ripped, torn, and infested with vermin, the wall paper stained, the room covered with dust and littered with debris, so that the ugliness is accentuated to the "point of obscenity," the resultant judgment of "yukworthiness" will not be a further critical judgment of an aesthetic sort.

When we call faces ugly, we may mean that they fail to satisfy certain conventional criteria of form and "composition", in which case we make a kind of "negative aesthetic judgment" about them. "The eyes are too small, the nose too long, the lips too full," we might add, thus giving an account of the way the face fails to succeed aesthetically. We might still find the homely face as animated by the spirit of its possessor pleasant enough to behold, even if deficient when considered as an aesthetic object merely. But if the facial features are so grossly deformed as actually to hurt the eye, and cause involuntary shrinking and disgust, we are attributing no further aesthetic property to them when we say so. Rather we have left the realm of the aesthetic altogether for the sphere of the disgusting, the revolting, and (in extremis) the obscene.

Attempted works of art that fail on aesthetic grounds so often manifest nonaesthetic flaws also, that it is easy to confuse the two types of defect. In particular, the work is likely to manifest moral or charientic flaws of its creator, so that they are attributable to the work itself only as "transferred epithets." "Obscene" when it is applied in this way to an art object attributes extreme vulgarity to the artist rather than an aesthetic flaw to his creation, though in all likelihood, some aesthetic defect will also be present. There may be some special cases where the work of art (or literature or drama) fails not because of the presence of an aesthetic "bad-making" characteristic, but rather because of the absence of aesthetic "good-making characteristics," and in these cases it will be easy to confuse the artist's moral or charientic flaws with aesthetic bad-making characteristics present in the created work, especially when those flaws are strong enough to produce a reaction of repugnance. Revulsion, however, is characteristically either moral, charientic, or yukky. It may well be, in fact, that there is no such thing as pure "aesthetic revulsion," properly speaking, that by the time an emotional reaction is strong enough to be revulsion it has imported elements from these other realms.

In those infrequent cases mentioned above when we condemn a work of art as an aesthetic failure even though we can identify no positive feature of the work that is a peculiarly aesthetic flaw, the aesthetic failing is a result of the absence of aesthetic virtues rather than the presence of transferred nonaesthetic flaws. Such a work of art either succeeds or it fails. When it succeeds it will manifest "beauty" or, more likely, some *other* aesthetic virtue; if it does not succeed, it will fail to achieve such positive effects, and its aesthetic value, therefore, will be nil. In that case it may simply fail to move us one way or the other. We will shrug our shoulders and say it

leaves us cold, and so far as the aesthetic dimension of our experience is
concerned that is an end to the matter. Such works of art will either have
positive aesthetic value or they will have no aesthetic value, but they do not
appear to have peculiarly aesthetic negative value (unless that phrase is used
simply to refer to the *absence* of positive aesthetic merits). There may, of
course, be negative elements in our experience, but these will not be,
properly speaking, aesthetic elements. The work might, for example, be
trite, hackneyed, exploitative, imitative, cheap, or vulgar, and these features might bore, anger, even disgust us. But the offense we take, in these
cases, is better understood as moral or charientic than as aesthetic revulsion.
Our negative aesthetic judgment will be, simply, "it did not work." When
we add that it was a phony, cynical, inept, unserious work as well, we are
passing a kind of moral judgment on its creator, just as to say that it is
vulgar and trite is, in part, to make a charientic judgment about its creator.
If the work also has features (such as intense ugliness) that trigger the yuk
reaction, then in giving voice to that reaction, we are no more expressing an
aesthetic judgment than if we gave full vent to our nausea itself while
blaming our revulsion on the object which was its occasion.[42]

The final three examples in the list of quotations are rather pure cases of
the type of obscenity that derives from the blatant violation of moral principles, and thus from shock to the moral sensibilities of one who embraces
those principles and beholds their naked transgression. An irresponsible
congressional or parliamentary debate is an open, public thing. One can sit
in the galleries and observe the bartering of principle for cheap political
gain. One might react with anger or disappointment if one read an exposé
of subtly concealed corruption "off-stage," but when one sees unveiled and
undenied surrender of principle for tarnished political reward right in the
public arena, then the very nakedness of the moral offensiveness is "almost
obscene." Similarly when an industry's "gross and bloated" profits in a
period of general economic hardship violates one's sense of justice in the
most direct and unvarnished way, consisting of a *patently* arbitrary inequality in the distribution of social burdens and benefits, the effect on one's
sensibility again is similar in its impact to a rude blow to the solar plexus.
Again, there is nothing subtle about obscenity either in its paradigmatic or
its (possibly) extended senses.

Finally, the word "nigger" is a blunt and insulting term of contemptuous
abuse and hatred. It is not apt to offend everybody, but it surely ought to
offend everyone, and at least as much as any other single *word* does. To call
it obscene then is to use the word "obscene" in its purely gerundive sense
(wholly to endorse revulsion as an appropriate response to it) rather than in
its partly predictive sense as a standard aptness word.

7. An alternative account of obscenity: The view of D. A. J. Richards

My account of the scope of obscenity differs from that given by David A. J. Richards in his analysis of obscenity, which in other respects is probably the most adequate account of the subject yet propounded.[43] Richards' account is similar to the present one in emphasizing the offense–endorsement character of judgments of obscenity and in leaving it an open question, not to be settled immediately by definition, whether any particular class of objects, actions, or depictions are "really obscene." But when Richards surveys the classes of entities generally agreed to be obscene, he extracts from them a relatively narrow common character that would exclude most of the items in our list of "extended uses." It is clear, I think, that Richards would treat talk of obscene profits, obscene debates, obscene ways of dying, obscene punishments, obscene pictures of wounds, obscene exultations in another's death, obscene parodies of human beings, and the like, as mere colorful metaphors of no particular theoretical significance.

Richards identifies the concept of the obscene with that of the "abuse of bodily function."[44] The conceptual complex from which the notion of the obscene derives, according to Richards, is that which attributes to all the various bodily parts and organs under voluntary control "sharply defined functions and ends,"[45] in the same sense as that in which knives and forks, for example, have their normal purposes and uses. The purpose of a knife is to cut; it is an unnatural "abuse" of a knife, therefore, to use it to pick one's teeth, or to stick it in one's ear. Similarly, according to an ancient tradition, "failure to [properly] exercise bodily function is unclean, polluting, an abomination, in short, obscene."[46]

> The obscene, thus, is a conceptual residuum of very ancient ways of thinking about human conduct . . . Obscenity within this view is a kind of vice, a wasting and abuse of the natural employment of bodily functions. Hence, a culture's definition of the obscene will indicate those areas of bodily function in which the culture centrally invests its self-esteem and in which deviance provokes the deepest anxieties. For example, incompetence with respect to excretory function typically defines the frailest members of society, infants and the senile . . .[47]

Richards differs from current spokesmen for the traditional Western concept of obscenity not in his analysis but in his application of it. Older moralists took masturbation, for example, to be the very model of an unnatural abuse of bodily function and therefore obscene and disgusting. Richards, on the other hand, has less restrictive and rigid conceptions of what bodily parts, especially sexual parts, are *for*. One of their functions at least, in his view, is to give pleasure. He finds nothing at all "unnatural," then, in

voluntary sexual acts of virtually all descriptions. He is not altogether beyond the molding influence of his culture, however, as he is the first to
admit. Thus, while he suggests that sexual pornography does not seem
obscene to him, coprophagy (eating feces) and eating vomit are quite
another story, these being plain abuses of the ingestive function.[48]

Richards' analysis has the substantial merit of leaving the obscenity of
any specific type of conduct an open question to be settled not by definition
but by argument over the appropriateness of disgust or repugnance. Disagreements are interpreted as deriving from differing conceptions of the
natural and proper functions of bodily parts and systems. His account also
has the merit of emphasizing the connection between the idea of the obscene and the idea of the impure and filthy, though perhaps he fails to
appreciate sufficiently that some yuk reactions are antecedent to, or independent of, religious taboos and metaphysical–theological doctrines. Richards' claim, however, that "abuse of bodily function" is the tacit criterion to
which we all appeal in applying the concept of the obscene will not with-
stand close scrutiny, for as a criterion it is doubly deficient, being at once
too broad and too narrow.

Richards' criterion is too broad because it would require that some actions be classified by some people as obscene, whereas in fact, those actions
would not be so classified. The official Roman Catholic condemnation of
contraception, as I understand it, rests on a doctrine, similar to that described by Richards, that bodily systems have "sharply defined functions
and ends." According to the Church, it is an unnatural abuse of the function of the reproductive system to have sexual intercourse while using
mechanical or chemical devices to prevent conception. For that reason,
artificial contraception is said to be wrong, immoral, and sinful, but to my
knowledge, no Catholic would call it "obscene" on those grounds. Obscenity, whatever else it involves, is an aspect of the way things appear. A
married couple making love in the privacy of their own bedroom while
using contraceptives that would be hidden from the view of an electronic
peeping Tom, are surely not behaving obscenely, whatever the moral quality of their conduct. Only when the offensive aspect of behavior is blatantly
obtrusive is it ever considered "obscene." To take one other example of a
similar but nonsexual kind, consider smoking. To the enemies of that messy
and unhygienic practice, it would seem at least as unnatural a use of the
respiratory system as onanism is of the reproductive organs, and almost as
unnatural an abuse of the lungs as coprophagy is of the digestive tract. Yet,
as far as I know, no one has thought to condemn cigarette smoking as
"obscene"—imprudent, reckless, thoughtless, even immoral, but no matter
how egregiously and publicly offensive, never obscene.

Richards varies the terms in which he formulates the ground of obscenity, and in one of its formulations he poses a criterion which is too broad in still another fashion. One of his favorite ways of stating the matter links obscene acts with the shame one feels when one fails to exercise bodily capacities *competently* (his word) "as dictated by standards in which one has invested self-esteem."[49] Richards' alternate formulations thus mix the distinct ideas of "competent performance" and "natural use and function" in a most confusing way. To use a knife to pick one's teeth is an unnatural use (or abuse) of a knife; to use a knife to cut, but then to cut roughly, unevenly, untidily, may be to use a knife in its natural and proper function, but to use it badly or (even) incompetently, and a would-be craftsman who has invested self-esteem in his work, will feel shame as a result. But there is nothing *obscene* in poor workmanship. Richards' criterion put in terms of "competent exercise of a capacity" would require the classification of private sexual failures—frigidity, impotence, premature ejaculation—as obscene and thus group them with such things as (say) acts of coitus performed publicly with animals.

Richards' statement (or statements) of the criteria actually used to determine obscenity is also too *narrow* since it leads to the exclusion from the category of the obscene, of acts and objects that are commonly and noncontroversially described as "obscene": "obscene parodies of men," inappropriate responses to deaths, obscene spectacles, bloated profits, shameless irresponsibility, blatantly unfair inequalities, public torture of victims and more. Some (but not all) of these uses of the word "obscene" may be extended beyond standard paradigms of usage, but if so, they have become fixed metaphors and not mere colorful but inaccurate idioms. They all point by analogy to something essential in the central uses of the term, and what they point to is something other than the unnatural abuse, or incompetent misuse, of bodily functions and capacities.

8. Summary: general characteristics of obscenity

It is time now to summarize our analysis of the concept of judgmental obscenity. According to the foregoing account:

1. Obscenity is an extreme form of offensiveness producing repugnance, shock, or disgust, though the offending materials *can* (paradoxically) be to some degree alluring at the same time.

2. The word "obscene" functions very much like the words "shocking," "repugnant," and "disgusting," either as a standard aptness word, nonstandardly as a purely predicative word, or as a purely endorsing (gerundive) word without predictive function, or, in some contexts, as a descriptive

conventional label. When applied to some object X in the sense of a standard aptness word, it asserts that X would disgust, shock, or repel the average person; it implies (subject to explicit withdrawal) that it so offends the speaker; and it endorses disgust, shock, or repugnance as the correct or appropriate reaction to X.

3. Common to its usage as a standard aptness word and a gerundive word is its employment to *endorse* the appropriateness of offense. It may be impossible conclusively to support such judgments of appropriateness with reasons, but considerations can often be presented that have the effect of inducing others—"relevantly"—to share one's feelings, and thereby come to appreciate their appropriateness.

4. The main feature that distinguishes obscene things from other repellant or offensive things is their *blatancy:* their massive obtrusiveness, their extreme and unvarnished bluntness, their brazenly naked exhibition. A subtle offensiveness is not obscene; a devious and concealed immorality, unless it is an *extreme* violation of the governing norms, will not be obscene; a veiled suggestiveness is not obscene. A gradual and graceful disgarbing by a lovely and skilled strip-teaser is erotically alluring, but the immediate appearance on the stage of an unlovely nude person for whom the audience has not been prepared is apt to seem, for its stark blatancy, obscene. And even for the most lascivious in the audience, wide screen projections of highly magnified, close-up, color slides of sex organs, will at the very least be off-putting.

5. There are three classes of objects that can be called "obscene": obscene natural objects, obscene persons and their actions, and obscene created things. The basic conceptual distinction is between the natural objects, whose obscenity is associated with their capacity to evoke *disgust* (the yuk response) and the others, whose obscenity is a function in part of their *vulgarity*. Obscene *natural objects* are those which are apt to trigger the yuk reaction. In our culture, at least, these are usually slimy, sticky, gelatinous things; excretal wastes, mucous products, and pus; pale, cold, lifeless things; and strange, unnatural, inhuman things. Obscene *persons and actions* are those which are coarse and vulgar to an extreme, or those which are brazenly obtrusive violations of any standards of propriety, including both moral and charientic ones. Ascriptions of obscenity to persons or their actions on the grounds of their immorality are nevertheless charientic, not moral, judgments. Blatant immoralities are one class of extremely vulgar or unseemly behavior. When we condemn them as morally wrong we pronounce moral judgment on them; when we condemn them as obscene (for having offended or shocked the moral sensibility) we make the most extreme kind of charientic judgment. In the latter case, we should no doubt

be prepared to make an adverse moral judgment as well, but we would have to supplement the purely charientic vocabulary to do so.

Obscene *created things* are blatantly shocking depictions or unsubtle descriptions of obscene persons, actions, or objects. Representations of disgusting (yukky) objects can themselves be disgusting to the point of obscenity in which case obscenity is an inherent characteristic of the representation itself. In other cases, however, obscenity is a "transferred epithet" referring indirectly to the vulgarity of the creator. In neither case is the ascription of obscenity to the created object a kind of aesthetic judgment.

6. There are three ways in which objects of any of these kinds can be offensive to the point of obscenity: by direct offense to the senses (some totally unrecognized object may yet be "obscene to the touch"); by offense to lower order sensibilities (an object recognized as a dank cavernous fungus or a slug or a dead body), or by offense to higher sensibilities. The latter category includes blatant exhibition of tabooed conduct (eating pork), or inappropriate responses (lewdly reveling in death), or revolting violations of ideals or principles (bloated profits, cynical irresponsibility). The corruption, perversion, depersonalizing, or mere "parodying" of a human being is likely to strike any observer as obscene in this third way,[50] as are the most amazingly obvious immoralities, done in crass disregard of ethical principles. Deliberately telling a gross and unvarnished lie clearly to deceive others and to help the speaker gain at their expense is "obscene," and will rightly shock the moral sensibility of a standard observer.

7. Prominent among the types of conduct that shock higher-order sensibilities are instances of inappropriate response to the behavior of others. There is a kind of second-order morality of response which is especially susceptible to obscene violation. Laughter at the misfortunes of others, for example, is obscene even when the misfortunes are deserved. Even passive witness to the intimately private conduct of others, when it is voluntary and avoidable, is obscene. Public hangings before huge crowds are obscene spectacles even when the crowd is appropriately solemn, insofar as they are intrusions upon privacy and violations of personal dignity. When the crowd is boisterous and lustful for blood, the spectacle is doubly obscene, as both intrusive and inappropriately responsive.

Voyeurism is another clear violation of the morality of response. Suppose Mr. and Mrs. *A* are having sexual intercourse in their room, while unbeknown to them *B* is peeking through the window. There is nothing obscene in what *B* sees, but the fact that he is seeing it is obscene. If a third person *C* perceives *B* peeking at the copulating couple, he beholds an obscene spectacle, and will be appalled.[51] But if *C*, on the other hand, exults at what he sees (Mr. and Mrs. *A* copulating while *B* lewdly peeks at them) then he becomes part of the obscene spectacle himself. But a late-arriving third observer D who stumbles on to that obscene situation might break up in ribald mirth. He is no longer close enough to the primary conduct to be shocked, so laughter will be his appropriate reaction to the bizarre chain of obscene vulgarities that unfolds before his astonished eye.[52]

I I

Obscenity as Pornography

1. Is pornography obscene?

There is no more unfortunate mistake in the discussion of obscenity than simply to identify that concept, either in meaning or in scope of designation, with pornography.[1] To call something obscene, in the standard uses of that term, is to condemn that thing as shockingly vulgar or blatantly disgusting, for the word "obscene," like the word "funny," is used to claim that a given response (in this case repugnance, in the other amusement) is likely to be the general one and/or to endorse that response as appropriate. The corresponding term "pornographic," on the other hand, is a purely descriptive word referring to sexually explicit writing and pictures designed entirely and plausibly to induce sexual excitement in the reader or observer. To use the terms "obscene" and "pornographic" interchangeably, then, as if they referred to precisely the same things, is to beg the essentially controversial question of whether any or all (or only) pornographic materials really are obscene. Surely, to those thousands or millions of persons who delight in pornographic books, pictures, and films, the objects of their attachment do not seem disgusting or obscene. If these materials are nevertheless "truly obscene," they are not so merely by virtue of the definitions of the terms "obscene" and "pornographic" but rather by virtue of their blatant violation of some relevant standards, and to establish their obscenity requires serious argument and persuasion. In short, whether any given acknowledged bit of pornography is *really* obscene is a logically open question to be settled by argument, not by definitional fiat.

The United States Supreme Court has committed itself to a different usage. In searching for definitions and tests of what it calls "obscenity," it has clearly had on its collective mind only pornography: not expressive oaths and intensifiers, not abusive curses and epithets, not profanity, (usually) not scatology, nor any other impolite language for which the term "obscene" is a conventional label; not objects disgusting to the senses, or non-sexual conduct and materials that offend the higher sensibilities; but *only* verbal, pictorial, and dramatic materials and exhibitions *designed effectively to be instruments of erotic arousal.* "Obscene" came to *mean* "pornographic" in the Court's parlance. Justice Harlan quite explicitly underwrote this usage in *Cohen v. California* in 1971.[2] Paul Robert Cohen had been convicted in a county court of disturbing the peace by wearing a jacket emblazoned on its back with the words "Fuck the draft." When the Supreme Court considered his appeal, Harlan wrote:

> This is not . . . an obscenity case. Whatever else may be necessary to give rise to the State's broader power to prohibit obscene expression, such expression must be, in some way, erotic. It cannot plausibly be maintained that this vulgar allusion to the Selective Service System would conjure up such psychic stimulation in anyone likely to be confronted with Cohen's crudely defaced jacket.[3]

If only erotic uses of language can be "obscene," then the most typical uses of the tabooed vocabulary of "dirty words" (for example, in angry insults) are not in the slightest degree obscene—an absurd consequence that the Court is apparently prepared to live with.

An even more bizarre instance of this distorted usage comes from a lower court that was committed to follow the Supreme Court's example. In the 1977 case, *Connecticut v. Anonymous*,[4] a high school student appealed his conviction under a statute that declares it to be criminal to make an "obscene gesture." The youth in this case had rashly insulted the occupants of a police cruiser. The gesture in question, in which one extends the middle finger, is an ancient form of insult called "giving the finger." The appellate court decreed that the gesture was not obscene (not even in the sense intended in the statute) because "to be obscene, the expression must be in a significant way erotic . . . It can hardly be said that the finger gesture is likely to arouse sexual desire. The more likely response is anger."[5] The reason why this opinion fills the ordinary reader with amazement is that, given the ordinary associations of the term "obscene" with offensiveness (disgust, shock to sensibility, etc.), the court seems to be saying that only sexy things can be offensive, a judgment that is either plainly false (if it is an empirical description of what things in fact offend people) or morally perverse (if it is a judgment about what kinds of things are appropriate objects of offense). It also seems to imply, as a matter of definition merely, that *all* erotically inciting materials are *ipso facto* intensely repugnant, a judgment that begs the question against pornography right from the start.

2. *Pornographic writing contrasted with literary and dramatic art*

A more difficult definitional tangle confronts writers who attempt to state (in a non-question-begging way) the relation between pornography, on the one hand, and literature and drama, on the other. Works of literature do have one thing in common, at least, with works of pornography: they both are found in books. But that is hardly sufficient to establish their identity, or even to relate them closely as species of some common, and theoretically interesting, genus. Books, after all, are an enormously heterogenous lot. Cookbooks contain recipes for preparing meals; telephone books enable one to discover the telephone numbers of friends or business firms; dictionaries explain meanings of words and prescribe standard spellings; pornographic books induce sexual desire; novels, plays, and short stories . . . Well, works of literature are something else again. The question that has divided literary critics into disputing factions is, "To what extent may pornography be judged as legitimate literature rather than merely ersatz eroticism?"[6] But this question, which has also interested the courts, presupposes an inquiry into the characteristic, and hence defining, functions of pornographic and literary works, whether books, plays, or films.[7]

The three leading answers to the question whether pornography can be literature are (1) that pornography and literature are as different from one another as novels are from telephone books, but that pornography (like telephone books) can be useful, for all that, provided only that it not be confused with literature; (2) that pornography is a corruption or perversion of genuine literature, properly judged by literary standards, and always found wanting; (3) that pornography is, or can be, a form of literature properly judged by literary standards, and sometimes properly assigned high literary merit by those standards. The debate is easily confused by the fact that there can be within the same work a criss-cross or overlap of "characteristic functions." An undoubted work of literature can incidentally excite sexual longing in the reader just as it can arouse anger, pity, or any other passion. And an undoubted work of pornography—pure hard-core pornography—may here and there contain a line of poetic elegance and be "well written" throughout. Moreover, books of one kind can be put to the "characteristic use" of books of another kind: one could masturbate to passages in Joyce, Lawrence, or the Old Testament, for example.[8] But then one can also use a novel as a guide to correct spelling (though that does not make novels into cryptodictionaries), or, for that matter, to sit on, or to prop doors open. Despite these unavoidable overlaps of properties and uses, one can hope, in principle, to describe accurately the characteristic functions of works of different kinds. Novels can be used as dictionaries and works of pornography as door props, but that is not what each is primarily *for*.

The most persuasive advocate of the first view of the relation between pornography and literature (and a writer who has in fact persuaded me) is Anthony Burgess. He is well worth quoting at length:

> A pornographic work represents social acts of sex, frequently of a perverse or wholly fantastic nature, often without consulting the limits of physical possibility. Such works encourage solitary fantasy, which is then usually quite harmlessly discharged in masturbation. A pornographic book is, then, an instrument for procuring a sexual catharsis, but it rarely promotes the desire to achieve this through a social mode, an act of erotic congress: the book is, in a sense, a substitute for a sexual partner.[9]

Burgess, of course, is talking about what other writers[10] have called "hardcore pornography" as opposed to "erotic realism." The former is the name of a category of materials (books, pamphlets, pictures, and films), now amounting to a flood, that make no claim, however indirect, to serious literary or artistic purpose and simply portray very graphically, and with unrestrained explicitness and enthusiasm, sexual acts and objects for all tastes. Erotic realism, on the other hand, is a category of literature in which sexual events, desires, longings, and so on, are portrayed, often vividly and often at length, but always as part of a serious literary effort to be true to life. Sexual thoughts and activities are, of course, a vitally important part of the lives of most people. They often determine who we are, whom we encounter, what happens to us, and in which direction our lives develop. Hence, they are naturally important, often supremely important, elements in the characterizations and plots of novels that are concerned to render truly the human condition, comment critically upon it, and evoke appropriate emotions in response to it. Works of hard-core pornography are not intended to do any of these things. Their aim is to excite sexually, and that is an end of the matter.

Hard-core pornography, Burgess reminds us, has something in common with what he calls "didactic works" of other kinds, for example, political propaganda in the form of fiction, stories whose whole purpose is to arouse anger at a tyrant, or revolutionary ardor, or charitable assistance.

> A pornographic work and a didactic work (like Smile's *Self-help*) have this in common: they stimulate, and expect the discharge of the stimulation to be

effected in real-life acts—acts of masturbation or acts of social import. They differ from a work of literature in that the purpose of literary art is to arouse emotions and discharge those emotions as part of the artistic experience. This is what Aristotle meant by his implied doctrine of catharsis. [11]

When we find the number we want in a phone book we have had a good "reference experience" but not a literary one. No one would think of confusing a telephone book with a novel; but the confusion of pornography with (erotic) literature is both common and pernicious. "Pornography," Burgess concludes, "is harmless so long as we do not corrupt our taste by mistaking it for literature."[12]

George Steiner, the leading spokesman for the second view, is less tolerant of pornography, perhaps because of his understandable impatience with the pretentious variety that mistakes itself for literature. To anyone who has surveyed the collections of hard-core pornography in any "adult" bookstore, Steiner's description of its standardly recurring features will seem right on target. He cites the limited number of basic themes and shrewdly notes how they correspond to the biological limitations on actual lovemaking, there being a severely limited number of "amorous orifices" in the human body, and "the mechanics of orgasm imply[ing] fairly rapid exhaustion and frequent intermission."[13] In any case, "dirty books are maddeningly the same."[14] Despite variations in trappings, race or class of the characters, or background settings, hard-core pornography always follows "highly conventionalized formulas of low-grade sadism [where one partner rejoices in his or her abject humiliation], excremental drollery, and banal fantasies of phallic prowess or feminine responsiveness. In its own way the stuff is as predictable as a Scout manual."[15] Or, we might add, as a dictionary or a telephone book.

High-grade pornography by well known writers with literary pretentions, insofar as it too is pure pornography, does no better. Steiner's verdict here too will seem to hit the target to anyone who has struggled through the more egregious works of Henry Miller, Jean Genet, or William Burroughs. Speaking of an all-star collection of "high porn" called the *Olympia Reader*, Steiner's patience collapses: "After fifty pages of 'hardening nipples', 'softly opening thighs,' and 'hot rivers' flowing in and out of the ecstatic anatomy, the spirit cries out, not in hypocritical outrage, not because I am a poor Square throttling my libido, but in pure, nauseous boredom. Even fornication cannot be as dull, as hopelessly predictable, as all that".[16] Fornication, of course, is by no means dull, unless one tries to make a full-time job out of it.

That "high porn" is still pure porn, no matter how you slice it, is a point well worth making in reply to all the pretentious critical hogwash that

would find some mysterious literary merit in the same old stuff when
served up by fashionable names. No one has made the point better than
Steiner. And no one has documented more convincingly the harm to imagination, to taste, to language itself that can come from mistaking pornography for literature. But, for all that, Steiner's essay is no answer to Burgess.
Literature is one thing, and pornography is another. If, nevertheless, pornography is judged by literary standards, it must always get low marks,
and if one persists in reading it and using it in the manner appropriate only
to literature, then one converts it into hideously bad literature, and the
results will be corrupting in a way common to *all* bad literature—slick
westerns, soap operas, tear-jerkers, mass-produced mysteries, and Gothic
romances. But there is no necessity that pornography be misconstrued in
this way, and little evidence that it commonly is.

An able defender of the third view, Kenneth Tynan, defines pornography in the same way Burgess does, so that there is an apparent contrast
between pornography and literature. Yet Tynan insists that when pornography is done well, that is to say artfully, there is no reason to deny it the
laudatory label of art. Pornography, he says, "is orgasmic in intent and
untouched by the ulterior motives of traditional art. It has a simple and
localized purpose: to induce an erection [or, presumably, the corresponding
effect in women, a substantial consumers' group oddly forgotten by Ty-
nan]. And the more skillfully the better."[17] So far, so good. There will be
no objection yet from Burgess. Moreover, quite apart from the question of
whether pornography can aspire to be literature without ceasing to be
pornography, it can be quite valuable, and not merely "harmless," just for
being what it is. Not everybody has a use for it, of course, any more than
everybody needs a dictionary or a phone book, but it can be extremely
useful for various well-defined classes of the population. Unlike some other
writers,[18] Tynan fails to mention geriatric depressives and couples whose
appetites lag to their own distress, but he does mention four other classes:
First, those with minority tastes who cannot find like-minded mates; second, those who are "villainously ugly" of face or body and "unable to pay
for the services of call girls";[19] third, "men on long journies, geographically
cut off from wives and mistresses," for whom pornography can be "a portable memory, a welcome shortcut to remembered bliss, relieving tension
without involving disloyalty";[20] and finally "uncommitted bachelors, arriving alone and short of cash in foreign cities where they don't speak the
language."[21] This too is an important point.

The next step in Tynan's argument is the one that makes a sharp break
with both Burgess and Steiner:

> Because hard-core performs an obvious physical function, literary critics have
> traditionally refused to consider it a form of art. By their standards, art is

something that appeals to such intangibles as the soul and the imagination; anything that appeals to the genitals belongs in the category of massage. What they forget is that language can be used in many delicate and complex ways to enliven the penis. It isn't just a matter of bombarding the reader with four letter words.[22]

It is a pity that Tynan neither quotes nor cites examples. The standard porn of the hard-core shops follows the patterns disclosed by Steiner so unswervingly that one suspects they were all composed by the same salacious computer. Readers are not simply bombarded with four-letter words; they are also assaulted by the same clichés—the trembling lips and cherry pink nipples, the open thighs and warm rivers of semen—in book after book. But what if hard-core pornography *were* done artfully? Would it be literature then in that (largely) hypothetical event?

There is a linguistic confusion underlying the question that is not easily sorted out. Almost *any* form of purposeful or creative human activity can be done either crudely or artfully. One can compose or perform music crudely or artfully; one can design or erect buildings crudely or artfully; one can write poems crudely or artfully. Music, architecture, and poetry are art forms. When they are done artfully, they are good music, architecture, or poetry; when done crudely, the result is (usually) bad music, architecture or poetry. Bad art, however, is still art. A badly written novel is still a novel, and a badly composed photograph is still a photograph. On the other hand, one can make a phone book or dictionary crudely or artfully; one can mend a blouse or repair a carburetor crudely or artfully; one can throw a baseball or shoot a basket crudely or artfully. But it does not follow that reference compilation, repair work, and sports are art forms. Surely they are not among the fine arts.

Still it is possible, I suppose, for one to *think* of dictionary making, auto mechanics, and baseball as art forms. Professional practitioners may well think of their work as simply an occasion for artful enterprise and achievement. But, even if we grant that (with some reluctance), it does not follow that the artful construction of telephone books is *literature*, or that the artful repair of eroded buildings is *architecture*, or that the artful fielding of the second-base position is *ballet*. Nor does it follow that the artful "enlivening of the penis" with language is literature. "A thing is what it is, and not another thing."

3. Artful pornography: the film Emmanuelle

The films of the French director Just Jaeckin are perhaps as good examples of artful pornography as one can find. His 1973 film *Emmanuelle* became within a year the most profitable film in the history of the French movie industry, and his 1975 sequel, *The Story of O*, employing a similar formula, seemed designed to break the record. Both films are produced with an artfullness that sets them off from almost all other essentially pornographic films. *Emmanuelle* is in many ways actually beautiful: It is set in exotic Bangkok whose picturesque streets and gorgeous gardens, and nearby jungles and mountains, are photographed with a wizardry that would win it awards if it were a travel documentary film. And, as one reviewer said of *The Story of O*, "It is filmed through delicate soft focuses and is so prettily presented that it might have been served up by Chanel."[23] The background music in *Emmanuelle* is sophisticated and erotic—perhaps the most suggestive music since Ravel's *Bolero*—and played sensitively by a full symphony orchestra. There are highly effective dance scenes, originally choreographed but in traditional Oriental patterns. For all its artfulness, however, *Emmanuelle* is no more a work of dramatic or literary art than a well-decorated and tastefully produced cookbook is a novel. Its sole theme or "plot" is the story of how the wife of an overworked French diplomat overcomes her boredom by abandoning herself to the sensual life with partners of all ages, genders, and races. Insofar as progression is suggested in the "story," it consists in her dawning appreciation at the end of the film of the attractions of group sex. Apart from that, the "story" is simply a hook on which to hang twelve or fifteen sexual adventures of the same stereotyped genres that are repeated monotonously in the literature of hard-core porn: coitus (as always punctuated with gasps and squeals) with a stranger in the darkness of a commercial airliner; coitus with another stranger in the locked restroom of the same plane; a sexual affair with another woman; a casual masturbation in a boring interval; a rough coital act granted as a prize to the victor in a Siamese boxing match (here a touch of sadomasochism), a simultaneous sexual encounter with several men, and so on. The film clearly satisfies Steiner's criteria of pornography and equally clearly fails to satisfy the Burgess–Aristotle criterion of dramatic art. Not that it tries and fails; it fully succeeds in achieving what it sets out to do.

Pornographic as it is, however, *Emmanuelle* is in no obvious way obscene. Artfulness and obscenity do not sit easily together. Sex acts are filmed in shadowy pantomime; the details are simulated or merely suggested. There is no close-up camera work focusing on sex organs or the contact that stimulates them. Male sex organs are not shown at all. (This omission is typical of the double standard that generally prevails in works of pornography meant to sell to large general audiences. The commercial assumption is that the audiences are primarily *men* who will be titillated by scenes of female homosexuality but repelled or threatened by parallel episodes with men, or even by the unveiling of the masculine sex organ.) There is, in short, very little that is gross or obtrusive in the film, or likely to diminish its aphrodisiac effectiveness.

4. Pornographic pictorial art, poetry, and program music

Although pornographic films and books, insofar as they are purely porno-graphic, can never aspire to the status of dramatic and literary art no matter how artfully they are produced, a quite different verdict seems to be re-quired for pornographic pictorial art. That surprising result is no real para-dox, however. Rather, it is explained by the empirical fact that the charac-teristic purposes of pictorial art and pornography can be jointly satisfied by one and the same picture. A painting of a copulating couple that satisfied the relevant standards for good painting would *ipso facto* be a work of pictorial art; it might be done in exquisitely harmonizing color, with prop-erly balanced composition, subtlety of line, successful lighting effects, and depicted figures of memorably graceful posture and facial expressiveness. Such a painting might also be designed primarily to stimulate the genitals of the observer. Insofar as it also achieved that goal, it would be a work of pornography. The defining features of literature and pornography, how-ever, mutually exclude one another for the reasons given by Burgess. To be sure, a long and complex literary work might contain whole sections that are purely pornographic, or contain art and pornography in various com-plex combinations and alternations. Such a work could be called both liter-ary and pornographic, just as a dictionary that contained chapters of a novel between each alphabetical section would be both a dictionary *and* a novel. But the literary and pornographic parts would be separate and distinguish-able, unlike the painting, which can be both pictorial art and pure pornog-raphy at the same time and as a whole. The point applies even more forcibly, I should think, to that much rarer genre, pornographic program music. It might be possible for a composer deliberately to set out to create a musical aphrodisiac and succeed in that aim, and also in the same work to create a genuine piece of music, even a work of high musical merit.

It is difficult to find any reason why a poem cannot in principle satisfy high literary standards and also achieve the deliberate aim of pornography, to arouse the reader. Very likely then lyric poetry should be classified with pictorial art and program music in this respect rather than with other species of literature. Still it is surpassingly difficult to find clear and non-controversial examples of works that are at once good or at least serious poems and also effective pornography; and that difficulty may reside in the nature of the two objectives and natural impediments to their successful cross-breeding. (Love poems, of course, are an altogether different matter.) [24] What *clearly* cannot be both literary art and pornography, if the argument thus far is sound, are works that tell *stories* and have subtly structured *plots*—short stories, novels, plays, dramatic films. Tragedies cannot be erotically arousing on balance and still achieve their essential goals, for the reasons given by Aristotle and Burgess. Pathos can be gripping, edifying, and saddening, but it is not possible for it to achieve its characteristic ends while also evoking erotic feelings in the reader or observer. Comedy is especially incapable of being pornography (though it may work its own purposes on erotic materials), because a laugh is a "discharge within the work," not a cause of further tensions to be discharged in "real life acts." The funny bone is not a sex organ.

5. Can pornography be art? The minimal relevance of the question

Interesting as the question may be for aestheticians and critics, why does it matter to a social philosopher whether pornography is art or something *sui generis?* Of course, insofar as American courts acknowledge a special social value, or "redeeming social importance" to works of art, even poor works of art, the relation between art and pornography is a question of vital practical importance. But interesting as the question is in its own right, and crucial as it may be for the application of American constitutional law, it has very little importance for the philosopher or social critic whose concern is to discover what restrictive legislation could be passed by an ideal legislature as determined by the morally correct principles for limiting individual liberty. One such principle is that severely offensive (disgusting, shocking, revolting) public behavior that is not reasonably avoidable may be prohibited as a kind of public nuisance. A legislature is generally thought to have the right to control offensive behavior, within carefully circumscribed circumstances, by means of the criminal law, even when that behavior (or depicted behavior) is not directly injurious to health or wealth. But what relevance to this right and its limits is there in the fact that the offensiveness in question is, or is not, attached inextricably to a work of art? After all, offensiveness is offensiveness whatever its source, and, if it is unavoidable offensiveness that confers the right of prohibition on the legislature, what relevance can the other characteristics of the offending object have?

There is surely *some* relevance in the fact that the offense stems from a work of art. As we have seen (Chap. 7, §2, Chap. 8, §2), both the civil and the criminal law of nuisance empower courts to weigh the degree (intensity and extent) of the offense caused by a given activity against the "reasonableness" of the offending conduct. One of the standards, in turn, for judging the reasonableness of offending or inconveniencing behavior is its general social utility, that is, "the social value which the law attaches to its ultimate purpose." Just as in nuisance law offensive noises and smells are not prohibited when they are the unavoidable concomitants of the operations of a socially useful industry, but are enjoined when they are the products of merely private diversions of little social value, so the criminal law might prohibit offensive materials and actions when they have no further "redeeming" social function, but permit them when the offense is the side effect of a socially useful purpose. The fact that publicly offensive, sexually explicit materials happen also to be serious works of literature is relevant to the social utility of the offending conduct (the creating and exhibiting of the offensive work) insofar as serious literary and artistic endeavors have social value and deserve to be encouraged in the public interest. The offense can be a price worth paying for the generally useful public practice of producing literary works, just as noise, smoke, and stench might be a price worth paying for the existence of boiler factories, power plants, and slaughterhouses. Where the offensiveness of pornography is not linked to a serious artistic intention, however, there may be no redeeming social value to counterbalance it (certainly none of an artistic kind), and in that case the offense principle, assuming that its other conditions are satisfied, would permit its prohibition.

But even pure hard-core pornography with no literary or dramatic pretensions, as Kenneth Tynan pointed out, can have a personal and social utility, so there is no "open and shut case" derived from the offense principle for banning it. The balancing of values in its case may be a close matter. The case for banning pornography that *is* art, on the other hand, insofar as it is derived from a carefully formulated offense principle, would be very weak. However much social value we ascribe to pure pornography on Tynan-like grounds, we must concede that works of literature, drama, pictorial art, and music have a much higher social value as a class (including both successful and unsuccessful specimens) than works of pure pornography, so that *their* legal prohibition would be a much greater loss. And so long as pornographic intent in a work of music or pictorial art does not have a *negative* social value, the value of these objects as works of art is undiminished by their aphrodisiac content or function. To make criminal the production or exhibition of any subclass of art objects would be to produce a "chilling effect" on the entire artistic enterprise and threaten to diminish its contributions to our civilization.[25]

The relevance of these considerations about the "reasonableness" or "social value" of offensive materials and actions is severely restricted, however, to those untypical situations in which the standards for determining the seriousness of the offense itself have been fulfilled. The "seriousness" of the offense, as we have seen, is a function of (1) how widespread the susceptibility to it is,[26] (2) how severe it will be in the typical case, (3) how much inconvenience would be involved in the effort to avoid it, and (4) whether or not the offended states of mind in question were voluntarily incurred, or the risk of offense voluntarily assumed. Surely, in most controversial instances of pornographic exhibition, either the offending materials do not offend intensely, or durably, or universally, and hence are not properly judged "obscene" in the first place (or at least not obscene enough); *or* they are reasonably avoidable, and hence not a serious inconvenience to anyone; *or* the risk of offense is voluntarily assumed by those who witness them, and hence no captive audience exists; *or* only those with abnormal susceptibilities to offense could reasonably have been expected to be offended in the first place. Moreover, some of these standards for determining the existence or degree of offense are often preemptive. In particular, if the only observers are willing observers, then it is wholly pointless to consider whether a film or book with explicitly sexual themes has social value or not, and the question of whether it is a genuine work of art becomes otiose. It is unfair to prohibit on pain of criminal punishment any object or behavior that is both harmless and in the circumstances inoffensive, whether it is a genuine work of art or not.

6. How can sex (of all things) be obscene?

The final question about the relation between obscenity and pornography is one whose perplexity is no less keen for being raised typically as a kind of afterthought. The question is not whether explicit depictions of sexual behavior as such are in fact obscene, but rather, how could sex, a department of life so highly valued by almost all of us, *possibly* be obscene? How is an extremely offended reaction to explicit sexual depictions even possible? In particular, how could sex, of all things, induce something like the "yuk reaction," an extreme form of disgust and repugnance? Even more puzzling at first sight, since the word "obscene" in its standard use endorses such disgust, how could the yuk reaction be the *appropriate* response to the unrestrained depiction of sexuality? These questions are profound and difficult and belong ultimately to the psychologist rather than to the philosopher, but the shadowy outline of their answers, at least, is visible. What is clear is that the answers must be of at least two kinds: (1) sexual explicitness (to use a vague generic term) violates a certain type of moral sensibility, and (2) sexual explicitness when extremely coarse and obtrusive can shock by reducing "psychic distance," even when moral sensibility is not involved. I shall consider these distinct factors in turn.

The word "obscene" is commonly applied to behavior thought to be immoral. When we use the word in this way, we do not reserve it necessarily for what we consider the most immoral behavior; secret, devious, or subtle private immoralities, no matter how seriously wrong they may seem to be, are rarely called "obscene" at all. (But see Chapter 10, note 25, p. 297.) Rather, we think of those immoralities that are absolutely open and shameless, and therefore "shocking" or "disgusting," as the typically obscene ones. The word "obscene" emphasizes how shocking they are to behold, as well as how flagrant they are as departures from a moral norm. Thus utterly cynical, obvious, or brazen falsehoods told with amazing aplomb before observers who know that they are intentional, are "obscene lies" even when they are only moderate departures from the moral norm. It is typically the grossly obtrusive offense to sensibility that elicits judgments of obscenity, whether the sensibility in question be moral, religious, patriotic, or merely gustatory or sensory.

Naturally enough, persons who hold certain moral convictions about sexual conduct will find blatantly obtrusive exhibitions or depictions of tabooed sexuality obscene, not *simply* because they violate moral standards but because they do so openly and blatantly. Given that such is the case, the sensibilities of these persons would command the respect, and, if only other things were equal, the protection, of the law.

This account, however, is still too vague to allay the puzzlement that generated this psychological inquiry. Hardly anyone holds the conviction that *all* sexual behavior as such is wrong, whatever the circumstances and whoever the actors. At most, people find illicit or unlicensed sex, sex out of marriage, solitary sex, or sex at inappropriate times and places to be immoral. Yet many people find the *depiction* or explicit *description* of any sexual conduct at all, licit or illicit, to be obscene. How then could the obscenity stem from the perceived violation of moral principle?

The answer, I suspect, must employ the distinction between *what is depicted*, which is not thought to be obscene, at least not on moral grounds, and *the act of depicting it*, which may under the circumstances be a blatantly offensive violation of moral norms. What is immoral (by the standards of some offended parties) in vivid depictions or unvarnished descriptions of the sex acts of real or fictitious persons, even when those acts in the depicted circumstances are entirely licit, are the "impure thoughts" in the minds of the beholders, which are in large part "desires in the imagination" for what would be immoral if realized. When the beholder finds the depiction obscene (on this account), he finds his own spontaneous concupiscence

disgusting, and it quickly curdles into shame and revulsion; or, if the beholder is part of a group, he or she may think of the inevitably impure ideas
in the minds of the others as repugnant, or may take the act of showing or
describing sex as itself immoral insofar as it is meant to exploit the weakness
of the audience and induce impure thoughts in receptive minds. So it is not
that what is depicted is thought to be immoral, but rather that the act of
depicting it in those circumstances, and the spectacle of its common perception, with those motives, intentions, and likely effects, is thought to be
immoral and—because the immorality is shameless and open—obscene.

The second explanation of how sex can come to seem obscene has nothing to do with anyone's conception of morality. Even persons who utterly
reject the prevailing sexual taboos may find some sexual depictions offensive to the point of obscenity. The reactions of such persons are to be
sharply contrasted with those of people with prudish moral sensibilities
who get trapped between their own salaciousness and shame. The disgust
of this second group is not moral disgust. Rather, it is the spontaneous
revulsion to what is overpoweringly close that is commonly produced not
only by crude pornography but by other kinds of experiences as well.
George P. Elliott has diagnosed the phenomenon well:

> Psychologically, the trouble with [artless] pornography is that, in our culture
> at least, it offends the sense of separateness, of individuality, of privacy . . .
> We have a certain sense of specialness about those voluntary bodily functions
> each must perform for himself—bathing, eating, defecating, urinating, copulat-
> ing—Take eating, for example. There are few strong taboos around the act of
> eating; yet most people feel uneasy about being the only one at the table who is
> or who is not, eating, and there is an absolute difference between eating a rare
> steak washed down by plenty of red wine and watching a close-up movie of
> someone doing so. One wishes to draw back when one is actually or imagina-
> tively too close to the mouth of a man enjoying his dinner; in exactly the same
> way one wishes to remove oneself from the presence of man and woman
> enjoying sexual intercourse.[27]

"Not to withdraw," Elliott adds, "is to peep, to pervert looking so that it
becomes a sexual end in itself."[28] Here he makes a different point and a less
tenable one. The point is (or should be) that if we are going to look without
being disgusted, we had better look from a proper distance, not that looking
at all is a "perversion". Not only erotically realistic art but also artful
pornography *can* satisfy the criterion of distance, and when it does we
identify imaginatively with one of the parties whom we watch rather than
thinking of ourselves as intrusive third parties or embarrassed "peepers."

Pornographers whose aim is aphrodisiac rather than emetic might well
consult Elliott for good tips. He tells us, with convincing examples, how
the problem of distance is solved in pictorial art, while implying that the

same solutions must be forever unavailable to the pornographer, but that is because he identifies pornography quite arbitrarily with the gross and artless kind. Distance is preserved in erotic pictorial art through the use of artificial stylized images, as in the throngs of erotic statues on Indian temples, by making the erotic image small, or by sketching it in with only a few details:

> One does not want to be close to a man while he is defecating nor to have a close-up picture of him in that natural, innocent act—not at all because defecating is reprehensible, only because it is displeasing to intrude upon. One would much rather have a detailed picture of a thief stealing the last loaf of bread from a starving widow with three children than one of Albert Schweitzer at stool. However, Brueghel's painting "The Netherlandish Proverbs" represents two bare rear ends sticking out of a window, presumably of people defecating into the river below, and one quite enjoys the sight—because it is a small part of a large and pleasant picture of the world and because the two figures are tiny, sketched in, far away.[29]

What should we say—or, more to the point, what should the law say— about those persons whose psyches are not accurately described by Elliott, persons with special kinky tastes who prefer their psychic distances short and their sexual perceptions large and detailed? Tiny Gulliver (as Elliott reminds us) is "revolted by every blemish on the breast of the Brobdingnagian wet nurse suckling the baby."[30] Even though the breast was pleasingly shaped and would have been delightful to behold had its proportions been suited to persons of Gulliver's size, it extended six feet from the nurse's body and its nipple was "half the size of a man's head." Swift makes his point well, and most readers are appalled in their imaginations, but what are we to say of the special reader who is sexually excited by the very thought of this normally emetic object? The law, of course, should say nothing at all, provided that satisfaction of the quirky taste is not achieved at the cost of direct offense to unwilling observers.

The more interesting point, however, is that the overwhelming majority of people do *not* enjoy being spatially or psychologically close to the physiological organs and processes deemed "private" in our culture. To revel in these objects is about as common a pastime, I should think, as reveling in the slinky, smelly things that most of us find immediately repellant to the senses and thus in an analogous way obscene.

Our discussion of the relation between (judgmental) obscenity and pornography can now be summarized. Obscenity and pornography are entirely distinct concepts that overlap in their applications to the world but by no means coincide. Obscene things are those that are apt to offend people by eliciting such reactions as disgust, shock, and repugnance. Moreover, when we call something obscene we usually wish to endorse some form of offense as the appropriate reaction to it. Pornography, on the other hand, simply consists of all those pictures, plays, books, and films whose *raison d'etre* is that they are erotically arousing. Some obscene things (e.g., dirty words and insulting gestures) are not pornographic. Indeed some obscene things have nothing whatever to do with sex. Human wastes and other disgusting objects fall into that subcategory of the obscene, as do acts of rejoicing in the misfortunes of others, racial slurs, shameless lies, and other blatant but nonsexual immoralities. Some pornographic things, for example artful paintings, are not obscene. Others, such as close-up, highly magnified photographs of sexual couplings are obscene, though their very obscenity tends to defeat their pornographic purpose.

In the absence of convincing evidence of its causal tie to social harms, pornography ought to be prohibited by law only when it is obscene and then precisely because it is obscene. But obscenity (extreme offensiveness) is only a necessary condition, not a sufficient condition, for rightful prohibition. In addition, the offending conduct must not be reasonably avoidable, and the risk of offense must not have been voluntarily assumed by the beholders. (No doubt additional conditions might also be added such as, for example, that reasonable efforts have been made to exclude children.)

The defining purposes of plotted fiction and dramatic literature cannot be satisfied by a work that is also properly denominated pornographic. On the other hand, there is no contradiction in the idea of a pornographic painting, musical composition, or (perhaps) poem. But the question whether or not art can be pornographic, while obviously important for American constitutional law, which places limits on what legislatures *may* do, is of less interest to critical public policy, which asks what legislatures *ought* to do from among the alternative courses permitted them. The Supreme Court has interpreted the first amendment as permitting legislatures to prohibit all obscenity that is not also art (or opinion).[31] Reasonable liberty-limiting principles also give special importance to works of art but prevent legislatures from prohibiting even obscene *non-art* provided that it is not imposed on unwilling audiences. It is quite unnecessary to determine whether (or to what degree) a given book or film is also art, when the only people who experience it are either unoffended or have voluntarily assumed the risk of offense in advance.

Finally, we considered how sexual conduct could possibly seem obscene to anyone, given the universal human propensity to derive extreme pleasure from it. Those who find pornography obscene, we concluded, do so either when it is done in circumstances that render it (by their standards) both immoral and blatantly and shamelessly obtrusive and thus shocking to moral sensibility, or else when it has reduced psychic distance to the threshold of repugnance or disgust, even when no moral considerations are involved.

7. The feminist case against pornography[32]

In recent years a powerful attack on pornography has been made from a different quarter and on different, but often shifting grounds. Until 1970 or so, the demand for legal restraints on pornography came mainly from "sexual conservatives," those who regarded the pursuit of erotic pleasure for its own sake to be immoral or degrading, and its public depiction obscene. The new attack, however, comes not from prudes and bluenoses, but from women who have been in the forefront of the sexual revolution. We do not hear any of the traditional complaints about pornography from this group—that erotic states in themselves are immoral, that sexual titillation corrupts character, and that the spectacle of "appeals to prurience" is repugnant to moral sensibility. The new charge is rather that pornography degrades, abuses, and defames women, and contributes to a general climate of attitudes toward women that makes violent sex crimes more frequent. Pornography, they claim, has come to pose a threat to public safety, and its legal restraint can find justification either under the harm principle, or, by analogy with Nazi parades in Skokie and K.K.K. rallies, on some theory of profound (and personal) offense.

It is somewhat misleading to characterize the feminist onslaught as a new argument, or new emphasis in argument, against the same old thing. By the 1960s pornography itself had become in large measure a new and uglier kind of phenomenon. There had always been sado-masochistic elements in much pornography, and a small minority taste to be served with concentrated doses of it. There had also been more or less prominent expressions of contemptuous attitudes toward abject female "sex objects," even in much relatively innocent pornography. But now a great wave of violent pornography appears to have swept over the land, as even the mass circulation porno magazines moved beyond the customary nude cheesecake and formula stories, to explicit expressions of hostility to women, and to covers and photographs showing "women and children abused, beaten, bound, and tortured" apparently "for the sexual titillation of consumers."[33] When the circulation of the monthly porn magazines comes to 16 million and the porno industry as a whole does $4 billion a year in business, the new trend cannot help but be alarming.[34]

There is no necessity, however, that pornography *as such* be degrading to women. First of all, we can imagine easily enough an ideal pornography in which men and women are depicted enjoying their joint sexual pleasures in ways that show not a trace of dominance or humiliation of either party by the other.[35] The materials in question might clearly satisfy my previous definition of "pornography" as materials designed entirely and effectively to induce erotic excitement in observers, without containing any of the extraneous sexist elements. Even if we confine our attention to actual specimens of pornography—and quite typical ones—we find many examples where male dominance and female humiliation are not present at all. Those of us who were budding teenagers in the 1930s and '40s will tend to take as our model of pornography the comic strip pamphlets in wide circulation among teenagers during that period. The characters were all drawn from the popular legitimate comic strips—The Gumps, Moon Mullins, Maggie and Jiggs, etc.—and were portrayed in cartoons that were exact imitations of the originals. In the pornographic strips, however, the adventures were all erotic. Like all pornography, the cartoons greatly exaggerated the size of organs and appetites, and the "plot lines" were entirely predictable. But the episodes were portrayed with great good humor, a kind of joyous feast of erotica in which the blessedly unrepressed cartoon figures shared with perfect equality. Rather than being humiliated or dominated, the women characters equalled the men in their sheer earthy gusto. (That feature especially appealed to teenage boys who could only dream of unrestrained female gusto.) The episodes had no butt at all except prudes and hypocrites. Most of us consumers managed to survive with our moral characters intact.

In still other samples of actual pornography, there is indeed the appearance of male dominance and female humiliation, but even in many of these, explanations of a more innocent character are available. It is in the nature of fantasies, especially adolescent fantasies, whether erotic or otherwise, to glorify imaginatively, in excessive and unrealistic ways, the person who does the fantasizing. When that person is a woman and the fantasy is romantic, she may dream of herself surrounded by handsome lovesick suitors, or in love with an (otherwise) magnificent man who is prepared to throw himself at her feet, worship the ground she walks on, go through hell for her if necessary—the clichés pile up endlessly. If the fantasizing person is a man and his reverie is erotic, he may dream of women who worship the ground *he* walks on, etc., and would do anything for the honor of making love with him, and who having sampled his unrivaled sexual talents would grovel at his feet for more, etc., etc. The point of the fantasy is self-adulation, not "hostility" toward the other sex.

Still other explanations may be available. "Lust," wrote Norman Mailer, "is a world of bewildering dimensions . . ."[36] When its consuming fire takes hold of the imagination, it is likely to be accompanied by almost any images

suggestive of limitlessness, any natural accompaniments of explosive unrestrained passion. Not only men but women too have been known to scratch
or bite (like house cats) during sexual excitement, and the phrase "I could
hug you to pieces"—a typical expression of felt "limitlessness"—is normally
taken as an expression of endearment, not of homicidal fury. Sexual passion
in the male animal (there is as yet little but conjecture on this subject) may
be associated at deep instinctive or hormonal levels with the states that
capture the body and mind during aggressive combat. Some such account
may be true of a given man, and explain why a certain kind of pornography
may arouse him, without implying anything at all about his settled attitudes
toward women, or his general mode of behavior toward them. Then, of
course, it is a commonplace that many "normal" people, both men and
women, enjoy sado-masochistic fantasies from time to time, without effect
on character or conduct. Moreover, there are pornographic materials intended for men, that appeal to their masochistic side exclusively, in which
they are "ravished" and humiliated by some grim-faced amazon of fearsome
dimensions. Great art these materials are not, but neither are they peculiarly degrading to women.

   It will not do then to isolate the most objectionable kinds of pornography,
the kinds that are most offensive and even dangerous to women, and reserve
the label "pornographic" for them alone. This conscious redefinition is what
numerous feminist writers have done, however, much to the confusion of
the whole discussion. Gloria Steinem rightly protests against "the truly
obscene idea that sex and the domination of women must be combined"[37]
(*there* is a proper use of the word "obscene"), but then she manipulates
words so that it becomes true by definition (hence merely trivially true) that
all pornography is obscene in this fashion. She notes that "pornography"
stems from the Greek root meaning "prostitutes" or "female captives,"
"thus letting us know that the subject is not mutual love, or love at all, but
domination and violence against women."[38] Steinem is surely right that the
subject of the stories, pictures, and films that have usually been called
"pornographic" is not love, but it doesn't follow that they are all without
exception about male domination over women either. Of course Steinem
doesn't make that further claim as a matter of factual reporting, but as a
stipulated redefinition. Her proposal can lead other writers to equivocate,
however, and find sexist themes in otherwise innocent erotica that have
hitherto been called "pornographic"—simply because they *are* naturally
called by that name. Steinem adopts "erotica" as the contrasting term to
"pornography" as redefined. Erotica, she concludes, is about sexuality, but
"pornography is about power, and sex-as-a-weapon," conquerors dominating victims. The distinction is a real one, but better expressed in such terms

as "degrading pornography" (Steinem's "pornography") as opposed to "other pornography" (Steinem's "erotica").

At least one other important distinction must be made among the miscellany of materials in the category of degrading pornography. Some degrading pornography is also violent, glorifying in physical mistreatment of the woman, and featuring "weapons of torture or bondage, wounds and bruises."[39] "One frightening spread from *Chic Magazine* showed a series of pictures of a woman covered with blood, masturbating with a knife. The title was 'Columbine Cuts Up'."[40] A movie called "Snuff" in which female characters (and, it is alleged, the actresses who portrayed them) are tortured to death for the sexual entertainment of the audiences, was shown briefly in a commercial New York theatre. The widely circulated monthly magazine *Hustler* once had a cover picture of a nude woman being pushed head first into a meat grinder, her shapely thighs and legs poised above the opening to the grinder in a sexually receptive posture, while the rest comes out of the bottom as ground meat. The exaggeration of numbers in Kathleen Barry's chilling description hardly blunts its horror: "In movie after movie women are raped, ejaculated on, urinated on, anally penetrated, beaten, and, with the advent of snuff films, murdered in an orgy of sexual pleasure."[41] The examples, alas, are abundant and depressing.

There are other examples, however, of pornography that is degrading to women but does not involve violence. Gloria Steinem speaks of more subtle forms of coercion: "a physical attitude of conqueror and victim, the use of race or class difference to imply the same thing, perhaps a very unequal nudity with one person exposed and vulnerable while the other is clothed."[42] As the suggested forms of coercion become more and more subtle, obviously there will be very difficult line-drawing problems for any legislature brave enough to enter this area.

Yet the most violent cases at one end of the spectrum are as clear as they can be. They all glory in wanton and painful violence against helpless victims and do this with the extraordinary intention (sometimes even successful) of causing sexual arousal in male viewers. One could give every other form of pornography, degrading or not, the benefit of the doubt, and still identify with confidence all members of the violent extreme category. If there is a strong enough argument against pornography to limit the liberty of pornographers, it is probably restricted to this class of materials. Some feminist writers speak as if that would not be much if any restriction, but that may be a consequence of their *defining* pornography in terms of its most revolting specimens.[43] A pornographic story or film may be degrading in Steinem's subtle sense, in that it shows an intelligent man with a stupid woman, or a wealthy man with a chambermaid, and intentionally exploits the inequality for the sake of the special sexual tastes of the presumed male consumer, but if that were the *only* way in which the work degraded women, it would fall well outside the extreme (violent) category. All the more so, stories in which the male and female are equals—and these materials too can count as pornographic—would fall outside the objectionable category.

May the law legitimately be used to restrict the liberty of pornographers to produce and distribute, and their customers to purchase and use, erotic materials that are violently abusive of women? (I am assuming that no strong case can be made for the proscription of materials that are merely degrading in one of the relatively subtle and nonviolent ways.) Many feminists answer, often with reluctance, in the affirmative. Their arguments can be divided into two general classes. Some simply invoke the harm principle. Violent pornography wrongs and harms women, according to these arguments, either by defaming them as a group, or (more importantly) by inciting males to violent crimes against them or creating a cultural climate in which such crimes are likely to become more frequent. The two traditional legal categories involved in these harm-principle arguments, then, are *defamation* and *incitement*. The other class of arguments invoke the offense principle, not in order to prevent mere "nuisances," but to prevent profound offense analogous to that of the Jews in Skokie or the blacks in a town where the K.K.K. rallies.

8. Violent pornography, the cult of macho, and harm to women

I shall not spend much time on the claim that violent and other extremely degrading pornography should be banned on the ground that it *defames* women. In a skeptical spirit, I can begin by pointing out that there are immense difficulties in applying the civil law of libel and slander as it is presently constituted in such a way as not to violate freedom of expression. Problems with *criminal* libel and slander would be even more unmanageable, and *group* defamation, whether civil or criminal, would multiply the problems still further. The argument on the other side is that pornography is essentially propaganda—propaganda against women. It does not slander women in the technical legal sense by asserting damaging falsehoods about them, because it *asserts* nothing at all. But it spreads an image of women as mindless playthings or "objects," inferior beings fit only to be used and abused for the pleasure of men, whether they like it or not, but often to their own secret pleasure. This picture lowers the esteem men have for women, and for that reason (if defamation is the basis of the argument) is sufficient ground for proscription even in the absence of any evidence of tangible harm to women caused by the behavior of misled and deluded men.

If degrading pornography defames (libels or slanders) women, it must be in virtue of some beliefs about women—false beliefs—that it conveys, so that in virtue of those newly acquired or reenforced false beliefs, consumers lower their esteem for women in general. If a work of pornography, for example, shows a woman (or group of women) in exclusively subservient or domestic roles, that may lead the consumer to *believe* that women, in virtue of some inherent female characteristics, are only fit for such roles. There is no doubt that much pornography does portray women in subservient positions, but if that is defamatory to women in anything like the legal sense, then so are soap commercials on TV. So are many novels, even some good ones. (A good novel may yet be about some degraded characters.) That some groups are portrayed in unflattering roles has not hitherto been a ground for the censorship of fiction or advertising. Besides, it is not clearly the *group* that is portrayed at all in such works, but only one individual (or small set of individuals) and fictitious ones at that. Are fat men defamed by Shakespeare's picture of Falstaff? Are Jews defamed by the characterization of Shylock? Could any writer today even hope to write a novel partly about a fawning corrupted black, under group defamation laws, without risking censorship or worse? The chilling effect on the practice of fiction-writing would amount to a near freeze.

Moreover, as Fred Berger points out,[44] the degrading images and defamatory beliefs pornographic works are alleged to cause are not produced in the consumer by explicit statements asserted with the intent to convince the reader or auditor of their truth. Rather they are caused by the stimulus of the work, in the context, on the expectations, attitudes, and beliefs the viewer brings with him to the work. That is quite other than believing an assertion on the authority or argument of the party making the assertion, or understanding the assertion in the first place in virtue of fixed conventions of language use and meaning. Without those fixed conventions of language, the work has to be interpreted in order for any message to be extracted from it, and the process of interpretation, as Berger illustrates abundantly, is "always a matter of judgment and subject to great variation among persons."[45] What looks like sexual subservience to some looks like liberation from sexual repression to others. It is hard to imagine how a court could provide a workable, much less fair, test of whether a given work has sufficiently damaged male esteem toward women for it to be judged criminally defamatory, when so much of the viewer's reaction he brings on himself, and viewer reactions are so widely variable.

It is not easy for a single work to defame successfully a group as large as

51% of the whole human race. (Could a misanthrope "defame" the whole human race by a false statement about "the nature of man"? Would every human being then be his "victim"?) Perhaps an unanswered barrage of thousands of tracts, backed by the prestige of powerful and learned persons without dissent might successfully defame any group no matter how large, but those conditions would be difficult to satisfy so long as there is freedom to speak back on the other side. In any case, defamation is not the true gravamen of the wrong that women in general suffer from extremely degrading pornography. When a magazine cover portrays a woman in a meat grinder, *all* women are insulted, degraded, even perhaps endangered, but few would naturally complain that they were *libelled* or *slandered*. Those terms conceal the point of what has happened. If women are harmed by pornography, the harm is surely more direct and tangible than harm to "the interest in reputation."[46]

The major argument for repression of violent pornography under the harm principle is that it promotes rape and physical violence. In the United States there is a plenitude both of sexual violence against women and of violent pornography. According to the F.B.I. Uniform Crime Statistics (as of 1980), a 12-year-old girl in the United States has one chance in three of being raped in her lifetime; studies only a few years earlier showed that the number of violent scenes in hard-core pornographic books was as high as 20% of the total, and the number of violent cartoons and pictorials in leading pornographic magazines was as much as 10% of the total.[47] This has suggested to some writers that there must be a direct causal link between violent pornography and sexual violence against women; but causal relationships between pornography and rape, if they exist, must be more complicated than that. The suspicion of direct connection is dissipated, as Aryeh Neier points out,

> . . . when one looks at the situation in other countries. For example, violence against women is common in . . . Ireland and South Africa, but pornography is unavailable in those countries. By contrast violence against women is relatively uncommon in Denmark, Sweden, and the Netherlands, even though pornography seems to be even more plentifully available than in the United States. To be sure, this proves little or nothing except that more evidence is needed to establish a causal connection between pornography and violence against women beyond the fact that both may exist at the same time. But this evidence . . . simply does not exist.[48]

On the other hand, there is evidence that novel ways of committing crimes are often suggested (usually inadvertently) by bizarre tales in films or TV (See Vol. I, Chap. 6, §5), and even factual newspaper reports of crimes can trigger the well-known "copy-cat crime" phenomenon. But if the possibility of copy-cat cases, by itself, justified censorship or punishment, we would have grounds for supressing films of *The Brothers Karamozov* and the TV series *Roots* (both of which have been cited as influences on imitative crimes). "There would be few books left on our library shelves and few films that could be shown if every one that had at some time 'provoked' bizarre behavior were censored."[49] A violent episode in a pornographic work may indeed be a causally necessary condition for the commission of some specific crime by a specific perpetrator on a specific victim at some specific time and place. But for his reading or viewing that episode, the perpetrator may not have done precisely what he did in just the time, place, and manner that he did it. But so large a part of the full causal explanation of his act concerns his own psychological character and predispositions, that it is likely that some similar crime would have suggested itself to him in due time. It is not likely that non-rapists are converted into rapists *simply* by reading and viewing pornography. If pornography has a serious causal bearing on the occurence of rape (as opposed to the trivial copy-cat effect) it must be in virtue of its role (still to be established) in implanting the appropriate cruel dispositions in the first place.

Rape is such a complex social phenomenon that there is probably no one simple generalization to account for it. Some rapes are no doubt ineliminable, no matter how we design our institutions. Many of these are the product of deep individual psychological problems, transferred rages, and the like. But for others, perhaps the preponderant number, the major part of the explanation is sociological, not psychological. In these cases the rapist is a psychologically normal person well adjusted to his particular subculture, acting calmly and deliberately rather than in a rage, and doing what he thinks is expected of him by his peers, what he must do to acquire or preserve standing in his group. His otherwise inexplicable violence is best explained as a consequence of the peculiar form of his socialization among his peers, his pursuit of a prevailing ideal of manliness, what the Mexicans have long called *machismo*, but which exists to some degree or other among men in most countries, certainly in our own.

The macho male wins the esteem of his associates by being tough, fearless, reckless, wild, unsentimental, hard-boiled, hard drinking, disrespectful, profane, willing to fight whenever his honor is impugned, and fight without fear of consequences no matter how extreme. He is a sexual athlete who must be utterly dominant over "his" females, who are expected to be slavishly devoted to him even though he lacks gentleness with them and shows his regard only by displaying them like trophies; yet he is a hearty and loyal companion to his "teammates" (he is always on a "team" of some sort.) Given the manifest harm the cult of macho has done to men,[50] to women, and to relations between men and women, it is difficult to account for its survival in otherwise civilized nations. Perhaps it is useful in time of war, and war has been a preoccupation of most generations of young men, in most nations, up to the present. If so, then the persistence of *machismo* is one of the stronger arguments we have (among many others) for the obsolescence of war.

The extreme character of macho values must be understood before any sense can be made of the appeal of violent pornography. The violent porn does not appeal to prurience or lust as such. Indeed, it does not appeal at all to a psychologically normal male who is not in the grip of the macho cult. In fact these pictures, stories, and films have no other function but to express and reenforce the macho ideology. "Get your sexual kicks," they seem to say, "but make sure you get them by humiliating the woman, and showing her who's boss. Make sure at all costs not to develop any tender feelings toward her that might give her a subtle form of control over you and thus destroy your standing with the group. Remember to act in the truly manly manner of a 'wild and crazy guy'."

In her brilliant article on this subject, Sarah J. McCarthy cites some horrible examples from *Penthouse* Magazine of the macho personality structure which is peculiarly receptive to, and a necessary condition for, the appeal of violent porn:

"There's still something to be said for bashing a woman over the head, dragging her off behind a rock, and having her," said one of the guys in the February 1980 *Penthouse* . . . "Women Who Flirt With Pain" was the cover hype for a *Penthouse* interview with an assortment of resident Neanderthals (a name that would swell them with pride).

"We're basically rapists because we're created that way," proclaims Dale. "We're irrational, sexually completely crazy. Our sexuality is more promiscuous, more immediate, and more fleeting, possibly less deep. We're like stud bulls that want to mount everything in sight . . ."

The letters-to-the-editor in the February *Penthouse* contains an ugly letter from someone who claims to be a sophomore at a large midwestern university and is "into throat-fucking". He writes of Kathy and how he was "ramming his huge eleven-inch tool down her throat." [Sexual bragging, pornography style.] Kathy "was nearly unconscious from coming." [Deceit and self-deception, pornography style.] Gloria Steinem writes in the May 1980 *Ms.*: "Since *Deep Throat*, a whole new genre of pornography has developed. Added to the familiar varieties of rape, there is now an ambition to rape the throat . . ."

Another issue of *Penthouse* contains an article about what they have cleverly called "tossing." A college student from Albuquerque, who drives a 1974

Cadillac and who is "attracted to anything in a skirt," tells how it's done. "How did you get into tossing?," the *Penthouse* interviewer asks. "It just happened," says Daryl. "I was doing it in high school two years ago and didn't know what it was. I'd date a chick once, fuck her in my car, and just dump her out. Literally."[51]

These repugnant specimens are not examples of make-believe violent pornography. Rather, they are examples of the attitudes and practices of persons who are antecedently prone to be appreciative consumers of violent pornography. These grisly sentiments are perhaps found more commonly among working class youths in military barracks and factories but they are only slightly more familiar than similar bravado heard by middle class Americans in fraternity houses and dormitories. These remarks are usually taken as meant to impress their male auditors; they are uttered with a kind of aggressive pride. The quotations from *Penthouse* capture the tone exactly. These utterly outrageous things are said publicly and casually, not in passion, not in hate, not in lust. They seem to say "That's just the way we machos are—for better or worse." Sarah McCarthy understands it perfectly—

> Though I'm sure male rage exists, just as female rage exists, it is probably not the main cause of rape. What we may be dealing with is the banality of rape, the sheer ordinariness of it as the logical end of macho, the ultimate caricature of our sexual arrangements. Some men may think that rape is just the thing to do. Its source could, in large part, be due to something as mundane as faulty sex education, rather than a wellspring of rage of mythic proportions. In many subcultures within the United States, violence against women has become acceptable, expected, even trendy . . .[52]

There is probably no more typical pure macho enterprise than gang rape, a kind of group rite among cultish "individualists," in some ways like a primitive puberty ritual in which insecure males "prove themselves" to one another, and the victim is but an incidental instrument to that end. In a chapter on rape and war in her *Against Our Will*,[53] Susan Brownmiller discusses the behavior of American troops in Vietnam. Various veterans are quoted to the effect that rape was widespread but rarely reported. One veteran who denied his own participation, had a terse explanation of the behavior of others: "They only do it when there are a lot of guys around. You know, it makes them feel good. They show each other what they can do. They won't do it by themselves."[54] Macho values thrive and spread in wartime battle zones. They become part of the process by which soldiers celebrate their cynical toughness and try to convince themselves and one another that they truly have it.

Would it significantly reduce sexual violence if violent pornography were effectively banned? No one can know for sure, but if the cult of macho is the main source of such violence, as I suspect, then repression of violent pornography, whose function is to pander to the macho values already deeply rooted in society, may have little effect. Pornography does not cause normal decent chaps, through a single exposure, to metamorphoze into rapists. Pornography-reading machos commit rape, but that is because they already have macho values, not because they read the violent pornography that panders to them. Perhaps then *constant* exposure to violent porn might turn a decent person into a violence-prone macho. But that does not seem likely either, since the repugnant violence of the materials could not have any appeal in the first place to one who did not already have some strong macho predispositions, so "constant exposure" could not begin to become established. Clearly, other causes, and more foundational ones, must be at work, if violent porn is to have any initial purchase. Violent pornography is more a symptom of *machismo* than a cause of it, and treating symptoms merely is not a way to offer protection to potential victims of rapists. At most, I think there may be a small spill-over effect of violent porn on actual violence. Sometimes a bizarre new sadistic trick (like "throat-fucking"?) is suggested by a work of violent pornography and taken up by those prone to cruel violence to begin with. More often, perhaps, the response to an inventive violent porno scene may be like that of the college *Penthouse* reader to "tossing": "I was doing it in high school two years ago, and I didn't know what it was." He read *Penthouse* and learned "what it was," but his conduct, presumably, was not significantly changed.

If my surmise about causal connections is correct they are roughly as indicated in the following diagram:

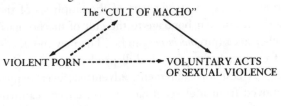

The "CULT OF MACHO"

VIOLENT PORN - - - - - - - - - - - - - -▶ VOLUNTARY ACTS
                                          OF SEXUAL VIOLENCE

──▶ = causal direction
- - -▶ = possible "spill-over effects"

The primary causal direction is not from violent pornography to violent real-life episodes. Neither is it from violent pornography to the establishment and reenforcement of macho values. Rather, the cult of macho expectations is itself the primary cause *both* of the existence of violent porn (it provides the appreciative audience) and of the real-life sexual violence (it provides the motive). The dotted arrows express my acknowledgement of the point that there might be some small spill-over effect from violent pornography back on the macho values that spawn it, in one direction, and on real-life violence in the other, but the pornography cannot be the primary causal generator. Sexual violence will continue to fester so long as the cult of macho flourishes, whether or not we eliminate legal violent pornography.

How then can we hope to weaken and then extirpate the cultish values at the root of our problem? The criminal law is a singularly ill-adapted tool for that kind of job. We might just as well legislate against entrepreneurship on the grounds that capitalism engenders "acquisitive personalities," or against the military on the grounds that it produces "authoritarian personalities," or against certain religious sects on the ground that they foster puritanism, as criminalize practices and institutions on the grounds that they contribute to *machismo*. But macho values are culturally, not instinctively, transmitted, and the behavior that expresses them is learned, not inherited, behavior. What is learned can be unlearned. Schools should play a role. Surely, learning to see through machismo and avoid its traps should be as important a part of a child's preparation for citizenship as the acquisition of patriotism and piety. To be effective, such teaching should be frank and direct, not totally reliant on general moral platitudes. It should talk about the genesis of children's attitudes toward the other sex, and invite discussion of male insecurity, resentment of women, cruelty, and even specific odious examples. Advertising firms and film companies should be asked (at first), then pressured (if necessary) to cooperate, as they did in the successful campaign to deglamorize cigarette smoking. Fewer exploitation films should be made that provide attractive models of youths flashing knives, playing chicken or Russian roulette, or "tossing" girls. Materials (especially films) should be made available to clergymen as well as teachers, youth counselors, and parole officers. A strong part of the emphasis of these materials should be on the harm that bondage to the cult of macho does to men too, and how treacherous a trap *machismo* can be. The new moral education must be careful, of course, not to preach dull prudence as a preferred style for youthful living. A zest for excitement, adventure, even danger, cannot be artificially removed from adolescent nature. Moreover, teamwork, camaraderie, and toughness of character need not be denigrated. But the cult of macho corrupts and distorts these values in ways that can be made clear to youths. The mistreatment of women, when its motivation is clearly revealed and understood, should be a sure way of eliciting the contempt of the group, not a means to greater prestige within it.

Rape is a harm and a severe one. Harm prevention is definitely a legitimate use of the criminal law. Therefore, if there is a clear enough causal connection to rape, a statute that prohibits violent pornography would be a morally legitimate restriction of liberty. But it is not enough to warrant supression that pornography as a whole might have some harmful consequences to third parties, even though most specific instances of it do not. "Communications from other human beings are among the most important causes of human behavior," Kent Greenawalt points out, "but criminal law cannot concern itself with every communication that may fortuitously lead to the commission of a crime. It would, for example, be ludicrous to punish a supervisor for criticizing a subordinate, even if it could be shown that the criticism so inflamed the subordinate that he assaulted a fellow worker hours later."[55] An even stronger point can be made. Even where there is statistical evidence that a certain percentage of communications of a given type will predictably lead the second party to harm third parties, so that in a sense the resultant harms are not "fortuitous," that is not sufficient warrant for prohibiting all communications of that kind. It would be even more ludicrous, for example, for a legislature to pass a criminal statute against the criticism of subordinates, on the ground that inflamed employees sometimes become aggressive with their fellow workers.

A more relevant example of the same point, and one with an ironic twist, is provided by Fred Berger:

> A journal that has published studies often cited by the radical feminists . . . has also published an article that purports to show that the greater emancipation of women in western societies has led to great increases in criminal activity *by* women. Such crimes as robbery, larceny, burglary, fraud, and extortion have shown marked increase, as have arson, murder, and aggravated assault. But freedom of expression would mean little if such facts could be taken as a reason to suppress expression that seeks the further liberation of women from their secondary, dependent status with respect to men.[56]

Of course, one can deny that violent porn is a form of valuable free expression analogous to scholarly feminist articles, but the point remains that indirectly produced harms are not by themselves sufficient grounds for criminalizing materials, that some further conditions must be satisfied.

Those instances of sexual violence which may be harmful side-effects of violent pornography are directly produced by criminals (rapists) acting voluntarily on their own. We already have on the statute books a firm prohibition of rape and sexual assault. If, in addition, the harm principle permits the criminalization of actions only indirectly related to the primary harm, such as producing, displaying or selling violent pornography, then there is a danger that the law will be infected with unfairness; for unless certain further conditions are fulfilled, the law will be committed to punishing some parties for the entirely voluntary criminal conduct of other parties. (For a fuller discussion, see Vol. I, Chap. 6, §5 on "imitative harms.") Suppose that A wrongfully harms (e.g. rapes) B in circumstances such that (1) A acts fully voluntarily on his own initiative, and (2) nonetheless, but for what *C* has communicated to him, he would not have done what he did to *B*. Under what further conditions, we must ask, can *C* be rightfully held criminally responsible along with *A* for the harm to *B*? Clearly *C* can be held responsible if the information he communicated was helpful assistance to *A* and intended to be such. In that case *C* becomes a kind of collaborator. Under traditional law, *C* can also incur liability if what he communicated to *A* was some kind of encouragement to commit a crime against *B*. The clearest cases are those in which *C* solicits *A*'s commission of the criminal act by offering inducements to him. "Encouragement" is also criminal when it takes the form of active urging. Sometimes mere advice to commit the act counts as an appropriate sort of encouragement. When the encouragement takes a general form, and the harmful crime is recommended to "the general reader" or an indefinite audience, then the term "advocacy" is often used. Advocating criminal conduct is arguably a way of producing such conduct, and is thus often itself a crime. An article in a pornographic magazine advocating the practice of rape (as opposed to advocating a legislative change of the rape laws) would presumably be a crime if its intent were serious and its audience presumed to be impressionable to an appropriately dangerous degree.[57]

Violent pornography, however, does not seem to fit any of these models. Its authors and vendors do not solicit rapes; nor do they urge or advise rapes; nor do they advocate rape. If some of their customers, some of the time, might yet "find encouragement" in their works to commit rapes because rape has been portrayed in a way that happens to be alluring to them, that is their own affair, the pornographer might insist, and their own responsibility. The form of "encouragement" that is most applicable (if any are) to the pornography case is that which the common law has traditionally called "incitement." Sir Edward Coke wrote in 1628 that "all those that incite . . . set on, or stir up any other" to a crime are themselves accessories.[58] Thus, haranguing an angry crowd on the doorsteps of a corn dealer, in Mill's famous example,[59] might be the spark that incites the mob's violence against the hated merchant, even though the speaker did not explicitly urge, advise, or advocate it. Yet, a similar speech, twenty-four hours earlier, to a calmer audience in a different location, though it may have made a causal contribution to the eventual violence, would not have borne a close enough relation to the harm to count as an "incitement," or "positive instigation" (Mill's term) of it.

Given that "communication" is a form of expression, and thus has an important social value, obviously it cannot rightly be made criminal simply on the ground that it may lead some others on their own to act harmfully. Even if works of pure pornography are *not* to be treated as "communication," "expression," or "speech" (in the sense of the first amendment), but as mere symbolic aphrodisiacs or sex aids without further content[60] (see Chap. 12, §2), they may yet have an intimate personal value to those who use them, and a social value derived from the importance we attach to the protection of private erotic experience. By virtue of that significance, one person's liberty can be invaded to prevent the harm other parties might cause to *their* victims only when the invaded behavior has a specially direct connection to the harm caused, something perhaps like direct "incitement." Fred Berger suggests three necessary conditions that expected harms must satisfy if they are to justify censorship or prohibition of erotic materials, none of which, he claims, is satisfied by pornography, even violent pornography.

1. There must be strong evidence of a very likely and serious harm. [I would add—"that would not have occurred otherwise."]
2. The harms must be clearly and directly linked with the expression.
3. It must be unlikely that further speech or expression can be used effectively to combat the harm.[61]

Berger suggests that the false shout of "fire" in a crowded theatre is paradigmatically the kind of communication that satisfies these conditions. If so, then he must interpret the second condition to be something like the legal standard of incitement—setting on, stirring up, inflaming the other party (or mob of parties) to the point of hysteria or panic, so that their own infliction of the subsequent damage is something less than deliberate and fully voluntary. Their inciter in that case is as responsible as they are, perhaps even more so, for the harm that ensues. Surely, the relation between pornographers and rapists is nowhere near that direct and manipulative. If it were, we would punish the pornographers proportionately more severely, and blame the actual rapist (poor chap; he was "inflamed") proportionately less.

It may yet happen that further evidence will show that Berger's conditions, or some criteria similar to them, are satisfied by violent pornography. In that case, a liberal should have no hesitation in using the criminal law to prevent the harm. In the meantime, the appropriate liberal response should be a kind of uneasy skepticism about the harmful effects of pornography on third party victims, conjoined with increasingly energetic use of "further speech or expression" against the cult of macho, "effectively to combat the harm."

9. Violent pornography and profound offense

The harm principle grounds for legally banning pornography do not appear sufficient. Does the offense principle do any better? Pornographic displays *can* be public nuisances, of course, and when the balancing tests tip in the nuisance direction, the offending activities may fairly be prohibited, or redirected to less offensive channels. The manner in which degrading and violent pornography offends women (and men who support women's rights) is substantially different from that in which erotica as such offend the prudish. The shame, embarrassment, shock, disgust, and irritation of the latter group can be effectively avoided if the erotic displays are concealed from their view. The offense to a woman's sensibilities when her whole sex is treated as grist for the meat grinder, however, is deeply repugnant to her moral sensibilities whether out of view or not. Feminist writers often make this point by means of analogies to racist literature and films.

Suppose some unscrupulous promoters decide that they can make large profits by pandering to the latent hatred against blacks which they suppose to be endemic in a substantial minority of the white community. Since explicitly racist remarks and overt racist behavior are no longer widely acceptable in American society, many secret black-haters might enjoy an occasional night at the movies where they can enjoy to their heart's content specially made films that lampoon minstrel-style "darkies" "with wide eyes as white as moons, hair shot straight in the air like Buckwheat's, afraid of everything—spiders, [their] own shadows, ghosts."[62] So much for comic openers. The main features could be stories of uppity blacks put in their place by righteous whites, taunted and hounded, tarred and feathered, tortured and castrated, and in the climactic scenes, hung up on gallows to the general rejoicing of their betters. The aim of the films would be to provide a delicious catharsis of pent-up hatred. It would be prudent, on business grounds, to keep advertisements discreet, and to use euphemistic descriptions like "folk films" (analogous to "adult films").

I don't imagine that many blacks would be placated by the liberal lawmaker who argues in support of his refusal to enact prohibitive legislation that there is little evidence of actual harm done to blacks by the films, that they do not advocate violence to blacks or incite mobs to fury, and that for all we know they will make the racists less dangerous by providing a harmless outlet for their anti-social impulses. Neither would many blacks be assuaged by the liberal assurance that we should all be wary of possible harmful effects anyway, continue to look for evidence thereof, and use educational campaigns as a more effective means of exposing the evils of racism. "That is all well and good," the blacks might reply, "but first we must lance this painful boil on our sensibilities. The 'folk films,' whether we are in the audience or not, are morally abominable affronts to us. Their very existence in our midst is a perpetual laceration of our feelings. We aren't present to be humiliated, but they degrade the very atmosphere in which we breathe and move."

The analogy to violent pornographic films is close though not perfect. (It is an interesting fact to ponder that although there undoubtedly is a large racist underground in this country, no promoter has yet found a way of exploiting it in the manner of our example.) The pornographic films do serve an erotic interest of their customers, and that gives them, *ceteris paribus*, a personal value greater perhaps than that of the "folk films," The racist films, on the other hand, may be easier to disguise as genuine works of drama, thus making it much more difficult for a line to be drawn between them and genuine attempts at dramas about odious people and their victims. The bare-knowledge offense in the two cases seems almost equally profound, going well beyond anything called "mere nuisance," to touch the chord of moral sensibility.

It does not express an unsympathetic attitude toward the offended parties, however, to deny a basis in either the harm or offense principles for the use of legal force to "lance the boil." Profound offense, as I have argued (Chap. 9, §4 and 8), is either an impersonal and disinterested moral outrage or else an aggrieved response on one's own behalf because of the unpleasant mental states one has been forced to experience. If it is an impersonal response, then it can warrant legal force against its cause only on the basis of the principle of legal moralism which is unacceptable to liberals. We would have to argue in that case that the very showing of violent films to appreciative audiences is an evil in itself and one of such magnitude that it can be rightly prevented by legal force if necessary, even though it is not the kind of evil that *wrongs* any one. (See Vol. IV, Chap. 27, on "free-floating evils"). If, on the other hand, the profound offense is a felt personal wrong voiced on one's own behalf as its "victim," then the complaint is that the offending materials cause one to suffer unpleasant states that are a nuisance to avoid. But that offense will not have much weight on the scales if one is not forced to witness the showings, or lurid announcements of the showings, and is not forced to take irritating and inconveniencing detours to avoid them. The offense principle, in short, will not warrant legal prohibition of the films unless the offense they cause is not reasonably avoidable, and bare-knowledge offense, insofar as it is mere offensive nuisance, *is* reasonably avoidable. It is only in its character as disinterested moral outrage that it is not reasonably avoidable, but we cannot ban everything that is thought to be outrageous, whether right-violating or not, without recourse to legal moralism.

This argument, I conceded, is subject to two strong qualifications. (See *supra* ,p.69.) It may be possible in certain untypical situations to go between its horns and thus escape its dilemma. A profoundly offended state of mind may be both disinterested moral outrage and also involve a sense of personal grievance, as when the offending cause is an affront to the offended party himself or a group to which he belongs. To feel personally degraded or insulted before others may well be to feel personally *wronged*, even though one's interests are unaffected and one's unpleasant states easily avoidable. The more difficult question is whether one truly *is* personally wronged when this happens, whether one's own rights have in fact been violated. The difficult cases I have in mind fall in between more extreme cases on either side that are easier to make judgments about. Consider hypothetical cases 1, 2 (a and b), and 3. Cases 2a and b are the difficult ones I have in mind.

> *Case 1.* A desecrates in private an icon that B regards as inherently sacred. B is morally outraged later when he learns about it. We can assume for the sake of the argument that A's action was morally wrong, but that it caused no harm to B (or anyone else). Neither was it, in any sense, directed at B. (A and B are total strangers.) Nevertheless, B suffers deep offense, as well as moral outrage, whenever he thinks about it. But B does not feel personally wronged. A did not violate *his* rights simply because he did something B morally disapproved of. B is neither the "target" of A's morally wrongful action, nor its victim.

> *Case 2a.* B is morally outraged (in at least the disinterested way) when he learns that A and his friends, all of whom resent B for no good reason, frequently insult him when they gather together in private, and maliciously ridicule him behind his back. A and his friends act wrongly, but not in a manner that harms B (there is, for example, no incitement or defamation against him), but their conduct *is*, in a sense, directed at B, and B is deeply offended to learn about it. He *feels* personally wronged, but is he in fact wronged? Have his rights been violated? He was the "target" of morally wrongful behavior, but was he its *victim?* A and his friends might rebut his grievance by saying: "We all happen to dislike you (whether or not for good reason is beside the point), and we get great collective pleasure from sharing that dislike. How does that violate your rights? Do you have a right not to be disliked or not to have that dislike shared by those who have it? In fact, our little private party, while understandably not to your liking, was none of your business."

> *Case 2b.* A and his friends are anti-semitic Nazi sympathizers who gather together privately and in secret in A's apartment, and spend an evening regaling themselves with abusive and mocking stories about Jews, and top off their evening of fun by showing old Nazi propaganda films against Jews, and even newsreels of Jewish corpses discovered in the newly liberated concentration camps. The latter cause general hilarity except for one odd chap in a corner who masturbates excitedly at depictions of torture instruments. We can safely assume that all of this is morally wrongful though not necessarily harmful behavior, and that it has Jews, as a class, as its "target." B is a Jew who learns of the party later, and is morally outraged, deeply offended, and in his estimation personally wronged by the immoral activities. But again we can admit that he was (part of) the target of those activities so that his offense was in a clear sense "personal," while doubting that he was the victim of those activities, one whose own rights were violated.

> *Case 3.* This is an easier case. A and his friends include at their party (in 2a) C, D, and E, who know nothing about B. A then deliberately lies to C, D, and

E by telling them that *B* is an exconvict, a child molester, and bad check passer. This utterly destroys *B*'s reputation for probity with *C*, *D*, and *E*, who eventually spread the libel widely among many other persons, including *B*'s customers. *B*'s business declines and his economic interests as well as his interest in his good name are harmed by the defamation. *B* later learns what has happened and is outraged. He was not only the target of wrongful behavior; he was its victim, the one whose rights were violated. He not only feels personally wronged; he clearly was personally wronged.

The moral I draw from these stories is that the targets of abuse in 2a and b were not in fact its victims, so that their profound offense, while both moral and personal, is not the sort of "wrongful offense" (a right-violating offense) that is a reason for criminal prohibition. I am realistic enough to expect that many readers will not share my "intuition," and that the matter is not easily settled by argument. Even if I concede, however, for the sake of the argument, that *B*'s rights *were* violated in 2a and b as well as 3 (though not in 1), there will be little gain for those who would invoke legal action against *A* (without resorting to legal moralism) in those cases. It would be an extraordinary extension of the offense principle to punish such activities even on the supposition that some parties' rights were violated by their bare-knowledge offense. That would be to consider the quite avoidable offended feelings of those parties to have more weight on the balancing scales than the freedom of others to speak their minds to one another in private. *B* may be even more offended to learn that his enemies have insulted or ridiculed him to other parties who may not even know him, and this case, I admit, is a more plausible if not entirely convincing example of a violated right, even without defamation. But all that is conveyed by these comments to the strangers who hear them is that *A* has a low regard for *B* (which is his right). They may also infer from this that *B* has a low regard for *A*. *B* surely will not be reluctant to express that disregard to any of *A*'s auditors who inquire, which, I should think, would also be *his* right.

Racist and porno films do not directly insult specific individuals, but rather large groups, thus diluting the impact of the insult, or at least its directed personal character, proportionately. The "folk films" might be more serious affronts in this respect than the porno films since their target is a much smaller group than half of the human race, and one which has historically been brutalized by slavery and cruel repression. A black man might be more likely to feel a *personal* grievance at the folk film he does not witness than a woman would to a porno film she does not witness, for these reasons.[63] This personal aspect of his offense would overlay the more general disinterested moral indignation he shares with the women who are offended by their bare knowledge of the existence of violent pornographic displays. Nonetheless, understandable as the black's felt grievance may be, the insulting film shown to a willing audience in a private or commercial theatre is in the same boat as the insulting conversations among willing friends in a private home or club. In both cases the conduct is morally execrable, but in neither case do liberal principles warrant state intervention to punish the mischief. If, however, I concede for the sake of the argument what seems to me to be dubious, namely that undeserved insults *wrong* the insulted party (violate his rights), and further (what is not doubtful) that he can be inflamed by the bare knowledge of them even though they occur behind his back, then I must make the further concession that these are relevant reasons under the offense principle in support of criminal prohibition. They cite, after all, a wrongful offense of the appropriate kind. But unless the balancing tests that mediate the offense principle are satisfied (and in these cases that would require that the offending conduct be of a kind that has virtually no redeeming personal and social value whatever), that relevant consideration can never be a sufficient reason.

The second accomodation our theory must make for profound offense is to acknowledge that severe restrictions should be made on announcements and advertisements. A black need not suffer the direct humiliation and stinging affront to his dignity and self-respect that would come from his being forced into the audience for a "folk film." He can simply stay away, and avoid the worst of it. But if the city is blanketed with garish signs announcing the folk films, or worse than that, signs that dispense with euphemisms and advertise "shows that put niggers in their place," then the affronts are no longer private; the offense is no longer avoidable; and its nature no less profound. The signs will be even more deeply offensive than those inviting participation in cannibalistic banquets in our earlier example (Chap. 9, §3 and 4), since they can be expected to inflame the blacks, who are the direct object of their insult, in the manner of fighting words, further frustrating them since violent response cannot be permitted. The offense of conspicuous advertisements, even nongraphic ones (though graphic ones are the worst), is so great that any restriction of them short of interference with the minimum basic right of communication is warranted.

In this and the preceding chapter we have distinguished three types of activities the bare knowledge of which can be profoundly offensive. The first category is illustrated by private desecration of cherished symbols like religious icons and national flags, and by the mistreatment in private of dead bodies. We are to think of these "private" activities as unwitnessed by others or witnessed only voluntarily by other participants or spectators. In the second category are the "Skokie-type cases," for example, a Nazi demonstration in Skokie or a K.K.K. march in Harlem. Spectators are deliberately sought out and taunted by the display of hated symbols of racial cruelty known to offend deeply those they insult. In the third category are racist "folk films" and violent porno films shown in privately owned and secluded places for the pleasure of anyone in the general public who wishes to buy a ticket. All three categories can cause bare-knowledge offense as well as equally "profound" offense to unwilling observers (if any). But they differ subtly in various other important respects.

The bare knowledge offense taken at "private desecrations" is not personal; that is, the offense is not taken because the offended party thinks of *himself* as wronged. (In fact he may admit that no one is personally wronged by the conduct he finds odious.) If he demands that legal force be used to prevent the outrageous behavior (anyway), the offending party might challenge him thus: "What concern is my behavior to you? You are morally outraged at what I have done, but I've done nothing *to* you except to morally outrage you. The outrage may or may not be justifiable, but it's no business of *yours* (or of anyone else for that matter) to intervene, either to enforce your moral judgment (which implies legal moralism) or simply because you find your own intense moral aversion unpleasant. You can always escape *that* unpleasantness by ceasing to dwell in your imagination upon unseen things. If you can't escape the annoyance that way, then you are suffering from a severe neurotic obsession and should seek help." The offense produced by the sacrilegious private conduct, in short, cannot be thought to be a wrong *to* anyone, even if it is morally wrong in itself. Hence, it cannot be rightly banned on liberal principles, no matter how repugnant it might be to think about.

In the other two categories, however, the bare-knowledge offense, while equally profound, is also personal. The folk film promoter's challenge "What concern is that to you?" can be answered by some people—"I am black. Your film mocks and insults blacks, and therefore mocks and insults me, my family, and my dear ones. That's how it concerns me." If it is plausible to think of a person as truly wronged by abusively insulting materials shown to others behind his back, (and I have doubted this) then the black person's bare-knowledge offense, and the woman's bare-knowledge offense at violent porn films, are not only profound, they are also wrongful (to them) in the sense required by the offense principle. There is then a reason of the appropriate kind for banning them, but that reason is not likely to be decisive in most cases when the actual offensive materials are not thrust upon any unwilling observers or advertised in prominent places and obtrusive ways. The offending materials usually have very little personal or social value, it is true, but they are instances of a general category (films or books) which we all have a very great stake in keeping free. The porno films, in addition, service certain erotic tastes, which kinky though they may be, are a source of important personal value to some, and an area of personal experience that has a strong claim to noninterference. Whatever minimal value the porno film may have, it is not nullified by any spiteful or malicious motives of its displayers. The theatre owner would prefer that women were never in the neighborhood to be offended. It is no part of his purpose to offend women; his whole aim is to make money from men. Indeed, it is in his commercial interest not to arouse the wrath of organized women's groups, for their unrelentingly pesky campaigns against him could in the end drive him out of business in search of a less stressful way of making money. If that happens in time to all violent porn displayers, the whole genre will be as empty as racial folk films are now, and for similar reasons. Even without the help of legislatures, the black community would make such a fuss about folk film theatres, that customers would prefer to stay at home with their own videotaped materials, and theatre owners would throw in the towel. But then the home films would be as clearly immune from criminal prohibition as insulting private conversations (no matter how abusive of third parties) and private voluntary sexual activity (no matter how kinky).

The third category, which includes the examples of Nazis in Skokie and Klansmen in Harlem, differ in two important respects from the second category. The offending behavior deliberately seeks out the audience that will be most intensely, most profoundly, and most personally offended, and imposes its offense on them as its sole motivating purpose. It is therefore spiteful and malicious through and through, thus lacking measurable social value. In the purest hypothetical cases, at least, where for some people the offense cannot possibly be avoided, and the menacing abuse of the displayed symbols is the sole "message" communicated, the offense principle clearly justifies prohibition, whether by preliminary injunction, by on the spot "cease and desist orders," or by general prohibitory statute. The difference between these cases and the violent porn cases are subtle; but small differences in mode and manner of offense can be the basis of large differences in the form of political response, and in the realm of criminal law policy, must inevitably be so. Wherever a line is drawn between permission and prohibition, there will be cases close to the line on both sides of it.

12

Pornography and the Constitution

1. The offense principle and the first amendment

We shall return in this chapter to the more traditional ways of discussing the moral and legal status of pornography from the period before people thought of treating its more egregious forms primarily under the headings of affront and danger to women. In particular we shall examine a leading alternative to our recommended liberal way of treating the problem, namely that which has prevailed in the American courts in so-called obscenity cases. As we have seen (Chap. 11, §1), whatever the word "obscene" might mean to the world at large, within the chambers of the Supreme Court it has a narrow meaning indeed, corresponding to what more common usage would call "pornographic". Nothing can be "obscene" in the Court's primary meaning unless it tends to cause erotic states in the mind of the beholder, and anything that does tend to produce that kind of "psychic stimulation" is a likely candidate for the obscenity label whether or not the induced states are offensive to the person who has them or to anyone else who may be aware of them. As we shall see, the court has occasionally departed from this narrow usage when it labels quite anti-erotic materials "obscene" because of the extreme and universal shock or disgust they produce. On these occasions the Court has recalled its liberal function to protect unwilling audiences from offensive nuisances. But on many other occasions the Court has spoken as if "prurient interest," offensive or not, is its real enemy, as if its tests of obscenity were intended to prevent and punish inherently evil mental states (invoking the illiberal principle of "legal moralism") or else to "protect" adults from the corruption of their own characters even when that corruption is produced by their own voluntary conduct and threatens neither harm nor offense to others (invoking a moralistic version of "legal paternalism"). The simple liberal approach would have been to ascribe to the word "obscene" the same meaning in the law that it has in ordinary usage, namely "blatantly repugnant," and to interpret anti-obscenity laws as having the traditional liberal function of preventing offensive nuisances, subject of course to the usual balancing tests. Instead the court chose to *mean* by "obscene," "lust-inducing," and to attribute to anti-obscenity statutes the quite illiberal functions of preventing sexy states of mind as an end in itself, and protecting autonomous adult citizens from moral corruption. I shall suggest that these two related mistakes—that of misdefining "obscene," and that of endorsing as constitutional the principles of moralism and paternalism—have led the Court to its present uncomfortable impasse in the law of obscenity.

Although this is not an essay in American constitutional law, it will be interesting to cast a quick glance at some extraordinary recent decisions of the Supreme Court about the permissibility of pornography, and in particular the various judicial formulae the Court has produced for dealing with the problem. Even a hasty survey will reveal, I think, that the Court has moved back and forth among our various legitimizing principles, applying now a liberal offense principle mediated by balancing tests and later a thinly disguised moralism, here flirting with paternalism, there sniffing for subtle public harms, and never quite distinguishing with any clarity among them. Moral philosophers, of course, have different objectives from courts of law. My purpose is to determine which governmental restrictions and suppressions are morally legitimate; the Supreme Court aims to establish which restrictions are permitted by the Constitution, especially the first amendment. (Still a third kind of concern, to be sharply distinguished from both of the others, is that of federal and state legislators who must decide which restrictions from among those that are consistent both with the Constitution and with principles of moral legitimacy it would be good policy to write into law.) Despite these different concerns, it should be possible to interpret each crucial formula in various leading court decisions in the terms of our own recommended liberal standards (derived in part from nuisance law), and to criticize the deviations. Where the Court's standards depart from our own, we can conclude either that the court has misread the Constitution or that the Constitution itself fails to satisfy our ideal prescriptions. We need not opt for one of these verdicts or the other, since this is not an essay in philosophical jurisprudence. A "legal positivist" no doubt would argue that the Constitution, for better or worse, is the law of the land, and that if it falls short of our moral ideals we should work for its amendment. A "natural law" theorist, on the other hand, would insist that all valid moral standards are tacitly incorporated by the Constitution, so that any interpretation that ascribes to it moral standards of an inferior or defective kind must be mistaken. Fortunately, my limited purposes in this book enable me to evade this vexatious jurisprudential issue.

When one approaches the problem of obscenity from within a first amendment framework, the distinction between action and expression is vitally important. Offensive conduct, as such, poses no particular constitutional problem. American legislatures are perfectly free to employ the offense principle, as mediated by the standards we have recommended, in prohibiting loud, raucous conduct, brazenly indecent conduct, public nudity, lewdness, offensive solicitation, and the like. But when the only "conduct" involved is the expression of some proposition, attitude, or feeling in speech or writing, or of whatever it is that gets "expressed" in art, music, drama, or film, then restrictive legislation would seem to contravene the explicit guarantees of the first amendment. And when the "conduct" in question is the mere possession of protected symbolic or expressive materials like books, pictures, tapes, or films, or the distribution or exhibition of such materials to willing recipients or observers, then its prohibition would also seem to violate the first amendment's strictures since it would render dangerous the creation of such materials and have a "chilling effect" on the spontaneity and freedom of expression generally. Moreover, expression is rarely valued or valuable in itself but only as part of the process of communication, and that process requires an audience. It follows that to deprive a symbol-user of his willing audience is to interfere with his "expression," and that is precisely what the first amendment forbids. The problem that presents itself to the Supreme Court then is this: how, if at all, can statutes that forbid and punish offensive obscenity be reconciled with the first amendment's "free speech" and "free press" guarantees when the offensiveness of the prohibited conduct resides in spoken or printed words, in pictures, plays or films?

Until the 1950s, the United States Supreme Court had never taken a clear stand on the question of whether "obscene" (i.e. "sexy," "lust-inducing," "erotic," etc.) materials and actions are protected by the first amendment's ban on statutes that "abridge the freedom of speech, or the press." By that time, both the federal government and virtually every state had enacted criminal statutes prohibiting obscenity, and more and more convictions were being appealed on the ground that these statutues were unconstitutional as violating freedom of expression. At the time the Court first decided to hear some of these appeals it might have appeared (as it does now to our privileged hindsight) that there were two broad alternative courses open to it.

1. It could hold that explicitly erotic materials, or the acts of distributing or exhibiting them, do qualify as "speech" or expression, and hence for protection under the first amendment. In that case, obscene expressions, like every other use of "speech," cannot be banned because of their expressive content (the proposition, opinion, feeling, or attitude that they express) but at most, only because of the manner in which they are expressed in the circumstances. Just as speech that is ordinarily free might be punishable if it is defamatory or fraudulent, or if it is solicitation, or incitement to crime, so obscene speech, while ordinarily free, might be prohibited if in its circumstances it is a public nuisance or falls under some other recognized heading of exception. Under this alternative, the exceptive headings that include defamation, fraud, and the like, do *not* include "obscenity" (in the Supreme Court's sense) as such.

Even if the Court took this first course it could allow that statutes prohibiting obscenity might nevertheless be constitutional if they are drawn with sufficient care. Statutes might, for example, prohibit public showings of obscene matter on the grounds that such materials are extremely offensive, but in that case, one would think that the Constitution would require satisfaction of something like our proposed balancing tests for the offense principle. That is to say that even admittedly "obscene" (that is, erotic) material cannot be prohibited if the offense is only moderate or sporadic, or if it is reasonably avoidable, or if its risk is voluntarily assumed, etc. One could easily imagine what a constitutional statute controlling pornography (sexual "obscenity") would be like. Only patently offensive exhibitions to captive audiences in public places or to children would be prohibited. In short, on this first alternative course, either there would be no statutes prohibiting "obscenity," or else the statutes would all be of the kind that control public nuisances and are legitimized by a properly mediated offense principle.

A model for this first interpretation of the constitutional status of obscenity can be found in the long sequence of Supreme Court decisions interpreting the "free exercise of religion" clause of the first amendment.[1] Normally, any conduct that is an essential part of what is recognizably a religious service or observance, or is required by a moral rule of a recognizably religious sect, is protected. Nevertheless, such conduct can be punished if it should happen to satisfy the definition of a crime, such as ritual human sacrifice, or incitement to crime in a sermon read from the pulpit. Given that the first amendment explicitly recognizes the distinctively important value of religious freedom, we can infer that there is a proportionately greater burden on those who would criminalize any conduct that is part of a religious observance. The more important a part of the religious observance is the conduct in question, the more important must be the "state's interest" (i.e., the harm, offense, or other evil for the aversion of which the prohibition is necessary). Thus, balancing tests of the sort we have found in nuisance law and then built into the offense principle are an essential element in the application of the first amendment to statutues that restrict religious liberty.[2]

2. The court could hold, alternatively, that purely pornographic materials do not qualify as speech or artistic expression, that in terms of the values enshrined in the first amendment, they are utterly without worth or significance. This is by no means a wildly implausible or "illiberal" alternative. It would be more implausible to interpret most works of pornography as expressions of "ideas," and while the line between erotic realism in drama or literature, on the one hand, and pure pornography on the other, is obscure, at least the clear cases of pornography are easily distinguishable from any kind of expressive art. So-called "filthy pictures" and hard-core pornographic "tales" are simply devices meant to titillate the sex organs *via* the mediation of symbols. They are designed exclusively to perform that function and are valued by their users only insofar as they succeed in that limited aim. For the pure cases (if only they could always be identified!) it would be as absurd to think of them as speech or art as it would be to think of "French ticklers," and other mechanical devices made solely to stimulate erotic feelings, in the same fashion.

This second alternative course for the Court then would be to deny pornography the protection of the first amendment on the ground that it is not "speech" in the requisite sense. It does not follow, however, that pornography is not protected by any part of the Constitution just because it is not protected by the first amendment; nor would it follow from the fact that it stands beyond the scope of the whole Constitution that it is morally legitimate to prohibit it unconditionally. If legislatures are free to bar individuals from wholly private and harmless indulgences just on the ground that they are "obscene" (sexually stimulating), then the exercise of that legislative freedom in many cases will lead to an invasion of the "privacy" of individuals, or (avoiding that troublesome word) of their liberty to control their own sexual experiences in any way they like short of harming or offending others. Unqualified prohibition of pornography may well be in this way a violation of individual rights even though, *ex hypothesi*, it does not violate first amendment rights.

Faced with this morally repugnant consequence, the Supreme Court following this second alternative might respond in either of two ways. It could look, if it were so disposed, elsewhere in the Constitution for an implicit right that is violated by the prohibition of private, consented to, harmless conduct in so basic a department of human experience as sexuality. In *Griswold v. Connecticut*,[3] for example, the Court discovered in the interstices of the first, fourth, fifth, ninth, and fourteenth amendments a hitherto unnoticed "right to privacy," which would perhaps be less misleadingly described as a right to personal *autonomy* in self-regarding and peculiarly intimate affairs. In *Griswold* the right to privacy was invoked to defend the sanctity of the marriage bed against laws that would prohibit the use of contraceptives. The same right was extended to unmarried persons in *Eisenstadt v. Baird*,[4] and to the viewing of pornographic films in one's own home in *Stanley v. Georgia*.[5] Once more the same right was invoked in *Roe v. Wade*[6] to strike down statutes that would deny to women the opportunity to have abortions and thus violate their "privacy," that is, their autonomy in respect to what is done to their own bodies. It may be stretching things a bit to use one label, "the right to privacy," for such a diversity of rights, except to indicate that there is a realm (or a number of realms) of human conduct that are simply nobody's business except that of the actors, and *a fortiori* are beyond the legitimate attention of the criminal law. Graham Hughes was encouraged by the trend of the Supreme Court "privacy" decisions to speak cautiously of "the maturing constitutional freedom to engage in discreet sexual stimulation or gratification."[7] What provides coherence to those motley decisions as a group, he suggests, "must be that there is something special about erotic activity that entitles a person to protection from the law unless the activity is being offensively thrust before members of the public."[8]

The second possible approach of the Court, if it were to exclude pornography from the scope of the first amendment, would be to conclude that there is no protection to be found anywhere in the Constitution for "obscene materials" even when they are used discreetly and restricted to adults. In that case, a judge might personally regret that the properly mediated offense principle is not written into the Constitution and urge legislatures to initiate the amendment process. Or he might advocate that those antiobscenity statutues that can be legitimized only by paternalistic or moralistic principles be modified or repealed. But as a justice sworn to uphold the Constitution as he understands it, he would not be free arbitrarily to strike down the offending statutes, odiously unfair though they may be.

The two generic alternative courses sketched above will not always be as distinct as they first appear, for they will overlap in mixed cases of pornog-

raphy-cum-art-or-opinion, and in instances of erotic materials that are bor-
derline-expressive. One would think that the chief need of the court in
these cases would be not for a criterion of "obscenity" but for a criterion of
"protectible expression," for where such expression is present *and* there is
no captive audience or children involved, then it doesn't matter how lurid,
tawdry, provocative, or unseemly the expression is; it cannot be forbidden.
The point is not that explicit sexiness *per se* is prohibitable if only we can
learn how to recognize and define it; but rather that expression *per se* is not
prohibitable (except where it is a nuisance), so we had better learn how to
recognize and define *it*.

2. *Critique of judicial formulae:* Hicklin *and* Roth

Until the United States Supreme Court took its first close look at the
problem of obscenity in 1957, the leading judicial precedent in the field was
an English one. In the famous case of *Regina v. Hicklin*[9] Lord Cockburn
formulated a test for obscenity that was "widely accepted in the American
courts well into the twentieth century."[10] Between 1868 and 1957 American
appellate courts commonly applied the *Hicklin* test in judging appeals of
convictions under vaguely worded federal and state statutes against obscenity.[11] Lord Cockburn's words were quoted over and over again during that
period: "I think the test of obscenity is this, whether the tendency of the
matter charged as obscenity is to deprave and corrupt those whose minds
are open to such immoral influences, and into whose hands a publication of
this sort may fall."[12]

The first thing to notice about the *Hicklin* formula is that it is a test of
obscenity, not a definition of the word "obscenity." Lord Cockburn apparently means by "obscenity" something like "objectionable treatment of sexual materials," so his "test" tells us how to determine whether a given
treatment of sex in writing or pictures is sufficiently objectionable to be
banned by statutes that forbid "obscenity."

It is important to notice next that Lord Cockburn's test appeals in no way
to an offense principle but rather to certain speculative harms that might be
produced by exposure to erotic materials. Reading dirty books and leering
at filthy pictures can "deprave and corrupt" persons who might otherwise
remain innocent and pure. Virgins will become libertines and harlots; virtuous men will become rakes and lechers. Even if the skeptical view of former
New York mayor Jimmy Walker is correct ("No nice girl was ever ruined
by a book") and pornography does not cause virtuous people to commit
sexual sins, it may yet strengthen the habit to dwell on one's sexual
thoughts, and be absorbed in one's sexual fantasies short of actual conduct.

That too might be a form of "corruption" or "depravity" by Victorian standards. The ultimate (and tacit) justification of the *Hicklin* test might have been derived from the harm principle, if Lord Cockburn had in mind "social harms" like the weakening of the social fabric that would come about if people generally abandoned themselves to lives of debauchery. There was no doubt an element of moralism involved too, since we can suppose that Lord Cockburn held lustful states of mind to be inherent evils whether or not they issue in harmful conduct. More likely still, the ultimate rationale is a blend of moralism and paternalism. Potential viewers of pornography need to be protected from "moral harm;" that is, harm to their characters. (See Book I, Chap. 2, §1 and Book IV, Chap. 33.) No matter that they voluntarily run the risk of corruption; they need to be protected from themselves. The Victorian justification for keeping pornography from adults, on this interpretation of motives, is precisely the same as our own noncontroversial rationale for keeping it away from children. Nowhere does Lord Cockburn express concern for the captive observer who might be caused offense; he is much too preoccupied with the danger to "those whose minds are open to such immoral influences" to worry about offenses to the sensibilities of those not in moral jeopardy.

There would appear to be more than a hint of the traditional British patronizing of the lower classes in Lord Cockburn's concern for those "into whose hands a publication of this sort may fall." Educated gentlemen no doubt can read pornographic books without fear of serious corruption, or corruption beyond that which motivates them in the first place, but what if the dirty book should just happen to fall into the hands of their servants, and be disseminated among ordinary workers and others (not to mention their own wives) who may be more susceptible to such influences? Perhaps Lord Cockburn's models for those "whose minds are open to such immoral influences" were alcoholics who can't hold their liquor and can't leave it alone. Perhaps he suspected that there is a similar class of "sex-addicts" who can get "hooked" on pornography and need ever greater stimulation to satisfy their growing needs, so that in the end mere pornography won't do, and illicit sexual conduct in ever-greater frequency takes its place. Such would not be the normal reaction to dirty books, of course, but only the response of those unnamed susceptibles "whose minds are open to such immoral influences."

Mr. Justice Brennan, when he came to write his groundbreaking majority opinion in *Roth v. United States*[13] in 1957, rightly found the *Hicklin* formula (as it had come to be interpreted) objectionable on three grounds: (1) it permitted books to be judged obscene on the basis of isolated passages read out of context; (2) it allowed the obscenity of a work to be determined by its likely effects on unusually susceptible persons; (3) it posited fixed standards of propriety regardless of time, place, and circumstances.[14] These three objectionable features had made it possible for courts in Massachusetts to uphold the ban on Dreiser's *American Tragedy*,[15] Lillian Smith's *Strange Fruit*,[16] and Erskine Caldwell's *God's Little Acre*,[17] and for federal prosecutors to attempt (unsuccessfully) to ban Joyce's *Ulysses*.[18] The "isolated passage" and "culturally invariant standard" part of the *Hicklin* test now seem to be simple mistakes, but the "susceptible person" standard seems especially wrong-headed in the light of our discussion of the mediating standards for determining the gravity of a nuisance which minimizes the seriousness of offenses to abnormally susceptible individuals.[19] *Hicklin's* concentration on the abnormally vulnerable moral character invites comparison with laws that would impose civil liability for frightening unusually skittish horses or laws that would ban the use of table salt on the grounds that some persons are allergic to it.

Whatever else Brennan would put into the new test for obscenity in his *Roth* opinion, he would certainly correct the three errors of *Hicklin*, and that he did. Henceforth, he decreed, a book can be judged obscene only if "the dominant theme of the material taken as a whole"[20] is so judged; and only if it is the likely effect of the materials on "the average person" (and not the especially susceptible person) that is taken into account[21] and only if "contemporary community standards"[22] (and not eternally fixed Victorian upper class standards) are applied to the work. The three key expressions—"dominant theme of the material taken as a whole," "average person," and "contemporary community standards"—became a fixed part of subsequent court formulations of an obscenity test, and while their vagueness did breed some mischief, they were clearly distinct improvements over *Hicklin*. Brennan had made a good start.

Unfortunately the rest of the *Roth* opinion caused a good deal of confusion, much of which remains to this day. Some of the trouble stems from the locutions "utterly without redeeming social importance" and "appealing to prurient interest," which are of course the fourth and fifth famous phrases of the *Roth* opinion. It is possible that Brennan intended his statement that obscenity is utterly without redeeming social importance to be a "synthetic judgment" giving low grades to some class of objects that can be independently identified and defined. But I suspect that his statement functions more naturally in his argument as part of the stipulation of a new legal *definition* of "obscenity." The other part of the definition is constituted by the "appeal to prurient interest" clause. So interpreted, he is saying: This is what we shall henceforth *mean* by "obscene," namely "whatever is produced for the sole purpose of arousing lustful thoughts and thus has no expressive value or function that is protected by the first amendment." Risqué novels are still literature, and the first amendment protects *all* literature. But pure pornography, whether it uses words or pictures, or both, is no kind of literature or art at all, good or bad, but rather some quite different kind of thing, properly classifiable with chemical aphrodisiacs and mechanical sex aids rather than with poems, plays, and the like. Radical opinions advocating more sexual liberty are expressions of opinion about sexual titillation, and, as such, they too are protected, even if they should happen themselves to be intended to titillate. "Mixed cases" of art-cum-pornography (if there are any such cases when one judges "dominant themes" of "whole works") are also to be treated as protectible expression. When you add "no value" to "small value" you get a diluted value, but even diluted values must be protected. This interpretation finds some support in a subsequent paragraph of the *Roth* opinion where what looks like a formal definition of "obscenity" is presented: "Obscene material is material which deals with sex [genus] in a manner appealing to prurient interest [difference]."[23] In other words, pornography. The generic part of the definition makes clear that it is the realm of the erotic only which is on the Court's mind; the phrase "appealing to prurient interest" serves to rule out various non-pornographic ways of portraying sex, "for example, in art, literature and scientific works."[24] The whole definition says simply that legal obscenity is pornography; then the "utterly without importance" clause adds "and nothing but pornography." The complete definition thus identifies legal obscenity, in effect, with *pure* pornography.

What remains vague is the meaning of "appealing to." Does it mean "intended to excite such interest" or "having the function, intended or not, of exciting such interest?" Very likely, intention and probable effect are each necessary and are jointly sufficient for a work to qualify as pornography. We must embrace this interpretation if we are to handle plausibly the case of the inept pornographer who tries to earn a living selling photographs of embarrassed and heavily garbed middle-aged relatives, under the mistaken impression that they will "turn on" lustful consumers. His appeal to prurience is genuine enough, just as the appeal to the mercy or charity of a hard-hearted skinflint might be genuine enough, but in neither case does it seem to be the sort of appeal that could hit its mark. The inept pornographer tried to make pornography but failed despite his evil intentions. So an "appeal," in the sense of simple intention, to the prurience of one's audience is not enough to constitute pornography. In addition the effort must be of a general character that can plausibly be expected to strike a responsive chord in . . . in whom? "In the average person in one's own contemporary community," say the earlier clauses about the "average person" and "community standards," thus filling out the definition.

If we are right about the Court's *definition* of "obscenity," what then is its *test* for determining obscenity? A chemist can tell us what he means by the word "acid" by citing a feature of the molecular structure of acids, for example that they contain hydrogen as a positive radical, or by mentioning other essential characteristics of all acids. But then when we ask him how we can go about telling an acid when we see one, he will give us answers of a different kind, theoretically less interesting, but more useful for our purposes, for example that acids are soluble in water, sour in taste, and turn litmus paper red. Similarly, a dictionary can explain the meaning of "drunk" and a physiologist can enumerate the biochemical characteristics that underlie all instances of drunkenness, but if we wish a useful and precise test of drunkenness, then we need something like a drunkometer machine and a metric criterion. The old *Hicklin* formula had not been meant to be a definition of "obscene," but to be more like a litmus test or drunkometer test for determining when obscenity is present. Just as the one test says that drunkenness is present when there is a certain percentage of alcohol in the blood, so the other test says that materials are obscene when they are capable of producing a certain effect on susceptible persons. Actually, the analogy is much closer to a test for determining when a substance is intoxicating than to a test for determining when a person is intoxicated. In each case what is being tested is the capacity of an object to produce effects of some measurable kind on a precisely defined class of subjects. Obviously the *Hicklin* test fails totally to do its assigned job in a satisfactory way. Does *Roth* provide a test that does any better?

Probably the best way of interpreting *Roth* is to conclude that it doesn't even attempt to supplement its definition of "obscenity" (as pornography) and its analysis of pornography (as nonexpressive) with a practical test for determining the presence of obscenity.[25] More likely the Court, both in *Roth* and its numerous *sequelae*, never even attempted to provide identifying tests of obscenity. The difficulty of doing so, in fact, filled it with collective despair, most piquantly expressed by Justice Stewart in *Jacobellis v. Ohio*[26] who said that he would not try to specify a criterion of "hard-core pornography," and "perhaps I could never succeed in intelligibly doing so. But I know it when I see it . . ."[27] It may be that no litmus test of "obscenity" is needed since pure unredeemed and unsupplemented pornography is indeed accurately characterized in general descriptive formulae[28] and is easily recognized by the ordinary men and women who sit in juries. Once we have it that a given book, for example, is pornographic, the only test that is needed is whether, "taken as a whole," it is also literature or opinion, that is, protectible expression. Pure pornography is easy to recognize; what are hard to spot are the "redeeming" units or aspects of expression in such impure admixtures as artfully pornographic films and erotic realism in novels.

When all five famous phrases are combined in the *Roth* opinion, there emerges, nevertheless, a formula that bears the superficial appearance of an identifying test. It is one of the predominant confusions of the Court in those subsequent decisions in which the *Roth* formula is refined, that it is unclear whether or not the Court intended the formula to provide a practical litmus test. Indeed, Justice Brennan refers to the standards as a "substituted test" for *Hicklin* in the very sentence in which he formulates it: ". . . this test: whether to the average person, applying contemporary community standards, the dominant theme of the material taken as a whole appeals to prurient interest."[29] The central source of the confusion in this formula, however, is not its obscure status or its imprecision as a test; it does no worse, surely, than *Hicklin* on those counts. Rather the confusion stems from the fact that it is not really a "substitute" for *Hicklin* so much as a mere modification of *Hicklin:* "average person" is substituted for unusually susceptible persons, "contemporary community standards" for eternally fixed Victorian standards, "the material as a whole" for isolated passages. These substitutions suggest that the *Roth* formula shares starting points, purposes, and initial assumptions with the *Hicklin* test, but just does its common job more carefully, avoiding undesirable side-effects.

But in fact the *Hicklin* test judges that sexual materials are sufficiently objectionable to be denominated "obscene" when they are capable of producing effects of a certain kind. Those effects are taken to be so evil in themselves that even responsible adults can be protected from their own choices and not permitted to run the risk of infection. The ultimate principles appealed to are, as we have seen, moralistic and paternalistic; the idea of offensive nuisance is not used or mentioned even implicitly. Can we believe that Justice Brennan, one of the Supreme Court's staunchest liberals, really intended to incorporate moralistic paternalism as a principle of constitutional jurisprudence? Can we believe that he thought that the state has a right to protect "the average person" from morally deleterious mental states ("itches") induced in him by materials he has freely chosen precisely because he wished to experience such states, when there is no clear and present danger of public harm and no third parties to be offended? The only answer to these questions, I think, is that Justice Brennan may not quite have understood what he was saying.

His confusions come out most strikingly in his use of the phrase regarding the "average person, applying . . . standards." Standards of what? And who, exactly, applies them: the average person or later, the court? There are at least three possible answers to these questions. First of all, if *Roth* really is but a small modification of *Hicklin*, the "standards" in question are norms for determining when materials have sufficient capacity to cause corruption or depravity. (The analogous question is when a beverage has sufficient capacity to cause intoxication in the "average person.") In that case the standards are not applied *by* the average person (as suggested by Brennan's syntax) but rather by the court *to* the average person. The Court's task, according to this interpretation, is to determine whether the likely effect of the materials on the average person would be a change in his character which, according to the standards of his (our?) community, would be corrupting or depraving. In effect, the plural term "standards," on this view, refers to two distinct standards: one for determining what the causal effects of the materials on the average person would be, and one for evaluating those effects as morally corrupting. The former standard would come from the social sciences, the latter from "the contemporary community."

Still, it is hard to believe, especially in the light of the opinions in later obscenity cases, that standards of offensiveness were not lurking somewhere in the penumbra of Brennan's opinion in *Roth*. These standards too vary from place to place, and change from time to time. On a second interpretation of *Roth* they too are among the "standards" that must be "applied." Quite apart from, or in addition to, their desirable or undesirable effects on traits of character, would the materials be likely to *shock* the average person? To answer this question about offensiveness, we must look to the standards of decorum in a given historical community that are held by its "average member" in such a way that their violation causes him shock or disgust (quite apart from the speculative effect on his own character).

The actual wording of the *Roth* formula, however, suggests a third interpretation, that the relevant "standards" are to guide yet another determination, namely whether the materials in question can be expected to *excite* ("appeal to") lustful thoughts in the average person ("prurient interest"). These standards too vary from community to community and from one culture to another. These standards too are in gradual constant change within one community over extended periods of time. With changes in the norms determining permissible conduct and dress come concomitant changes in the customary effects of different styles of dress and deportment on observers. Grandpa was excited even by bare ankles, dad by flesh above the knee, grandson only by flimsy bikinis. According to this third interpretation, a court must look at a contemporary community and decide what it takes then and there to excite the average person to a certain level of lust, and that will depend, in part, on what the average person is accustomed to see, to do, to experience.

Which of these three interpretations of the *Roth* formula is correct? My conclusion is that the court simply hadn't thought these matters out, that there is some plausibility in each interpretation, that ambiguities in judicial language here reflect uncertainties and conflicts in judicial thought. If the first interpretation is the correct one, then Justice Brennan, like Lord Cockburn before him, was basically a moralistic paternalist, endorsing the propriety and constitutionality of legislative efforts to protect citizens from harm to their own characters, quite apart from other consequences. Since it is difficult to believe that Justice Brennan, of all people, held such a view, the first interpretation is perhaps not very convincing. On the second interpretation, the Court was applying the offense or nuisance principle to the question of obscene materials, but—astonishingly—without the mediating maxims that would protect the privacy of willing consumers. The third interpretation is perhaps the one that is closest to the Court's conscious intentions, because it understands the *Roth* formula to be a test of when something is pornographic, hence "obscene" in the Court's sense, quite apart from further questions about its effects on sensibility and character. On this interpretation, as on the other two, the concept of obscenity is a relative one, varying on this reading with the average person's susceptibility to lustful feelings. In a way, this interpretation of the formula makes it even more disappointing to the liberal than the others. In the Court's view, so understood, there is no question about a legislature's right to ban lust-inducing materials, and no explanation why "obscenity" defined in this way (as pornography) and determined by these varying standards may be prohibited. The unwritten assumption apparently is that if legislatures think lustful states of mind are inherently evil (quite apart from harm or offense), that is sufficient.

3. Critique of judicial formulae: from Roth to Paris Adult Theatre

From the language of the majority opinion in *Roth* it would appear that the offensiveness of materials has nothing to do with the question of whether they are obscene and properly subject to legislative ban. Obscenity *means* pornography, and pure pornography without redeeming literary or scientific admixture totally lacks qualification for first amendment protection. What then is the test of whether a given set of materials—a book or a film— is truly pornographic? Whether a court, applying prevailing community standards to the average person, finds that "the dominant theme of the materials taken as a whole appeals to prurient interests." Not a word about whether they are repulsive, abhorrent, disgusting, or shocking to anyone.

Not a suggestion that the state's legal interest in their regulation might derive from their character as nuisances.

Five years later, however, in *Manual Enterprises v. Day*[30] the Court recalled the concept of offensiveness, and added it, as a kind of afterthought, to the *Roth* formula. The Post Office Department had barred from the mails on the grounds of obscenity three magazines (*Manual, Trim,* and *Grecian Guild Pictorial*) that specialized in photographs of nude or nearly nude male models. Manual Enterprises, the publisher of all three, appealed to the Supreme Court objecting that, among other things, the publications were "body-building magazines" and therefore not obscene. Justice Harlan, the author of one of the two opinions supporting the petitioner in this case, sidestepped the question of whether the materials could be judged obscene on the grounds that they appealed to the prurient interests of the average (male) homosexual rather than the "average person" (the question of relevant audience that was finally settled in *Mishkin v. New York*, in 1966)[31] and gave emphasis instead to the question of offensiveness: "These magazines cannot be deemed so offensive on their face as to affront current community standards of decency—a quality that we shall hereafter refer to as 'patent offensiveness' or 'indecency.' "[32] Justice Harlan then went on to spell out a "twofold concept of obscenity" according to which "patent offensiveness" and "appeal to prurient interest" are each necessary and jointly sufficient for obscenity.[33] Only one of these "distinct elements"[34] (at most) was present in the body-building magazines; hence they were not obscene, however much they may have excited homosexual lust. The presence of both elements is determined by the application of community standards: offensiveness by standards of decorum or "customary limits of candor,"[35] prurience presumably by standards of average susceptibility. "In most obscenity cases," Harlan rushed to reassure us, "the two elements tend to coalesce,"[36] and what obviously appeals to prurience will on that account alone be "patently offensive."

The next steps in the evolution of the *Roth* formula occurred on one strange day in 1966 when the Court handed down decisions in *Ginzburg v. United States*,[37] *Mishkin v. New York*,[38] and *A Book Named "John Cleland's Memoirs of a Woman of Pleasure" v. Attorney General of Massachusetts* ("*Memoirs*" v. *Massachusetts*, for short).[39] The *Mishkin* case makes the best transition from *Enterprises v. Day*, so I shall begin with it. This case settled the problem of relevant audience which Justice Harlan had put aside in *Enterprises*. Mishkin was appealing a conviction and a sentence of three years in jail and a $12,000 fine for violation of a New York state criminal statute prohibiting publication, possession, and distribution for sale of obscene materials. The books in question described sado-masochistic sexual acts, fetishisms, lesbianism, and male homosexuality. It was clear that the "average person"[40] would be repelled rather than aroused by such materials and that the books, therefore, made no appeal to the prurience of the "average person" at all. In a 6–3 decision, the Supreme Court upheld Mishkin's conviction anyway, and reformulated the *Roth* criteria at the same time: "Where the material is designed for and primarily disseminated to a clearly defined deviant sexual group, rather than the public at large, the prurient-appeal requirement of the *Roth* test is satisfied if the dominant theme of the material taken as a whole appeals to the prurient interest in sex of the members of that group."[41] Thus were the equal rights of sado-masochists, fetishists, and homosexuals to be free from stimulants to their own kind of lustfulness vindicated in the highest court. Apparently, "patent offensiveness" is determined by the standards of the "average person" (even when no average person is in fact offended), while the prurient interest test is applied to the special audience at which the materials are aimed.

One would think that, as a general rule, the more special the audience addressed, the greater the offensiveness as measured by the standards of the general public. The average person is more offended (shocked, disgusted) by homosexuality than by heterosexuality, more repelled still by bestiality than by human homosexuality, etc. On the other hand, as a general rule one would expect that the more special the audience addressed, the smaller the total amount of lustfulness induced. It would follow then that the more fully the offending materials satisfy the "patent offensiveness" test, the smaller the amount of prurience they actually produce in the community as a whole—at least for the more familiar sorts of sexual deviance. In a limiting case, the offensiveness might be extreme but the lust actually stimulated so minuscle as to be insignificant, in which case the materials would satisfy only one of the two necessary conditions for obscenity. Apparently, however, the Court recognizes no lower limit to the amount of prurience that must be stimulated by a book in order for it to be judged obscene. Given satisfaction of the "patent offensiveness" standard, any increase in the next amount of prurience is an evil that a legislature is entitled to prevent. Where offensiveness is extreme, then, the appeal to the prurient interest standard hardly seems necessary at all. In fact, sale or display of the offending materials might be prohibitable as nuisances anyway in that case; minimal appeal to prurience is necessary only if the prohibition is made on the grounds of "obscenity." But what importance is there in a mere name?

The addition of the "patent offensiveness" component to the *Roth* formula saves the Court from another kind of severe embarrassment that would result from the applications to certain hypothetical cases, at least, of a test for obscenity that makes no reference to offensiveness at all. Without the offensiveness component, the *Roth–Mishkin* criteria would require only that socially valueless materials appeal to the prurient interest of some audience, no matter how special or small, in order to be judged obscene. In that case, if there are seventeen people in the entire United States who achieve their sexual gratification primarily by fondling stones, then a magazine aimed directly at them which publishes lurid color photographs of rocks and pebbles would be obscene. As it is, the Court is saved from such an absurdity by Justice Harlan's afterthought of offensiveness. Since the *Mishkin* decision, a sex magazine for rock fetishists would qualify as obscene only if it published, for example, pictures of naked people rubbing up against a variety of sandstone, limestone, basalt, and marble rocks in various erotic postures suggesting abandonment to ecstasy. Then no doubt the deviant cultish magazine would be fully obscene by both the "prurient interest" standard (minimally satisfied) and the "patent offensiveness" standard, though it might yet be "redeemed" by scientifically serious articles about geology interspersed among the photographs.

    Ginzburg v. United States,[42] decided the same day as *Mishkin*, took a wholly unexpected new path for which *Roth* had not prepared observers of the Court. That path led the Court into a thicket from which it subsequently retreated, and it led Ralph Ginzburg, to his astonishment and despair, to prison for a five-year term. Ginzburg had been convicted of violating the federal statute against obscenity by publishing among other things the magazine *Eros* and the book *The Housewife's Handbook on Selective Promiscuity*.[43] He appealed, and the Supreme Court spent most of its time during oral argument trying to apply the newly interpreted "three pronged" *Roth* formula to the publications to determine whether they were truly obscene. To be obscene, a majority agreed, the materials must appeal to their audience's prurient interests, be patently offensive by community standards of decorum, and be "utterly without redeeming social importance." Ginzburg's lawyers were especially concerned to argue that respectable literary and journalistic materials were intermixed with the avowedly pornographic materials, thus establishing some redeeming social value in the materials taken as a whole. But none of this mattered, according to the decision which the Court dropped like a bombshell on March 21, 1966. Justice Brennan argued in his majority opinion that Ginzburg's publications could be found obscene because of the "leer of the sensualist" that permeated the *advertising* for the publications.[44] If the Court had considered it solely on the basis of the *content* of the publications, he admitted, this would have been a close and difficult case, but the emphasis of Ginzburg's advertising made all the difference.[45]

    A close examination of Justice Brennan's decision reveals the usual uncritical mixture of appeals to moralism, paternalism, and the oddly unmediated offense principle. Justice Brennan, employing his own *Roth* formula (at that time in *Memoirs* the three-pronged test),[46] must first decide whether the materials are pornographic. Do they "appeal" to the prurient interests of prospective readers? Well, of course they do; their own advertising explicitly makes such an appeal.[47] The materials are "openly advertised to appeal to the erotic interest of their customers."[48] To be sure, in court Ginzburg's lawyers had argued that some of the articles and stories conferred a redeeming social importance to the publications taken as a whole, but this doubtful claim, Brennan argues, is belied by Ginzburg's own sales pitch where his "appeal" is made. The advertising is "relevant to determining whether social importance claimed for material in the courtroom was, in the circumstances, pretense or reality—whether it was the basis upon which it was traded in the marketplace or a spurious claim for litigation purposes."[49] And it must be admitted that there was not a single mention of literary values, scientific studies, or moral–political advocacy in Ginzburg's advertising; "[T]he purveyor's sole emphasis is on the sexually provocative aspects of his publications . . ."[50] This then is Brennan's first argument: In "close cases" the advertising for publications may be used as evidence of whether or not the materials appeal exclusively to prurient interest, that is, are purely pornographic, meaning legally obscene.[51] When in doubt, judges should take the defendant's own words into account as evidence of the obscene content of his publications. This last-minute rationalization, which could not possibly have been anticipated at the time of the criminal conduct, sent Ginzburg to prison for five years. Subsequent publishers of pornography took warning. Their advertisements used euphemisms and code words like "adult books" and "erotic literature," but their books were as "dirty" as ever. This decision sent one man to prison, but changed little else.

Justice Brennan's opinion did pay some homage to the offense principle, as indeed it had to, since "patent offensiveness" was now one of the three prongs of the revised *Roth* formula. But his words are very sparse on this subject: "The deliberate representation of petitioners' publications as erotically arousing . . . would tend to force public confrontation with the potentially offensive aspects of the work; the brazenness of such an appeal heightens the offensiveness of the publications to those who are offended by such materials."[52] Perhaps these cryptic words do make a good point. An unavoidable sign in large red letters on a billboard in a crowded place that shrieks "Filthy Pictures For Sale" will be predictably offensive to anyone who would be offended by the filthy pictures themselves, and no doubt also to a great many who would not be offended by a private perusal of the advertised products. Still, the advertisement for the filthy pictures could hardly be as offensive as the filthy pictures themselves would be if *they* were on the public billboard. In comparison with the latter impropriety, the shrill advertising is a mere peccadillo. In any case, advertising can be regulated by explicit statutes that put advertisers on warning. No such statutes were violated by Ginzburg's advertisements; he was jailed, in effect, for conduct that he could not have known to be criminal.

The final argument in Brennan's opinion for the relevance of advertising to the determination of obscenity is a moralistic-paternalistic one of a special kind. (See Vol. IV, Chaps. 30 and 31.) "*Eros* was created, represented, and sold solely as a claimed instrument of the sexual stimulation it would bring. Like the other publications, its pervasive treatment of sex and sexual matters rendered it available to *exploitation by those who would make a business of pandering to 'the widespread weakness for titillation by pornography.' "*[53] The latter phrase is especially revealing. It is not pornography and erotic stimulation as such that are the object of Brennan's wrath, but rather "the sordid business of pandering—'the business of purveying textual or graphic matter openly advertised to appeal to the erotic interest of their customers.' "[54] Brennan here follows the Model Penal Code[55] in taking an "oblique approach" to the problem of obscenity. That approach is well-explained by Louis B. Schwartz.

> The meretricious "appeal" of a book or picture is essentially a question of the attractiveness of the merchandise from a certain point of view: what makes it sell. Thus, the prohibition of obscenity takes on an aspect of regulation of unfair business or competitive practices. Just as merchants may be prohibited from selling their wares by appeal to the public's weakness for gambling, so they may be restrained from purveying books, movies, or other commercial exhibition by exploiting the well-nigh universal weakness for a look behind the curtain of modesty.[56]

Customers, in short, need protection by the state from enticing advertisements that "exploit their weaknesses," whether the weakness be for erotic fantasy, gambling, or whatever. (But why not then also for cigarettes, sweets, and fried foods?)

In treating the desire for titillation by pornography as a "weakness," Brennan seems to be making a contestable moral judgment that permits him in effect to incorporate part of the conventional sexual morality into the law. Suppose that a regular customer for pornographic materials were to deny that his need and taste is a weakness? "I don't think of the titillation I crave as a temptation to do something evil by my own standards," he might say. "Rather it is an appetite like any other, entirely innocent in my eyes. I seek it in good conscience, and find it patronizing indeed to be told that my moral sense needs correction, or that my moral resolution needs reenforcement by the law." Another user might have moral reservations. He might admit that he is sometimes ashamed of his pornographic indulgences, but deny vehemently that his moral struggles are anyone else's business. Certainly, he will say, they are not the law's business. Both of these users might admit that they have a need for erotic titillation, while denying that every need is a "weakness" that renders them incapable of governing themselves without outside help.

The reasonableness of these replies to Justice Brennan is underscored by the contrast between the taste for titillation and the genuine weakness of the alcoholic for whiskey, the drug addict for heroin, perhaps even the cigarette smoker for nicotine. An advertising sales pitch aimed directly at alcoholics encouraging them to strengthen their habit would be unfair not only to one's more scrupulous competitors in the liquor business (one of the Schwartz's prime concerns)[57] but also to the poor wretches one is trying to exploit. Their addiction is a weakness in the sense that it is something they regret and try to resist themselves, something that is objectively bad for them, as they would be the first to admit. Similarly cigarette advertisements aimed directly at teenagers can fix a fatal habit on unsuspecting innocents from which many will find relief only in a painful and premature death. But these analogies fail to provide convincing models for the willing consumer of pornography. The tenability of the principle of moralistic paternalism is a matter to which justice cannot be fully done here. It suffices to point out that Brennan's final argument for the relevance of advertising to determinations of obscenity tacitly invokes that principle.

We need not linger long over the last of the three obscenity cases decided by the Supreme Court in March, 1966.[58] *John Cleland's Memoirs of a Woman of Pleasure* was much more widely known by the name of its central character, *Fanny Hill*. The book, first distributed in England in 1750, was published anew in the United States in 1963. Obscenity charges were promptly brought against it by the Commonwealth of Massachusetts whose Supreme Court, in a 4–3 decision, officially declared it obscene.[59] Many expert witnesses, including distinguished professors of English and history, testified that the book was not utterly without redeeming value, although its similarity to more recent works of pure hard-core pornography was marked. The sole issue in the case, according to Justice Brennan's majority opinion, was whether the book actually is obscene as determined by the *Roth* formula, and he decided that it was not.[60] The main significance of the opinion stems from Brennan's explicit endorsement of the "three pronged test"—appeal to prurient interest, patent offensiveness, and utter absence of redeeming social value—as the proper criterion of obscenity, naturally evolved from his own *Roth* formula laid down nine years earlier. That criterion came to be called "the *Memoirs* criterion," or "the Fanny Hill test" more commonly than "the *Roth* formula" in the years following.

The next landmark obscenity decision left the formula for obscenity unchanged, but was important for its judgment on another matter. *Stanley v. Georgia*[61] raised the issue whether mere possession in one's own home of an admittedly obscene film, where there is no attempt to sell it or distribute it further, could be grounds for prosecution. In a resounding 9–0 decision the Court emphatically denied that it could. Justice Marshall derived the right to possess obscene materials from a more general right to privacy implicitly guaranteed, he claimed, by the first and fourteenth amendments, and made explicit in *Griswold v. Connecticut*.[62] Civil libertarians applauded the result, as well they should have, but in a cooler hour many of them had some misgivings about Justice Marshall's reasoning, for the privacy Marshall invoked was not so much a personal privacy as a set of rights derived from the "sanctity of the home." The appellant, Marshall wrote, "is asserting . . . the right to satisfy his intellectual and emotional needs in the *privacy of his own home*. He is asserting the right to be free from state inquiry into the contents of *his library* . . . If the First Amendment means anything, it means that a State has no business telling a man, sitting alone *in his own house*, what books he may read or what films he may watch."[63] But though the state has no business investigating the contents of a person's library or bedroom, there is nothing in the Marshall opinion to deny that the state has business inquiring into the contents of a person's boat, or automobile, or luggage, or his pockets, briefcase, or wallet. The confines of one's home can make very narrow boundaries for the area of one's privacy.

The next important day in the history of the Supreme Court's struggle with the riddles of obscenity, was June 21, 1973, when the Court decided both *Miller v. California*[64] and *Paris Adult Theatre I v. Slaton*.[65] By that time the membership of the Court and undergone a new change and a "conservative" majority had emerged under the leadership of Chief Justice Warren Burger. There had been a great outcry in the country against pornography and excessively "permissive" Supreme Court decisions. Chief Justice Burger and his conservative colleagues clearly wished to tighten legal controls on obscenity to help "stem the tide," but they also felt bound to honor the Court's own precedents and particularly the *Memoirs* formula. The result was a pair of 5–4 decisions in which the opinion of the Court delivered by Chief Justice Burger gave some lip service to the *Memoirs* test while modifying each of its three prongs. Henceforth: (1) whether materials appeal to prurient interest is to be determined by the application of local community standards rather than national standards,[66] (2) the use or display of sexually explicit materials may be deemed patently offensive even when it involves only willing adult observers in a commercial theatre (nor can the privacy of the home be equated "with a 'zone' of 'privacy' that follows a distributor or a consumer of obscene materials wherever he goes."[67] Furthermore, not all conduct directly involving "consenting adults" only has a claim to constitutional protection.[68]; (3) a finding of obscenity requires not that the materials be utterly without redeeming social value but only that they lack "serious literary, artistic, political, or scientific value."[69]

The intended consequence of this decision clearly was to permit more aggressive prosecutions of pornographers while maintaining continuity with earlier Court tests for obscenity. Recourse to a local community norm rather than a national standard for applying the "prurient interest" test permits local courts to find persons guilty for distributing materials that could not plausibly be found obscene in other, more sophisticated, jurisdictions. In denying that there is a movable zone of privacy that follows a person wherever he goes and that private transactions between consenting adults cannot be patently offensive, the Court permits local authorities to prevent the display of pornographic films in public theatres no matter how discreetly they are advertised, no matter how effectively customers are forewarned, no matter how successfully children are denied admittance. By insisting that a book with sexual themes must have serious literary, artistic, political, or scientific value if it is to qualify for first amendment protection, the Court allows successful prosecutions of such borderline works as *Fanny Hill* which had a certain elegance of language and an incidental interest to critics and scholars of history and sociology, although it was basically pornographic in intention. *Fanny Hill* admittedly was not *utterly* without social value, but it could hardly be said to have *serious* literary value.

Burger then did achieve his double goal. He tightened the screws on obscenity and maintained fidelity to the Court's basic *Roth–Memoirs* approach. In so doing, however, he reduced that approach to something approaching absurdity. The substitution of local community standards in effect makes it difficult to publish anywhere materials that would violate the most puritanical standards in the country. Publishers will have to screen out-of-state orders more carefully than Larry C. Flynt did when he routinely mailed a copy of his publication *Hustler* to a person who had ordered it by mail from a town in Ohio. He was subsequently tried for violation of the Ohio obscenity statutes and sentenced to 7–25 years in prison.[70] How could a national publisher or film producer hope to distribute his book or film nationally when he might misjudge the "community standards" of one small town somewhere and thereby end up in jail? Publication would be commercially feasible only when the materials were unchallengeable any-

where in the country. Willard Gaylin describes these absurdities and ineq-
uities well when he writes that:

> The principle established by the Supreme Court . . . was intended to let local
> communities set their own standards, allowing diversity to flourish as the
> people of each area wished. Instead, . . . what community control does is to
> set the limits for nationally distributed literature and television at the level of
> the bluest-nosed small town critic.[71]

The Burger Court's second modification of the *Memoirs* formula is, from
the moral point of view, even more absurd, for at a stroke it restricts
personal privacy arbitrarily to the confines of one's home and denies constitutional recognition of the *Volenti* maxim. (But of course it is always possible that it is the Constitution that is absurd, not the five-man majority of
the Supreme Court.) The third "modification" is more than a mere tighten-
ing or adjustment of the Roth "utterly without redeeming social value"
formula; it nearly guts the theory of the first amendment that Justice Brennan had employed when he formulated that clause. That people should be
free to make serious efforts to produce works of art and literature, political
and moral judgments, and scientific discoveries; that they should be free to
innovate and experiment, to depart from or defend orthodoxies; that they
should be free to fail and thus to produce bad art or to be in error, if that's
what it comes to, as they themselves choose and see fit: *that* is what has
"social value" and is defended by the first amendment.

The Burger "modification" seems to limit constitutional protection to
good novels and films, seriously valuable political commentaries, and importantly correct scientific reports and theories. If future courts take his
words seriously, they shall have to strip protection from most novels that
deal with sexual themes, since assuredly most of them, like most other
novels, lack "serious literary importance." The Court's message to writers is
a discouraging one: If you plan to write a novel that contains explicitly
sexual scenes that an average person in a remote community would judge to
be titillating or shocking, you had better make sure that it has important
literary value; if it turns out to be merely mediocre on literary grounds,
your publisher may end up in jail. How could anyone seriously believe that
this is the way the first amendment protects the enterprise of literature?

4. Starting over again:
some tips from Justice Brennan

Justice Brennan, whose opinion in *Roth* sixteen years earlier had set the
Court on the serpentine path that led to *Miller* and *Paris Adult Theatre*, lost

his patience finally with that basic approach, and in a ringing dissent to *Paris Adult Theatre* urged a new beginning.[72] Chief Justice Burger's majority opinion, Brennan wrote, was not a "veering sharply away from the *Roth* concept," but rather simply a new "interpretation of *Roth*."[73] The *Paris Adult Theatre* decision, while ostensibly tougher on pornographers, nevertheless shares in equal degree the primary defects of the earlier decisions. First, Justice Brennan argued, these cases rely on essentially obscure formulas that fail to "provide adequate notice to persons who are engaged in the type of conduct that [obscenity statutes] could be thought to proscribe."[74] "The underlying principle," as Chief Justice Warren had written earlier, "is that no man shall be held criminally responsible for conduct which he could not reasonably understand to be proscribed."[75] No one now can predict how the Supreme Court is going to decide close obscenity cases, of which there are in principle an endless number, and the resulting uncertainty not only makes "bookselling . . . a hazardous profession,"[76] but also "invites arbitrary and erratic enforcement of the law."[77] Secondly, it creates a chilling effect on all writing that deals candidly with sexual matters, since at any point the wavering and uncertain line that separates permissible from impermissible expression may veer suddenly and leave a writer unprotected on the wrong side of the line.[78] Finally, Brennan concluded, constant need to apply obscure formulas to materials accused of obscenity imposes a severe burden on the Supreme Court amounting to a kind of "institutional strain."[79] Brennan is therefore forced to conclude that no amount of tinkering with the *Roth–Memoirs–Paris Adult Theatre* formulas will ever lead to definitions of obscenity sufficiently clear and specific to avoid these unfortunate byproducts.

How then can the Court find a new approach? Brennan suggests a strategy. "Given these inevitable side-effects of state efforts to suppress what is assumed to be *unprotected* speech, we must scrutinize with care the state interest that is asserted to justify the suppression. For in the absence of some very substantial interest in suppressing such speech, we can hardly condone the ill effects that seem to flow inevitably from the effort."[80] What is the alleged "state interest" that makes the unobtrusive and willing enjoyment of pornographic materials the state's business to control and prevent? That interest could not be the prevention of harm to persons caused by other persons, since the conduct at issue is freely consented to, and that kind of private harm is excluded by the *Volenti* maxim. It cannot be the protection of children, since there is no controversy about the state's right to prevent the dissemination of obscene materials to juveniles, and the fact that the Paris Adult Theatre had effectively excluded children from its performances had been deemed irrelevant by the Georgia Supreme Court in its ruling that was upheld by the Burger majority opinion.[81] It cannot be the prevention of offensive nuisances, since the materials in the Paris Adult Theatre had not been obtruded on unwilling witnesses nor advertised in luridly offensive ways. "The justification for the suppression must be found, therefore, in some independent interest in regulating the reading and viewing habits of consenting adults."[82]

The implicit rationale for such regulation is not hard to find, and it has been present all along in the background of *Roth* as well as *Hicklin*, in *Memoirs* as well as in *Paris Adult Theatre*. Even when some lip service is paid to the requirement of offensiveness, the ultimate appeal has been to the principle of *moralistic paternalism*. How else can we explain why the Court recognizes a state interest in proscribing pornography *as such*, even when privately and unobtrusively used by willing adults? Moralistic paternalism, however, is extremely difficult to reconcile with the Constitution, which the Court has interpreted in other cases to permit responsible adults to go to hell morally in their own way provided only they don't drag others un-willingly along with them. "In *Stanley*," writes Brennan, "we rejected as 'wholly inconsistent with the philosophy of the First Amendment' the no-tion that there is a legitimate state concern in the 'control [of] the moral content of a person's thoughts.' "[83] Brennan concludes then that there is no legitimate state concern in preventing the enjoyment of pornography as such, but that there may be valid state interests in regulating the "manner of distribution of sexually oriented materials,"[84] these being, presumably, prevention of the corruption of children, protection of captive audiences from offense, and the preservation of neighborhoods from aesthetic decay. Brennan thus ends up precisely where years earlier he could have begun: with a concept of pornography as a potential source of public nuisance subject to control by statutes that satisfy the provisions of a properly medi-ated offense principle. Where pornography is not a nuisance, and (we must now add) not a threat to the safety of women, it can be none of the state's proper business.

13

Obscene Words and their Functions, I

1. Classification of tabooed words

The word "obscene," in addition to its uses as a vehicle for expressing and/or endorsing repugnance, shock, or disgust, and (in American legal contexts) for referring to pornography, is used as a conventional label for a particular class of words. These words, which have their counterparts in virtually every human language,[1] tend to cause great offense. Obscene utterances, unlike other offensive uses of language, however, shock the listener entirely because of the particular words they employ, quite apart from any other message they may be intended to convey. By virtue of certain linguistic conventions, well understood by all users of the language, these words, simply as words, have an inherent capacity to offend and shock, and in some cases even to fill with dread and horror. Indeed one might even go so far as to say that shocking others is what these words are *for*, how they are understood to function in a language. They are able to do this job because of word-taboos that have a powerful inhibiting force in the community, but not so powerful that they are never defied. By virtue of an almost paradoxical tension between powerful taboo and universal readiness to disobey, the words acquire their strong expressive power. The utterance of one of these words for any purpose in an inappropriate social context is sure to produce, as if by magic, an extraordinary emotional response in one's listeners, most of whom treat the word with a kind of exaggerated respect, anxiety, and even fear. The magic in obscene words, and its social effects, is what this chapter is primarily about.

The difference between obscene words in a strict and narrow sense, and other merely impolite words, is one of degree, and we shall cross its boundaries often when it suits our convenience and when differences in principle are not involved. The leading naughty-to-obscene words in English can be quickly enumerated. They include religious profanities—"God," "Christ," "Damn," "Hell," and many others that are now archaic, such as "zounds," "sblood," etc., or which are profane when used "in vain" in more pious, especially Roman Catholic countries, for example the cognates in other languages for "Virgin," "Holy Mother," and the names of angels, saints, and holy places. All of the "profane words" have perfectly proper religious uses, of course, but they are impolite-to-obscene when used for unworthy purposes—swearing trivial oaths, cursing enemies, forming expletives of anger—or when employed in blasphemies. In addition to profanities, the list of obscene terms in English includes various vulgarities, most of which can be subsumed under two headings, the scatological and the sexual. In the former category are the various vulgar terms for urine, excrement, and the excreting organs, of which "piss," "shit," "crap," "turd," and "ass" are perhaps the most prominent. These are the "dirty words" in a strict or narrow sense. In a wider sense, now less common as the older attitude toward sex as "dirty" diminishes, "dirty words" also include the vulgar terms for the sex organs and the sexual act. Among the more prominent of these terms in contemporary English are "cock," "prick," "tit," "cunt," "screw," and the word that is generally thought to be the chief obscenity in the language, "fuck." A miscellany of other terms are also recognized to be usable only for impolite purposes—"bastard," and "son of a bitch," which have survived as terms of abuse long after the taboos and attitudes that gave them their initial shock value have receded; "fairy," "faggot," and other terms for homosexuals; "red," "Commie," "Facist" and similar terms for hated political ideologies, which come to be used indiscriminately in epithets of political opprobrium; "Nigger," "Kike," "Dago" and similarly contemptuous labels for ethnic groups, and still others.

The class of words that are either obscene, totally disreputable, or naughty enough to be forbidden is thus surprisingly diverse and heterogeneous. The class is wide enough, as we have seen, to include sexual vulgarities (which are probably still the most offensive terms as a group), other "dirty words," political labels, ethnic slurs, terms whose whole function is to insult, and religious blasphemies and other profanities. In addition there are merely "naughty words" that are weakened or watered down obscenities. There is a great danger in lumping all these words together as if they all had the same sources and functions, for one might easily extend a point that applies to one subgroup to cover all the others. It will be better to classify the terms and trace the origin of each type independently, and thus avoid the danger of embracing simplistic half-truths. The most cónvenient classification of obscene-to-naughty words and phrases has already been suggested. It divides them into two main categories: profanities and vulgarities. The profanities in turn can be subdivided into blasphemies, vain swearings, and curses, and the vulgarities into scatological, sexual, and "other" subclasses. Admittedly, the line between the two main genera of forbidden words is often blurred. Some obscene vulgarities may shock in the manner of desecrations even though they employ no "profane words," and some profanities when uttered on inappropriate occasions may seem "obscene" in the sense of "revolting" and "disgustworthy." When profanity and obscenity are combined in the same utterance the effect is often vastly multiplied, as for example when one shouts scatological or sexual obscenities in a sacred shrine as insults addressed to God, and thus in one exclamation manages to be super-profane and super-obscene. In such combined expletives, the greater the obscenity the more severe is the profanity and vice-versa.[2] Nevertheless, profanity and vulgarity have different origins and characteristically offend in different ways. Let us consider the leading species.

2. Profanities

The profane words have at least three characteristic functions apart from their licit uses in prayer, religious ceremony, theological discourse, and so on. The tabooed uses are to blaspheme, to swear, and to curse.

Blasphemies. In its widest sense, a blasphemy is any irreverence shown toward anything that is regarded as sacred. Apparently the word originally referred only to the ultimate shocker: cursing or reviling God. But in the more common derivative sense, a blasphemy need not be a cursing or reviling, and in this wider usage, it need not be restricted to disrespect to God. When the deity is the object of blasphemy, the blasphemous expression can be *any* "indignity offered to God in words, writing, or signs, such as speaking evil of God, also the act of claiming the attributes or prerogatives of God."[3] Thus the utterances "God is cruel," "God is an Englishman," and "I am God," are blasphemous in most contexts, as are inappropriately familiar references, such as "J. C.," "Big Daddy," and "Holy Spook." It is rude to be overly familiar with anyone, and to be presumptuous with a deity is the ultimate in bad manners. In some traditions, as we shall see, it is blasphemous even to mention the (true) name of the deity, much less to use it in an offhand, familiar, or derisive fashion.

The concept of the *sacred* is clearly the basic idea underlying our conception of a blasphemy. In a strict sense corresponding to its original uses, the sacred is the holy, and the deity Himself is the one truly sacred thing. Now the word is more commonly used in a somewhat broader sense to refer to anything "hallowed by association with the divine, the consecrated, or the like; worthy of religious veneration, as in 'the sacred name of Jesus' or 'Jerusalem's sacred soil,' hence *entitled to reverence and respect*, venerable, as in 'old age is sacred' or 'a sacred memory.' "⁴ In a looser sense still, the sacred is any object, religious or not, that is thought to be entitled to the highest respect, as when one speaks of "the sacred memory of my mother," "the sacred soil of the fatherland," or "the sacred mission of science." Whatever else the sacred is, it is no laughing matter. The sacred is something not to be joked about or treated lightly, something beyond mockery, presumption, and indignity. Something or other is sacred, in this sense, to almost everyone, atheists and theists alike. The person to whom nothing at all is sacred is the person who can laugh at anything—the sufferings of children, the victims of genocide, and libels on his loved ones, as well as mockery of his gods.

It is because most people hold some things to be sacred, in the broad sense at least, that blasphemous epithets and other conventional expressions of disrespect can be so powerfully offensive, and so effective as insults, exclamations, oaths, and the like. Most of the conventional blasphemies in English are anemic survivals from a day when people believed in eternal punishment and were genuinely terrified by their own sins. Blasphemous utterances then were not mere habitual devices for speaking with emphasis, as they have since become. Rather they were electric with danger, emotionally charged and crackling with magic. In devout countries, the language of blasphemy is still powerfully expressive. The narrator in Ernest Hemingway's *For Whom the Bell Tolls* wisely observes:

> There is no language as filthy as Spanish. There are words for all the vile words in English and there are other words and expressions that are used only in countries where blasphemy keeps pace with the austerity of religion. Lieutenant Berrendo was a very devout Catholic. So was the sniper. They were Carlists from Navarra and while both of them cursed and blasphemed when they were angry, they regarded it as a sin which they regularly confessed.⁵

Where religious doctrines have lost much of their hold on the masses, the sacrilegious terms survive but they don't frighten and they don't offend. The blasphemous insult says in effect, "I mock and deride whatever you think is holy," but if the recipient of the insult does not hold sacred the objects explicitly mentioned in the malediction, then no extreme offense is caused and the utterance falls flat. The Spanish soldiers in Hemingway's novel are forever spitting (or worse) on the memory (or in the milk!) of one another's mothers, or charging one another's mothers with whoredom (or worse), or blaspheming one another's hallowed shrines; and what could be more emphatic to a Spaniard than a blasphemous oath?

> "Listen," Andres said. "I am alone. I am completely by myself. I obscenity [expletive deleted] in the midst of the holy mysteries that I am alone. Let me come in."
> "He speaks like a Christian," he heard someone say and laugh."[6]

It does not exhaust the meaning of blasphemous utterances, however, to point out that they offend by expressing disrespect or contempt for something (anything) that the listener might hold sacred. "Your mother was a whore" is not the paradigm blasphemy, shocking and enraging as it might be. The original blasphemies, in an earlier time when religion was "austere," did more than merely offend, as any vulgar insult might offend. The penalty for blasphemy in biblical times, after all, was death by stoning, which suggests that the punished words were thought to be not merely offensive but dangerous to the collective interest or positively *harmful* in themselves. A solemn interdiction had been laid upon sacred words when used for the purpose (or with the effect) of blasphemy, and disobedience threatened the whole community with divine vengeance. For that reason, blasphemy was not merely offensive but *dreadful*, that is, likely to be accompanied in the speaker's mind, and to arouse in all listeners, a great dread of awful consequences. The dread sticks to the offending words themselves, whatever the intention that accompanies their use, whether they be used innocently or perversely, whether they be used or merely mentioned, whether the listener has the appropriate beliefs or not. (What convinced atheist can say "May God strike me dead" without at least one extra palpitation of the heart?) In a believing age the blasphemous expressions were dangerous magical instruments to be handled with the care our age reserves for explosives.

Many writers, impressed by the verbal magic of blasphemy, its capacity to evoke dread, and the sternness of its punishment in an earlier day, trace its force to ancient "name-taboos." The term "taboo" is a word in the language of a Polynesian tribe, the Tongas, for stringent prohibitions of certain actions, possessions, or words that are perceived to be threats to the safety of the community, and for the isolation of spiritual pollutors or those especially vulnerable to sorcery or contamination. "Taboos may be designed to prevent 'pollution', as in prohibition of the use of certain foods, or . . . touching a corpse, or to secure certain privileges or properties, as when a field is secured against trespass. The taboo is commonly imposed by chiefs and priests, and among the Polynesians is indicated by a sign or mark,"[7] as when the house of a dead chief, for example, is marked with the sign of taboo. Sir James Frazer in his classic work *The Golden Bough*[8] found analogues to the Polynesian systems of taboos in cultures all over the world, and survivals of taboos and their supporting belief-systems even in modern Europe. Each person in a primitive tribe feels himself constantly threatened not only by the visible dangers in nature, but by evil spirits who may be malevolent, capricious, or vindictive. The tribe itself is even more endangered by threats to the safety of its chief or king who must therefore be protected by even more stringent safeguards. Hence a king is often secluded, and his subjects prevented from entering his presence or touching him. This will protect him, and the whole community that depends on him, from baneful influences, black magic, and spiritually tainted atmospheres. Strangers especially are a source of evil magic and contamination, threatening not only kings but all subjects. Contacts with strangers can be survived only if purificatory ceremonies are held promptly. Eating and drinking are always dangerous, since "at these times the soul may escape from the mouth, or be extracted by the magic arts of an enemy present."[9] An elaborate system of taboos on various objects and methods of eating, and special rituals of spiritual decontamination are therefore required for everyone's safety, and especially for that of the king, who in some tribes may not even be seen, by anyone, eating or drinking. Not only are kings tabooed (for their own good and the public safety) and strangers too, but also mourners for a period after the death of a close relative, warriors after their return from lethal combat, other man-slayers, hunters and fishermen after a kill, and women during menstruation and at childbirth.

Moreover, the personal possessions and garments of tabooed persons are considered unclean or polluted, and therefore untouchable. The possessions of a king cannot be touched because they are *sacred*, while the materials of other tabooed persons are untouchable because they are *polluted*, but the operation and effect of the taboo is the same in both cases, and the common aim is to prevent fatal mischief from evil spirits.[10]

Frazer lays great emphasis on the point that there are two main classes of tabooed persons and things:

> Thus in primitive society the rules of ceremonial purity observed by divine kings, chiefs, and priests agree in many respects with the rules observed by homicides, mourners, women in childbed, girls at puberty, hunters and fishermen, and so on. To us these various classes of persons appear to differ totally in character and condition; some of them we should call holy, others we might

pronounce unclean and polluted [morally speaking]. But the savage makes no
such moral distinction between them; the conceptions of holiness and pollution
are not yet differentiated in his mind. To him the common feature of all these
persons is that they are dangerous and in danger, and the danger in which they
stand and to which they expose others is what we should call spiritual or
ghostly, and therefore imaginary . . . Taboos act, so to say, as electrical insula-
tors to preserve the spiritual force with which these persons are charged from
suffering or inflicting harm by contact with the outer world.[11]

Kings, priests, and chiefs are holy persons who must be protected from the
contamination or deliberate sorcery of others, whereas mourners, hunters,
menstruating women, and the rest are spiritual contaminators from whom
all of the rest of us must be protected.

Still another universal superstition traces the etiology of spiritual pollution not only to persons and things but to bare words, particularly personal
names. Words have an independent causal potency in the world; their bare
utterance in some contexts can contaminate, wound, or damn. And just as
one can harm a person from a distance by sticking pins through a doll that
bears his image, so can one harm a person by doing things to his name,
which is another kind of "image."

Unable to discriminate clearly between words and things, the savage commonly fancies that the link between a name and the person or thing denominated by it is not a mere arbitrary and ideal association, but a real and substantial bond which unites the two in such a way that magic may be wrought on a
man just as easily through his name as through his hair or any other material
part of his person. In fact, primitive man regards his name as a vital portion of
himself and takes care of it accordingly.[12]

Frazer gives an abundance of examples from all over the world of the
primitive conception of a name as a literal part of oneself, and of name-
taboos designed to protect ordinary persons from evil magic performed on
their names. "Every Egyptian received two names, which were known
respectively as the true name and the good name, or the great name and the
little name; and while the good or the little name was made public, the true
or great name appears to have been carefully concealed."[13] The secondary
names were thought not to be a literal part of the person himself, so they
could be freely divulged and commonly used both in personal address and
in third person reference without danger to their possessor's safety. The
primary names, on the other hand, were kept deep secrets. In many tribes
names of close blood relations were also tabooed. Close relatives "are often
forbidden, not only to pronounce each other's names, but even to utter
ordinary words which resemble or have a single syllable in common with
these names."[14] One can't be too careful! Finally, the names of the dead
(who as deceased persons are now sensitive spirits quick to avenge affronts)

are especially dangerous and must also be tabooed. "Among the aborigines of Victoria the dead were rarely spoken of and then never by their names; they were referred to in a subdued voice as 'the lost one' or 'the poor fellow that is no more'."[15] Such taboos, it can be imagined, did not contribute much to the keeping of accurate historical records.[16]

The ubiquitous taboos that banned mention of the names of kings and other sacred persons, and even the names of the gods, had precisely the same purpose, according to Frazer, as those that forbade mention of the "true names" of ordinary persons. Even greater precautions must be taken, however, to protect kings and sacred priests from misuses of their names, since harm to such important persons affected the whole tribal community, its practices, and its institutions.

Let a sorcerer get hold of the name of a king, and a whole people might be ruined. Gods, in turn, are thought to be super-kings with no immunity to word sorcery. "Hence just as the furtive savage conceals his real name because he fears that sorcerers might make an evil use of it, so he fancies that his gods must likewise keep their true name secret, lest other gods or even men should learn the mystic sounds and thus be able to conjure with them."[17] It would surely be rash to attribute such motivation to the biblical Hebrews for their elaborate taboo on the mention of the "incommunicable name" of the Supreme Being. But the unmentionability of divine names was an ancient taboo in the Near East and there might well have been some acculturation from the practices of the Egyptians with whom the Hebrews were all too well acquainted. More likely, Frazer's explanation misses the mark when applied to the monotheistic Jews whose motive may have been closer to one we discussed earlier, namely a desire not to offend the Almighty Himself by affecting an unwarranted familiarity with Him. If it would be presumptuous to address a mighty human king as (say) "George," it would be downright insolent to address an infinite being by his true name at all. And in any case, when one deals with so awesome a thing as the name (a kind of detachable and controllable part) of an infinite being, one does not wish to take any chances. The best way to handle it with care is not to handle it at all. One cannot but tremble with awe in its presence.

There are then two different ways in which blasphemy (and something very much like blasphemy) can offend. Expressions of disrespect toward something treasured by the listener as deserving of the highest respect offend by debasing personal values and ideals. This kind of "blasphemy" however does not directly require that any specific *word* be used. "Your late mother was a prostitute," and "I spit on the soil of Jerusalem" do not use any profane words. The other kind of blasphemy requires the use—even the mere *mention* will do—of forbidden words, and offends in large measure because it uses those words. For this kind of blasphemy an explanatory account in terms of name-taboos and word magic is probably required. For blasphemous utterances of this kind to be powerfully expressive, the words in which they are uttered must be so charged with terror that their very utterance for a light or unworthy purpose should evoke fear and trembling. Today one can still be impious or irreverent—disrespectful in one's talk of what is "entitled to reverence"—but the linkage of disrespect to specific marks and sounds is now much weaker. Our profane words, having literally lost their supposed magic, survive as "mere explosive noises" that are used habitually, absentmindedly, and without passion. Many commentators have regretted this development as a decline in the expressiveness of our language, and one of these writers adds (not very hopefully) that "Whenever and wherever good people agree to clothe certain names and terms in sanctity and set them apart as too holy for common use, they are making some swearwords for their neighbors."[18]

Vain swearings. One of the major personal problems in previous ages was deciding when to believe the assertions and accept the promises of others when mendacity was rife and one's own important interests were at stake. Equally difficult was the correlative task of convincing others that one is telling the truth and means what one says. One very useful device was to put up collateral. "Here you may take this calf, or this horse, or this piece of gold, and hold it in reserve during the period of my promised performance, and if it should turn out that I am lying, and that I do not do what I hereby promise, my possession will be forfeited to you. That way you are protected against the possibility of my dishonesty and I am motivated by the fear of personal loss to keep my word." That might be all very well to reassure the promisee, but what will guarantee the promiser that the promisee will not run off with his collateral? Perhaps a third party can be trusted to hold the forfeitable possessions, in escrow so to speak, until the promise is discharged. But the problem of guaranteeing the trustworthiness of the third party then arises. Sooner or later powerful governments were instituted among men, and the power of the state could be invoked to guarantee loans, enforce agreements, and sanction contracts. Until state offices took on such functions, individual bargainers and testifiers somehow had to rely on words to create trust all by themselves. Those early days in the infancy of political power and large-scale commerce saw the flowering of the art of swearing the "oath asseverative."

The first element in a sworn oath is the *solemn vow* which gives an otherwise casual remark or weak statement of intention a formal dress and a special status. Then comes the citing of *witnesses*. "I solemnly vow that if

you help me harvest my crops next week then I shall help you harvest
yours the week after, and in witness thereof I call upon all those who are
herewith gathered . . ." That means that I cannot subsequently deny that I
made the promise if I should fail to perform. The third element is a *swearing
to forfeit* some treasured possession in case of nonperformance. This is the
part that calls for eloquence and ingenuity. The oath to help with the crops,
if it were elegant, might continue in such fashion as this: "I swear by the
faith of all those who love me which shall be forfeit if I am foresworn. I
swear by the loyalty of my wife; may her confidence in me be forever
forfeit if I break this oath. If I lie now, may some terrible misfortune befall
my children, etc., etc."

The fourth and final element is the *invocation of a sanctioning power or
authority* who will enforce the forfeiture if the vow is broken. According to
Burgess Johnson, primitive man "made his first attempt to bolster up his
own word by loudly inviting the forces of nature to punish him if he had
slipped from the truth. A little later on he invoked magic which was much
the same thing, because there was magic behind the flood and the lightning,
the landslide and the falling tree."[19] And then as time went on, Johnson
speculates

> . . . if he found that Mr. and Mrs. Bab in the next cave began to eye him
> skeptically when he told them about the fish which had got away, he not only
> invited the hanging rock to fall upon him in case he lied, but touched it with
> his finger as a sort of challenge, which somehow strengthened his case, and the
> neighbors listened with greater credence. If he said he hoped he might grow
> blind if he had stretched the truth and touched his eyes at the moment of
> speaking, or if he invited death by violence and laid his hand upon a spear or a
> dagger, his word was trusted even more. At long last he called upon the gods.
> Lars Porsena [the Etruscan King] had to call upon nine of them, which does
> not speak well for his reputation among his neighbors.[20]

To animistic primitive people who believed in the magic of the word and
gesture, it was hardly necessary to call upon the gods as sanctioning authorities. No one in his right mind would tempt fate even so much as to
appeal to hanging rocks, if he were not speaking the truth.

In time, the imagination of man spun so many variations on the four
stock elements of the oath that some poetic souls took to swearing to no
practical purpose.[21] In particular, the witnesses, the forfeits, and the sanctioning forces were subject to imaginative articulation. "As God is my
witness," "As the heavens are my witness," "I swear before all the stars in
heaven," "I swear before all the angels and saints," and so on. This part of
the oath is swearing *to* or swearing *before*, and there is in principle no limit
to the objects of these prepositions. Forfeitures too are rich in poetic ramifi-

cations: "I cross my heart and hope to die," and "May God blind me" (the origin of the threadbare British epithet "Blimey") are commonplace. Homer did much better than that:

> Zeus, most glorious, greatest, and all ye other immortals Whiche'er first of the folk does violence unto the pledges, So may their brains be poured out here on the earth, as the wine is, Theirs and their children's as well—their wives be slaves unto others.[22]

Swearing *on* or *by* is sometimes a reference to sanctioning force ("I swear on this alter," "I swear by God") but more often a reference to promised forfeiture. The ancient Roman youth swore *by* his virility, promising to forfeit his testes if he lied. (Hence the derivation of the word "testify," "testimony," "testament.")

Under the impetus of colorful language, promised forfeitures evolved into declared logical consequences: "If what I say is false, then my name is not John Doe and fish have wings." (Since my name *is* John Doe, and fish manifestly do *not* have wings, it follows that I speak truly). The mechanism of the transition was straightforward enough. The earlier oaths said in effect: "If I speak falsely may some dreadful thing befall me. I could not want the dreadful thing, therefore I could not speak falsely." It was a small extension of this way of speaking to swear that "If I speak falsely then some dreadful falsehood about me is in fact true, and since I could not want it to be true, I could not speak falsely." Thus, "As I am a gentleman and a scholar, I swear that . . ." (in effect making forfeit a true and valued description), "What I say is true or my mother is a whore," "I'm a dog if I do," or "I'm a Jew else" (said in Shakespeare's *Henry IV*).

The art of swearing was no doubt well enough developed before the rise of the great world religions, but it was given a great new impetus when people could invoke gods as sanctioning authorities. Religious sites, shrines, relics, and sacred objects were new and effective things to "swear on," and gods were not mere enforcing powers, they were authoritative persons, like fathers and kings. Johnson traces the transition to religious oaths:

> Long after men had begun to pray to their gods, in their oaths they continued to swear "on" or "by" some visible person or thing which was powerful or dangerous or deemed magical. Such an oath, sworn on a tiger skin, invited death by a tiger in case of falsehood; or if on an anthill it implied a similar invitation to the ants. A man swore "by" anything which had power to harm him.

> The first man to swear by his gods must have created quite a sensation. A little later he strengthened his oath by touching an image of the god or one of that god's possessions and inviting the god to injure him if he swore falsely. Finally,

in medieval times, so little respect came to be felt for a simple oath uttered in the name of a god or saint that no formal oath was really binding unless the swearer at the same time touched a relic or other sacred object.[23]

Invoking the religious sanction to enforce promises and guarantee truthfulness was the final culmination of a development that had relied on word-magic at every previous stage. Spirits who reside in hanging rocks, anthills, and tiger skins can be manipulated by mere linguistic means to inflict punishment on liars and false promisers. Nature itself can be thrown out of joint by false vows and spring back with violence on the malefactor. These procedures, of course, are all magic, no matter how you slice them. Nature in fact obeys its own laws and stands aloof from the games people play, and there are no lingering "spirits" about at all. From the point of view of a more sophisticated (monotheistic) religious believer it is impious in the extreme to attempt to use the deity for the same purposes as those for which primitive man had always used natural objects and the spirits of animals. After all, God is not just another kind of tiger skin or anthill. And from the presumed point of view of the Supreme Being himself, attempts to manipulate Him for every trivial human purpose, just as if He were some magical talisman rather than an infinite person with His own free will, are utterly comtemptible. "I'll be damned if I don't," says the false swearer, but that does not *make* God damn him as though his very words had a magical potency to which even God is subject. God can damn whom He chooses; His judgments are not simply automatic movements of humanly constructed magical machinery. How could anyone think that a Supreme Being could be so easily bound by words and actions that are not His own? Who does the swearer think he is?

Swearing by God or by His sacred symbols then has been thought to be a kind of blasphemy, not in the sense of uttering unmentionable names and thereby unleashing fearsome forces (the magic sense), but in the sense of being disrespectful, presumptuous, even insolent to that which is entitled to reverence, of dealing lightly with what is sacred. Underlying that judgment is the whole history of oath-swearing with its essential elements of verbal magic and the absurd presumption that a person can make terrible things happen in nature simply by uttering certain words in the wrong frame of mind. So long as one's vows serve one's private interests alone, then swearing by God is a kind of profanity. But God is generally thought to be a willing party to certain grand public vows made for large public purposes. The "sacred oath" which mutually independent tribes substituted for the exchange of hostages as sanctions for treaties has been one such exception; the oath of office (sworn in the U.S. on a holy bible) is one that survives to this day. Swearing in these cases is not thought to be using the Lord's name in vain.

Curses. The "oath denunciatory" is a form of language older than swearing and even more essentially related to magic. We can imagine that one of the first uses to which man put words, when words were presumably little more than grunts and snarls, was to hurl them like missiles at their enemies. Burgess Johnson tells us that to this day primitive tribesmen "cringe and leap aside" when their neighbors fling curse words at one another, and all who stand between the curser and his target "duck their heads so that the words might fly harmlessly over."[24] There is little doubt that our primitive ancestors did not clearly distinguish between words as mere symbolic expressions of evil wishes and as real weapons that could inflict harm all by themselves on those who are "hit" by them, even on innocent bystanders who are unintended objects of harm. Johnson describes the belief of Irish folklore that a curse, once uttered and released on its flight, must land somewhere. If it misses its target it may float in the air for seven years before lighting on its intended victim, or it may become a "wandering curse" and follow its victim in the form of an evil temptation or an illness. In many tribes it was believed that a verbal missile that hits no human target would boomerang and return to the person who launched it, inflicting its harm on him.

For such reasons primitive people learned to aim their curses with great care. Curses were often accompanied by pointing gestures. Also,

> They became more effective if the evil-wisher could touch the person of his foe; and if he lacked the reach or the courage to do that, he might still add to the force of his wish if he touched one of his enemy's intimate possessions, and ever since the shadowy Pleistocene years man has directed an evil wish by touching his thumb to his own projecting nose, and pointing with all outstretched fingers toward his enemy.[25]

The most feared curse-aiming device in all history has been the baleful glower or "evil eye" which has been thought in almost all human societies to be a magical gift of certain evil persons. Spitting toward the foe was also effective for "spittle carried the venom of the curse."[26]

The earliest curses, like the earliest oaths, invoked no gods. Evil wishes, if expressed and aimed in the right way, were a potent enough magic even without divine help. "May you go blind," "May you perish," and "The plague take you" must have been typical examples. But once theology had been invented, the vocabulary of cursing was immensely enriched and enemies could be damned, consigned to hell, subjected to the sadism of the devil or the power of the Almighty. Johnson reminds us of the eloquent example of high-powered cursing provided by Jehovah in the Old Testament in his angry remarks to Adam, Eve, the serpent, and Cain, among others. By the seventeenth century the art of cursing derived from biblical models was so highly developed that it needed no evil eye, spittle, or other props, to do its job. The famous excommunication of Spinoza by the elders of the synagogue of Amsterdam in 1656 is a case in point:

> By the sentence of the angels, by the decree of the saints, we anathematize, cut off, curse and execrate Baruch Spinoza, in the presence of these sacred books with the six hundred and thirteen precepts which are written therein, with the anathema wherewith Joshua anathematized Jericho; with the cursing wherewith Elisha cursed the children; and with all the cursings which are written in the Book of the Law; cursed be he by day, and cursed by night; cursed when he lieth down, and cursed when he riseth up; cursed when he goeth out, and cursed when he cometh in; the Lord pardon him never; the wrath and fury of the Lord burn upon this man, and bring upon him all the curses which are written in the Book of the Law. The Lord blot out his name under Heaven. The Lord set him apart for destruction from all the tribes of Israel, with the curses of the firmament which are written in the Book of the Law. There shall no man speak to him, no man write to him, no man show him any kindness, no man stay under the same roof with him, no man come nigh him.[27]

A formal and official excommunication is no mere trivial personal thing, and received doctrine denies that it is a taking of the Lord's name in vain. Indeed it is to cursing what an oath of office is to swearing. But ecclesiastical authority does not permit private enterprise in the business of cursing or swearing. Again the primary explanation for this prohibition is that invoking God in a curse (as in an oath) is a presumptuous and disrespectful use of His name. God will punish whom He pleases as an exercise of His own free will, not as an automatic response to the bidding of human enemies employing verbal magic. Just as in the case of swearing, however, there is another explanation for the fearsome dreadfulness that once attended curses but does no more. Cursing as a traditional human activity has always been intimately connected with superstitious beliefs in word magic, and as those beliefs have declined in our time (without altogether disappearing), the expressiveness of curses has diminished apace. We no longer believe that we can be blinded merely by the use of words, no matter what the words are, even when they are accompanied by baleful glowers, spitting, pointing, or touching, and even when they invoke the name of God. We believe that simple curses as such are *harmless* no matter how much they may offend as profanities. That belief is very new in human history.

Johnson suggests still another source of the traditional shock value of curses using theological language. In primitive tribes the gods are thought of in human terms and thought to have no special immunity to sorcery, black magic, or the verbal magic of curses. We have seen already how that conception helps explain the primitive origins of the fear of blasphemy in a pre-monotheistic age. Similarly, there has always been an uneasiness at language that curses by invoking a god since it reminds one of the alarming thought that gods can be cursed too. No curse has been thought to be more virulent than that of a dying man, and respect for that potency, according to Johnson, is behind the ancient practice of providing "sanctuary" in a holy place, a custom that is far older than Christianity.

> A fugitive was safe in a temple, not because his death there would profane so holy a place, but because in the temple he was a god's guest, and his dying curse would harm a god, so that diety protected him as long as he remained. What might happen to him afterwards was unimportant.[28]

In summary, the shock value of profane words in the past has essentially depended on implicit beliefs in word magic—sorcery, verbal manipulations of nature, or the efficacy of words and gestures as weapons. It was because of such beliefs among pre-monotheistic peoples, that profane words were strictly *tabooed* in the first place, and because of the taboos that their use could evoke shock and dread. Loss of the expressive force of profanity in our own age is largely a consequence of the decline in the belief in verbal magic (though word superstition still lingers in the viscera even of the enlightened).[29] "Profanity" can still offend the pious, at least in its extreme form, when it is understood really to *profane*, that is to express disrespect for something deemed worthy of the highest honor or reverence. But this form of offensiveness no longer has any essential connection with the use of any particular forbidden words. Most uses of so-called profane words are understood by listeners to have neither the intent nor the effect of genuine profanation. ("I'll be damned if it isn't Charley Brown!," said in surprised and joyful greeting, expresses disrespect for no one.) And those profane expressions which are genuinely disrespectful are so for reasons other than that they contain "profane words." It is in fact possible to be blasphemous without using a single profane word as when one says "Your deity is cruel and treacherous; I dispise him and believe that he should be defied." Nevertheless the conventionally profane words are still useful for providing emphasis and for other expressive purposes. "I'll be damned if it's not Charley Brown!" is more emphatic than "Charley Brown, what a pleasant surprise!" One might argue that profane words are more emphatic simply because they are the terms in the language that are understood to provide emphasis. Some terms must be assigned that job, after all, and prevailing "linguistic conventions" make the assignment to these words. But what needs explaining is why just *these* words are the ones to which the assignment is made. And the answer to that question must be that these words still carry the aura of social disapproval inherited from an earlier day when they were explicitly condemned by moral (and not merely "linguistic") rules, and an earlier day still, when fear of word magic made them unconditionally tabooed.

3. Vulgarities

There is no need here to make as thorough a survey of the various species of vulgar words as we did for the subclasses of profanities. For the most part there is very little mystery about why the vulgarities offend, and the connection between them and ancient traditions of verbal magic is much less direct. The scatalogical terms are the least problematic class. Such words as "shit," "crap," and "ass" are very expressive and very widely used, though of course not in polite company or in formal discourse (e.g., a political speech, a sermon, or a commencement address). To use them in formal contexts would be like wearing overalls or a bathing suit to a formal dinner. Everybody who understands the language knows that that is simply not done. Precisely because they are forbidden in formal and polite contexts, they are powerfully expressive in informal contexts. Indeed, for a laborer at his workbench to say "alas, what a disappointment", or "I find myself in disagreement," or "I am indifferent," when he could say "oh, shit!," or "That's a pile of shit," or "I don't give a shit one way or the other," would be almost as much of a solecism as wearing a tuxedo or a formal gown to a picnic lunch in the park. One need not go far afield to discover why the scatalogical terms are proscribed in polite contexts by rules of etiquette. They are out of favor there because of the natural response to their literal referents, the processes and products of bodily elimination. Urine and feces are dirty, smelly, disgusting, unclean things. All civilization rests on our ability to dispose of bodily waste products and prevent stench and filth, thus infestations of vermin, and the epidemics and plagues that come with their accumulation. Control of the excretory organs is the first moral lesson taught infants and the most powerful inhibition implanted in them. No wonder the symbols for excreta are used to evoke something like the revulsion with which we respond to the real thing. Reference to the real thing is sometimes a necessary part of serious discourse, however, and when that is so we invent playful euphemisms for children like "peepee" or "poop," or resort to the sober scientific vocabulary of "bowels," "rectum," "feces," "urine" and the like.

There is a certain clarity then in our understanding of how scatological vulgarities work and how they offend. One is naturally tempted, therefore, to use the scatalogical terms as models for understanding the sexual vulgarities, and to think of them as one undifferentiated collection of "dirty words," all offensive for the same sort of reason. That is the mistake made by Edward Sagarin in his groundbreaking and otherwise excellent book, *The Anatomy of Dirty Words.*[30] Following the lead of Benjamin Lee Whorf and other anthropologists, Sagarin is rightly impressed by the way language generally follows cultural attitudes and then turns around, so to speak, and reinforces those attitudes. He is equally impressed by what he takes to be the "anti-biological bias" of the attitudes expressed in the obscene parts of our vocabulary. "There is no explanation," he writes, "for the appropriation of the biological dirty words for nonbiological negative qualities other than the simple and apparent one: the processes, the parts of the body, and the products are looked down upon, and therefore the improper language can properly be used only for other characteristics and persons held in low esteem."[31] Here Sagarin lumps scatological and sexual vulgarities together as "biological dirty words"; he assumes that the general attitude toward sex is not significantly different from that toward excretion (both are "dirty"); and he claims that it is equally irrational to think of the products of excretion as dirty as to think of the processes of sex as dirty. He misses the mark in all three contentions. Very few people these days still think of penises, vaginas, and acts of coitus as dirty. Surely those who are most prone to use sexual vulgarities are themselves the least likely to think of sex as filthy or disgusting. In fact they are more likely than others to pursue sex relentlessly and promiscuously. Nobody pursues excreta relentlessly and promiscuously! That is because excreta are smelly, dirty, and disgusting. If that is a mere "cultural prejudice," it is an extremely useful one for purposes of public hygiene. In fact it is no mere prejudice at all but a rational judgment supported as we have seen by the best reasons. Sagarin is right when he judges that the puritanical attitude toward sex is irrational, but because he wrongly lumps it together with the universal attitude toward exreta, he is forced to judge the latter as irrational too.

Sagarin's error is not a gross one. There have been many and still are some who think of sex in terms similar to those in which most of us think of stinking filth, and Sagarin is able to appeal to some prima facie evidence for his assimilation of the two chief forms of vulgarity. He refers to the expression "I don't give a shit," for example, and finds that it means roughly "I just don't care a hoot." He then continues—

> The same expression is used with the word "fuck": "I don't give a fuck." The parent of both of these expressions is probably "I don't give a damn" coming from the slang expression for "tinker's damn (or dam)" which was synonomous

with "worthless." In the two modern versions, the same expressions are used, with the epitome of worthlessness being found in the product of excretion and the act of sexuality.[32]

Surely there must be a better explanation for the phrase "I don't give a fuck" than that. It taxes credulity to think of the millions of youths in army barracks, factories, and lumber camps, who are the leading users of sexual vulgarities, as persons who regard the "act of sexuality" as "the epitome of worthlessness"! Think of the soldiers in army barracks who distribute the sexual vulgarities liberally through all their conversation, as others might sprinkle salt on their boiled potatoes. Does this express their "contempt of sex and all things biological?" Nothing could be further from the truth. These lusty cursers are for the most part young men living in an artificial isolation. Most of them have no regular contact with women. They are often sex-starved, and always sex-obsessed. Their typical constant use of the word "fuck" and its forms ("fucking" is the chief intensifier in their language, an adjective that can modify any noun, and even fit in between the syllables of individual words) is a way of defanging, defusing, taming their lusts and obsessions, of controlling the fearsome thing by fearlessly using the word for the thing. Everyone uses the obscene terms habitually when only other soldiers are present, for in numbers there is a kind of strength, and a kind of harmless bravado. "The extremely obscene remark or joke," writes Peter Farb, "which is often signaled by an unusually gross and obscene vocabulary, often hides by means of laughter the speaker's anxiety about certain taboo themes in his personality or his culture."[33] In our culture most young people are anxious about their sex lives. Obscene words not only "hide" that anxiety, they fight and deny it.

It is precisely the prohibition against use of the sexual vulgarities in polite society (often loosely called a "taboo") that makes a word like "fuck" so powerfully expressive, not the association to its literal biological reference. Or, to put the point differently, it is the many "taboos" that govern sexual conduct itself that make the vulgar words that refer to it so shocking, not an antecedent attitude toward sex as dirty or disgusting. It has always been in the highest interests of society to control the powerful sexual drives of its members and thereby keep lines of descendance and inheritance clear, families well defined, the births of infants who cannot be cared for prevented, and epidemics of venereal disease averted. Those social interests are at least as powerful as those that are served by regulating human waste disposal. But whereas the taboos regulating excretion are securely internalized in all adults and firmly in control of wayward impulses, the taboos governing sexual behavior are in constant conflict with sexual drives that will not be repressed once and for all. The tension between drive and inhibition is always in the background of consciousness, causing in many young people a turmoil of anxiety. In times of weakening norms and changing expectations, that underlying anxiety is intensified by uncertainty and the general fear of making a fool of oneself. The compound of low self-confidence, uncertainty about the rules, threatened pride, and tension between wish and taboo can be a torment for the exorcism of which obscene words are often useful. It is this whole background that gives a word like "fuckin" its great expressive power as an intensifier, not its role, as Sagarin puts it, in "the internalization of the negative attitude toward all things sexual."[34] If there is a "negative" or hostile attitude expressed in the young male's habitual use of sexual obscenities, the target is *certainly* not sexual behavior as such, put probably rather *women*, who become sour-grape objects of scorn and scapegoat objects of resentment.[35]

4. Derivative uses of obscenity (A): vulgar reference

The primary use of naughty-to-obscene words is to shock, offend, or disgust persons. Only by virtue of their essential capacity to cause offense, can these words serve various useful purposes. The first of these is to make reference, albeit in a vulgar way, to the excretory and sexual activities, objects, and organs. The exclamation "Oh, shit!" doesn't *refer* to anything; its sole function is to blow off steam. "That's a pile of shit!," said of some previously affirmed proposition, does not make a direct reference to feces; rather it employs an analogy or metaphor to discredit something which is not literally excrement. But in the expressions "I am going to take a shit" or "Clean up that pile of dog shit," the vulgar term simply substitutes for the non-vulgar terms "defecate" and "feces" and refers to precisely the same activity and object. Vulgar terms thus provide an alternative vocabulary for describing or referring to things for which we already have neutral antiseptic words.

How useful is it to have such an alternative vocabulary? Apparently most speakers of our language find the vulgar terms useful to the point of indispensability. They are known and understood by all native speakers, even those who would never dare use them. "In some instances," Sagarin claims, "these words are unquestionably the sole vocabulary that many people have at their command to describe the processes [of sex and excretion]."[36]

> The medical terms, the clumsy phrases, and the euphemisms are all inadequate for everyday speech. They cannot suffice for unstilted conversation among people, for a free communication of thought, or even for the inward

thought processes in which one verbalizes to oneself. Simple words are required, and if they were not available (as once they were not) they would have
to be invented.[37]

Sagarin's point is sound but he probably has his historical order reversed.
Very likely the simple "four-letter words" were once the plain and home-
spun vocabulary of the masses and wholly inoffensive in their everyday use.
Only later did they fall into disfavor, and get replaced by evasive euphemisms and complex latinate technical terms. It is not probable that thirteenth
century English peasants spoke of "defecation," "bowel movements," "coitus," and "copulation" whenever they wished to refer to excretion and
sexual intercourse, and then invented the simpler terms later as a more
convenient shorthand.

The utility of the vulgar terms in their referential use consists not chiefly
in their brevity, but rather in the attitudes they are uniquely capable of
expressing, simply because they *are* vulgar. There are times when we wish
to be emphatically plain and matter of fact, and suggest not the slightest
skittishness or squeamishness, no moralistic aloofness, no sententiousness or
sentimentality. A rose is a rose, a spade is a spade, and shit is shit. That is
simple street talk without pretension, without regard to delicacy and other
refinements and affectations. Sometimes—not always, but sometimes—this
sort of no-nonsense mood is entirely reasonable, and even if it were not, we
would wish to have a vocabulary to give it expression. That is one of the
ways in which vulgarities are useful. They tell listeners that the speaker is a
plain blunt man or woman with no patience for evasive and fancy words.
Sometimes—not always, but sometimes—we wish to wear only undershirts and go barefoot. The vulgar words are the undershirts and bare feet
in our vocabularies.

The scatological and sexual vulgarities also form an essential part of the
language of irreverence and disrespect. They are the "disphemistic" terms
par excellence, the offensive and disrespectful substitutes for neutral terms
that have the same referents. (See Chap. 15, §1 for a fuller discussion.) Just
as some straightlaced and conventional persons find it useful in some circumstances to have euphemisms (e.g., "lovemaking" for "sexual intercourse," "bathroom" for "toilet," "passing water" for "urinating"); other
persons find it useful in challenging prissiness and mindless conformity to
have disphemisms available, like "fucking" for "sexual intercourse," "shit-
house" for "toilet," "pissing" for "urinating." It is no accident, as we shall
see below, that words for biological functions tend to come in convenient
triple packages, the neutral word for straightforward businesslike reference,
the euphemism for sedative purposes, and the obscene word with the same

meaning—the disphemism—for flaunting one's irreverence, or disrespect for convention.

5. Derivative uses of obscenity (B): vivid description, intensification, and colorful speech

Because the naughty-to-obscene words are tabooed and therefore offensive, their shock value can be borrowed for the purpose of adding spice and vinegar to discourse that is not essentially obscene. Of course it is not necessary to use obscenities to be colorful, but it is often helpful. Examples are legion but the following are personal favorites. "I was terribly frightened" is an accurate but unimaginative expression compared with "I was scared shitless", and "I was shitting green" is better still ("green" being a synonym for "unripe" or "unready").[38] The military expression "snafued" cleverly encapsulates an idiom that is colorful partly because it employs a tabooed word. This acronym ("Situation Normal: All Fucked Up") is much more effective than "Once more there has been a characteristic blunder." "I'll be damned" is very shopworn indeed, though it is still more effective than "I *am* surprised"; much better still is "I'll be dipped in a bucket of shit!" Similarly, "It's as cold as a witch's teat," or "It's as cold as a well digger's ass in Idaho!" A woman can rebuff the rude and unwanted attentions of a man by telling him to go to hell or, somewhat more imaginatively, to "get lost," but it would be much more effective to tell him to "take a flying fuck at a rolling doughnut." A final example is a Spanish guerrilla's expletive in *For Whom the Bell Tolls*. He does not say "I'd like to see thousands of fascists killed"; he says "I would like to swim ten leagues in a strong soup made from the *cojones* [vulgar term for testes] of all of them."[39] All of these examples, before they become hackneyed through overuse, involve genuinely creative and incongruous images, but the comic punch in each case is carried by a single forbidden word. The obscenity adds just the right touch of irreverence to drive the message home.

It is the taboo on naughty words, the convention that renders them naughty, that makes it possible for them to play their role in colorful idioms so effectively (and to perform their other derivative functions as well). The word itself, coming without warning, accentuates the element of surprise. The word "fuck," for example, because it is a stringently tabooed sound, sets off an alarm. It is as if printed in red; it can't be ignored; it unfailingly calls attention to itself. In so doing it calls attention, by a kind of spill-over effect, to the words with which it is associated, underlining their message, and that is precisely what it is to intensify or emphasize—the role assigned to obscene terms in colorful idioms.[40]

The use of obscenity in imaginative and vivid phrases is one kind of *slang*, but only one kind. While all such obscene phrases are slang, not all slang by any means is obscene. Yet even non-obscene slang is slightly disreputable, something to be avoided when language is used on formal occasions. The *Oxford English Dictionary* defines slang in part as "language of a highly colloquial type, considered as below the level of standard educated speech . . ." Some colorful idioms begin as slang and then through constant use become respectable fixed idioms. Others are clever inventions of respected writers or speakers that never have the stigma of "slang" in the first place. Others begin as slang and never achieve a higher status even though they become fixed parts of the language. H. L. Mencken explains the distinction "insofar as any distinction exists at all" between slang and sound idiom:

> Slang originates in the effort of ingenious individuals to make the language more pungent and picturesque—to increase the store of terse and striking words, to widen the boundaries of metaphor, and to provide a vocabulary for new shades of difference in meaning. As Dr. Otto Jesperson has pointed out, this is also the aim of poets (as indeed it is of prose writers), but they are restrained by considerations of taste and decorum, and also, not infrequently, by historical or logical considerations. The maker of slang is under no such limitations: he is free to confect his neologism by any process that can be grasped by his customers, and out of any materials available, whether native or foreign.[41]

Tabooed words, it seems clear, are *one* of the resources of the inventive slangist. "Scared shitless" and "all fucked up" are now standard permanent bits of slang, widely used because of their aptness, but never likely to be accepted as good usage. In these respects they join such non-obscene slang phrases as "flat-foot," "fuzz," "guy," "bonehead," "to burp," "to neck," "to frisk," "to bust," "to have guts" and "dope" (for fool), "egghead," "nerd" and "wimp."

6. Derivative uses of obscenity (C): expressions of strong feeling

Swearing undoubtedly has a definite physiological function, as Robert Graves has written,

> for after childhood, relief in tears and wailing is rightly discouraged, and groans are also considered a signal of extreme weakness. Silence under suffering is usually impossible. The nervous system demands some expression that does not affect towards cowardice and feebleness, and as a nervous stimulant in a crisis, swearing is unequalled. It is a Saturnalian defiance of destiny.[42]

What Graves says about swearing applies equally well to obscene exclamations, and the point applies with appropriate modifications to expression of a wide range of emotions in addition to suffering and despair—anger, rage, hate, disgust, desire, longing, frustration, fear, relief, joy, and surprise.

The superior expressiveness of profane and obscene epithets cannot be denied. Consider "Holy shit!" as an exclamation of surprise. Not even "wow!" or "I'll be damned!" can equal this ingenious compound of the sacred and the repulsive. "Oh shit!" similarly is our most pungent and economical expression of disappointment. "I don't give a shit" most emphatically expresses a kind of angry "indifference" or rejection. "Oh fuck it!" uses the chief naughty word non-referentially as an expression of frustration, disgust, and dismay.

Graves' example of expressing pain and suffering by means of curses and obscene epithets is an especially important one, however, for it reveals the distinctive way in which tabooed words express various unpleasant emotions. The odd thing about certain obscene and profane exclamations is that they are defenses against the very feeling that they express, thus giving with one hand what they take away with the other. Obscene exclamation is not a passive expression of suffering, as a mere moan or groan is, not a pathetic plea for relief, but an active grappling with pain. The obscene words used are the distinctive vocabulary of disrespect and defiance, of conscious and deliberate taboo-violation. Using the tabooed word to give vent to the pain is both to express the pain and to deny it at the same time, a way of complaining about one's situation while still asserting control over it.

It is worth repeating that the taboos that make obscene expressiveness possible are word-taboos. In general one is forbidden to use "shit" or "fuck" not because, or not only because, of what these words refer to, when they refer to anything at all. When they are used in a non-referential exclamatory fashion as in "Oh shit!" or "Fuck it!," it is the word in and of itself that is naughty. If one prints the exclamations leaving letters out of the naughty words so that the reader knows perfectly well what word is intended, then the taboo is not strictly violated. For many years only the first letter of a "four letter word" could be printed, and it sufficed in the context, together with three dashes, to suggest the intended obscene word in all its horror. Why is "f--- it!" less offensive than "fuck it!" and "oh s---!" less offensive than "oh shit!" when the reader knows with certainty that the former are but poor fitting disguises of the latter? Using the blank schema conveys to the reader that it is really the four-letter word that is intended but since that word is not actually printed, the taboo—rigid like all real taboos—remains unviolated.[43]

In examining the way in which tabooed words express feeling it will be useful to compare, for any given feeling, how pre-linguistic noises like grunts, laughs, sighs, and groans, conventional non-obscene interjections like "gee!," "wow!," and "ouch!," and obscene epithets like "oh shit!" and "fuck it!" can be expressive. Consider first the feeling of sad regret or disappointment at the occurrence of some event. Such a feeling can be vented directly by a kind of cross between a sigh and a grunt which in the context can be taken by an observer to be a spontaneous, even involuntary, indication of disappointment—if not an "expression" then at least a revelation or "giving away" of what is experienced. The sounds that escape from the "expresser" give natural vent to his feelings, but they are not part of any *language* that he speaks. If he wishes to convey his feeling in language he can assert that he has the feeling and go on to describe it, or he can use those parts of speech that are called interjections (exclamations or ejaculations) to give direct vent to the feeling in a manner similar to that of the "natural" pre-linguistic expression, without asserting or describing anything at all. He may, for example, utter the English word "alas!" which is as much a word in the language as "oops!" or "ouch!" or "wow!," although—like them—it is not used to refer to anything. Interjections are not meaningless sounds; they have a definite job to do that is assigned by the conventions of a language, just as a referential term like "man" or "table" has a task, though a quite different one, also assigned by the rules (definitions) that report and govern usage. "Man" and "table" are used to refer to men and tables respectively; that is what they *mean*. "Alas!" is not used to refer to anything; rather it is used to express sadness and disappointment. Given the conventions of English, it can no more be used to convey a feeling of joyous merriment than "man" can be used to refer to cockroaches or "table" to steam engines. The conventions that report and govern how given interjections work are themselves definitions of a sort, stating what C. L. Stevenson called "the emotive meaning" of a word. "People groan in all languages," Stevenson reports, "but say 'ouch' only in English. In learning French, one must learn to substitute 'helas' for 'alas,' but one may sigh just as usual."[44] What Stevenson says is true because "ouch" and "alas" are words in English whose meaning is wholly emotive; "helas" is a word in French that is an emotive synonym of "alas"; and sighs and groans, since they "communicate naturally" without help from any linguistic conventions, are words in no language at all.[45]

A third way of expressing disappointment is to use a word from the obscene part of the English vocabulary and say "oh shit!" This would be to express the feeling just as accurately as the word "alas!" would. No one who understands English would misconstrue what was being said since this idiom is understood to be a more forceful way of expressing what "alas!" expresses. Because of the conventions that determine its "emotive meaning" it can no more express joyous merriment than "alas" or a deep sigh can. But "Oh shit!" is much more emphatic than "alas!" because it exploits another expressive mechanism. Since the word "shit" is tabooed, one is saying in effect: "I am so keenly disappointed, that my violation of a word-taboo seems a matter of very little importance. I don't even care whether I am impolite and vulgar if that is the cost of giving this feeling proper expression." The existence of the word taboo is in this way necessary for the intensified expression. If it were to weaken and disappear, "Oh shit!" would become no more expressive than "alas!" and we should have to find some new way of saying what "Oh shit!" says now.

In short, the expressiveness of obscene epithets has a double source. When a person has obviously been frustrated by a turn of events and utters the words "Oh shit!," everyone who understands English knows (1) that nothing is being asserted or described; (2) feelings are being expressed; (3) those feelings are negative ones drawn from a limited range of feelings that include sad, frustrated, and enraged disappointment; (4) the feelings expressed cannot be those of glee, joy, etc. The speaker may be an actor in a play or a deceitful con man telling an "emotive lie." He may not be experiencing disappointment at all, but only feigning it. Nevertheless it is disappointment that he *expresses*, and it cannot be otherwise given the conventions of the English language. All of the above is to say that "Oh shit!" has an emotive meaning in the same way "damn!", "alas!" and "good heavens!" do. But in addition "shit" is tabooed; because of other conventions, perhaps better called rules of etiquette than rules of language, it shocks, offends, rings a bell, and calls attention to itself when uttered in inappropriate contexts. "Oh shit!" then functions like "alas!" or "damn!" as an interjection for expressing disappointment, but because of a word-taboo it becomes a maximally intensified "alas!," an "alas!" underlined in red. Similarly, "Oh, fuck it!," like "curse it!," expresses a kind of frustration, disgust or dismay in voicing a rejection of something. But because of the more stringent taboo it violates, it becomes a maximally intensified "curse it!" or "the hell with it."

Emotive meanings are either *laudatory*, like "hurray!" and "terrific!," *derogatory*, like "boo!" and "alas!," or *neutral*, like "wow!," "gee!," and "whew!," which express such feelings as surprise and excitement. Emotive terms can express *feelings*, like "alas!" (sad disappointment) and "terrific!" (excited joy), or *attitudes* such as "good!," "freedom," and "justice" (pro-attitudes) and "lousy!," "tyranny," and "unfair" (con-attitudes). There are no "neutral attitudes," because an attitude is an essentially polar stance, being for or against something, being in favor of or opposed to. Some emotive words are *purely emotive*, like the interjections "hurray," "boo," "wow," "gee," "whew," "great," "alas," and so on. Stevenson calls the emotive meaning of such words "*independent emotive meaning*" since the interjections have no descriptive meaning that could be the source or basis of the emotive meaning. On the other hand, most emotive words are more complicated, having both descriptive components (which Stevenson often calls "cognitive meaning") and emotive components. Thus the complex word "democracy" means something like "government by the people either directly by majority vote or through elected representatives." But in addition to this descriptive meaning, the word "democracy" conventionally expresses a laudatory emotive meaning, that is a favorable attitude toward that which is referred to by the descriptive meaning. When the emotive meaning of a word is dependent on antecedent attitudes toward the thing designated by the word (as is true for the most part of "democracy") Stevenson calls it *dependent emotive meaning*, and "to whatever extent emotive meaning is *not* a function of descriptive meaning, but either persists without the latter [as in interjections] or survives changes in it [because of 'inertia' or 'lag'], let us say that it is 'independent.' "[46]

The paradigmatic obscenities "shit" and "fuck" are words with both descriptive meanings (referring to feces, defecation, or coitus) and emotive ones. The emotive meanings express either feelings or attitudes, depending on the idioms of which they are a part. "Oh shit!" expresses angry disappointment (a feeling), but "that's a crock of shit!" expresses a con-attitude. "Fuck," on the other hand, is more typically used in idioms that express attitudes ("Fuck you" expresseses hostility, "all fucked up" expresses a kind of opposition or rejection). The feelings and attitudes expressed by these terms in all their uses are derogatory. A tricky problem is that of determining the extent to which the emotive meanings of obscene words are dependent or independent of their descriptive meanings. The scatological obscenities seem to differ sharply from the sexual ones in this respect. The general attitude toward human waste products is extremely negative. Excrement is "filth"; it smells bad; it is disgusting (and even "disgustworthy"). Because of that universal attitude toward the thing designated by the word, the emotive meaning is highly derogatory and the term becomes suitable for metaphorical application to persons and things that are despised. Furthermore, because of the stringent taboo against making the sound or putting the marks on paper, the speaker or writer can exploit the shock value of the word to intensify the feeling expressed. By and large then, the emotive meaning of "shit" is *dependent* on prevailing attitudes toward the word's literal referent. The word "fuck," which is an even greater shocker, seems to derive its derogatory expressiveness primarily from its role as taboo-breaker, since sexual intercourse, the referent of its descriptive meaning, is hardly the object of a universal contempt, disgust, or derogatory attitude.

In its case, the word-taboo and the conventional sexual morality that lies behind (far behind) it, alone account for its *independent* emotive meaning.

Sometimes the word "shit," of course, is used as a pure interjection understood to have no descriptive meaning at all, but even in these cases, its emotive meaning derives by association from general attitudes toward its literal referent in other uses. More commonly, "shit" is used metaphorically in phrases that acquire their impact from a double source: transfer of emotive meaning from the literal to the figurative object *and* exploitation of the word-taboo for emphasis. Thus, "bull shit" is applied to pompous overblown rhetoric, and "chicken shit" to small-minded meanness in the application of rules, especially in a bureaucracy. The metaphor in each case is striking: the large turds for the overblown exaggerations, the tiny droppings for the small-mindedness, and excrement in each case for the worthless and disgusting. But "bull excrement" and "chicken droppings" would use the same metaphors with less effect. What they miss is the expression of tough-mindedness and disrespect for convention that is expressed by all deliberate taboo-violation. The word "shit" in this as well as all other uses helps the speaker to put on the manner of toughness and disrespect for prevailing pieties. He tells the world by such language that he is a no-nonsense person, a straight-shooter, free of sentimentality, impatient at evasive trumpery and cant.

Something like Stevenson's account of emotive meaning was borrowed by the United States Supreme Court to bolster its decision in the fascinating case of *Cohen v. California*.[47] Paul Robert Cohen, it will be recalled (Chap. 11, §1), had been convicted for violating the Los Angeles municipal code's prohibition of conduct that "maliciously and willfully disturbs the peace or quiet of any neighborhood or person by offensive conduct." At the height of the opposition to the Vietnamese War, Cohen spent some time in a public corridor of the Los Angeles Municipal Court House, outside the courtroom where other war resisters were being tried. His "offensive conduct" consisted entirely in his wearing a jacket emblazoned with the words "Fuck the draft." One way of applying the offense principle to this case would have led to an affirmation of Cohen's conviction. The Court *might* have argued that Cohen's first amendment rights were not violated since he was not convicted because of the substantive content of the message on his jacket, but only because he used an inherently offensive word unnecessarily in expressing that message. Captive observers had to see the word "fuck," which was bound to shock and offend most of them, and was thus bound to be a minor nuisance (it might have argued) in the circumstances. The content of Cohen's message, on the other hand, was simply "Down with the draft," the sort of political opinion preeminently protected by the free-speech clause of the first amendment. If there had been two youths in the corridor one of whose jackets was emblazoned with the words "Down with the draft!" and the other with the words "Oh fuck!," only the latter could be convicted under a statute that is consistent with the constitution. Cohen was convicted for using an obscene word publicly, the argument concludes, not for expressing his political opinions.

Justice Harlan, speaking for the five man majority of the Court, rejected that approach. In the first place, he argued that *Cohen v. California* was not an "invasion of privacy case," which is apparently the way one says in jurisprudential lingo that the "reasonable avoidability" standard for the application of the offense principle has not been satisfied—"Observers could effectively avoid further bombardment of their sensibilities simply by averting their eyes". Secondly and more interestingly, Justice Harlan argued that to express what Cohen wanted to express, and what he had a first amendment right to express, it *was* necessary for him to employ the word "fuck." "Down with the draft" says something different from "Fuck the draft," and only the latter says what Cohen intended to convey. Harlan's reasons might well have come from Stevenson:

> Much linguistic expression serves a dual communicative function: it conveys not only ideas capable of relatively precise detached explication, but otherwise inexpressible emotions as well. In fact, words are often chosen for their emotive as well as their cognitive force. We cannot sanction the view that the Constitution, while solicitous of the cognitive content of individual speech, has little or no regard for that emotive function which, practically speaking, may often be the more important element of the overall message sought to be communicated.[48]

Cohen, Justice Harlan concluded, had no alternative to the language of obscenity for accurately expressing to the public "the depth of his feelings against the Vietnam War and the draft."[49] Only a stringent word-taboo can confer on a word a shock value that makes it an adequate vehicle for the expression of the deepest negative feelings.

14

Obscene Words and their Functions, II

1. Derivative uses of obscenity (D): invective and provocation

Another basic form of language usage, distinguishable from but not altogether unrelated to those we have already considered, is invective or personal vituperation. Invective has various uses—expressive intensification, badinage, calumny, insult, challenge, and provocation, among them. For many of these uses obscene words can advance the purposes of the speaker, but in many cases they are inessential, and sometimes downright self-defeating. Our aim in this section is to sort out these various connections, but we shall begin by noting the relation between some of the commonest styles of invective and even older forms of malediction.

It is but a small step from cursing and swearing (the latter being a kind of hypothetical self-addressed curse) to sheer vituperation, or undisguised, straightforward, categorical name-calling. Burgess Johnson traces this development succinctly:

> A man may tell his enemy to go to the dogs, to live in their kennels and fight with them for offal, and he is uttering an ancient curse. "May you go" is the enacting clause. Or he wishes him to *become* a dog, which is also a curse, invoking more of ancient magic. But when he says his enemy *is* a dog, that is name-calling; and it too follows precedents established behind the mists of early time.[1]

Name-calling in time became one of the most highly developed linguistic arts, though its basic forms and the other kinds of basic insults are usually artless enough. Johnson divides primitive insults into four very general categories. (My own classification will differ from his by consolidating some of his categories and adding others.) According to Johnson, primitives likened their enemies to lower animals; their appearances or characteristics were described in unflattering terms; they were accused (with no suggestion whatever that the accuser had substantiating evidence) of shameful acts; their ancestors (especially parents) were likewise abused. Name-calling in all these modes, of course, survives in our civilized time. Obviously only a small percentage of insults in these categories involve the use of obscene or naughty words either essentially or accidentally. "You are a pig" is not obscene; neither is "Your mind is a garbage heap." The "shameful acts" whose imputations define Johnson's third category of insult are, on the other hand, almost entirely sexual in character and charged to enemies in thoroughly indelicate language. Similarly, one's ancestry is questioned by insults to one's mother's honor, or such traditional epithets as "son of a bitch" and "bastard," originally conventional vehicles for accusing someone's mother of sexual infidelity.

Johnson's list omits at least one traditional category: the charge that one *is* a sexual or excretory organ, expressed in vulgar terminology. It is insulting enough to be called an animal, like a horse. It is even more insulting, though insulting in the same way, to be called part of a body like an "ass." And to call another part of an animal's body, like a horse's ass, is to combine the worst of both worlds to very good effect. Edward Sagarin interprets this familiar category of obscene insult as expressing contempt for all things biological, but again he misses the mark. Men call other men "pricks" not because they are transferring to their enemies the contemptuous or shameful attitudes they feel toward their own sex organs, but rather because it insults a person to be likened to a depersonalized organ, vital and demanding, yet utterly brainless. "Prick" is a term of contempt reserved for mindless fools. It functions in much the same way as the animal-insults "donkey," or "turkey." When it refers literally to the penis it can even be an affectionate term, as can "dog" when it is used literally to refer to a dog, but when applied metaphorically it is an insult, implying peremptory mindlessness like that of a yipping puppy demanding attention.

Tabooed words can lend color and vivacity to vituperation as they can to oaths, curses, exclamations, avowals, and jokes. It is a dull insult, for example, to call a person stupid, but it is an insult with a flair to say that "he has his head up his ass." It is especially effective to use obscene vulgarities in reenforcing combinations, stringing together tabooed idioms with no rhyme or reason except to build up a kind of venemous momentum, maximally exploiting the shock value of each new tabooed phrase as it builds upon its predecessor. Barracks insults often employ this breathless device to give emphasis to the unbounded character of the hostility they express. If such insults were uttered in polite society, in our day and age, they would probably be more shocking than any other uses of language available to speakers. Even in the barracks room where no obscenity shocks, such insults let off steam more effectively than any others, expressing, if not evoking in return, powerful aggressions, as for example when one soldier shrieks at another—"You mother-fucking, sister-raping, masturbating, cock-sucking, son of a bitch!" That epithet is imaginative and virulent, employing build-up, climax, rhythm, even internal rhyme, as well as the essential highlighting that comes from taboo-infraction.

Many of the same devices are available to the non-obscene vituperator, and while the dirty word may be essential to the most emotional insults, it is by no means essential to the most colorful ones. Two literary examples will be sufficient to prove that point. The first is a typical outburst from Thomas Mendip in Christopher Fry's *The Lady Is Not For Burning*. Speaking to Hebble Tyson he prefixes his message with some choice invective: "You bubble-mouthing, fog-blathering, chin-chuntering, chap-flapping, liturgical, turgidical, base old man!"[2] Not a naughty word in that sequence, but what an explosion of impatient anger! My favorite example of non-obscene vituperation, however, is better known. It is from Shakespeare's *Henry IV*, Part One:

> *Falstaff:* Now Hal, what time of day is it, lad?
>
> *Prince Hal:* Thou art so fat-witted with drinking of old sack and unbuttoning thee after supper and sleeping upon benches after noon, that thou hast forgotten to demand that which thou would'st truly know. What a devil hast thou to do with the time of day? Unless hours were cups of sack, and minutes capons, and clocks the tongues of bawds, and dials the signs of leaping-houses, and the blessed sun himself a fair hot wench in flame-coloured taffeta, I see no reason why thou shouldst be so superfluous to demand the time of the day.[3]

The resources of obscenity, at least in our time, run dry long before it can achieve anything resembling Shakespearean eloquence.

Obscenities can play a variety of roles in the language of invective, but contributing color and flair is not very prominent in the list. One function of obscene words in invective is that of general intensifiers in denunciations and objurgations. A few "fuckin's," "shits," and "asses" sprinkled throughout a rebuke, a scolding, or an accusation suggest that the speaker means business. The denunciatory message he means to communicate is so important to him that he is willing to violate the taboos that normally restrain his talk so that his anger and seriousness of purpose can come across. The dirty words themselves refer to nothing in such usage. Their sole function is to ring a bell, to highlight, to underline, to fix attention.

Oddly enough, obscene vulgarities can sometimes play the very opposite role in that form of language play called "badinage," "persiflage," or "manly banter." This sort of playful teasing talk is a highly sublimated and ritualized exchange of aggressive attitudes. The speakers are normally good friends and confident of one another's good will. They use expressions that would normally be thought to be insults, but in contexts that make their intentions clear. Persiflage is verbal sparring done for the fun of it. It stands to aggression as controlled flirting does to sex. The obscene words in locker room badinage are grudging terms of affection simply because they are recognized as familiarities of the sort that could not be used among strangers or in formal contexts without expressing genuinely angry emotion. That they are used here in a jocular way signals that the discourse is playful and not seriously threatening.

When invective has a more serious insulting purpose, obscene language often increases its effectiveness. "You prick" is a more expressive insult than "You mindless animal" or "You mindless organ." "You cunt" is a savage mockery, more effective than "You brainless personification of a sex organ" (even). These are contemptuous epithets *par excellence* exceeding even "fool," "ass," "clown," "donkey," "turkey," and "insect," partly because of the vivid metaphor employed, and independently because of the word-taboos whose violation contributes shock value. In contrast to these epithets of contempt are a group of morally denunciatory insults that include "skunk," "swine," "louse," and "rat," as well as the quasi-obscenities "bastard," and "son of a bitch." These simple insults express fear and even a kind of respect. They say of a person that he is evil and mean, but in attributing a dangerous power to him they confer a grudging respect.[4] It is interesting that the only sexual vulgarities that charge meanness or ruthlessness are terms like "bastard" that originally insulted a person by attributing infidelity to his mother. That innocent bastards should necessarily be mean and nasty is an ancient superstitious belief no longer held by anyone; yet through a cultural lag, the term "bastard" still expresses personal anger.

2. The uses of invective

Name-calling, a form of pure insult, must be contrasted with *calumny* or malicious and usually false statements seriously meant to hurt someone's reputation. "You are a son of a bitch!" is paradigmatic of a pure insult, since no one could seriously believe that it is literally true. Nobody objects to it on the ground that people will believe that one's mother was a dog and think less of one as a result. "Your mother was a whore!" said in anger by a person who obviously did not know one's mother and has no access to any evidence about her life is also taken to be a pure insult, either without truth value or understood not to be literally meant. If it stings and enrages, it is not because it threatens to hurt anyone's reputation. A newspaper column that charges that you are a member of an organized crime syndicate, or that you often drive your taxi while drunk, threatens not only your reputation as a businessman or a taxi driver, it threatens your very livelihood, or even your freedom. Because of these tangible effects on your interests you may sue the newspaper for defamation and collect damages in compensation for the harm done your reputation and your pocketbook. Defamatory utterances (libel and slander) can cause people to have beliefs about you that lead them to act toward you in harmful ways. Pure insults, on the other hand, do not harm you by conveying information to third parties. As we shall soon see, they function characteristically in a quite different way.

Still another category of invective, neither calumny nor pure insult but bearing resemblance to each, is what might be called the "factually based put-down." This form of vituperation is not a way of damaging a person's reputation with third parties by maliciously conveying false information about him. Unlike calumny it achieves its whole purpose through face to face confrontation whether or not third parties ever learn of it. But unlike pure insult it does purport to make serious factual imputations; it is not purely a venting of hostile spleen. The point of the factually based put-down is to remind the addressed party of some defect or flaw in his own makeup, thought by at least the speaker to be shameful, and to make him feel bad about it. The mercilessly derisive taunts of the school yard are perhaps the most familiar examples. "You're a cripple, ya, ya!" chanted to a child with a club foot is a prime instance of the genre. So is "You're retarded, ya, ya" spoken to a child who is indeed retarded. On the other hand, "You blockhead!" or "You idiot!" spoken in anger or frustration to a person of obviously normal competence is a pure insult since no one would take it to be a serious claim of literal truth. Obscene words have very little role, if any at all, to play in derisive taunts. "You're a fuckin cripple" adds more hostile emphasis but only at the cost of decreasing the derision and weakening the focus on factuality. On the other hand, "You fuckin idiot!" obviously intensifies an insult without distorting or confusing its function.

A pure insult may simply be a way of expressing one's hostility and nothing more, or it may be a more formal announcement of one's antagonism and thus a kind of analogue in interpersonal affairs to the breaking off of diplomatic relations between nations. Insults are signs that the normal constraints of civility have been lifted, and thus they are warnings that violent consequences might follow. In some cases they come very close to being threats of violence—not quite curses ("May the plague take you" or "May God punish you"), not quite statements of fixed intention ("I'm going to bash your brains in")—but more like contingent threats, quasi-threats, or near-threats ("I have such a low regard for you that I have half a mind to beat your brains out," or "For two cents I'd . . . ," or "If I weren't such a gentleman, I'd . . . ," or "If you weren't so pathetic, I'd . . ."). The insult is usually one thing ("You son of a bitch") and the near-threat another, but the two are normally so closely linked that the occurrence of one is a sign that the other is in the offing. Perhaps in some particularly contentious groups a conventional understanding takes the insult itself to express a "near-threat."

The insult itself, as we have seen, can use obscene or non-obscene words, and can consist in simple name-calling or in ritualistic accusations that are not likely to be understood as ordinary statements of fact. "Son of a pig!" does not purport to make a factual claim, but neither does the "accusation" of incest expressed in the standard pure insult of the ghetto, "You mother-fucker," or the "imputation" of coprophagy in the ultimately contemptuous retort, "You eat shit," or similarly shocking charges of pederasty, sodomy, bestiality, and the like. The closest these ritualistic uses of language come to genuine cognitive content is in their suggestion that the speaker's esteem for his auditor is so minimal that he is prepared to believe the worst about him; no form of degradation would be so extreme that the insulted party might not have engaged in it. "I wouldn't be surprised to learn even that . . ."

Ordinary charges and villifications, on the other hand, are to be con-trasted with pure name-calling and ritualistic accusations. We do not often charge another party, to his face, with being a coward, a liar, a cheat, or a murderer, without the intent that he take us very seriously indeed as makers of truth-claims. Serious villifications, it is interesting to note, are not normally made in obscene language. Not only are the tabooed words unnecessary, but they are also misleading insofar as they suggest that the language used is merely that of ritualistic accusation instead of a serious moral judgment. "You practice incest with your mother, a dreadful sin" makes a serious moral charge in appropriately somber language. If the same charge were made by means of the familiar obscene epithet of the ghetto, it would sound more like a pure insult than a genuine imputation. Genuine accusations can be made more in sorrow than in anger, or with no accompa-nying emotion at all; pure insults (which are more often obscene than not) are expressions of hostility through and through.

Ritualistic accusation and name-calling are not the only ways in which insults can express extreme disrespect for their objects. A third way is to disparage, or express scorn, ridicule, or contempt for the various things assumed to be sacred or blessed to the party insulted, to express a readiness to rejoice, for example, if harm came to his loved ones. The Spaniard tells his enemy that "I spit in your mother's milk." Any European knows that he hits a vulnerable place when he says "Your mother is a whore." The Oriental imprecation "May a goat shit on thy grandmother's grave" strikes with effectively comic disrespect at something deemed sacrosanct by an ancestor worshiper. A curse is not the same thing as a pure insult, but it can be equally "insulting" insofar as it employs a common mechanism of disrespect, namely the disparagement of what is held dear or holy. An ancient Cuban insult, addressed presumably to a person thought to be pious, is "I spit on the twenty four feet of the apostles."[5] The Arab says simply "Thy religion be damned."[6] By such means the pure insulter tells his enemy: "I loathe all that is holy to you." Such loathing can be expressed, sometimes quite effectively, in non-obscene language, but its effectiveness is magnified greatly when its terms are drawn from the tabooed vocabulary, for the obscene words are *par excellence* the vehicles of disrespect in any language. The language of obscenity *is* the language of irreverence, scorn for conventional norms, and contempt for pious sensibility. Its use, therefore, will make almost any pure insult more insulting than it would otherwise be.

A fourth class of insults aims at establishing and exploiting the inferior status of the addressee relative to that of the speaker. These can be called "symbolic dominance claims" for their purpose is to cite or to help establish a relationship between the insulter and his foe in which the former is dominant and the latter is subordinate. The insulted party is meant to be shamed or humiliated by having his nose rubbed in his degraded status relative to the speaker. The insult usually describes what the speaker thinks of as an appropriately submissive posture for the person he addresses, in which the subservience is total and unqualified. The very most shocking obscenities, being total and unqualified expressions of disrespect for social norms, are especially fit vehicles for this use.[7]

One of the more puzzling of all the insulting idioms, and one whose origins are lost in the mists of antiquity, is the expression "Fuck you." When one stranger addresses it to another in the course of an argument it is an emphatic (and certainly obscene) gesture of defiance, and if not a formal challenge to violence, at least a substantial escalation of heat and passion. If all insults are of our first three types—either name-callings, ritual accusations, or expressions of scorn for what is deemed precious—then "Fuck you" is not an insult. But in the broadest sense of "insult" ("an act, remark, etc. meant to hurt the feelings of self-respect of another; affront; indignity"), it certainly is an insult. I suggest that it belongs in our fourth class of conventional insults which includes such other symbolic dominance claims as "Kiss my ass" (that would be an appropriately degrading posture for you), and "I spit on you," (with or without the accompanying act). Common to insults in this fourth class is the assertion of the vast superiority of the speaker over the person insulted, a superiority so marked that unbounded contempt is an appropriate attitude in the speaker, and humiliating gestures of self-degradation and obeisance are appropriate postures for the one insulted.

Carl Sagan speculates that the phrase "Fuck you" is an anachronistic survival from our pre-human past:

> Squirrel monkeys with "gothic" facial markings have a kind of ritual or display which they perform when greeting one another. The males bare their teeth, rattle the bars of their cage, utter a high-pitched squeak, which is possibly terrifying to squirrel monkeys, and lift their legs to exhibit an erect penis. While such behavior would border on impoliteness at many contemporary human social gatherings, it is a fairly elaborate act and serves to maintain dominance hierarchies in squirrel-monkey communities . . .
>
> The connection between sexual display and position in a dominance hierarchy can be found frequently among the primates. Among Japanese macaques, social class is maintained and reinforced by daily mounting: males of lower caste adopt the characteristic submissive sexual posture of the female in oestrus and are briefly and ceremonially mounted by higher-caste males. These mountings are both common and perfunctory. They seem to have little sexual content but rather serve as easily understood symbols of who is who in a complex society.
>
> In one study of the behavior of the squirrel monkey, Caspar, the dominant animal in the colony and by far the most active displayer, was never seen to copulate, although he accounted for two-thirds of the genital display in the colony—most of it directed toward other adult males. The fact that Caspar was highly motivated to establish dominance but insignificantly motivated toward sex suggests that while these two functions may involve identical organ systems, they are quite separate. The scientists studying this colony concluded: 'Genital display is therefore considered the most effective social signal with respect to group hierarchy. It is ritualized and seems to acquire the meaning, "I am the master." It is most probably derived from sexual activity, but it is used for social communication and separated from reproductive ability . . .'
>
> The behavioral as well as neuroanatomical connections between sex, aggression, and dominance are borne out in a variety of studies. The mating rituals of great cats and many other animals are barely distinguishable, in the earlier stages, from fighting. It is commonplace that domestic cats sometimes purr loudly and perversely while their claws are slowly raking over upholstery or lightly clad human skin. The use of sex to establish and maintain dominance is sometimes evident in human heterosexual and homosexual practices (although it is not, of course, the only element in such practices), as well as in many (obscene) utterances. Consider the peculiar circumstances that the most common two-word verbal aggression in English, and in many other languages, refers to an act of surpassing physical pleasure; the English form probably

comes from a Germanic and Middle Dutch verb *fokken*, meaning 'to strike.' This otherwise puzzling usage can be understood as a verbal equivalent of macaque symbolic language, with the word 'I' unstated but understood by both parties. It and many similar expressions seem to be human ceremonial mountings . . . such behavior probably extends much farther back than the monkeys, back through hundreds of millions of years of geological time.[8]

Sagan's account is both vague and highly speculative, but I know of no other explanation of the idiom "Fuck you" that is remotely plausible.

3. The doctrine of fighting words and its difficulties

Like most emotive uses of language, pure insults are not only expressive but also evocative; they can be relied upon to elicit an attitude in the insulted party similar to the one expressed by the insulter. For that reason they lend themselves to manipulative purposes. The anger expressed by the insult may be only feigned anger. Even a cold-blooded deliberate use of an insulting epithet might predictably bring forth an angry response from the person insulted. For that reason the vocabulary of insulting expressions, obscene and non-obscene, are handy instruments for manipulating passions and provoking violence. One party can use them to taunt another (as he might also flaunt insulting symbols and gestures) for the purpose of goading him into an unpromising attack or a humiliating withdrawal. Pure insults, in short, are dangerous weapons.

Insulting words might elicit insulting or violent responses in either of two ways: they might directly arouse anger in the listener or they might function as formal invitations to combat. The former method is *provocation;* the latter is *challenge.* Provocations are essentially causal mechanisms. They exploit the known tendency of a certain class of words to evoke emotional responses, and the presumed tendency of certain classes of persons (nearly *all* persons in some circumstances or other) to respond passionately to them. Walk up to any male stranger on the street and call him "mother-fucker," and he will assuredly react with some emotion or other—fear, terror, or anger. He will clench his fingers and (perhaps involuntarily) make a fist; his pulse beat will increase suddenly; he may begin to sweat. Your words alone, uttered in an appropriately menacing fashion, will produce these psychological and physiological effects in him. Such effects are not invariant and certain. The propensity of human beings to react passionately to insults is not like the tendency of sugar to dissolve in water. Typical human responses to insults are sufficiently predictable, however, to permit us to speak of "causal tendencies," "verbal instruments," "manipulation," and "goading." Even that ideal legal construction, "the reasonable man," will sometimes boil up with anger that overwhelms his usual self-control when confronted with causally potent insulting language. In such a case the insult "provokes" him into violent language or action in return.

Challenges work in a somewhat different manner. The challenging language does more than merely express hostility and evoke a similar antagonism in the listener. In virtue of its recognized symbolism, it is a way of doing something directly in the world, a way of acting and bringing about changes in the relations between people, simply by speaking words. A challenge, in short, is a kind of linguistic performance, an instance of what J. L. Austin called a "performative utterance."[9] When Doe says to Roe: "I cordially invite you to dinner next Wednesday," Roe's status as well as Doe's are now automatically changed. Roe becomes an *invitee*, and Doe an *inviter*, and a new sort of social relationship between them has sprung into existence. In a broad sense, a new *moral* relationship has been created, since a new pattern of rights and obligations has now been formed. Similarly, when a licensed clergyman says, as the culmination of an appropriate ritual, "I hereby pronounce you man and wife" or "I hereby baptize you John Paul Doe," new legal relationships spring into reality: a couple is now married, or a person now has a correct name. The mere utterance of certain words in certain circumstances, as if by magic, brings new facts into the world. The "verbal magic," of course, is not magic at all. We all understand that in virtue of certain linguistic conventions, certain utterances have certain consequences. Changing the world in certain ways is what utterances of those types are *for*. Thus when Doe says to Roe, "I hereby challenge you to a fight," or when he uses other words or symbolic gestures to do the same, he has significantly altered the relationship between Doe and Roe, just as much as if he had done something to Roe without the aid of language, for example bestowed a gift on him, or robbed, pushed, kissed, or saluted him, or as if he had used language to bind him, invite him, baptize him, or marry him to someone.

It may be a mistake to describe the great variety of customary rules for challenging as *linguistic* conventions. We can look up the words "I challenge you" in a dictionary and in that manner learn what the phrase means and what it is used for. But there are many symbolic techniques for challenging that do not use the word "challenge,"[10] and indeed many that use no *words* at all. These techniques derive from customs that vary widely from group to group and time to time. Outsiders can learn of them by direct observation, or word of mouth, or by reading reports of social workers, sociologists, or anthropologists, but they are not likely to get far by consulting dictionaries, even for accounts of challenges that do employ words. For the clearest accounts of symbolic challenges one might well turn to the history books for descriptions of practices that are now obsolete. In the old West, a cowboy on a spree could issue a generalized challenge to all the patrons in a tavern by placing a chip on his shoulder so that anyone who knocked it off would by that very action start a good spirited brawl. Alternatively, a person could issue a challenge of fisticuffs to a specific party as the culmination of a heated exchange of words, by very deliberately picking up a chip, placing it on his shoulder, and inviting the enemy to knock it off. In that way the advantage of surprise, which normally goes to the initiator of an attack, is nullified and the fight can proceed on fair terms. The medieval practice was to remove from one's hand a leather glove covered with metallic plates (a gauntlet) and throw it down in front of a hated party as a challenge to combat. The prevailing rules permitted the enemy himself to "take up the gauntlet," or for some third party to take it up on his behalf and thus undertake his defense. The cowboy and medieval rules for challenging were clear and, at least now in retrospect, precisely describable, but the practices that gave meaning to the symbolic gestures are now extinct. (Walk up to a stranger in a bar with a chip on your shoulder today and very likely he won't even notice. If you call it to his attention, he will probably be either confused or amused, but he won't feel challenged. If you throw your leather glove on the floor he might politely retrieve it for you, but more likely he will withdraw in vicarious embarrassment at what seems to him a pointless temper tantrum.)

How can one challenge another party to combat these days, when gauntlets and chips have passed into desuetude? There are still some symbolic gestures that are generally perceived as insults,[11] and of course one might employ the explicit performative utterance "I hereby challenge you," though the latter is an example of a challenge by means other than insult. Are there conventions, however, according to which *some* name-callings, ritual accusations, expressions of scorn for what is deemed precious, or symbolic dominance claims (the main forms of pure insult) are clear symbolic challenges? The American courts apparently think so and have formulated their answer, vague and tentative as it is, in the doctrine of "fighting words." (See Chap. 9, §7.)

The doctrine finds its origin in the Supreme Court case of *Chaplinsky v. New Hampshire.*[12] Chaplinsky, a Jehovah's Witness, had been arrested after his distribution of literature on the streets of Rochester, New Hampshire, had occasioned a public disturbance. While he was being escorted to the police station for booking, he turned to the City Marshall and in great anger uttered the following immortal words to him: "You are a Goddamned racketeer" and "a damned Fascist, and the whole government of Rochester are Fascists or agents of Fascists." There was not a single obscene word in

Chaplinsky's tirade. His utterance had the superficial form of an imputation, but angry charges of communism and fascism are pretty generally
understood to be mere name-callings or ritual accusations, especially when
addressed in anger to politicians or public servants, and in any case no suit
for libel was ever initiated. The words were understood without question to
be pure insults, as opposed to serious calumny, factually based put-downs,
or defamation. Chaplinsky was convicted of violating a statute prohibiting
any person from addressing "any offensive, derisive, or annoying word to
any other person who is lawfully in the street or other public place." The
conviction was appealed all the way to the highest court where it was
unanimously upheld. Justice Frank Murphy's opinion expressed the doctrine that subsequently became influential, but which still has not become
clear:

> There are certain well-defined and narrowly limited classes of speech, the
> prevention and punishment of which have never been thought to raise any
> constitutional problem. These include the lewd and the obscene, the profane,
> the libelous, and *the insulting or 'fighting' words—those which by their very utterance*
> *inflict injury or tend to incite an immediate breach of the peace.* It has been well
> observed that such utterances are no essential part of any exposition of ideas,
> and are of such slight social value as a step to truth that any benefit that may
> be derived from them is clearly outweighed by the social interest in order and
> morality.[13] [Emphasis added.]

It is not immediately clear whether Justice Murphy thought of "fighting
words" as effectively provocative ones merely—words whose "tendency" is
to incite or causally produce a violent response from the person addressed—
or as performative utterances, verbal equivalents of the gauntlet, the chip,
or the finger. If the latter, they are first steps in a violent episode, as
properly prohibitable themselves as initial punches or personal "declarations
of war." The latter interpretation of Murphy's words is supported by Thomas I. Emerson in his important work on the philosophy of the first amendment. Emerson's basic principle for interpreting the free speech clause is
stated succinctly at the start of his book. "The central idea of a system of
free expression," he writes, "is that a fundamental distinction must be
drawn between conduct which consists of 'expression' and conduct which
consists of 'action'. 'Expression' must be freely allowed and encouraged.
'Action' can be controlled subject to other constitutional requirements, but
not by controlling expression."[14] When he comes to discuss *Chaplinsky* later
in the book he writes:

> Under the expression–action theory, the only point at which the communica-
> tion could be classified as action is when the communicator in effect participates
> in an act of violence. This can be said to occur only when the provocation takes

the form of a personal insult delivered face to face. Such "fighting words" can be considered the equivalent of knocking a chip off the shoulder—the traditional symbolic act that puts the parties in the role of physical combatants. It is in short the beginning of action. But the classification of provocative or insulting words as "action" is limited to direct encounters. Thus, if such language is used in the course of a speech addressed generally to the audience, even though the speaker refers to specific persons, organizations, or groups, the communication must still be considered "expression." Unless the speaker singles out members of his audience, and addresses insulting or fighting words to them personally, the communication cannot be said to constitute part of action. Applied in any other way the "fighting words" doctrine becomes a "bad tendency" [mere causal provocation] test.[15]

Enough distinctions have now been made to permit us to construct a chart or a "road map" to the relevant areas of language use:

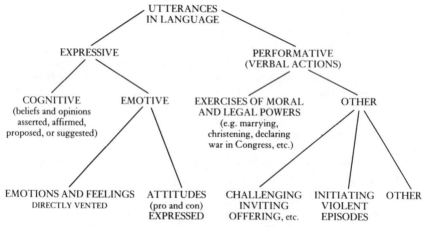

Mere expressions, even when wholly cognitive, can causally precipitate violence, as for example when they function as calumny or serious accusations. Expressions of pure emotion can be provocative too, for example laughing gleefully at a funeral. Expressions of favorable and unfavorable attitudes, being "for" or "against" something, can cause—indeed in some cases are *likely* to cause—disagreeing parties to become very angry. These instances are all examples of what the law calls "provocation" or "incitement," eliciting hostile responses from others by virtue of the known tendency of one's expressive language to produce such effects generally among certain classes of listeners. But the doctrine of fighting words, as Emerson understands it, is not about merely "provocative" language, or words with "bad tendencies." That doctrine applies to nothing on the purely expressive side of the chart. Rather, it applies to a subclass of "verbal acts," uses of words to *do* things rather than (or in addition to) merely *expressing* things.

That subclass contains the informal analogues to such legal performances as bringing a marriage, a name, or a state of war into existence, namely those that constitute a part—the first part—of violent episodes. Just as legal rules require that only persons with the appropriate authority utter the correct words in the correct manner in the appropriate circumstances if the utterance is to succeed in producing the intended effect, so recognized and accepted customs require that "fighting words" be spoken by a certain class of persons (infants, drunks, and incapacitated persons, among others, are excluded), that they have content within an acceptable range (to say simply "I don't like you" is not, or not yet, to utter fighting words), that they be uttered in a certain spirit (one that excludes playful badinage, for example) and in appropriate circumstances (not in the sanctuary of a church, for example). When the appropriate words are uttered "felicitously,"[16] that is in accordance with the governing conventions, then, on this interpretation, a state of hostilities automatically comes into existence between the speaker and the individual he addresses.

There is no doubt an element of truth in all this. Adversaries no longer have the *code duello*, nor the conventions governing gauntlets and chips— universally recognizable, nonverbal ways of announcing that henceforth a state of violence exists between them. Nevertheless, *some* verbal insults in *some* groups do seem to be intended and received as challenges, or as "verbal acts" initiating hostilities. The problem is to say *which* insults have this character in the absence of clearly understood, generally used symbols. *Chaplinsky* is not a very good guide to our inquiry, and even the helpful start in Emerson's commentary does not take us far.

The first deficiency in the *Chaplinsky* precedent is that it permits the classification as "fighting words" of insults that are highly implausible candidates for that category. Justice Murphy's opinion does not contain a formal criterion for determining when utterances are fighting words, but if there is an implicit criterion in his remarks, it is a standard that interprets the angry charges of "Fascist" and "racketeer" made directly to a police officer by a person who is in custody and presumably constrained physically, to be a linguistic act of violence, "words which by their very utterance inflict injury or tend to incite an immediate breach of the peace." Chaplinsky's words share the "bad tendency" of all insults to provoke ire in the one insulted, but even the City Marshall did not take them to constitute by their very utterance the beginning of violent action, for there is no record that he or anyone else responded with violence. "Racketeer" and "Fascist," like the "pinko" and "Commie" of a later period, are standardized forms of political invective when addressed to public officials, and no more incendiary than more generalized insults like "bastard," "pig," "rat," and "son of a bitch." Murphy's implicit criterion of fighting words then–if he had such a thing–was much too broad.

The second defect in the *Chaplinsky* criterion as interpreted by Professor Emerson is the very opposite one that it is also too narrow. The requirement that fighting words be a "personal insult" delivered directly to the party insulted seems to exclude from the category of fighting words our third class of insults, those aimed not directly at the person of the party addressed but rather at other persons, causes, or ideals that he is presumed to hold dear. Actually, the third class of insults is the most important one of all in the quest for fighting words. It is entirely possible, in fact, that *all* fighting words are insults in this third category. Mere name-callings are not understood to be automatic triggers of violence; neither are ritual accusations and symbolic dominance claims which normally elicit, at most, rejoinders in kind. A verbal assault on all that the addressee holds holy, on the other hand, is another story. In one community or another, at one time or another, attacks on the integrity of the addressee's father, the fidelity of his mother, the chastity of his daughter, or the memory of departed dear ones or ancestors, gestures of contempt for his religion or the leaders of his church, insults to the memory of fallen saints and martyrs, or to the larger ethnic group of which he is a member (especially to the memory of its "sacred" sufferings and tribulations) have all been generally understood to be fighting words. Even here and now, to tell a black that blacks are fit for nothing but slavery and that emancipation was a mistake, or to tell a Jew that Hitler's "final solution" was a noble effort that should have succeeded, is to "start a fight" by the use of words. It is also, in many cases, automatically to evoke ire by means of the "bad tendency" of the words employed, but that is another matter. Genuine fighting words, as Emerson understands them, do more than *cause* anger. They can initiate hostilities even when they fail to evoke anger, by appealing in effect to the self-respect of the addressed party, or his "sense of honor"—his conviction that he has a *duty* to respond violently to a certain class of insults whether he really wants to or not, even whether he is angry or not. Failure to respond in the conventional way, he believes, would be to acquiesce without effective protest in the desecration of his ideals, which would be a humiliation not only to him but to the treasured cause in whose vindication he feels he must fight. It seems to him that his silence would be a symbolic ratification of the insult, something which would shatter his personal integrity.

These are the thoughts that lead a person to interpret an insult as "fighting words." They may not be reasonable beliefs; indeed by some transcultural objective standard they might not *ever* be reasonable. But they often are understandable, and in the clearest cases, perfectly predictable, and it is their naturalness and predictability in a given cultural group that constitutes part of the test of whether or not they are authentic fighting words in that group. The initiation of violence for the reasons just described is another sort of response, utterly different in kind, from simply being goaded by taunts into losing one's temper (as in "provocation" or "incitement") or from acting to avoid the shame of being thought cowardly (as in declining a challenge under the *code duello*), and it is doubtful that *merely personal* insults ever occasion it. In any case, if there are any fighting words at all in our community, then they must include insults to what is held precious, whether or not they include personal insults too.

Another required emendation to the Emerson account of fighting words would be a clarification of the tricky analogy of the chip on the shoulder (and the dropped gauntlet). Whatever the historical origin of the practice of placing chips on shoulders and knocking them off, the phrase "having a chip on one's shoulder" is now a fixed metaphor of very derogatory import. We think of the person with a (metaphorical) chip on his shoulder as being truculent and quarrelsome, or as being excessively sensitive and insecure, even sullen, testy, and irritable. It is very definitely not a good way to be. Sometimes we say of a person that he has a chip on his shoulder not in general, but about this or that sensitive topic—property taxes, welfare cheaters, or his treatment by the army during the Vietnamese War. Perhaps all of us have a chip on our shoulders about something or other, some topic which others must treat warily, and it is not so clear that having such specific sensitivities is necessarily a bad way to be. Acute sensitivity respecting some matters, in fact, may be as proper as it is unavoidable. It is important to understand this point if we are not to be misled by what is currently ordinary language into assuming that the party with the metaphorical chip on his shoulder is somehow at fault right from the start.

The question now arises: If we use the chip analogy to elucidate the "fighting words" doctrine, is it the *putting on* or the *knocking off* of the chip that constitutes "the beginnings of action"? Both of these alternatives must be distinguished from simply *having* a chip on the shoulder (in respect to some specific matter) in the sense of the popular idiom. The person who simply has a chip (sensitivity) has not deliberately put it on with the intention of *challenging* people in general or any specific person. His vulnerability to ordinary causal provocation may be greater than that of most people, a fact that might even serve the defense of a person charged with inciting or provoking him to violence. His own dispositions as such, however, are clearly not the "beginnings of action" we are looking for. In contrast, the person who deliberately *puts* on the chip, like the medieval knight who casts down his gauntlet, has issued a challenge. One could take the user of fighting words to be issuing a challenge by verbal means, and his utterance to be a linguistic performance having the same force as a challenge to combat. To challenge another to participate in a joint action, however, is not the same thing as actually commencing that joint action, unless the circumstances are such that the second party has no choice but to accept. Among the nobility in the heyday of the duel the recipient of a challenge had very little choice indeed but to accept, for the alternative was lasting disgrace and humiliation among all the members of his class. (See Vol. I, Chap. 6, §1.) At best that sort of consequence is only approximated in any contemporary Western subculture, and the legislators and judges who make our laws have every motive to keep that approximation minimal. In prohibiting violent responses to insults they *give* insulted parties "a choice" to refrain from violence. It is not in virtue of being *challenges* that some insults become fighting words, for in our time challenges to violence are not themselves automatic precipitants of action. It is not *putting on* the chip, therefore, that is the start of the violent episode.

The best way to use the chip analogy to explain "fighting words," then, is the one Emerson suggests. What starts the altercation is the verbal equivalent of *knocking off* the chip. It is just as misleading to interpret fighting words as acceptances of challenges, however, as it is to think of them as issuings of challenges. If the chip analogy is to be at all useful we must forget about challenges altogether (and that of course requires abandoning the gauntlet analogy too). The chip knocked off by fighting words is not one that has been deliberately put on for the purpose of challenging. Rather it is a transparent sensitivity of a sort generally known to be common to all members of an identifiable class of people. The insulted party is a person who finds himself with a figurative chip on his shoulder as he may find himself with a quite literal wart on his back; for better or worse it is a part of himself. The "chip" is by no means a formal challenge to all comers, so much as an unavoidable vulnerability he hopes no one will ever exploit. Surely, he does not advertise to the world that whoever wants a fight need only insult him in a certain way and he will be obliging. If he does call attention to the chip it will be as a warning.

Fighting words then, if there are such things in a given group, are performative utterances, which, like formal declarations of war, automatically bring into existence a state of violent hostility between two persons. The person to whom the words are uttered, if he understands the way the words function in the language, will take them to be intended precipitants of his own violent response and also as expressions of the readiness of the speaker himself to become violent in turn, even as expressions of the speaker's intention to be violent in any case. The words are verbal equivalents of the first shoves and pushes of a fight. As such they are fit objects of state prohibitions since they are not verbal expressions of opinion, belief, emotion, or attitude, so much as verbal doings in the world, and as actions they can be prohibited without interfering with freedom of expression. Moreover, as violent actions—declarations of private war between individuals— their prohibition would be supported by sound public policy, at least where the quarrel they initiate is likely to become a public disturbance.

To forbid utterances of fighting words, however, is not by the same token to permit open-ended, uncontrolled, violent responses to them. (See Chap. 9, §7.) The law can consistently forbid all acts of violence, verbal and physical, except those committed in self-defense (or defense of others, or of property, etc.). The person who receives fighting words, insofar as they resemble declarations of war, *can* plausibly cite self-defense if retreat is impossible or too dangerous, and his antagonist has advanced on him menacingly, but at no point in the ensuing struggle is he permitted to strike a blow that is not reasonably necessary for his own protection even if it should seem necessary to protect his "honor." Legislatures could permit more reactive violence than traditional self-defense rules would allow, but the mere prohibition of fighting words does not logically commit them to do so. In any case, insofar as the law limits the violent options of the insulted party, just so far does it weaken the whole social–linguistic practice of "private war." If the law resolutely requires the insulted party to turn on his heels and walk away (if that can be done safely) or else stand his ground with clenched fists waiting for the other to attempt the first physical blow, then it weakens the force of the precipitating utterances themselves. Then, insofar as the community is law-abiding, violence will *not* be the automatic response to "fighting words" and it will therefore not be the predictable response to them. When that time comes, the words will be mere anachronisms without performative effect; as fighting words they will no longer exist. The case is not implausible that we are approaching that state in this country, but so long as certain things are known to be thought "sacred" by certain identifiable groups in the population, so long as some causes are beyond tolerable scorn and mockery, that day has not yet arrived.

It is worth mentioning, in conclusion, another deficiency in the doctrine of fighting words as shaped by the *Chaplinsky* precedent. We can distinguish between the *target* of an insult, the person, group, or cause that it disparages, and the *addressee* of an insult, the particular person or persons to whom it is addressed. *Chaplinsky* requires that to count as fighting words an insult must have a particular individual as its addressee, and must insult him personally rather than some third party or parties, or some impersonal cause. We have already criticized the requirement that the target of the insult be identical with its addressee; we must now register some reservations about the requirement that the addressee be a single individual. I have already argued that the most plausible candidate for fighting words are insults of the third class whose targets are other than, and in a sense larger than, the mere individual to whom the insult might be addressed. The most plausible subsets in this category for targets of fighting words are *groups* (e.g., families, nations, ethnic groups) and *institutions* (e.g. churches, religions). A parade of men carrying Nazi emblems, and wearing military uniforms with swastikas on their armbands in a largely Jewish community, is an insult to a whole people (and its unspeakable persecution and suffering) and therefore an insult of the third category to each individual Jewish observer. The same point would apply to a parade of virulently anti-Catholic Ulsterman in an Irish neighborhood in Boston, or to Ku Klux Klansmen in Harlem. But the insult in question is not addressed to a particular Jewish individual but rather to the whole crowd of Jewish observers. One would think that insulting words addressed by one *group* to another would be more incendiary, and from the social point of view, even more worth preventing than similar words addressed from one individual to another. If the words and symbols in question satisfied all the other criteria of fighting words and were not serious expressions of political opinion and attitude except incidentally, derivatively, and bare minimally, it does not seem relevant that they are addressed to a group rather than to a singled-out individual.

4. The useful but limited role of obscenity in invective

One of the most common ways of exploiting the offensiveness of obscene words and the shock value of violating the taboo on their usage is to employ them as elements in the various forms of invective. Indeed their suitability for this function renders them nearly essential for achieving some of the purposes of invective. For other purposes they are usually helpful but inessential, and for others still, their presence actually tends to defeat the goal for which the invective is employed.

Where obscenity seems almost necessary is where invective has an especially hostile character. Obscene words (and profane ones too) add sting to rebukes and scoldings, angry near-threats, and other forms of abuse. They remove all doubts about the seriousness of the speaker's aggressive feelings. Serious insulting purpose, where the expression of genuine hostility is essential, virtually requires at least a sprinkling of tabooed words. As conventional vehicles of impiety and disrespect, they play a leading role in disparagements of what is held dear or holy by the person addressed. And insofar as certain sexual postures, vividly describable in vulgar language, are deemed the most degrading symbols of submission and inferiority, the sexual obscenities play a central role in symbolic dominance claims.

In the expression of the most extreme, unlimited hostility, however, conventional obscenities are absolutely required. Such "unbounded emotions" as sheer hatred and utter contempt cannot be given expression in measured or guarded language. Only the maximally shocking words can do them justice. Inevitably, however, these words become ritualized standard forms for expressing the "unbounded feeling" in question: they lose some of their venom. Taboos slow the weakening process down, by keeping the obscenities out of regular public usage, but still there is constant pressure on the language to produce more expressive, more nearly "unbounded" forms. In this respect obscenity shares in the general tendency of our language toward emotional inflation. Superlatives become super-superlatives; "great" becomes "stupendous," which yields in time to "colossal," which grows into "supercolossal," and so on. The vulgar words, which shock simply as sounds or marks apart from whatever referential meaning they may have, are limited in number and combination. The ultimate insults, therefore, not only require such words as intensifiers; they require that sacred taboos of taste and morals be deliberately smashed and that the *content* of the uttered insult, quite apart from the words that express it, be maximally revolting and offensive.

For the enthusiastic *positive* feelings—the states of mind for which we invent new senses for such words as "great," "stupendous," etc.—and also for such positive emotions as love and joy, the obscene vulgarities would never do as intensifiers and magnifiers. Their use for such purposes would inhibit the expression of the feeling in question by bringing in extraneous associations with hostility, disrespect for social norms, and utter defiance. For the negative emotions, however, they can increase expressiveness simply by being taboo infractions. The very willingness to shock with words gives evidence of the state of mind being expressed.

There are at least three categories of invective which require that obscenity not be used if the aim of the invective is to be achieved. Calumny or defamation is more likely to succeed without obscene intensification. If one's serious purpose is to harm another by tarnishing his reputation, it will sound more objective, less personal, to keep obscenities out of one's defamatory language. Similarly, genuine imputations and villifications demand a more serious tone and disinterested style. Obscenities would suggest mere ritual accusation or name calling. Finally, obscenity detracts from the tone of malicious merriment and thus weakens the derision expressed in factually based put-downs. For the purposes of pure insult, however, obscenity is almost always useful, and never self-defeating.

5. Derivative uses of obscenity (E): obscene wit and the "dirty joke"

The final "derivative use" of conventionally obscene words is in the "off-color story" or "dirty joke." A disproportionate part of what we laugh at concerns the realms of sex and excretion, a fact that is less surprising when we consider that these are the areas where our strongest taboos and other moral norms operate. Funny stories with tabooed themes are like folk songs and other folk art, in that they get transmitted from generation to generation by oral tradition, and their original authors are often unknown. These folk tales often employ conventionally obscene words, but that is by no means always and necessarily the case. Some risqué stories can maintain their comic punch even when told in antiseptic language, and even when obscene words are essential, very often the primary source of their comic function is their descriptive meaning, that is their (irreverent) reference to sexual or excremental behavior itself. In this section we shall first consider how comic wit and humor about sexual and other tabooed things operate, and then what contribution obscene words as such can make to obscene humor.

Since the primary function of obscene words is to offend and one of their more important derivative functions is to provide direction and sting to insults, one might expect that a characteristic use of the dirty joke is to express aggression or hostility. To be sure jokes make us laugh, and sometimes jokes have a butt at whose expense we laugh, someone the joke "makes fun" of. The danger for the theorist, however, is to mistake the special case for the essential function. Not all laughter is personal and barbed, and laughter at dirty jokes is characteristically free of acrimony and rancor. There is no reason why a dirty joke cannot at the same time be a kind of weapon—satirical, biting, caustic, or ironic; but more often risqué humor is simply good fun, a source of spontaneous delight at what is ludicrous, incongruous, or clever.

Another very special use of the dirty story does not even involve laughter, and yet some theorists, following Freud, have attached great importance to it, almost as if it explained the very nature of dirty jokes. Freud noticed that dirty jokes are often employed as a tactic of "verbal seduction." In his day if a man told such a tale to a lady, he gave her "the option of rejecting (by not laughing or 'not understanding') the verbal approach."[17] If she responded with a sly giggle or with hearty laughter, her reaction would be interpreted as an encouragement to further advances. If the dirty joke graphically portrayed sex organs or flagrantly used forbidden words, then it could be regarded as a kind of "verbal rape." Unquestionably there have been bounders and cads who have employed off-color stories, sometimes with great subtlety, to achieve such practical goals, but the fact that jokes are as frequently told by males to males or females to females, and the fact that a solitary reader can burst into laughter upon reading such a tale in a book, and quite without erotic stimulation, show that the characteristic function of sexual humor is as independent of seductive strategy as it is of aggressive attack.

For the purpose of explaining off-color stories a more promising emotion than anger or lust is *anxiety*. Many of us to an extreme degree, and perhaps most of us to some degree or other, feel vaguely threatened by, and hence anxious about, behavior that is tabooed in our culture, and references to bodily functions, incest, homosexuality, and the like, naturally bring the anxieties to the surface. Some persons hide the anxieties from themselves and others by means of laughter, or lay the anxieties to rest temporarily through the verbal relief of the joke. The dirty story functions for these persons as an instrument of therapeutic self-defense. Others, as Peter Farb points out, in effect "foist off" the anxieties on their listener by telling dirty jokes that specially fit the speaker's own most troubling anxieties. "Jokes on these themes are usually embarrassing to a listener who lacks the [particular] anxieties [in question]."[18] Such a listener, according to Farb, will likely think of the speaker's behavior as "sick," reserving his laughter, and his more favorable judgment, for jokes that deal with anxieties he shares.[19] Of course it is true that laughter discharges tension and thus gives a kind of relief, but this cannot be the whole story, for it neglects the fact that the joke, in order to work in this therapeutic fashion, must be perceived as *funny*, or amusing in its own right.

Max Eastman has pointed out that the things that strike us as funny are of two basic kinds. What he calls "ludicrousness" is perceptual humor, amusement at things that "look funny," the clown's facial expression, or Chaplin's walk, or spatially incongruous juxtapositions like that referred to by Abe Martin when he remarked that "ther's few funnier sights than a full set o' whiskers in bed."[20] The earliest laughter at the ludicrous, Eastman reminds us, is the baby's gleeful response to the adult who makes a non-threatening funny face at it. The second kind of funny thing is a temporal process which culminates in a surprising way, a kind of practical joke played on the mind. This grows out of the experience of the infant who, once he has been put in a playful mood, will laugh gleefully at an adult who teases him by offering him a toy with one hand and then snatching it away at the last minute with the other. The two ways of amusing a child,

Eastman maintains, correspond to the two most famous philosophical definitions of the comic. Laughter at the frightful face made playfully fits Aristotle's definition of the comic as "some defect or ugliness which is not painful or destructive." Corresponding to the teasing or practical joke is Kant's account of laughter as "the sudden transformation of a strained expectation into nothing." Very often, in the latter kind of humor, the surprising twist that releases the laughter is not only a playful trick but also the provision of a substitute result that is more welcome than the one that was expected, so that the joke is "a trick played on our minds—a playful disappointment of their momentary expectation, *and* a pleasure offered to their underlying trends."[21]

A "dirty joke," like any other kind of funny story, can employ ludicrously incongrous images that are funny in the Aristotelian way. (Think of the potbellied colonel locked out of his hotel room by an angry courtesan, with nothing more than a bath towel to protect his dignity.) But insofar as the joke is a *story*, a narrated sequence of events leading up to a comic climax, it fits the Kantian mold. Expectations are created and then suddenly disappointed in a kind of practical joke on the mind, and then (often) by some verbal sleight of hand, a substitute reward is provided. The process, of course, is not simply the mechanical application of some formula. If it is to evoke sudden laughter the trick must be played with dexterity and wit ("verbal felicity or ingenuity and swift perception, especially of the incongruous," according to *Webster's* third edition.)[22] Appreciation of the joke's dexterity and wit then adds another layer of pleasure to the "tickled" victim of the trick.

Most theorists of humor have grasped the Kantian point that funny stories cause laughter by tricking the expectations of the reader or listener, and thus releasing him from a kind of "tension." Laughter itself is metaphorically conceived as a "triggered explosion" in which the tension of a coiled spring is released, thus offering "relief." There are, notoriously, dozens of theories about the workings of the trigger mechanism and the nature of the relief, all of which seem to apply to some but not to all of the major types of humor.[23] Whatever the nature of the "mechanism" of laughter, the phenomenon itself, at least often or even characteristically, maintains a certain independence from other psychic states and systems. The "tensions" that are exploited by the joke may include some general anxieties that the laughing person carries with him as part of his permanent burden—anxieties associated with the subject matter of the joke, for example, or nervousness connected with his suspicions of the story teller. (Is he being derisive? or seductive? Will he embarrass himself or me or others?) But if the story is to be received as genuinely *funny* and responded to as such, it must create and then discharge its *own* "tensions," and not merely draw on the standing anxieties of the audience. Laughter, according to Arthur Koestler, is an "activity detached from any utilitarian purpose . . . a *luxury reflex* unconnected with the struggle for survival, a kind of biological luxury . . ."[24] In a given case, of course, laughter can have a biological or psychological function. It can relieve aggression, allay anxiety, or relax an overly tense musculature. But the comic can do these useful things for us only by amusing us first, and amusement is a response to what is funny. Funny objects, in turn, are states and sequences that we might find ugly or unpleasant if we perceived them in a deadly serious mood. But when we are in the requisite playful state, as we are fortunately much of the time, then certain harmlessly ugly sights please rather than hurt the eye; absurd incongruities delight rather than offend the understanding; and slight of hand tricks on the mind please rather than anger their "victims."

Dirty jokes are no exception to the generalization made by D. H. Parker[25] about comic stories and plays: Comedy typically involves a standard (principle, rule, or norm) and an object or performance that fails somehow to measure up to the standard. In some cases we adopt the point of view of the standard and "laugh down" at the discrepant object or person, as when we delight in the undignified fall of the pompously powerful. In other cases we take the opposite viewpoint, that of the comically discrepant object itself, and we laugh at the standard, as for example when we laugh at cute children masquerading as adults, or in a quite different example, we laugh at a risqué story, and thus have some fun at the expense of the sexual conventions violated in the tale. Parker, I think, was mistaken to suggest that *all* laughter is laughter *at* something or other. The human mind is capable of taking rich comic pleasure in the apprehension of pure incongruity (disparity, discrepancy, disproportion) as such, without necessarily "taking sides" between a standard and a violative object. Still, the identifications to which Parker refers are especially likely to occur in the case of the obscene story, so Parker's distinction will be useful in the attempt to classify types of dirty jokes by the various forms of comic response to which they characteristically appeal.

Some dirty jokes are forms of whimsical humor, playful tricks in language. They are narrated and received in a spirit of sly waggishness. In order to enjoy stories of this kind a person must have a somewhat less than reverent attitude toward the moral norms and standards violated in the story. In Parker's terms, one identifies with the violative object and gently mocks the violated norms. The characteristic spirit, however, is not acidly derisive; an amused chuckle is not an angry snort. Comedy above all else is fun.

In many dirty jokes, naughty evasions of sexual norms occur both in the story and in the very act of telling the story, and in others (especially those that achieve their comic effect by playing on hidden meanings) mischievous norm-violation in the telling is the whole source of the amusement. The obscene pun is a rather pure example of the latter genre. Despite its light-hearted spirit, the obscene pun is thought to be subversive by moralists, Farb tells us, "because it cleverly attacks the sacredness of taboo words, and it manages to do so with apparent innocence."[26] Our delighted response is like that of the mischievous school child who has tricked the teacher by adhering to the letter of some trivial prohibition while totally circumventing its motivating spirit. The main fun is at teacher's expense, and if she has any sense of humor and any appreciation of wit and dexterity, she will slyly smile herself. Similarly, "A speaker who says 'She was only a fisherman's daughter, but when she saw my rod she reeled' is really launching a sneak attack upon verbal taboos by the use of a pun."[27] Since the words are ambiguous, listeners may respond to different messages in appropriately different ways, but when a listener laughs, he "thereby becomes accomplice to challenging the taboos of his speech community."[28]

Puns are generally considered a lowly form of humor because they require little ingenuity to construct, and one often sees through their transparency to their very simple internal mechanisms. Dirty limericks on the other hand are a prankish form of wit that employs the resources of meter, rhyme, and bizarre imagery, to play the same kind of joke, though with less semblance of "innocence," on word taboos and other sexual norms. Their trickery is clever, setting us up in one way then springing their trap in the final line in such a way as to delight any playful mind. Even obscene practical jokes, when sufficiently inventive, can tickle the playful mind. It is said that when the full-scale replica of Michaelangelo's equestrian statue of Marcus Aurelius was unveiled at Brown University some seventy years ago, in a formal ceremony with bands and visiting celebrities, a great fountain of water spurted from the horse's phallus on to the crowd. Working by dark of night, a group of undergraduate pranksters had drilled a hole in the end of the iron phallus and filled the horse's hollow body with water. Then they plugged the hole and connected the plug to the string used during the ceremony to draw back the curtain and reveal the statue in all its glory. It is said that the horse passed water for two days. The laughter caused by this prank clearly could not have occured if the pranksters had drilled their hole anywhere else. Involvement of the horse's phallus (a "tabooed organ") made the joke at once naughty and clever. Without its central role in the incident, the prank would have been merely pointless and destructive.[29]

A second class of dirty jokes is so-called *risqué* humor and off-color stories that characteristically evoke prurient snickers and smirking giggles. Perhaps *any* kind of dirty joke can be responded to in this way, though some jokes are typically told with the intention of producing such responses, and may be specially suited to produce them, having very little appeal of any other kind. The important point though is about the nature of the comic response. The jokester takes seriously the taboos that he exploits, and he expects his audience to do the same. Then he sneakily violates them. The response is self-conscious and mixed with shame—furtive smirks and snickers. The pleasure is taken in what is acknowledged to be a kind of dirty-mindedness. (See Chap. 15, §2.) There will often be genuine arousal produced by the story's erotic content, to which the person responds with characteristic ambivalence. He can wallow in lust as long as he allows himself to feel ashamed at the same time. In Parker's terms he is laughing at the norms but not in an unreserved and whole-hearted way. His own laughter frightens him and he will swallow it instantly if teacher should look his way. Indeed he is capable of switching perspectives in an instant, coming to think of his laughter as directed at the foibles of the violative object. He does that because he still takes the violated norms so seriously that he cannot long laugh at *them* with a clear conscience. And so the laughter is either sneaky and shameful, or hypocritical and smarmy. Not a pleasant thing to behold.[30]

A third kind of dirty joke (or type of response to any dirty joke) is ribald humor, those earthy tales that produce hearty and robust laughter. Eastman distinguishes between what he calls "the dirty-minded smirk of the Victorians and the hearty sexual laughter of the Elizabethans," and "the naughty snicker of the hothouse-bred modern from the merry outdoor laughter of the olden times."[31] The latter is the humor of people who have no reverence for prohibitive norms, and indeed of people who have no such norms governing their linguistic and much of their sexual behavior. Their laughter releases no "tension" from sources external to the joke; it expresses no derision and allays no anxiety. It is simply a kind of fun of the sort that is common to all humor—ludicrous images and ingenious tricks on the mind that spontaneously tickle the fancy of a playful spirit. That the jokes happen to be about sex and other "bodily functions" needs no special explanation, since these are central areas of human experience often in the forefront of awareness and attention.

Eastman rejects Freud's theory because (as he puts it) "it sins against humor in making it all furtive."[32] Freud's view is yet another theory that identifies the whole genus with one of its eccentric subspecies. Some jokes *do* amuse by tricking our internal censor and thus releasing tension, but the same joke may amuse others whose censors are long gone on holiday, by simply tricking the mind in a way that naturally elicits delight. Eastman illustrates the point with the following joke:

> A woman got on the train with nine children, and when the conductor came for her tickets she said: "Now these three are thirteen years old and pay full fare, but those three over there are only six, and these three here four and a half." The conductor looked at her in astonishment.
> "Do you mean to say you get three every time?" he asked.
> "Oh no," she said. "Sometimes we don't get any at all."[33]

This joke easily fits into one of Parker's explanatory categories. It makes us laugh, in a good-natured way, at the woman who inadvertently reveals her preoccupation with sex, and thus brings out a disparity between conduct and pretension. If we are delighted by such incongruity for its own sake (as all playful spirits are) we can think of the story as funny without identifying firmly either with violative object or violated standard. More repressed persons may find the humor clouded by their own anxieties and embarrassment at the very subject matter of the joke. Eastman contrasts his "Victorians" and "Elizabethans" in this regard, in commenting on the train joke:

> Is it not clear that the tripping of your mind in what it starts to make of the phrase "every time" is the jocular element here, and that the improper allusion to the sexual act is merely protected by this element, and rendered admissible to your polite speech? And is it not equally clear that whether your speech is polite and in the habit of repressing such allusions or not, will make no difference to the witty value of the joke? If you have that habit, you will enjoy it with a somewhat smirking giggle, if not, you will enjoy it with a jovial laugh.[34]

The "smirking giggle" is the expression of playful amusement mixed with a little embarrassment, derived partly from your secret feeling that the joke is not only on a fictitious lady, but also to some degree on *you*. Not only guilt, but shame and personal embarrassment, among various other states, can mix with amusement to make a smirk instead of a laugh. Eastman's main point, however, is that genuinely jovial laughter is possible too, at the dirty joke as well as other things.

6. The useful but limited contribution of obscene words to obscene humor

Some comic stories with sexual themes can be told in utterly antiseptic language, and yet be "dirty" because of their content, their "improper" reference to tabooed things and events. It is not the *form* of the reference that makes the stories "obscene," not the particular *words* employed, but what is said. If we were to tell the same jokes with dirty words substituted for the euphemisms, there might be some small gain in what Eastman calls the "pleasure in reality frankly spoken"[35] produced typically by effective ribaldry. But the comic point in these tales does not turn upon the language used and would be amusing even without the added element of ribaldry. In other stories, like Eastman's train story told above, the substitution or intrusion of dirty words would actually spoil the comic effect.

Obscene language, then, is by no means essential to all obscene humor and quite incompatible with some of it. Many other dirty jokes, however, centrally involve the use of dirty words. To some degree at least, in these cases, the words themselves, and not just what they refer to, contribute to the comic point, which could not be made as well, if at all, in neutral language. Often the dirty words *refer* to objects and activities that are tabooed, but even in these instances, it is the independent emotive meaning, and not merely the emotive force that derives from our attitudes toward the objects referred to, that supports the humor. In other cases, the dirty word is not used to make reference, even vulgar reference, to anything, but rather to express strong feeling, contribute color, or make an insult in ways that cannot be done in non-obscene language.

The contributions of obscene words to obscene humor can be merely helpful, making an already funny story funnier still, or essential, making funny a story that would not otherwise be remotely amusing. In the former category are stories told in obscene language where the main comic point is in the narrated events and images (the same as the linguistically antiseptic stories). The obscene words nevertheless make a strong contribution by highlighting and emphasizing, and expressing the (highly irreverent) attitudes of the speaker toward the events he narrates. They add spice and seasoning and magnify comic impact, though the comedy is in the narrated events themselves. One can hardly overstate the tactical importance to effective story-telling of the proper manipulation of *emphases*. The humorist, as Burgess Johnson points out, is one who has "artistry in the placing of emphasis and the determining of its proper quantity."[36] To achieve the proper comic effect, it is essential to manipulate the listener's expectations, build up in him the right degree of attentive tension, and then spring the trap on him. The story can fail if language gives insufficient emphasis at critical points or if it intrudes with verbal red herrings at just the wrong places. Nothing is more deadly than "cloying exaggeration and wearisome overstatement,"[37] which as Johnson notes, generally indicate a lack of humor:

> Little boys and traveling salesmen and a lot of other people are not aware of that important truth. They put in the old-fashioned curse word or the four letter obscenity at the moment of [comic] climax and think that it *alone* caused the laughter. So next time they put in more curse words or more obscenities and expect the laughter to be louder. I have even known them to leave out the

real point altogether in their eagerness to insert the tabooed words, and then look about eagerly for applause.[38]

Johnson's point is of course well taken. Indeed there are even risqué stories that require manipulation of expectation through subtle adjustment of emphases in such a way that the interjection of one single obscenity would spoil everything. Nevertheless, there are a myriad of other dirty jokes whose comic impact would be much diminished without the high-lighting provided by obscene words at critical junctures. Some of these can be called "dirty" only because dirty words have provided unexpected emphasis in a story not otherwise concerned with sexual or scatological themes, and others are called dirty anyway because of their content, but dirty words help the humor along. It is time for examples (one of each).

> One day in Cleveland John Smith began hearing voices. "Go to Las Vegas, Go to Las Vegas," they kept saying. Six months later the voices had not relented, and Smith, at his wit's end, took a plane to Las Vegas, and checked in at a hotel. Then the voice started again. "Go to the casino," it said. Smith did not like to gamble, but after a couple of days of constantly reiterated direction, he succumbed in despair. "Go to the roulette table," the voice said, in a tone that had become stern and peremptory. "Bet one hundred dollars on red." Smith did as he was told, and the ball landed on red. "Bet it all on black," said the voice with impressive calm. Smith obeyed and again he won. Now the voice had taken on a deep, sepulchral, even mystic tone of serene confidence. It echoed through his mind so loudly, he was surprised that it was not audible to everyone. "Again, bet everything on red," it decreed. Smith no longer hesitated. Again he won. And so it went, as a crowd began to gather. Soon his winnings were over a million dollars, and the owner of the casino himself stood nervously at the table, fearing that one more turn of the wheel would break the bank. Smith started to pocket the money, but the voice spoke again in a God-like manner: "Put it all on red." The wheel went around and round, and the ball finally came to rest on . . . BLACK. And the voice said "Oh, shit!"

Suppose that the voice had said "alas!" There would still have been some amusement in the story, but hardly an explosive release of laughter. Even gods might say "alas." But "oh shit!" is a very human thing to say in moments of great disappointment. These words in the story make it instantly clear that Smith was not let down by a god or a mystic phenomenon, but by his own very human and vulnerable self.

A second example of the helpful if not essential use of dirty words is a story that would be dirty anyway (and funny anyway), but which is given a comic boost by its obscene language.

> A traveling salesman, between trains in Chicago, meets a girl at the railroad station and says, "Look, I've got to catch another train in half an hour so I

don't have time to fuck around. Do you screw or don't you?" The girl replies, "Well, I'm not usually that kind of person—but you just talked me into it."[39]

Imagine the story told with "time to waste" substituted for "time to fuck around," and "go to bed" substituted for "screw." The comic point would still remain. The girl could no more attribute her seduction to the persuasive eloquence of the salesman in that euphemistic version than she could in the obscene original. But the incongrous contrast between motive and rationalization and hence between conduct and pretension would be blurred, and the comic focus weakened.

There are many other examples of dirty stories that would have no comic point at all without their obscene words. The whole point of these stories derives from the use of the forbidden words. In some cases, the stories would be called dirty anyway because of their content or subject matter, but without the dirty words they could not be funny. Most of the jokes in this category are concerned with the norms of linguistic propriety, rather than norms governing sexual behavior. As we have seen, obscene puns are ways of mocking and subverting these norms which also manage to tickle the funny bone when they are sufficiently dextrous and witty. Other jokes are more complex than puns, but employ similar principles to similar ends.

> An inexperienced newspaperman was scolded by his editors for composing excessively wordy headlines. The following day he learned that a man had escaped from a mental institution, run amok, terrorized a neighboring town, and raped a woman. In all its flavorful detail, the reporter zestfully wrote his story . . . and sent it to press with the headline: NUT BOLTS AND SCREWS.[40]

Here the obscene word is employed to make vulgar reference to sexual activity. Not only is there spontaneous delight in the wit of the triple equivocation, the concluding word, perfectly suited to provide emphasis, drives home the comic twist and makes fun of a purely linguistic taboo.[41] The reporter, about whom the story is told, does not violate any *other* kind of taboo.

A second example of the genre is the following:

> Just after the triumphant conclusion of World War II, a large unit of the British army assembled in a public square in London for a military ceremony that featured the presentation of medals for valor by no less than King George himself. All went well until the royal family confronted the final hero, Corporal Grinsby, of the Twentieth Infantry Regiment.
>
> The king addressed Grinsby in the same tired, florid rhetoric he had used in previous presentations. "Under intense enemy fire, he . . ."
>
> "Shit," whispered Grinsby.

"Indifferent to his personal safety he . . ."

"Shit" said Grinsby, more audibly.

"Quiet, man," rebuked the king. "Remember that the queen is here."

"Showing valor above and beyond the call of duty . . ."

"Shit," said Grinsby in a strong voice, now clearly audible.

"For God's sake, man," said the scandalized monarch, "I implore you to watch your language. The queen is right here, and she can hear you! Please don't embarrass the queen!"

At that point Queen Mary stepped forward and shouted: "Fuck him, George; if he doesn't want the Goddamned medal don't give it to him!"

There is humor in this story on several levels. Both of Eastman's basic kinds of humor are represented, each indispensably dependent on a dirty word. We chuckle throughout at the ludicrous image of an enlisted man saying "shit" to his monarch. What a comic cartoon could be drawn of the corporal stiffly at attention and the formally garbed king with an astonished look on his face. Then the surprise twist that takes us off guard at the end (if the storyteller is dextrous enough) and explodes our tension, functions to mock the queen's authority and allows us to have fun at her expense. More than that, we relish the breathtaking incongruity of a violation of a basic rule of linguistic civility by the very paragon of propriety and majestic dignity. Even if our laughter does not mock the norm or its illustrious violator, we relish the disparity for its own sake. Imagine substituting "Don't bother with the man, your highness" for "Fuck him, George"! Without the offending word, ludicrously conjoined with the proper name, there could be no joke.

15

Obscene Words and Social Policy

1. Context and paradox

As a useful approximation to the truth, I asserted in our earlier discussion that the primary function of obscene words is simply to offend, and that by virtue of that basic function, obscene words have a number of other derivative uses. But that cannot be *quite* right. The more exact truth about obscene words is more complicated and even somewhat paradoxical. It is probably more accurate to say that the primary or immediate effect of obscene words is to conspicuously violate taboos, and that obscenities, by virtue of their function as taboo-breakers, have unavoidable immediate effects on the feelings of listeners to which we can refer compendiously, though somewhat misleadingly, as "offense." In general contexts the unprepared listener will be put in an unpleasant state. He will be shocked, alarmed, made anxious or uneasy, angered, annoyed, or repelled; he will be at the very least alerted, aroused, "put on his toes." Obscene words *sometimes* do this partly by virtue of their literal references (dependent emotive meaning), and even non-obscene words used to describe or narrate inappropriate subject matter can have the same effect. Obscene words, however, standardly have such effects, even when they refer to nothing at all, and they have that impact simply and entirely because they violate taboos against the uttering of certain sounds or the writing of certain marks. In defying the taboos against the very utterance of the proscribed sounds, we underline, emphasize, call attention to ourselves and what we are doing or saying, express disrespectful attitudes either toward the norms themselves, or our listeners, or the subject of our discourse, and so on. That in turn enables us, depending on other contextual features, to achieve such "derivative" purposes as deep expression, counter-evocation, suppression of pain and conquest of fear, the disowning of assumed pieties, effective badinage, emphatic insult, challenge, provocation, and even, as we have seen, seduction, amusement, and the triggering of waggish or ribald laughter.

Even this fuller account of the function and uses of obscene language needs serious qualification, and attention to a paradox. First, the qualification. The first and fundamental thing that obscene words do is to defiantly violate norms, but the norms they violate are *contextual* rather than absolute prohibitions. In more religious times and places, to utter the unutterable name of God or other profanities *ever* was to commit a dreadful sin.' The prohibitions against sexual and scatological obscenities, however, are typically not so far-reaching. Everyone knows and understands these terms and their practical uses. Almost everyone is prepared to use them with some trusted friends when sufficiently provoked. There are some contexts in which it is universally understood that they are permissible, and others in which they are actually *de règle* or even *de rigueur*. In the barracks room they cannot reasonably be expected to offend listeners, though of course they are recognized by anyone who understands the language as words which may not safely be used in public contexts or formal situations. They are words whose general shock value enables them to perform useful derivative tasks even among those who are in no way shocked or offended by them. Even the most hardened muleskinner or dogface, however, will be shocked if he hears (say) his mother, or (say) the President of the United States in a televised address, use one of the forbidden words. Linguistic norms are part and parcel of an elaborate structure of norms of propriety, norms which prescribe what may be done or said, by whom, to whom, and in what situations. Overalls may not be worn at a formal dance; it simply is not done. Nor may construction workers wear tuxedos to work; that "is not done" either.

The "paradox" grows out of our bold assertion that the primary and immediate job of obscenities is to violate the general taboos against their own use. Looked at in a utilitarian light, it is as if the main point in having the taboos in the first place is to make possible their violation so that certain "derivative" purposes can be achieved. What seems paradoxical is that if we all understood the rationale of the rules in this way, then none of us would take them very seriously as independently grounded norms, and in that case their "magic" would disappear and they could no longer achieve their useful derivative purposes. In that case a kind of moral fiction or "noble lie" is needed to sustain their usefulness, a cost that seems to many (as we shall see in section 4) to be excessive for the purchased benefits.

And yet the benefits are impressive. Perhaps chief among them is that obscenities enable us to express personal disavowals of prevailing pieties in a uniquely emphatic manner. Obscenity, as we have seen, is above all else the language of impiety, irreverence, and disrespect. Sometimes we are tempted to use it to convey a disrespectful attitude towards a particular person, or our rejection of a particular platitude. Others use it habitually to reject the prevailing norms of propriety generally, to express a certain attitude toward life, and to convey an image of cynical tough-mindedness. Such persons want us to know that *they* have no reverence for "bullshit stuff"; *they* see through sentimentality, patriotic cant, and the like. Let the pious pussyfoot around hard truths; they want us to know that *they* are always prepared to believe it and tell it "like it is," because they are tough, hard-boiled straight-shooters, not mealy-mouthed hypocrites. And so they pepper their talk with obscenities. That shows that they are vulgarians, but so much the worse, they reply, for the conventions that define vulgarity.

2. A distinction between distinctions: euphemism–cacophemism versus prophemism–disphemism

Nobody, however, can plausibly subject everything to disrespectful mockery. Just as we wish to have terms of disrespect, indeed emphatic disrespect, so we need complementary terms of respect, and (unless we are the sort to whom nothing is sacred), terms of esteem and veneration. If Jones is appropriately called an "asshole," so Smith is best referred to as "Mr. Smith," or "Father Smith," or (as the case may be) "Your Honor," or "Mr. President." The neutral attitude which we have toward most people is perhaps best expressed simply by "Smith" or "Jones." Because of this variation in our attitudes, our language provides us with triads (and even sometimes quartets or quintets) of terms, sometimes (but not always) subtly modulated to reflect a full range of possible attitudes, pro and con, as well as simple businesslike neutrality toward precisely the same referent. Most people die, but some are said to "croak," and others to "pass away." They are then called simply "the deceased," or "the lately departed" or "the corpse" or "cadaver." Most couples have sexual intercourse, but some are said to "fuck," and others, (more delicately) to "make love," or "go to bed" or "sleep together." All people defecate; but some "take craps," others "move their bowels," still others "relieve themselves," and children "sit on the potty." These things are done in "lavatories," "bathrooms," or "shithouses." In short, some spades are simply spades and best so-called; others are digging implements; and others are "bloody shovels."

A given neutral term may have dozens of descriptive synonyms. Some of these may also be emotively neutral. The others, however, are all conventional vehicles for the expression of what can be called with deliberate vagueness, "positive" or "negative" attitudes. These include respectful and disrespectful, approving and disapproving, favoring and disfavoring, liking and disliking, and softening and toughening attitudes, and many other types of polarized responses. Speaking very loosely at first, we can label the terms expressing positive attitudes "euphemisms" (from the Greek *euphemos*, good-sounding, auspicious) and those expressing negative ones "cacophemisms" (from the Greek *kakia*, evil and *phemos*, sounding) despite the largely heterogeneous character of both groups of terms. Then we can note immediately that obscenities are one subclass of cacophemisms (the most extreme ones) and that wherever there is a cacophemism for a given neutral term, there are likely to be one or many corresponding euphemisms as well.

The situation is more complicated, however, than one simple distinction can suggest. Failure to appreciate the motley character of the classes of polar responses I have called "positive and negative attitudes" can distort our understanding of the way in which conventionally obscene words serve as cacophemisms. In the chart below I try to make a further distinction among these "attitudes." There are two classes of negative attitudes that obscene and other vulgar words commonly express. They are hardly ever used to condemn or express reasoned disapproval—and never to express *moral* condemnation or disapproval—of that to which they refer. But they commonly express either dislike (of their referents), on the one hand, or disrespect (of rules or listeners), on the other. The word "shit" and its close relations are the favorite vehicles for expressing distaste or dislike, and the supreme obscenity "to fuck" is the best example of a word that standardly expresses disrespect. When one refers to excrement as "shit," very likely one is expressing one's distaste, especially if one's utterance is accompanied by appropriate gestures or facial expressions. The word "shit" is an effective instrument for this expressive task mainly because of the general attitudes widely shared in our culture toward its literal referent, that is, because of its dependent emotive meaning. But "shit" is also an *obscenity*, condemned by a verbal taboo, and like all obscenities it exploits its own prohibition to express disrespect too. The word "fuck," not having negative dependent emotive meaning derived from association with its literal referent, is a purer case of the expression of disrespect. When that term is used typically, what is expressed is a tough attitude that rejects piety and sentimentalism, in the spirit of "telling it like it is." Obviously, the attitude so described is better called *disrespect* (impiety, irreverence, etc.) than disapproval, distaste, or dislike.

Many writers, including the authoritative Gershon Legman, use the term "disphemism," instead of our "cacophemism," as an antonym for "euphemism."[2] It is good to have another term available, since we can use it to help mark the distinction between words expressing disapproval, distaste, or dislike for their referents, which we can now call *disphemisms*, and terms expressing disrespect for norms, which we can continue to call (extreme) *cacophemisms*. Unfortunately, the term "euphemism" will then be ambiguous, serving in one sense as an antonym of "cacophemism" and in another sense as an antonym of "disphemism." The ambiguity can be eliminated, however, if we are willing to tolerate the neologism "prophemism" (ugh!) as the correlative to "disphemism" and let "euphemism" be the antonym of "cacophemism." Since all obscene words can function as cacophemisms and only some (mainly the scatological ones) as disphemisms, our major interest here will be in the function of cacophemisms and euphemisms. The distinction between our basic distinctions is charted in the diagram below.

1. PROPHEMISTIC VS. DISPHEMISTIC TERMS

Words that are:		Words that are:
honorific		pejorative
approbatory		disapprobatory
expressive of liking	vs.	expressive of disliking
laudatory		condemnatory
endorsing		derogatory

Like "lady," "statesman," "attorney," "public servant," "making love"	Like "bitch," "bureaucrat," "shit," "shyster," "nigger," "carnal sin"

2. EUPHEMISTIC VS. CACOPHEMISTIC TERMS

Words that are:		Words that are:
respectful		irreverent
pious		contemptuous
cultivated		uncouth
refined		rough
gentled		coarse
prettified	vs.	blunt
softened		unsoftened
cushioned		direct
indirect		rude
delicate		vulgar
decorous		indecorous
tactful		tactless

Like "powder room," "throw up," "pass away," "tinkle," "go to bed with"	Like "the can" (or "the crapper"), "puke," "croak" (for "die"), "piss," "fuck"

Allen Walker Read defines cacophemism as "the rhetorical device of speaking ill of a thing, as in calling one's clothes duds, one's horse a nag, any woman a bitch."[3] His examples are a perfect illustration of the confusion between cacophemism and disphemism. In the slangy American English of the 1930s, "duds" was a mild cacophemism for clothes, as "grub" was for food, and "dame" was for a woman. But "nag" is a (gentle) disphemism for a horse; "poison" or "garbage" are not so gentle disphemisms for food; "bitch" and "broad" are vulgar disphemisms for a woman. When we use prophemisms and disphemisms we speak good or ill of their referents; we laud or derogate, praise or condemn. When we use cacophemisms, however, we do not necessarily speak ill of anything. Cacophemistic language is a rough and raw, blunt and vulgar way of saying anything—good, evil, or neutral—of a thing. Not all of it is obscene by any means; witness "grub" and "duds" for example. Some is *extremely* vulgar, but not quite obscene (that is, not quite categorically tabooed in polite society), likely to offend but not to shock, like "puke," "guts," "fart," "stink," "belly," "croak," and "burp." A genuinely obscene word, in virtue of the taboo its utterance violates, is as cacophemistic as a word can be. But that is still something else than "speaking ill of a thing."

3. The reaction to excessive euphemization

People naturally find some perfectly accurate descriptive terms unflattering and displeasing. It is therefore considered good manners for others to avoid these terms as much as possible, and when one cannot avoid speaking the unpleasant truth, to find descriptive synonyms that strike the ear as less blunt, though they say the same thing as the unflattering term. In this way we generate a stream of euphemisms, in comparison to which the original descriptive term seems ever more coarse, until that term, originally neutral, becomes itself a cacophemism. The words "fat" and "old" are good examples of this process. It is now considered to be blunt almost to the point of uncouthness to refer to a fat person as "fat." And while there are a few rather disphemistic ways of saying the same thing ("potbellied," "fat-assed," "lard-assed," "gross"), there are few other terms that are as cacophemistic now as the straightforward unadorned "fat." Yet there are at least a dozen euphemisms that are quite acceptable, even to a fat person of the most delicate sensibility: "stocky," "portly," "stout," "pudgy," "chubby," "heavy-set," "corpulent," "bulky," "plump," and "beefy." The closest thing to a neutral description, the latinate "obese" (once a primarily medical term), is now going the way of "fat," a term of unwelcome frankness.

William Safire describes the similar evolution away from the straightfoward "old" (and it goes without saying, the cacophemistic "geezer" and the disphemistic "fogey.") "Old people did not like that description of themselves, and liked 'aged' or 'aging' not much more; soon they came to be called the elderly: Even this euphemism seemed unduly doddering, so we were treated to 'senior citizen' and 'golden ager,' and old women keep their chins up by calling themselves 'mature'."[4]

In his famous discussion of the process of euphemization in *The American Language,* H. L. Mencken has great fun with the word "toilet" and its relatives.[5] The word "toilet" as a term designating a room reserved for urination and/or defecation began its career in English as a euphemism (a "ludicrous gossamer of speech," as Mencken puts it disphemistically) for "franker terms," now mostly forgotten. But euphemisms can fool people only so long, and in time become ever more indelicate in their turn, stimulating the need for new euphemisms. "Toilet" changes its status from euphemism to "neutral term" and even finally to a "slightly soiled" cacophemism. The process of euphemization is so continuously renewed that it is hard to know at any particular time what is neutral and what isn't. Soon the tenderminded began using "retiring-room," "washroom," and "public comfort station," as well as "little boy's room," "little girl's room," "men's room," "ladies' room," "restroom," "head" (of the ship), "bathroom" (even when it contains no bath), and even "powderroom." Powderroom indeed! No wonder there is a countertendency in the language to strip and debunk by using such coined cacophemisms as "the john"[6] and "the can." And for those who delight in "truth frankly spoken," there is the obscene cacophemism "shit-house." There are few if any disphemisms for "toilet," and no prophemisms either, although "comfort station" comes close.

There is hardly any limit to the number of devices that are employed to soften references to anxiety-producing topics, and cushion the jolt of such references to vulnerable sensibilities. Foreign terms like "toilet" (in English) and "W.C." (in French) are commonly used. Antiseptically clinical scholarly and scientific terms are coined from parts of ancient languages and borrowed by nonscholars and nonscientists in the interests of delicacy. In this category belong "micturation," "defecation," "phallus," and "coitus." Then there are circumlocutions such as "in a delicate condition," "house of ill-repute," and "carnal connection," and mendacious evasions like "bathroom" and "sleep with."

One interesting category contains euphemisms coined especially for children—"tummy," "fanny," "wee-wee," "tinkle," "wee-wee stick," and so on. For generations it has been the custom of parents not to refer to "private parts" and their biological functions at all with their children, or at least no more than necessary. And when reference cannot be avoided, it must be made in specially invented children's language in which the cuddly-cute terms of reference are free of all associations of adult vulgarity. Even impeccably neutral scientific terms like "penis" and "urinate" must be avoided so that the shock of straightforward reference might be cushioned.[7] We must note here a point of some importance about this kind of euphemization and its imprinting effects on the developing sensibilities of the child. If an infant were told bluntly to sit on the toilet and shit, instead of sit on the potty and make poo-poo, he would of course not know the difference, since he is learning the language as well as hygiene from his parents, and no word will seem any more appropriate than any other for the processes he is experiencing. The coarse cacophemisms, in that case, will never acquire their magical hold over him, and linguistic taboos during a critical period of development will have little force. Given these facts, infantile euphemization frequently becomes a silly masquerade, with the parents acting as if they already had a tender regard for infant sensibilities that do not yet exist, but are in fact being created. Toilet training, in short, is also language training and linguistic-taboo training. Because of euphemization at the earliest stage of language-acquisition, words like "shit" can acquire their expressiveness later in life.

In respect to processes of excretion and sexual behavior, as in many other areas, our language is richer in euphemisms than in neutral and cacophemistic terms of reference. There are not many more obscenities for toilet and lavatory than "shit-house" but as we have seen, there is a great profusion of euphemisms. "Fuck" and "screw" remain the perennial cacophemistic obscenities for coitus, joined from time to time by occasional slangy terms that come and go with fashion, but euphemisms abound. In other areas where people try to rub the coarseness off referential words, much the same is true. Mencken devotes all of his subchapter on "euphemism" to words for trades and vocations, on the one hand, and words for ethnic groups on the other.[8] He reminds us there that rat-catchers prefer to be called "exterminating engineers," though they will settle for terms like "exterminator," and "pest controller." Similarly, corpse embalmers can choose among "mortician," "undertaker," "funeral director," "embalming surgeon," and so on. When Mencken wrote, the more respectable name for Jews was "Hebrews," and Negroes were becoming "Afro-Americans." Where negative terms for trades and ethnic groups proliferate, they tend to be disphemistic rather than cacophemistic, terms of disapproval and dislike rather than blunt taboo-breakers expressing disrespect for proprieties. Thus "heinie," "kraut," "frog," "mick," "limey," "dago," "wop," "hunkie," "kike," "sheenie," "spic," "nigger," and "coon" tend to be terms of abuse, reeking of hostility, and not merely impolite vulgarities. "Attorney" is a dignified euphemism for lawyer, but "shyster" is not merely an impolite no-nonsense way of referring to a lawyer (not merely a lawyer with his more glittering title removed), but rather a way of referring to a lawyer with dislike and disapproval. Much the same is true of the disphemisms "quack" and "butcher" (as applied to a physician).

Part of the point of using cacophemisms, even obscene ones, is to correct the imbalance caused by an excess of euphemism, and thus disavow emphatically the artificiality and sentimentality that are byproducts of super-scrubbed language. To be sure, the neutral words of reference, where they still exist, can often permit a speaker to make reference without what he takes to be excessive piety and deference. We can still say "lawyer," "doctor," and "government employee" instead of "attorney," "physician," and "public administrator," if we choose. But if too many people are using the euphemisms, then there may be no better way to disavow pompousness than to say "sawbones," "mouthpiece," or "bureaucrat."

The late great American philosopher Curt J. Ducasse, after he retired from Brown University, rarely used either a euphemism or a neutral term to refer to his own death and dying. Instead of "pass away" or "die" he said "croak"; instead of "dead body," he said "carcass." We have already seen (Chap. 10, §6) how these vulgar cacophemisms border on obscenity. Ducasse would use them to make a point. He objected to hypocritical failures to face up to death, deceptive ways of avoiding the subject, and efforts in language always to avoid suggesting it except in awed whispers and linguistic camouflage. His negative words were cacophemisms rather than disphemisms because they did not express negative feelings about their referents, but rather expressed negative attitudes of the speaker about the prevailing attitudes of his listeners toward the referent, namely that it was something to be covered up and disguised. Similarly, a person who prefers "fuck" to "intercourse" or "make love" will be expressing not his distaste for sexual intercourse but rather his contempt for the attitudes of others toward sexual intercourse, and the person who habitually employs a less reverent term for lawyer than "attorney" or "counsel," may be objecting not to lawyers, but to a conception of lawyers as models of respectability especially deserving of titles of honor and respect.

Two decades or so ago, black leaders undertook a campaign to replace the delicate foreign euphemism "Negro" (Spanish for "black") with the vaguely cacophemistic term "black" as the official name for Americans of African descent. The campaign was completely successful and now "black" is the accepted neutral name. Black leaders made the change because they thought that blacks had been so affected by white prejudice that they unconsciously thought of their distinctive racial characteristics as something to be ashamed of, "covered up," and referred to only with softening euphemisms. The new term boldly affirmed what had previously only been indirectly admitted, and thus by embracing what had been a cacophemism, the black community gave a boost to black pride. The term "nigger" could not have achieved the same result, of course, because it is not a cacophemism, but rather an extreme disphemism. "Nigger" expresses contempt for blacks; "black" expressed contempt for prevailing attitudes, white and black, *toward* blacks.

In summary, obscene referential words are always cacophemistic and only sometimes disphemistic as well. They are sometimes, but only sometimes, used to express "negative attitudes" toward their literal referent (disphemism), but they always express disrespect toward prevailing pieties (cacophemism). More often than not, obscene disphemisms are used to express negative feelings toward things other than their literal referents, as when another person's beliefs or arguments are called "a lot of shit." These metaphorical transfers of attitude are perhaps the most common way in which scatological obscenities are employed in living discourse. Similarly, sexual cacophemisms are often used to exploit the shocking effect of taboo-infraction and transfer the irreverent attitude thereby expressed to objects and contexts that are in no way sexual. Thus "Get your fucking rifles," said by the sergeant to his troops, is a kind of cacophemistic metaphor, invoking the disrespect originating in one context of reference, to give color and emphasis to expression in a wholly unrelated context.

4. Two strategies for ridding the language of obscene words

Although all natural languages have obscene words, a language without obscenities is nevertheless conceivable. What would it be like if obscene words disappeared from our language? There are two ways in which the disappearance could come about, and for each there are writers who advocate that it become our deliberate policy, while a third view urges that obscene expressiveness be protected and preserved. The disappearance might happen (and *should* happen according to the first view) if everybody took seriously the word-taboos that create obscenity and stopped violating them. The tabooed words would fall into desuetude and no new ones would take their places. The second path to linguistic purity would be followed if no one took the word-taboos seriously. People would so commonly use naughty words that the emotive luster would rub off them and they would lose their capacity to shock and offend. The words would survive but they would become clean through overuse. The model for this second process (or second strategy for enemies of obscenity) is what has already happened to profanity. The standard speaker of American English in the final decades of the twentieth century can no longer be shocked by "goddam," "hell," or "damn." "May God blind me," once the most electric of the vain oaths, is now the mild cockney intensifier "gorblyme," its origin known only by lexicographers and amateur scholars. A third possibility, also advocated as a policy by some writers, is to keep alive the tensions between practice and taboo that make obscene expressiveness possible by encouraging first the one, then the other, as they threaten to get out of balance. This third way is the course of those who, like Robert Graves, Burgess Johnson, and H. L. Mencken, value the contribution that only obscenities can make (through what I have called their "derivative functions") to artful and accurate expression.

The first path to linguistic purification is of course that advocated by the traditional "rigid moralist," or "puritan" as he is often called. The puritan's primary concern has been with the sin of specific writings and utterances here and now, not with the future goal of an obscenity-free language. Indeed if the puritan thought the matter out, he might not welcome the total disappearance of obscenities, for that might in time deprive some of his chief moral preoccupations of their point, and like the newspaper reporters who covered Richard Nixon for many years, he might miss having his bête-noire to kick around. Moreover, if it became impossible to speak obscenely for lack of linguistic resources, then the pure-minded could hardly get moral credit for their consistent use of clean language, and it would be harder than ever to distinguish the sheep from the goats by their speech behavior. Nevertheless the emergence of a language without obscenities is what would happen if the puritan got his way in every particular case, even if that consequence is not part of his conscious objective in opposing obscene utterance.

The hopelessness of the "puritan program" (if we can speak of such a thing at all) is obvious. Suppose that the puritans won political power on a platform that promised to stamp out the obscene words once and for all and keep them from ever returning. We can imagine the most heroic and draconian methods, book burning, capital punishment, paid informers, and so on, and in due time perhaps most citizens might not recognize even "the chief obscenity in our language" as an English word at all. But that four letter word is still one of the only simple single-word locutions we have for referring to sexual intercourse, and as long as sexual intercourse itself continues, a simple direct word for it would inevitably be coined. The question then is whether *that* word would be thought to be obscene. In the climate of thought promoted by puritanism, new obscenification would be inevitable. That is partly because the puritanical attitudes toward sexual behavior itself would continue and naturally transfer to the words that refer to it, and partly because strengthened verbal taboos would quickly convert mere distasteful vulgarisms like "screw" into words like "fuck," so absolutely prohibited as to horrify by their very sound.

Stamping out dirty words would be much easier than keeping them out. New words are constantly generated through the mechanisms of slang, and where there is a need, many of these will be cacophemistic or disphemistic to an extreme. So long as verbal taboos remain in place (and on our present hypothesis they will actually be strenghtened), extreme cacophemism will be tabooed. To their sometimes useful vulgarity will now be added the element of guilty taboo-infraction, so that they will become indistinguishable in their functions from their obscene counterparts in earlier days. There will never be any great difficulty in coining cacophemisms. So long as there are standards of respectability and decorum that people take seriously, so long as the "nothing sacred attitude" remains rare, and piety *about anything at all* persists, there will be ways of thumbing our noses through language. Newly tabooed words will not only offend because of what they mock; they will also achieve an increased momentum of offensiveness through their violation of the newly strengthened verbal taboos that forbid their use. The prohibitive rules tend to be self-defeating, since the stronger the taboo the more useful its infraction.

Because word-taboos tend to convert merely vulgar cacophemism into obscenity, the puritan program, in order to succeed, would either have to weaken the taboos (which of course it could not do and still be the puritan program) or else attempt to banish all cacophemism whether presently obscene or not. Suppose the goal of the puritanical censorship were the extreme one of purging all harsh and softening terms, euphemisms as well as cacophemisms, from the language. Honorific and pejorative terms (prophemisms and disphemisms) are no doubt inevitable and many of them are even useful to the puritan cause, so of course they could stay. Rude and delicate words, however, are not necessary for normal descriptive purposes, and would be rooted out systematically. Only "spades" would be left; "digging implements" and "bloody shovels" both would vanish. A possible puritanical motive for such an extreme campaign would be the plausible fear that the euphemisms, if allowed to persist, would tend to convert their contrasting terms into cacophemisms. If there are only neutral and euphemistic words, the neutral word in each pair will be the relatively harsh one, and those who seek blunt rude words will fasten on it for their purposes. In time the "neutral word," commonly preempted for cacophemistic uses, will come to offend the ears of the relatively fastidious. Those who tire both of tuxedos and overalls will have to design new neutral suits, and the old objectionable triads will return. Stringent verbal taboos would add the element of guilty infraction to the roughest terms in the triads and soon they would seem obscene.

Could the effort to prevent this by uprooting *both* euphemisms and cacophemisms possibly succeed? A language strictly policed to prevent the rise of harsh and delicate words would be one that required the rejection root and branch of the very distinction between respectability and vulgarity. It would be the linguistic analogue of a regime of classless uniformity in manners and dress. No one could be prim and proper; no one could be raffish and unconventional. These very concepts, mutually symbiotic as they are, would vanish in time. Moreover, everyone would be deprived of useful linguistic tools. Piety and impiety, decency and indecency, would alike be difficult to express in any direct and simple way. That would be a loss, of course, only to those who have such attitudes in the first place, but efforts to eradicate those attitudes would be difficult struggles, and their unlikely success a lamentably Pyrrhic victory.

The more probable form, therefore, of a puritan campaign against cacophemism, would be one that tolerated or encouraged euphemism. But a language all of whose descriptive terms were either neutral or euphemistic would suffer its own instabilities. As we have seen, there would be constant pressure on the neutral terms, in virtue of their *relative* coarseness, to become new cacophemisms. Hence there would have to be strong counterpressure on them. They would have to be abandoned and forbidden as soon as they showed the slightest infection of vulgarity. There would be a natural tendency to avoid corruption by using the euphemisms instead of the neutral terms for one's "neutral purposes." As they were used more frequently in this fashion, the euphemisms themselves would become commonplace and subject to the corruption of contrast. New euphemisms would have to be formed, and the turnover rate would accelerate. Soon we would have euphemisms in Victorian profusion, and there would be no recognizing a neutral word as such, since no word would be neutral for long.[9]

There is no more unlikely an ally for the puritans than the enlightened sociologist, Edward Sagarin. Yet Sagarin, for quite distinctive reasons of his own, argues that we should all cease using the currently dirty words. Unlike the puritans, Sagarin explicitly urges this boycott as a tactic designed to cause the death by desuetude of the offending terms. According to Sagarin, both the user of obscenity and the puritan whom he shocks, are expressing what he calls "the anti-biological bias" built into the words themselves. The puritan hears the sound "fuck" and is genuinely horrified at the awesome taboo-infraction. The speaker, however, picked that word to express his "unhealthy" attitudes toward sex, since such attitudes, as he well knew, are built into the sense of the word. An emancipated person who thinks of sex as a normal incident of life, of no more interest morally, say, than a handshake, would not want to use the obscenity, because he does not share the attitudes it expresses. If he nevertheless uses that word from habit or sloth, he inadvertently gives currency to anti-sexual attitudes (according to Sagarin), and plays into the puritan's hands. Sagarin, therefore, is not encouraged by the new freedom—

> Only a campaign to change the language [by eradicating altogether the current obscenities] . . . will save modern man from the fate that—win, lose, or draw in the struggle against censorship—the liberal must lose in the struggle against puritanism . . . Unless one changes the very structure of the language in which obscenities are used, the wider are these words spread among the people, the more will their rigid attitudes toward the body and its functions be reenforced . . . The puritans are losing every battle but they can be cocksure of winning the war.[10]

The title of the chapter in which this argument occurs is well named—"To the Victors Belong the Soiled."

We have already made enough distinctions to enable us to locate the confusions in Sagarin's position. To start, his view seems to be that obscene words are mainly disphemistic—derogatory ways of referring to biological parts and processes and transferring the derogation by metaphor to other disliked persons and things. The present view, on the contrary, is that obscene words are primarily cacophemistic, coarse ways of speaking which, in violating stern prohibitions, tend to shock the hearer and permit such derivative uses as insult, ribaldry, and so on. On the present view, moreover, the distinction between scatological and sexual obscenities is taken seriously. Both are cacophemistic, but the scatological obscenities, in virtue of the near-universal and hygienically useful distaste for digestive waste products, are *also* disphemistic, and highly suitable for metaphorical insults. Thirdly, Sagarin interprets the negative emotive meaning of obscene epithets as entirely dependent on associations to their literal referents and thus ignores the phenomena of "independent emotive meaning" and "emotive inertia or lag."

The sexual obscenities may very well owe their *origin* to unhealthy attitudes toward sex. It is, of course, no accident that it is the sexual words and not (say) the respiratory ones that became obscene. It was because of the increasingly puritanical attitudes toward sex, that the simple, blunt, Anglo-Saxon referential terms turned into cacophemisms that had to be replaced by more delicate circumlocutions. Then the cacophemisms became so rude that they were rigidly tabooed, and that made them obscene. None of that would have happened but for the triumph of negative attitudes toward sex. So far, Sagarin is right. But there are many different kinds of "negative attitudes." The feelings toward sex were never the same as those toward excretion—simple distaste and repugnance. Rather sex was always thought to be powerfully attractive, indeed diabolically attractive, a wicked temptation to be fought and repressed. Because of independent emotive meaning, the taboo against sexual obscenity lagged behind changes in the public attitudes toward sex. These attitudes, to say the least, have diversified over the centuries. Most people, even in this enlightened age, are spontaneously horrified by the sound of the word "fuck," even though they may have no tendency whatever to think of sex as wicked. The horror comes mainly from violation of the taboo, not from association to the biological subject matter.

Even many of those who are sensitive and reticent about sex and are likely to be embarrassed when the subject is raised even in antiseptic language, have "negative attitudes" that must be *contrasted* with those of the puritan. Sex is not wicked to these people, but private.[11] They feel uncomfortable or threatened by talk that seems likely to probe into their intimacies and render public what they would rather not be known. So talk of sex startles and alerts them, and puts them on their guard. When the talk is coarse and vulgar these effects are multiplied. Sexual obscenities, therefore, maintain their potency in such company, but even if they were to disappear permanently from the language, the shyness about sex which they exploit would not go away. It would be to put the cart before the horse to explain the embarrassed diffidence as the consequence of the obscene language. Rather it is a prior condition that obscene language feeds off of.

There is no good reason, then, to think that increased use of sexual obscenities plays into puritans' hands by spreading and reenforcing puritanical attitudes toward sex. Obscenity performs its diverse functions in human life primarily because it exploits the taboo against its own usage, and even though that taboo may have *originated* in puritanical attitudes, it can, because of emotive inertia, survive widespread weakening and changing of those attitudes. Because the taboo is so very powerful, it gives the forbidden words their basic symbolic function: use of those words is the quickest, easiest, most extreme way that one can be vulgar by the use of language. It is vulgarity, not sexuality as such, that shocks.

The second long-range policy for dealing with obscenity aims at the same goal[12] sought by Sagarin (and ironically by the puritans) but employs a reverse strategy. One must not think that the phenomenon of obscenity can be eradicated by strengthened word-taboos. According to the second approach, the word-taboos must be undermined if obscenity is to be eliminated, and this calls for a deliberate "strategy of talking dirty."[3] The top strategist of this policy is Allen Walker Read who would have us get rid of the taboos by defying them, for "When one refrains from using the stigmatized words, one is not ignoring the taboo but is actively abetting it."[4]

Read has no hesitation in identifying the enemy as the word taboos themselves. He wisely distinguishes what he calls "taboo of concept" (which is bad enough) from "taboo of word" (which is even worse), and anticipates Stevenson's doctrine of independent emotive meaning and emotive inertia by pointing out that taboo of word is often entirely independent of taboo of concept. The rigidity and independent power of word-taboos is explained by the way they are learned in childhood: "the hushed awe that surrounds these words, the refusal of information concerning them, or the punishment . . . for an inadvertent use of them."[5] Use of the words in the teeth of the terrifying taboos, however, brings its own rewards, and these explain the persistence of the terms despite the ban on them. The reward is itself the effect of the taboo, namely the thrill of the forbidden. Read refers to it as a "fearful thrill," "the zest of the forbidden," "the sly, lip-licking pleasure in obscenity," and "a titillating thrill of scandalized perturbation." Without the taboo, the thrill would be impossible, and the stronger the taboo, the greater the thrill in violating it.

"Why," Read asks, "should not the taboo be self-defeating?"[16] Why, that is, shouldn't the proscribed words simply disappear, as both Sagarin and the puritans hoped, and thus lead to the demise, in turn, of the now pointless taboo? Read's explanation combines his notion of the "fearful thrill," with what we have called the "derivative functions of obscenity." He calls the latter "inverted taboo," and makes it clear that he is as opposed to it as he is to everything else associated with verbal taboos:

> Here we come to a quirk . . . Some people respond [to taboos] with redoubled use of the words. They wish to feel the thrill of doing the forbidden to express the jangled state of their nerves, or to clothe an insult by what they feel are fitting terms. This is not a breaking of the taboo, but an observance of the taboo in a manner contrary to the normal. It may be called "inverted taboo."[19]

This is precisely the place where Read's argument goes wrong. If a taboo says that one *may not* use a certain word *ever*, and one proceeds with all deliberateness to use that word publicly in order to exploit its shock value for some ulterior purpose, one clearly *violates* the taboo. If doing what a taboo forbids is not breaking the taboo, what could possibly count as breaking it? To insist that a violation of a word-taboo is actually an "observance" of the taboo, if only it is done to achieve some intended effect, is to torture language. Why then does Read work himself into such an impossible position? I think it is because he senses that word-taboos are such that violating them frequently strengthens them. To show how the use of an obscenity can be a uniquely effective insult, or a uniquely suitable way to give vent to one's "jangled nerves," or to gird oneself to resist pain, or to express the depths of one's conviction about the evil of a war, to express contempt, irreverence, or symbolic dominance, to provoke, or challenge, or amuse with cacophemstic wit—is to show how word-taboos are useful, and how they can be exploited for reasonable ends. Artifacts that are known to be useful tend to be used, and used frequently. Read understands how the instrumental employment of a word tends to strengthen the norms that make its utility possible, but concludes, quite unwarrantedly, that any use of obscenity that strengthens word-taboos must (therefore) be an "observance" rather than a violation of the taboos. A better term than "observance" would be "exploitation," since a given use of a word can exploit the very taboo it violates. Read senses how useful effects depend upon the same taboos that make certain evils possible. But instead of drawing up a balance sheet to compare the benefits and evils that both depend on the existence of the taboos, he feels impelled to treat the benefits as if they were of no account, and by affixing the confused label "inverted taboo," to dismiss them.

Still, Read is much closer to the truth than Sagarin when he recommends a strategy for doing in the taboos. Judicious employment of obscene words for useful purposes may strengthen the taboos in the way I have indicated, but Read is right when he affirms that the *overuse* of obscenities can weaken them. We should set ourselves to use the forbidden words more and more frequently, he says, but *not* in colorful insults, ribald jokes, and the like, for such exploitations of the taboos will only reenforce them. Neither should we be loud, ostentatious, or flamboyant in our use of the dirty words, for that sort of vulgarity will overstimulate the resentment of our auditors and set no example for them. Nor should we be furtive and self-conscious, or appear to be ashamed, for that would appear to court smirks and snickers, and actually promote "dirty-mindedness." Apparently Read would have us use obscenities *only* as referential terms,[18] to speak very matter-of-factly of "shitting" when we might otherwise say "defecating" or "going to the bathroom," and of "fucking" when we mean copulation. This would be a return to the unadorned speech habits of our rude ancestors before it ever occurred to them that everyday words for everyday things would not do. Shamefulness pertaining to sex and bodily functions then would weaken, and the simple designative terms for these things would become less suitable for their derivative uses as "inverted taboo."

> The solution lies in adjusting oneself to the use of these words without shame. The use must be unostentatious to avoid "inverted taboo," and it must be recalled that language is not the property of any one person but that such changes must take place gradually by general consent. A beginning can best be made in the home, so that each of these words will not be a little festering sore in the adolescent's mind.[19]

Read's strategy is a familiar one, that of using cacophemisms as if they were neutral terms so that in time they do become neutral terms. We have already mentioned examples of this. "Negroes" campaigned successfully to be called "blacks" and thereby succeeded in removing some self-contempt produced by the word "black" when it *was* a cacophemism; and Ducasse squeezed some of the horror out of death by routinely using the word "croaking" without emotion as a purely referential term. Read would use the word "fuck" in the same spirit in the hope that elevation from its cacophemistic status would diminish the shame which persons in our culture associate with sex. When "black" was a cacophemism, it was something that could not politely be said of a person, as if dark skin color was something too shameful to mention. Similarly Ducasse thought that the cacophemistic vocabulary for death helped preserve the irrational horror of dying in our society. Again, if the main words for sexual behavior are cacophemistic, indeed if there are no simple straightforward neutral terms in the language for it, but only awkward circumlocutions ("sexual behavior"), foreignisms ("coitus"), and sugary euphemisms ("making love"), then that naturally suggests that there must be something in the practice itself that is "too shameful to mention." The verbal taboo against the obscene word reflects a prevailing attitude toward the word's real-life referent, but it also preserves and reenforces that attitude, and therein lies its evil. Words, of course, are not the only source by any means of the objectionable attitudes, and as long as those attitudes persist, even after linguistic reforms, they will tend to generate new rude vulgarisms for the now respectable "fuck," which in turn could become new obscenities. Read presumably is aware of this danger, and would reply that language is only one of the fronts where the war against unhealthy attitudes is fought, and that eternal vigilance is required there even in the aftermath of victories.

5. An analysis of dirty-mindedness

Just what exactly is it that both Sagarin and Read find so regrettable in the bare existence of an obscene vocabulary? What are the attitudes that they find so "unhealthy"? Which are the "derivative uses of obscenity" Read has in mind when he uses the pejorative phrase "inverted taboo"? Despite his misleading language, Read makes his motives clear. The true object of his attack is the complex of attitudes that is sometimes called "dirty-mindedness." (We have already encountered them in our consideration of "smirking dirty jokes" in Chap. 14, §5.) Writing shortly after the original publication of *Lady Chatterly's Lover*, he praises D. H. Lawrence's "straightforward sincerity" in the use of conventional sexual obscenities, and contrasts it with the motives of other novelists who use dirty words as "inverted taboos." The latter are trading on sex as a "dirty secret." "So tenaciously do some people hold to the taboo that it arouses the suspicion that they want above all to preserve the tickling pleasure that they get in obscenity."[20]

The peculiar phenomenon of dirty-mindedness requires a deep split in a person's character. The word-taboos that make obscenity possible must be very important to him, but his attitudes toward them are profoundly ambivalent. On the one hand he thinks that sex *is* dirty, or at least that sexual obscenities *really are* dirty words. On the other hand, he loves to wallow in what he takes to be dirty, if not at the time of wallowing, at least in cooler moments. That is what makes possible his "secret thrill." The thrill comes as a consequence not simply of doing what is known to be forbidden, but also of violating one's own standards. Hence the thrill is characteristically sly, scandalized, and fearful; sneaky, self-conscious, and shameful. The dirty-minded obscene person does not shamelessly exult in his bawdy language; nor does he use it naturally without self-consciousness. His furtive giggle has the element of genuine embarrassment in it; he is not really proud of himself.

The dirty-minded person has only partially internalized the taboos that he violates. They are his own norms to a degree, and that is why he is capable of feeling shame, and in certain public contexts, embarrassment. (If he is caught peeking through a keyhole, he will not only be fearful of punishment or disapproval, he will blush with shame. He will feel that he has let himself down and not been true to his own "ego-ideals.") The taboos, however, remain partially uninternalized, external, and alien. That is what explains how easily and frequently the dirty-minded person violates them, and how real his tickling pleasure is.

What makes this familiar picture so unattractive to us? I think that we are repelled by the lack of whole-heartedness in the dirty-minded person's pleasures. We sense the way in which his self is split, and find him lacking in moral integrity (literally wholeness or oneness). When he supresses either of his conflicting sides then we see him as a hypocrite. When we get some insight into his motives we find him evasive, self-manipulative, and devious. He is engaged in a constant struggle to deceive himself. He cannot really look himself in the eye. In his relations to his own conscience he is

like the servile sycophant who alternately fawns and cheats. These character defects are not pleasant to behold, self-regarding though most of them
are. We loathe the person who lacks proper respect for those who deserve
it, but we feel contempt for the person who lacks respect for himself.
Moreover, we cannot help suspecting that the person who is devious in his
relations to his own "better self" will be deceitful and hence hurtful in his
relations to others.

Read is on solid ground then when he argues that a universal matter-of-
factness in the use of presently tabooed words will take the shame out of
them, and pull the rug out from under the dirty-minded obscenity-
monger. Read's program would undermine not only the repugnant habits of
mind that are called "nastiness," "indecency," and "shameful dirty-mindedness," but also the parasitic virtues of "decency" and "clean-mindedness."
The latter presumably are defined not only negatively, in terms of the
absence of dirty-mindedness, but also positively, in terms of the disposition
to be shocked and offended by dirty words, censorious of those who use
them, and consciously superior to indecent persons. If the taboos that make
dirty-mindedness possible are destroyed, then clean-mindedness, so understood, would vanish too. But that would surely be a net gain. The point
was made well by Bertrand Russell in 1929—

> What I have observed among the children in my school has shown conclu-
> sively, to my mind, the correctness of the view that nastiness in children is the
> result of prudery in adults. My own two children (a boy aged 7, and a girl aged
> 5) have never been taught that there is anything peculiar either about sex or
> about excretion, and have so far been shielded to the utmost possible extent
> from all knowledge of the idea of decency, with its correlative indecency . . .
> Other children . . . however, who came to us at the age of 6 or 7 had already
> been taught to regard anything connected with the sexual organs as improper.
> They were surprised to find that in the school such matters were spoken of in
> the same tone of voice as was employed about anything else, and for some time
> they enjoyed a sense of release in conversations which they felt to be indecent;
> finding, however, that the grown-ups did nothing to check such conversations,
> they gradually wearied of them, and became nearly as clean-minded as those
> who had never been taught decency[21] . . .

The message is clear: stop teaching "decency," and both it *and* indecency
(dirty-mindedness) will in time vanish.

This plausible thesis of Russell and Read, radical as it once seemed, is
now widely accepted. Confined to attitudes toward sex and bodily function—extra-linguistic phenomena—it is entirely sound. Applied to obscene
language, it also has a point. If we all use the proscribed words openly and
matter-of-factly, *and* if we cease holding unhealthy attitudes toward the
non-linguistic phenomena referred to by those words in their matter-of-fact

employment, then the repugnant frame of mind called dirty-mindedness will diminish and in time approach extinction. Moreover, Russell and Read are surely right in thinking of this projected consequence as a good thing. But a possibility remains which they have overlooked. Obscene words might still remain and be useful long after they have ceased to be "dirty," just as profanities have remained widely used expressive devices long after they ceased being frighteningly dangerous effective sacrileges.[22] That is the possibility made much of by the third view about the obscene vocabulary, which we must now consider.

6. The case for retention of the obscene vocabulary

The common position to be extracted from the writings of Robert Graves, Burgess Johnson, and H. L. Mencken is that the useful derivative functions of obscenity make it desirable that obscene vocabularies be preserved and strengthened in their expressive power, even if this requires bolstering word-taboos that have nothing else to be said in their favor. The problem for this common view is this: how can we preserve obscene words for the sake of their expressive benefits, while correcting the unhealthy attitudes toward their literal referents in virtue of which the words became "obscene" in the first place? How can we have obscenity without dirty-mindedness? How can we have shocking words that are not "dirty"?

Robert Graves is well aware that the weakening of verbal taboos will weaken the expressive power of tabooed words, which distresses him since he values expressive obscenity and profanity, yet he can find no rational basis outside of language itself for the taboos that make obscene and profane words possible. He finds consolation, however, in the easy-going hypocrisy of the "nice people" in society that allows them to pay homage (but not excessive homage) to groundless taboos that they don't really believe in. Describing only his own partially emancipated circle of intellectuals, Graves captures the delicate balance perfectly:

> To consent uncritically to the taboos, which are often grotesque, is as foolish as to reject them uncritically. The nice person is one who good-humoredly criticizes the absurdities of the taboo in good-humored conversation with intimates; but does not find it necessary to celebrate any black masses as a proof of his emancipation from it . . . the society in which I move . . . is an obscene society: that is, it acquiesces emotionally in the validity of the taboo, while intellectually objecting to it.[23]

The attitudes described by Graves permit the survival of obscene words with only slightly diminished expressive power, but at an exorbitantly high cost. His "nice people" are hardly more attractive than the dirty-minded sorts who troubled Read. Indeed, they are a kind of "equal and opposite" counterpart of the dirty-minded, equally lacking moral wholeness, and equally committed to hypocrisy, but in an opposite fashion. The dirty-minded person has an emotional need for what his intellectual judgments disapprove; the nice person "emotionally acquiesces" in prohibitions which are rejected by his intellectual judgments. The nice person is by no means as repugnant to behold (at least for other nice people to behold), but he shares with his counterpart a lack of personal dignity and wholehearted-ness. He doesn't have his moral act together because his emotions, in this case moralistic rather than appetitive emotions, remain stubbornly beyond the control of his considered judgments. An ideal society would bear only a partial and superficial resemblance to Graves's "obscene society." It would consist of persons who have intellectually *and* emotionally rejected the historical *bases* of our word-taboos while preserving enough of their vitality to make possible the benefits of obscene language when occasions call for it.

Burgess Johnson suggests that as old words lose their magic through deflation of the taboos on their use, new ones can be coined to take their places. In order to satisfy the "natural craving for emphasis" served in the past by profanities and obscenities, the new terms "must startle, because they shock; or they must be ominous, threatening harm or arousing awe at the mention of mighty Beings; or they must cause discomfort because the hearer is not sure what they mean, but from the sound of them suspects the worst."[24] One of the causes of the weakening of the expressive power of the old naughty words that operates independently of the rejection of the intellectual bases of taboos, according to Johnson, is the tendency in our "noisy" society to exhaust superlatives by over-using them. "Emphasis destroys itself; words of power are shouted to death faster and faster in this age which is deafened by loud noises of all sorts."[25] This phenomenon, which Johnson labels "superduperness"[26] creates new everyday employment for words like "awful" (even where there is no awe) "horrible" (where there is no horror), "terrible" (where there is no terror), "splendid" (where there is no splendor), and "great" (where there is no distinction). The more often these words are applied to the commonplace, the less able they are to do justice to genuinely extreme states of affairs and overwhelming emotions on those rare occasions when they do occur. In order to preserve the power of language to provide emphasis where it is most needed, we must either slow down the self-defeating inflation of superlatives or else keep generating new terms to keep up with the demand. Ever the realist, Johnson opts for the latter course.

His most interesting suggestion is that profanities and obscenities can be manufactured out of nonsense words and sounds without prior meaning.

(Short sharp words are the best.) Many others have had this idea. One of Dumas' characters, for example, used "Malaka!" as his favorite epithet of malediction. Johnson likes that word too, and quotes a critic with approval:

> It has the advantage of meaning nothing, and that is precisely what a swear word should mean. It should be sound and fury, signifying nothing. It should be incoherent, irrational, a little crazy like the passion which evokes it . . .[27]

A striking disadvantage, of course, to such privately coined words is that while they can relieve the speaker of his emotions, they can not have as powerful an effect on the listener as may have been intended.[28] They can strike the reader as colorful, forceful, and mysterious, but they can hardly shock or offend him. They cannot even seem naughty until some sort of public convention takes form excluding their use from polite contexts. If one wished to make "Malaka!" a genuinely useful epithet, one would have to use it oneself in appropriate public contexts, induce as many others as possible to do so as well, make the sound seem as ominous and disreputable as possible to the uninitiated, and then (wearing another hat) condemn it publicly as rude and ill-mannered. In time its appropriate dictionary definition might be "Exclamation; generally considered vulgar," or "Impolite epithet." By that time the word would have secured a place in the language as a rough cacophemism without cognitive meaning. But that is a long way still from being obscene!

It may in fact be impossible to coin a new term that is rendered obscene *ab initio* by a purely linguistic taboo even though the term has no unwelcome extra-linguistic associations. In that case we had better hold on to our present profanities and obscenities, such as they are. To be sure, changes in religious beliefs and the weakening of prudery have drained them of some of their electricity, but they maintain a surprising amount of shock value anyway, simply through linguistic inertia. Even in an atheist community speakers of English can get surprising expressive mileage from saying (with appropriate tone and gestures) "damn!," or "Go to hell!," or "For Christ's sake!" It is still a powerful linguistic assault, even in the most enlightened communities, to call someone a "son of a bitch,"[29] or "bastard," though neither speaker nor audience will think of the "honor" of anyone's mother when he hears these conventional terms. And the supreme obscenity, while perhaps less shocking than it formerly was, maintains the power to stun libertines as well as prudes, sexual sophisticates as well as puritans, a power that renders it almost as useful as ever for various respectable derivative purposes. Centuries from now it may have lost its strength altogether through overuse (though I certainly hope not), but in the meantime, it will be impossible to coin an equally expressive shocker from whole cloth. As sexual enlightenment proceeds, the emotive meaning of a word like "fuck" will become more and more independent of the attitudes and beliefs that gave it its original impetus. But independent emotive meaning can have a life all its own, and while no more immortal than any other conventional meanings, it may persist into the indefinite future. May it long survive the last remnants of fearful superstition, prudery, and "dirty-mindedness"!

16

Obscene Words and the Law

1. Bare utterance and instant offense

What, if anything, should the law say about the use of obscene words? Not even the principle of legal moralism would justify a wholesale ban on uttering or writing obscene words any place, any time. The everyday obscenities of everyday people, as Burgess Johnson put it, "result not so much from bad morals as from bad manners, added to a more superficial ailment which may be called a disease of the vocabulary. If we classify this with hoof-and-mouth disease or with chronic belching, we can approach the subject with less confusion of mind . . ."[1] The essence of bad manners is their offensiveness; words uttered in the solitude of one's home or in the company of trusted intimates offend no one and thus are not bad manners. The state might as well make it a crime ever to be naked even in bath or bed (because nudity in public is offensive) as to make *every* use of obscene words into a crime.[2]

There was a time, of course, when profane oaths were thought to be a form of public endangerment provoking the gods to angry retaliation against a whole tribe. The proscribed words in those days had an awesome emotional impact because of the presumed danger to everyone implicit in their use. If we still held the appropriate superstitious views, we might plausibly invoke the public harm principle in support of wholesale criminal prohibition enforced by extreme penalties. The relevant superstitions, however, have now virtually disappeared, so that bad language, once shockingly dangerous, is now at most only shockingly rude.

Neither the general rules of good manners nor the more specific forms of etiquette have ever been thought, in modern times, to need enforcement by the criminal law (excepting of course the use of obscene language). The reason for this is probably that (a) offenses against manners are usually too trivial to require criminal regulation, and that (b) those violations of manners that would be thought to be non-trivial are quite efficiently controlled by social (nonpenal) sanctions. Few people deliberately court the disapproval and low regard of their fellows. So the use of obscene words in contexts where they give social offense is infrequent. And even when it does occur, attempting to stamp it out by means of the bulky and cumbersome apparatus of the criminal law would almost invariably be a cure far worse than the disease.

For the most part, the instant offense caused by exposure to the public utterance or printing of obscene words is an altogether evanescent phenomenon. As offenses go it is mild and brief, and its repetitions reasonably avoidable. In the universe of personal offensiveness, it is the counterpart of a single mosquito bite. It comes; we wince; it goes; that is all. To suppose the contrary, as our laws and traditions sometimes have done, is to assume that our population contains significant numbers of people with psyches so fragile that the bare exposure to an offending word can be either injurious or so profoundly shocking as to cause deep and enduring distress. Indeed, Victorian ladies, if so unfortunate as to be exposed to the worst obscenities, were expected to fall into a faint of mortification and take to their beds. Whatever the truth about the real states of mind of Victorian women, anyone in this day and age who responded in such a fashion would be thought pathologically sensitive. Use of the criminal law to protect abnormal susceptibilities, as I argued earlier (Chap. 8, §1), is not easily justified by a plausibly mediated offense principle. In any case, it is a good thing that people are not that vulnerable. Otherwise obscene words would be like dangerous firearms, and we would all be armed to the teeth with powerful weapons for wounding one another. Obviously the more realistic tactic for preventing such a situation has been to toughen up prospective victims rather than to attempt to disarm the public by rigorous supervision of language. There would be no need for gun control if we all had hides too thick to be penetrated by bullets.

Traditionally the classes of persons thought to need protection even from the very sound or sight of a single obscene word have been "women and children." Sometimes this phrase creeps into the criminal ordinance itself, as when legally obscene and boisterous behavior is said to require a feminine or juvenile audience; sometimes it lurks in the background of legislative debates or appears in judicial interpretations. Justice Harlan, in stating the legally relevant facts in the case of *Cohen v. California*, was constrained to mention that when Cohen wore his jacket emblazoned with the words "Fuck the draft" in a hallway of the Municipal Court Building in Los Angeles, "There were women and children present in the corridor."[3]

Why should the presence of women and children have any legal importance? There are several possible explanations, none very convincing. It might once have been supposed, at least among the upper classes, that it is part of the conventional sense of obscene words that they are linguistic devices for offending women not men. Women, after all, were expected to be genteel and refined. Their place was the home where they were insulated from the rough and ready manners of the man's world. However plausible that understanding might have seemed in another day its absurdity is manifest in the present time. Barriers between men and women have been crashing down as women by the millions enter the labor market. In any event, this interpretation of the conventional use of obscene words never was really plausible. Men have never been immune from the impact of tabooed words. In all-male settings the obscene terms were not just meaningless sounds. Perhaps they approached that point in military barracks, boiler rooms of ships, mines, foundries, and other places that never saw a woman, but there were always other contexts in which men too— even soldiers, sailors, and miners—could be shocked or offended by tabooed words. Some of these contexts were sexually mixed, like church services and formal dances; some were all-male, like legislative debates, judicial hearings, board meetings, and college classes. The distinction between formal contexts where obscene words offend and informal contexts where they do not never coincided neatly with the distinction between contexts with and without women. Today the alleged correspondence is hardly even a statistically significant correlation.

Another explanation, taken seriously a century ago when it was already quaint, is downright bizarre today. Some may once have thought (or tacitly presumed) that the utterance of a single obscene word in the presence of a lady could *defile* her. Sexual obscenities in particular were presumed to have a magic potency no less effective than that once associated with profane oaths. A single exposure to the very sound of the word could make even the involuntary auditor (provided she was a female or a child) unclean. Naturally husbands and fathers in the possession of such dreadful magic were concerned to keep "their" women pure and innocent. Obscene utterances and inscriptions could morally contaminate, if not utterly corrupt them. To speak obscenely in the presence of a young lady then was an offense in the same category, though of lesser magnitude, as deflowering a virgin.

This implicit rationale hardly fooled anyone, except perhaps some judges and legislators. To think of a bare sound or vocable, or a bare mark on a page with no known meaning, as having the power automatically to corrupt any (female or juvenile) persons unfortunate enough to lay eye or ear on it, would be to give credence to so flagrant a superstition that even its tacit assumption would be impossible. On the other hand, if the corruptible youth or maiden could be instantly defiled only by a word whose sense they understood, then the implicit rationale confronts a familiar dilemma. Either the maiden or youth does not recognize the word as tabooed, in which case she is not defiled by it, or else the word is already in her recognition-vocabulary, in which case she is already impure.

A watered-down version of the argument from moral corruption is somewhat more plausible. Obscene utterances, in this view, do not instantly defile by a kind of word magic; rather they contribute to the gradual coarsening of a woman or child. Each use of an obscene word in her presence will make her more immune to offense, toughen her sensibility, and make her less "lady-like" in her responses. She may in time even become less inhibited about using the forbidden words herself. This argument, since it avoids reference to instant defilement, is empirically more plausible than the other, but its moral plausibility is negligible, to put it mildly. It leaves the harm and offense principles behind and tacitly resorts to a form of moralistic paternalism buttressed by a sexual double standard. Responsible adults (if they should just happen to be females) are to be "protected" from the corruption of their own moral sensibilities (by coercive measures used against other parties) whatever their own degree of responsibility for it or consent to it. Furthermore, the alleged "corruption" consists of dispositions admittedly shared by most adult males in the same community. It is morally repugnant enough to treat adults generally as if they were children; it is more odious still to treat all and only female adults in that fashion.[4]

On the other hand, parents have a quite respectable interest in shaping the moral sensibilities of their own *children*, and quite legitimately turn to the law in many areas for help. For example, even where pornographic performances and materials may freely be presented to consenting adults, most parents would be outraged if the law did not make an exception for children. The rationale for the exception is not perfectly clear but it probably resembles the following argument. How children are exposed to the phenomenon of sex during their most impressionable period is likely to have a profound influence on their sexual attitudes and practices in later life. Parents who are interested in inculcating what they think are wholesome attitudes in their children will take a dim view of pornography, and suspect that its purveyors are usurping an exclusively parental educational function. Much pornography, as is now widely recognized (See Chap. 11, §7–9) expresses hostile or contemptuous attitudes toward women. Most pornography imports wildly unrealistic expectations about the nature of sexual response.[5] Very likely no parents would make pornographic works their textbook of choice in the sexual education of their offspring. Laws forbidding the dissemination of pornographic materials among children thus function to protect the interests of parents in the moral education of their children.

Exposure of children to obscene *words*, on the other hand, has no important effect as such on the child's developing moral dispositions. Rather it is a routine part of his or her language training. It is probably no exaggeration to say that every single normal adult in this country can list the leading obscenities as part of his own recognition-vocabulary. Exposure to those words is a necessary link in learning what they mean and how they are used. After all, children have to learn the word in order to learn that it is "nasty." The ideal of complete protection of their purity, if effectively achieved, would render the obscene words extinct in one generation, thus causing our descendants the bother of having to invent new ones. It is important that children learn that shock is a predictable response to obscene utterance in some contexts but not in others, so that they can avoid giving unnecessary and unintended offense while they learn the useful techniques of expressing deep feeling, making colorful insults, ribald jokes, and the like, through apt employment of obscene words. Children learn all these things in the first instance by exposure to adult usage, and from some adults they learn a central feature of that usage—how to be shocked themselves.

2. *Offensive nuisance and harassment*

The offense principle then cannot justify the criminal prohibition of the bare utterance of obscenities in public places even when they are used intentionally to cause offense. The single mosquito bite is simply too trivial a thing. A swarm of mosquitos, on the other hand, biting continuously as they relentlessly pursue their victim, is quite another thing. The difference between mere offense and offensive nuisance is that the offended party in the case of nuisance cannot escape the offense, or cannot escape it without incurring unreasonable inconvenience, expense, or harm to his other interests. In effect, then, he has no choice but to suffer his unpleasant states of mind or incur harm or inconvenience. He usually elects to suffer the nuisance, but not without a sense of deep grievance. If the use of obscene words can rightly be made criminal, it can only be when it is an unjustified, deliberately imposed nuisance, that is when (a) the words are used deliberately to shock, annoy, or offend their auditor for no respectable ulterior purpose (as when their motive is spiteful, vindictive, or malicious); (b) the auditor has not consented to the conduct in question and makes every reasonable effort to escape it; and (c) the words used, by virtue of their quality or quantity, were antecedently likely to cause intense and durable offense to their auditor and this was known to their user. This form of nuisance, in short, is a kind of *harassment*, and the fact that it employs obscene words is by no means essential to its moral gravamen.

Criminal codes should include as crimes forms of deliberate conduct meant to cause severe and/or prolonged annoyance, even without actual harm or the threat of harm to the victim. The authors of the *Model Penal Code* sensibly propose the inclusion of a crime called *harassment* (to supplement other crimes called "assault," "reckless endangerment," and "terroristic threats") which they define as follows in section 250.4:

> A person commits a petty misdemeanor if, with purpose to harass another, he: (a) makes a telephone call without purpose of legitimate communication; or (b) insults, taunts or challenges another in a manner likely to provoke violent or disorderly response; or (c) makes repeated communications anonymously or at extremely inconvenient hours, or in offensively coarse language; or (d) engages in any other course of harmful [*sic*] conduct serving no legitimate purpose of the actor.[6]

It is important to notice that this section of the code attaches no special significance to obscene words as such. Their use is simply one of the ways in which a person can cause an offended state to arise in the consciousness of another person. When that state cannot be reasonably avoided or extinguished by the second person, it amounts to a nuisance, and when that nuisance is deliberately and maliciously imposed, especially through repetition or through an extended "course of conduct," it is harassment. All four parts of section 250.4 can be violated without the use of a single obscene word, and conversely the use of an obscene word when it does not satisfy these conditions is (or ought to be) legally innocent. (It goes without saying that language that does satisfy any of the four conditions may also and incidentally be obscene.)

The catch-all condition of section 250.9 (part d) would make better sense if to the phrase "harmful conduct"[7] it added words from an earlier draft— "offensive or alarming." Then it would include not only harassment that incidentally harms some of the victim's interests but also those that remain mere nuisances without actual danger of harm. Consider a pure case of harassment under this heading that consists in a certain employment of obscene language. Suppose that a woman is approached by a man on the street. Perhaps he is a stranger, perhaps a mere acquaintance, perhaps a known "enemy." [The sex roles in the example are essential. Male harassers are much less likely to pester other males for fear of violent response; women are less dangerous victims. Moreover most male harassments of other males could plausibly be subsumed under 250.4(b)]. The man instantly begins to sputter sexual and scatological obscenities in nonsense patterns without rhyme or reason. Alarmed or merely annoyed, the woman turns her back and walks away at a brisk pace. The man continues right behind her on the sidewalk, bombarding her with endless repetitions of obscene words jeeringly chanted. Then as she begins to walk faster in the direction of her home and sanctuary, his obscenities begin to form into sensible patterns. He makes reference to bodily waste products, organs, and processes in obscenely vulgar ways. He uses obscene intensifiers to express strong emotion. He makes obscene "propositions" to the lady he pursues. He slanders her with false accusation in obscene language. He uses obscene words to insult her in all the basic ways—name-calling, ritual accusation, scorn for what she holds dear (e.g., the memory of her parents) and symbolic dominance claims (e.g., "Fuck you"!) Finally he tells dirty jokes in a smirking, dirty-minded way. At last she makes it to her home, enters, and slams the door in her pursuer's face. The annoyance is over and no actual harm was done—except perhaps to her sense of security. Under the rule of 250.4 (b), as I have reformulated it, a crime was committed against her anyway, and she might well lodge charges against the obscene harasser.

Note however that the offense in this hypothetical example could have been as great, or failing that, great enough for criminal liability, had no obscene words been used at all. Suppose we repeat the story with expletives deleted. The man begins to follow the lady, aggressively chanting nonsense syllables at her. Then he switches to real words and shouts "table!", "table!", "table!", "chair!", "chair!", "arm!", "leg!", "intercourse!", "defecation!", and so on, over and over again. Then, just as she becomes convinced that he is a raving lunatic (though not an obscene one), he begins to make sense, but what sense! He implores her to go to bed with him and describes various eccentric sexual acts in vivid though antiseptic language. Her pace quickens. Then he expresses profound feelings of love, frustration, hatred, and despair in emotional but non-obscene terms. Then he accuses her of vicious wrongdoing, insults her, puts her down, and asserts his own natural dominance over her, all in "clean language." Finally he regales her with comic tales of illicit amours, all in entirely acceptable language. Throughout the chase, lasting let us suppose for the better part of an hour, she pleads with him to stop, warns him, emphatically expresses her annoyance, and desperately tries to escape him. He has every reason to believe she is not pleased. On the other hand, *he* is highly pleased by the whole thing. He may try to meet her again the next day.

Absence of actual obscene language in the second version of our tale may require that we have more evidence than would otherwise be necessary of "intense and prolonged offense," and lack of consent and reasonable effort to escape (though where that evidence is abundant, as in our example, liability is unproblematic). Why should that be? I think the explanation is that obscene language is coarse, vulgar, disrespectful of prevalent norms generally, and therefore, when conjoined with other contextual elements, *alarming*. A straightforward request for sex may annoy a woman, but when it is made in obscene, disrespectful language it is bound to do more than that. Who knows (she may wonder) what this gross vulgarian may do next? He seems to mean business. Fear and anxiety are the worst of the "offended states" from which we are protected by the offense principle, and the ones that are most likely to cross the line of genuine harm. Notoriously, the human psyche can be injured in various subtle ways by being made to carry an excessive load of fear and anxiety, and "paralyzing" fear or anxiety can injure any person's interests. Even without reasonably supposed danger, however, inescapable annoyance, revulsion, and disgust, when imposed maliciously and inescapably, can be more than one person should be required to endure from another.

The priority of fear and anxiety among legally preventable offended states explains a good deal about the *Model Penal Code's* approach. It explains, for example, why some violations of the harassment section require "repeated" communications or extended "courses of conduct" (parts c, d, and probably b) while others (a and possibly b) require only a single message or utterance. Why should a single telephone call, for example, when it is made in order to harass, suffice for liability,[8] whereas other communications, even when anonymous, made at inconvenient hours, and in obscene language, require repetition? Part of the reason, of course, is that a telephone call can be an extension of an enemy's self into the protected privacy of a person's own home. When harassed outside the home one can always retreat until one reaches one's domestic sanctuary, but there is no way to escape the peremptory rings within the home that does not involve unreasonable sacrifice of the householder's convenience or safety. Another part of the reason, however, for attaching special significance to harassment by telephone is that anonymous or unwelcome telephone calls are ominous; we have no control over them, or access to the caller. They occur unpredictably and jarringly. For all we know they will go on forever. For all these reasons they tend to be not simply more annoying but more frightening than visible harassments. And when they are accompanied by obscene language, they can be terrifying. Hence many state statutes forbidding harassment by telephone explicitly require "vulgar, profane, obscene, or indecent" language.[9] The point to be emphasized here is that the law protects people from maliciously produced fear and anxiety, not from the shock or disgust that is produced directly by a single perceived infraction of linguistic taboos.

3. Obscenity on the public media: F.C.C. v. Pacifica Foundation

Another form of "intrusion" into the privacy of the home remains to be considered, that which comes over the air waves and appears on our television and radio sets. Normally it would be absurd to think of television and radio programs as "intrusions," since we voluntarily choose to install the receiving units in the first place, to turn them on, and to dial a particular channel. Moreover, we can always change the channel, turn off the set, or remove it from our homes. Unlike intruding telephone calls, sound trucks with blaring loudspeakers, and other forms of intrusive harassment, the television and radio entrance into our homes is subject to our own exclusive control. Obscene messages might yet be communicated to us, but our offended reaction need only be the instantaneous transient kind caused by momentary exposure. Unlike the response to obscene telephone calls, it will contain no element of fearful anxiety, and no expectation of prolonged or repeated occurrence despite our best preventive efforts.

Nevertheless, regulative agencies and courts have invoked a theory of nuisance to justify coercive measures against obscene broadcasts, and have even spoken in terms that suggest that obscene words on the air waves are a form of harassment. The leading case thus far is *Federal Communications Commission v. Pacifica Foundation*,[10] which was decided by the United States Supreme Court in 1978. Five years earlier, radio station WBAI-FM in New York, owned and operated by the Pacifica Foundation, had presented a discussion program on "The use of language in our society," as a part of which a twelve minute recording was played of a comic monologue by George Carlin called "Filthy Words." The monologue is a satirical mocking of the F.C.C.'s prohibition against the use of "seven filthy words"—"words you couldn't say on the airways." Carlin pronounces each of the words in turn, savors them, comments on them in mock-scholarly fashion, and illustrates their uses in dozens of everyday idioms. Carlin has an extremely sensitive ear for ordinary speech, a natural talent for speaking in various dialects, and an exquisite sense of comic timing. His audience, obviously somewhat tense in the beginning, responds to the main part of the mono-logue in a way to gladden any comedian's heart. As far as a listener can tell, robust guffaws predominate over smirking giggles.

The record was played at two o'clock on a Tuesday afternoon. The station received no complaints, but somewhat later the F.C.C. received a letter from a man who claimed to have heard the broadcast over his car radio while driving with his young son. The letter protested that "any child could have tuned in to that garbage." The F.C.C. forwarded the letter to the station for its comment. The station management replied that the mono-logue "had been played during a program about contemporary society's attitude toward language" and had been preceded by a warning that it contained "sensitive language" which some listeners might find offensive. Moreover, it said, "Carlin is not mouthing obscenities; he is merely using words to satirize as harmless and essentially silly our attitudes toward these words." Nevertheless, the F.C.C. in a Declaratory Order, "granted the complaint," and informed the offending station that it "could have been the subject of administrative sanctions," such as revocation of license, monetary forfeiture, or denial of license renewal. Though they were not mentioned, criminal sanctions were also among the Commission's options, since section 1464 of Title 18 of the United States Code provides that: "Whoever utters any obscene, indecent, or profane language by means of radio-communica-tion shall be fined not more than $10,000 or imprisoned not more than two years, or both." In fact the Commission imposed no formal sanctions but let the station off with the warning that the complaining letter was now in its file for further consideration in case there should be more complaints of a similar kind. In conjunction with this order, the Commission issued a Memorandum Opinion designed to clarify its standards for regulating lan-guage on the air waves. It characterized the language of the Carlin mono-logue as "patently offensive though not necessarily obscene." [!] It ac-knowledged that the recording had some "literary value," and that it did not wish to prohibit its broadcast absolutely but only at hours when "there is a reasonable risk that children may be in the audience." Offensive language, the Commission claimed, should be regulated by "principles analogous to those found in the law of nuisance where the law generally speaks to *channeling* behavior [in this case to a different time of day] more than actu-ally prohibiting it."

The Pacifica Foundation appealed the Declaratory Order, which was then overturned by the United States Court of Appeals for the District of Columbia. From that judgment the F.C.C. appealed to the Supreme Court. The judgment of the Appellate Court was there overturned and the Com-mission's original order upheld in a 5-4 vote.

Justice Stevens' majority opinion has a reasonable tone and does a decent amount of squirming—he is surely no enemy of first amendment freedoms—but manages nevertheless to make several subtle but substantial errors in reasoning. The first of these is confusing the instant offense that comes from momentary exposure to indelicate language with the more intense, more durable, and less escapable offense that constitutes nuisance. This mistake occurs during Stevens' discussion (IV, A, 13) of why radio and television "of all the forms of communication have received the most limited protection." The first reason, he says, for the special status of broadcasting is that it invades the privacy of the listener's own home, "where the individual's right to be let alone plainly outweighs the first amendment rights of the intruder." There follows this remarkable passage:

> Because the broadcast audience is constantly tuning in and out, prior warnings cannot completely protect the listener or viewer from unexpected program content. To say that one may avoid further offense by turning off the radio when he hears indecent language is like saying that the remedy for an assault is to run away after the first blow. One may hang up on an indecent phone call, but that option does not give the caller a constitutional immunity or avoid a harm that has already taken place.

Suppose you have the radio on while you are working in the house. While your attention is occupied, you do not notice that the program you were listening to has been replaced by another. Suddenly you hear a stream of obscene language. In disgust you switch the station to a musical program or turn it off altogether. "Too late!" says Justice Stevens; "the harm has already been done." On the contrary, no *harm* whatever has been done, and as for the offense, that was the "simple mosquito bite" that we have already argued is beneath the law's attention. Justice Stevens thinks of momentary exposure as more like a "blow" in an "assault," as though it were of the same degree of seriousness as a punch in the nose delivered by an uninvited stranger who storms into your house and forces you to flee. At the least that expresses a somewhat exaggerated respect for the power of mere words!

Justice Stevens' analogy to the harassing telephone call ignores the essential difference that one cannot escape the harasser by simply hanging up, for there is nothing to prevent him from calling right back again. Even if the call will not be repeated, you have no way of knowing that it will not, and thus there is no way of preventing fearful anxiety. For all you know the mysterious caller may not stop short of other forms of mischief. His indecencies, if any, are part of more elaborate linguistic behavior designed to taunt, frighten, insult, or solicit. Unlike the naughty words on the radio, his message is personal, directed squarely at you, indeed like a punch in the nose. No listener can feel *personally abused* by an unaddressed monologue he happens to overhear on the public air waves. Justice Stevens then has not only confused instant offense with offensive nuisance; he has compounded the confusion by mistaking them both for harassment.

The confusion does not stop there. The second reason for the relatively unprotected status of broadcasting, Stevens tells us, is that it is "uniquely accessible to children, even those too young to read." That is one of the factors, he argues, that distinguishes the present case from *Cohen v. California:* "Although Cohen's written message might have been incomprehensible to a first grader, Pacificas' broadcast could have enlarged a child's vocabulary in an instant." Justice Stevens does not go on to explain how a child can be harmed by having its vocabulary enlarged. The sexual and scatological obscenities are standard elements of the language known to every single normal adult member of the linguistic community and bound inevitably to become part of the vocabulary of every child. If the child has never heard the word before he may be curious about its meaning. He will ask a parent and be told that it is a naughty word that polite people do not use, and that he must *never* use. If the parent's tone is appropriately scandalized, that will give the child a fair idea of the emotive impact of the word, the first step in learning what the word is for, and how to use it. It is difficult to see anything objectionable in this educational process.

Justice Stevens' solicitude for the juvenile auditor of radio programs is misplaced. There is indeed a valid concern with the way the subject of sex is introduced to children and the way in which their basic attitudes and responses toward it are formed. The law rightly protects the parents' right to supervise the upbringing of their children in that respect free of the distorting influence of the pornographers. The mistake Stevens makes is to confuse the realm of erotic feelings and conduct with the realm of merely linguistic education, and to employ standards appropriate for the former in the regulation of the latter.

The confusion begins when the Court looks at the statute it is attempting to interpret. As we have seen, title 18 of Section 1464 forbids the use of "any obscene, indecent, or profane language by means of radio communication." Carlin's monologue used no profanities; so far it is innocent. As for obscenity, the monologue fails to satisfy the Court's own odd definition; surely there was no appeal to prurience, no plausible effort to arouse erotic feelings in the broadcast. The objectionable language, Stevens concludes, must be neither profane nor obscene, but rather "indecent," which term "merely refers to nonconformance with accepted standards of morality." If the words had been part of a larger pattern meant to induce lustful states in the minds of the auditors, perhaps there would be ground for parental concern and state intervention (though lustful states are known to all children above a certain age and are hardly a matter to get excited about, and below that age, for example among preschool children, a pornographic monologue would be incomprehensible). But "indecent words" are *only* objectionable because in violating linguistic taboos they tend to cause offense. Like belching, drippy noses, and dirty clothes, they are vulgar, and children should learn to find vulgarity displeasing. But children must first learn what vulgarity *is*, how to recognize it when they hear it, before they can be trained to avoid it. That process has nothing to do with erotic experiences or sexual education. At most, overexposure to "indecent words" without compensatory guidance may have deleterious effect on a child's developing manners, but soon the child will learn that bad manners displease others, and that awareness will tend to be corrective. In any case, it is hard to understand how momentary exposure to mere words, simply as such, can have a very marked effect, much less a profound impact,[11] on the developing child's moral character.

Justice Brennan in his vigorous dissenting opinion appears to me to get much the better of the argument. Not only are Stevens' appeals to the privacy of the home and the possible presence of children defective; his opinion apparently gives only the scantiest weight on the other side to the interests of "both those who wish to transmit and those who desire to receive broadcasts that many—including the F.C.C. and this Court—might find offensive." The privacy of the home in general may indeed outweigh the rights of a stranger to free expression, but given the easy avoidability of radio messages, the privacy interest hardly sits on the scale at all in this kind of case. The free expression interest in this case, however, remains strong. Not only did Carlin wish to entertain his listeners and earn money thereby, he can also be presumed (as the Court *did* presume) to have had a satirical intent. He wished, presumably, to convey persuasively the thesis that obscene words are "harmless" and that the prevailing attitude toward them is "essentially silly." If Robert Paul Cohen's intense political opinion was deemed inseparable from the form of its expression, surely Carlin's must be so deemed equally. Neither the words "the draft is evil" nor the words "attitudes toward obscene words are silly" express the full messages conveyed by the actual words of the political protester and the moral satirist.

A rechannelling of the Carlin broadcast might also inconvenience a part of the substantial audience who appreciate and welcome the comedian's wit and share his moral convictions about the silliness of attitudes toward "dirty words." The size of Mr. Carlin's enthusiastic audiences suggest that their total numbers must be in the millions, yet the Court shows little concern for their interests. Justice Brennan lectures his colleagues sternly about a vein in their opinions that he finds disturbing—"a depressing inability to appreciate that in our land of cultural pluralism there are many who think, act, and talk differently from the members of this Court, and who do not share their fragile sensibilities." He refers not only to the sophisticated intellectuals who cheer Carlin in night clubs and the middle class college students who buy his records, but also the black ghetto communities for whom the "dirty words" are part of ordinary parlance:[12]

> Today's decision will thus have its greatest impact on broadcasters desiring to reach, and listening audiences comprised of, persons who do not share the Court's view as to which words or expressions are acceptable and who for a variety of reasons, including a conscious desire to flout majoritarian conventions, express themselves using words that may be regarded as offensive by those from different socio-economic backgrounds. In this context, the Court's decision may be seen for what in the broader perspective, it really is: another of the dominant culture's inevitable efforts to force those groups who do not share its mores to conform to its way of thinking, acting, and speaking.

4. The case against regulation of indecent language on the air waves

The weakness of Stevens' efforts to apply a nuisance theory to public broadcasting, conjoined with Brennan's case for the importance of the interests of communicators and minorities at whom their messages are aimed, undermine the argument for government regulation of broadcast words as such. More generally they strongly support the view, briefly stated in Justice Stewart's independent dissent, that only broadcast obscenity in the Court's odd special sense of "pornography," and not "indecency" in the special sense of infractions of linguistic taboos, is rightly subject to regulation by government commissions or courts, and that even erotica are subject at most to "rechannelling" rather than outright prohibition, since the state's sole concern with it is to keep it from children.[13]

What then is to prevent obscene language from taking over the air waves altogether? The advocate of the offense principle can place his confidence in the capacity of a free marketplace of competing licensed broadcast stations to prevent this from happening. Given that *most* listeners are offended by vulgar language (is this a tautology?), and particularly by pointless vulgar language used routinely, it will not be in the commercial interests of most stations to use it except in special infrequent contexts (for example in panel discussions about attitudes toward language). People who expect a given station to be unpleasantly offensive will stop turning to that station altogether, and its ratings will drop. Perhaps the station in question will continue to appeal to a definite minority audience of sufficient size to support its profits, but so long as most people find vulgarity offensive, that recourse is not available to *all* stations, or even to most stations. The economic mechanisms are well explained by a recent commentator:

> If obscene broadcasts repel sizable groups of people, as the [F.C.C.] Commission assumes, entrepeneurs are likely to capitalize on their revulsion. The force of competition in radio in recent years, far from encouraging sameness, has developed specialty stations: all news, black, classical, country and western, rock, underground. To the extent then that obscenity offends the segment of the radio audience which supports any particular specialty, the F.C.C. need not fear that all stations will adopt an "obscene" format.[14]

On the other hand, if it should come to pass that so many people became immune to the offensiveness of vulgarity that *all* commercial stations would find it in their interests to "go obscene," then it would be a very strained and problematic sense indeed in which the obscene words would continue to be *vulgar* at all, and in any case there would be less support than ever from the offense principle for protecting the extreme sensitivity of the diminishing handful of persons still subject to offense. These persons would cease altogether being radio listeners, but would remain free, of course, to communicate in their own archaic tongue with one another.

Notes

7. Offensive Nuisances

1. American Law Institute, *Model Penal Code, Proposed Official Draft* (Philadelphia, 1962), Section 1.04.
2. An offense is said to constitute a violation, as opposed to any kind of crime, if no other sentence than a fine, or fine and forfeiture, or other civil penalty is authorized upon conviction by the law defining the offense, and conviction gives rise to no disability or legal disadvantage based on conviction of criminal offense. (Section 1.04, pt. 5.)
3. In this connection it should be noted that the most common generic synonym for "crimes" is neither "harms" nor "injuries," but "offenses."
4. Herbert Wechsler, "Sentencing, Correction, and the Model Penal Code," *University of Pennsylvania Law Review* 109 (1961): 473, 474.
5. The North Carolina law copied an English statute of 1533 (enacted during the reign of Henry VIII) that made it a felony punishable by death to commit "the vice of buggery." For "vice of buggery" North Carolina substituted "the abominable and detestable crime against nature not to be named among Christians" whether committed with "mankind or beast." In 1869 the penalty was reduced to imprisonment of "not less than five nor more that sixty years."
6. Zechariah Chafee, *Free Speech in the United States* (Cambridge, Mass.: Harvard University Press, 1964), p. 51. Chafee provides another good example (p. 286)—a Montana sedition law from World War I—

   > Thus Montana imposed a penalty of twenty years in prison for various insults to the Constitution, the uniform, and the flag, which were considered too trivial to be federal crimes, until Congress in 1918 inserted the whole Montana law into the middle of the Espionage Act. Nothing could show better the way state war legislation works than the fate of Starr of Montana, as described by a United States judge. "He was in the hands of one of those too common mobs, bent upon vindicating its

peculiar standard of patriotism and its odd concept of respect for the flag by compelling him to kiss the latter. In the excitement of resisting their efforts, Starr said: 'What is this thing anyway? Nothing but a piece of cotton with a little paint on it and some other marks in the corner there. I will not kiss that thing. It might be covered with microbes.' The state authorities did nothing to the mob, but they had Starr convicted under the Montana Sedition Act for using language 'calculated to bring the flag into contempt and disrepute,' and sentenced him to the penitentiary for not less than ten nor more than twenty years at hard labor."

7. William L. Prosser, *Handbook of the Law of Torts*, 2d ed. (St Paul: West Publishing Co., 1955), p. 390, n. 7.
8. William L. Prosser, *Handbook of the Law of Torts*, 4th ed. (St. Paul: West Publishing Co., 1971), p. 573.
9. *Restatement of the Law of Torts*, Section 822, comment j (American Law Institute, 1939).
10. Prosser, *op. cit.* (footnote 8).
11. *Ibid.*, p. 597.
12. *Ibid.*, pp. 597–99.
13. *Ibid.*, pp. 599–600.
14. *Ibid.*, pp. 577–78.
15. *Ibid.*, p. 593.
16. *Ibid.*, pp. 597–98.
17. *Medford v. Levy*, 31 W. Va. 649 (1888).
18. Prosser, *op. cit.* (footnote 8) pp. 598–99.
19. *Ibid., p. 599.*
20. *Ibid.*, p. 600.
21. There is an unfortunate tendency in human nature to elevate lower order sensibilities to the status of moral or religious ones, thus masquerading what is in origin little more than a reflexive aversion as some sort of rational or sacred principle. J. S. Mill cited a standard example of this in *On Liberty*, chap. 4, para. 13:

> To cite a rather trivial example, nothing in the creed or practice of Christians does more to envenom the hatred of Mahomedans against them than the fact of their eating pork. There are few acts which Christians and Europeans regard with more unaffected disgust than Mussulmans regard this particular mode of satisfying hunger. It is, in the first place, an offense against their religion; but this circumstance by no means explains either the degree or the kind of their repugnance; for wine is also forbidden by their religion, and to partake of it is by all Mussulmans accounted wrong, but not disgusting. Their aversion to the flesh of the "unclean beast" is, on the contrary, of that peculiar character, resembling an instinctive antipathy, which the idea of uncleanness, when once it thoroughly sinks into the feelings, seems always to excite even in those whose personal habits are anything but scrupulously cleanly. . . ."

22. Helen Lynd, *On Shame and the Search for Identity* (New York: Science Editions, 1961), p. 33.
23. *Ibid.*, p. 32.
24. Michael D. Bayles, "Comments," in *Issues in Law and Morality*, ed. Norman Care and Thomas Trelogan (Cleveland: Case Western Reserve University Press, 1973), p. 125, n. 4.

25. *Webster's New International Dictionary*, 3d Edition, 1961.
26. *Ibid.*
27. See *Chaplinsky v. New Hampshire* 315 U.S. 568 (1942). This case is discussed in detail, *infra*, chap. 12, §5.
28. Paul A. Freund, "Privacy: One Concept or Many?," in *Nomos XIII: Privacy*, ed. J. R. Pennock and J. W. Chapman (New York: Atherton Press, 1971), p. 102.
29. Fowler V. Harper and Fleming James, Jr., *The Law of Torts* (Boston: Little, Brown, and Co., 1956), vol. I, p. 681.
30. *Loc. cit.*
31. *Griswold v. Connecticut*, 381 U.S. 479 (1965). This case is discussed in detail, *infra*, vol. 3, chap. 17, §8.
32. Freund, *op. cit.* (footnote 28), p. 192. See also Hyman Gross, "Privacy and Autonomy" in the same volume, pp. 169–81.
33. Elizabeth L. Beardsley, "Privacy, Autonomy and Selective Disclosure," in *Nomos XIII: Privacy*, ed. J. R. Pennock and J. W. Chapman (New York: Atherton Press, 1971), p. 56. Letter variables revised to accord with the convention of this book.
34. *Ibid.*, p. 58.
35. And they cannot be reasonably expected to be very much subject to his control. As Beardsley notes:

> Of course sounds which (like thunder) are not produced by the intentional acts of human beings, or which (like subway clatter) could reasonably have been predicted by X to be part of an environment into which X has chosen to enter, or which (like the roar of compressed air drills and *perhaps* like some recorded music) have a redeeming social utility, have come to be accepted: questions about "violations of privacy" are often not so much as thought of, as far as most of the din of modern life is concerned." (Beardsley, *op. cit.*, p. 58.)

36. This point is well appreciated by Ernest Van den Haag in his "On Privacy" in *Nomos XIII: Privacy*, ed. J. R. Pennock and J. W. Chapman (New York: Atherton Press, 1971), pp. 150ff. One should point out that *if* the analogy to landed property rights is perfect, then even an unconsented-to intrusion of delightful and appreciated sounds and activities into the private domain is a technical violation of privacy on the model of trespass.

8. Mediating the Offense Principle

1. Donald VanDeVeer includes among his mediating standards for the offense principle an independent "Proportionality Standard" to the effect that the claim to restraint is proportionately stronger to the extent that the offense is "severe, conducive to further impairment [harm proper] of those offended, and difficult to reverse; and conversely." See his "Coercive Restraint of Offensive Actions, *Philosophy and Public Affairs*, vol. 8 (1979), p. 192. In virtue of my proposed balancing tests, *all* of my standards are "proportionality standards."
2. See my *Social Philosophy* (Englewood Cliffs, N. J.: Prentice-Hall, 1973), p. 44, and " 'Harmless Immoralities' and Offensive Nuisances" in my *Rights, Justice, and the Bounds of Liberty* (Princeton, N. J.: Princeton University Press, 1980), p. 88.
3. *Rights, Justice, and the Bounds of Liberty, op. cit.*, p. 88.
4. For a penetrating discussion of an actual case of this description, see Zechariah

Chafee, *Free Speech in the United States* (Cambridge, Mass.: Harvard University Press, 1964), p. 161.

5. As indeed the laws in many states do. Section 722 of the New York Penal Law, for example, specifies punishment for "disorderly, threatening, insulting language or behavior in public places, and acts which annoy, obstruct, or are offensive to others." A showing of a clear and present danger of substantive harm is presumably not required. In 1939, in a typical prosecution, one Ninfo, a Christian Front street orator, was convicted under this statute for saying "If I had my way, I would hang all the Jews in this country. I wish I had $100,000 from Hitler. I would show those damn Jews what I would do, you mockies, you damn Jews, you scum." See David Riesman, "Democracy and Defamation: Control of Group Libel," *Columbia Law Review*, 42 (1942), pp. 751ff. Riesman discusses not only offensive insults to groups, but the more complex question of group defamation.

6. VanDeVeer, *op. cit.* (footnote 1), p. 180, argues that protection of individuals from (minority) group insults would "open the door to coercive restraint of more or less innocent activities in a way that seems intolerable." The "intolerable" consequence he foresees is indeed daunting: "It is not at all improbable that *some* would be bound to be upset, alarmed, angered, or irritated by the abusive insulting behavior which, as they see it, is involved in jokes about Polish people, Jews, WASPS, women, the Pope, Pakistani families, or references to 'old fogeys,' 'hot-blooded Latins,' 'knee-jerk liberals,' 'fascist conservatives,' 'male egos,' or 'old wives' tales.' " (*Loc. cit.*) These are hardly entailed consequences, however, of the offense principle as judiciously mediated by the balancing tests I have proposed. There are differences in degree in upsets, alarms, anger, and irritation, differences in degrees of "innocence," and social and personal utility. VanDeVeer has given examples of trivial offense produced by free exercise of the highly valuable right of free expression. There is no reason to think the balancing tests would yield such counterintuitive results. Perhaps VanDeVeer is employing the foot-in-the-door version of the slippery slope argument (pardon the mixed-up metaphors) suggesting that unscrupulous legislators and judges might be tempted to misapply the offense principle, but that is another matter.

7. In respect to the billboard example, Michael Bayles points out that it would be unnecessary and uneconomical to prevent such evils by making it a crime to put up lurid billboards. Instead, the legislature could give statutory authority to officials to require that the picture be taken down, reserving punishment and abatement only for disobedience to the order. As Bayles ruefully notes, however, the Model Penal Code would permit imprisonment for up to one year for displaying an obscene billboard! See Michael D. Bayles, "Comments," in *Issues in Law and Morality*, ed. Norman Care and Thomas Trelogan (Cleveland: Case Western Reserve University Press, 1973), pp. 122, 124.

8. It is easy to overstate this point, as I have in the past. (See sources in footnote 2). It is an overstatement to say that "No respect should be shown for abnormal susceptibilities." Rather one should say that the more "abnormal" the susceptibility, the less weight it has on the scales, so that an excessive sensitivity is easily outweighed by a socially valuable activity. On the other hand, one must not neglect to discount the "social value" of the offending activity when it can

be done in such a way as to avoid the offense. VanDeVeer (*op. cit.*, pp. 184–85) gives examples of the numerous ways the law has already found to respect abnormal vulnerabilities without compromising valuable activities: ". . . laws prohibiting blowing automobile horns or otherwise disrupting quiet in hospital zones, as well as requirements that motorists give right of way to blind persons . . . or proper access to public institutions for those in wheelchairs."

9. William L. Prosser, *Handbook of the Law of Torts*, 4th ed. (St. Paul: West Publishing Co., 1971), p. 578. For the bronchitis example, Prosser cites *Judd v. Granite State Brick Co.*, 68 N.H. 185, 37A, 1041 (1804). For the skittish horse example, he cites *Rozell v. Northern Pacific R.R. Co.*, 39 N.D. 475, 167 N.W. 489 (1918).

10. Prosser, *loc. cit.*

11. David A. Conway, "Law, Liberty and Indecency," *Philosophy* 49 (1974): 143.

12. For whatever it is worth, I am cheered by the agreement with this view of the law of nuisance from which I have derived so much stimulation. Prosser reports a case of private nuisance in which the defendant was a tuberculosis hospital and the plaintiff a home owner in the neighborhood. The plaintiff's suit was successful even though the fear of contagion which was the basis of the nuisance was judged by the court to be "unfounded." Virtually all of the home owners in the neighborhood suffered from constant and intense anxiety that interfered with "the enjoyment of their land," and that very real anxiety constituted a nuisance, according to the court, even though unsupported by evidence of danger.

13. The preceding four paragraphs have been taken verbatim from my "Reply" to Michael Bayles in *Issues in Law and Morality*, ed. Norman Care and Thomas Trelogan (Cleveland: Case Western Reserve University Press, 1973), pp. 137–39. Reprinted in my *Rights, Justice, and the Bounds of Liberty* (Princeton, N. J.: Princeton University Press, 1980), pp. 96–109.

14. Prosser, *op. cit.* (footnote 9), p. 597.

15. For classic statements of the value of free expression, see Zechariah Chaffe, *op. cit.* (footnote 4) and Thomas I. Emerson, *The System of Free Expression* (New York: Random House, 1970). For penetrating discussions of the derivation of the right of free expression, see Thomas M. Scanlon's two articles, "A Theory of Free Expression," *Philosophy and Public Affairs*, vol. 1 (1972), and "Freedom of Expression and Categories of Expression," *University of Pittsburgh Law Review* 40 (1979).

16. John Stuart Mill, *On Liberty*, chap. 2.

17. Sometimes linguistic obscenities in the manner of expression are to be classified as essential to what is being expressed, and not merely extra "nose-thumbing" for its own sake. See *Cohen v. California*, 91 S. Ct. (1971) and my discussion *infra*, chap. 11, §1, chap. 13, §6, and chap. 16, §1. On this point my earlier view (*Rights, Justice, and the Bounds of Liberty*, *op. cit.*, pp. 100–102) was mistaken.

18. David Conway, *op. cit.* (footnote 11), pp. 139–40.

19. *Ibid.*, p. 140.

20. VanDeVeer, *op. cit.* (footnote 1), p. 186.

21. Prosser, *op. cit.* (footnote 9), p. 600.

22. *Pace* Chief Justice Warren Burger and the United States Supreme Court majority in *Paris Adult Theatre I v. Slaton*, 413 U.S. (1973).

23. American Law Institute, *Model Penal Code* (Philadelphia, 1962), §251.1.
24. *Ibid.*, §213.5.
25. *Ibid.*, §251.3.
26. Louis B. Schwartz, "Morals Offenses and the Model Penal Code," *Columbia Law Review* 63 (1963): 675.
27. *Ibid.*, p. 673.
28. *Ibid.*, p. 675.
29. Bayles, *op. cit.* (footnote 7), p. 118.

9. Profound Offense

1. Robert Paul Wolff, *The Poverty of Liberalism* (Boston: Beacon Press, 1968), p. 24.
2. Louis B. Schwartz, "Morals Offenses and the Model Penal Code," *Columbia Law Review* 63 (1963), as reprinted in Joel Feinberg and Hyman Gross, eds., *Philosophy of Law*, 2d ed. (Belmont, Calif.: Wadsworth Publishing Co., 1980), p. 215, n. 14.
3. Pa. Stat. Ann. tit. 18, §4211 (1945).
4. Schwartz, *op. cit.* (footnote 2), 210.
5. *Loc. cit.*
6. *Ibid.*, p. 211.
7. *Loc. cit.*
8. For fuller lists of suggested "person-making characteristics," and fuller discussion, see Joseph Fletcher, "Indicators of Humanhood: A Tentative Profile of Man," *Hastings Center Report*, Vol. 2 (1972), Laurence C. Becker, "Human Being: The Boundaries of the Concept," *Philosophy and Public Affairs*, Vol. 4 (1975), Mary Anne Warren, "On the Moral and Legal Status of Abortion," and Michael Tooley, "In Defense of Abortion and Infanticide." The Warren and Tooley articles are both included in *The Problem of Abortion*, 2d ed., ed. Joel Feinberg (Belmont, Calif.: Wadsworth Publishing Co., 1983).
9. Kurt Baier, "The Liberal Approach to Pornography," *University of Pittsburgh Law Review* 40 (1979), p. 620.
10. Baier, *op. cit.*, p. 621, spells out a corollary to this point:

> Disgusting behavior *offends* the senses of those who encounter it because it disgusts them. In such cases, what offends is what disgusts, i.e. the direct physical onslaught on the senses. Disgust, offense to a person, and so a [true] offense, can be avoided by preventing such onslaught. If I love the smell of burnt rubber, I can avoid offending and becoming guilty of an offense by making sure that the smell does not escape and bother my neighbors. I do not offend them by boasting of my unusual predilections or inviting them to sniffing parties. There is no standard of propriety violated by my indulging my taste.

11. For an example of a similar odd conviction, see Bertrand Russell, *Unpopular Essays* (New York: Simon and Schuster, 1950), pp. 75–76:

> I am sometimes shocked by the blasphemies of those who think themselves pious— for instance the nuns who never take a bath without wearing a bathrobe all the time. When asked why, since no man can see them, they reply: "Oh, but you forget the good God." Apparently they conceive of the Deity as a Peeping Tom whose omnipotence enables Him to see through bathroom walls, but who is foiled by bathrobes. This view strikes me as curious."

12. John Stuart Mill, *On Liberty*, chap. 4, para. 12.
13. *Loc. cit.*
14. Kurt Baier, *op. cit.* (footnote 8), pp. 621–22.
15. Louis Schwartz, *op. cit.* (footnote 2), p. 210.
16. J. S. Mill, *op. cit.* (footnote 11). In chap. 4, para. 12, Mill writes:

> . . . the opinion of a majority, imposed as a law on the minority, on questions of
> self-regarding conduct is quite as likely to be wrong as right, for in these cases public
> opinion means, at the best, some people's opinion of what is good or bad for other
> people, while very often it does not even mean that—the public with the most
> perfect indifference, passing over the pleasure or convenience of those whose con-
> duct they censure and considering only their own preference. There are many who
> consider as an injury to themselves any conduct which they have a distaste for, and
> resent it as an outrage to their feelings . . . when does a public trouble itself about
> universal experience? In its interferences with personal conduct it is seldom thinking
> of anything but the enormity of acting or feeling differently from itself . . .

17. H. L. A. Hart, *Law, Liberty, and Morality* (Stanford, Calif.: Stanford University Press, 1963), pp. 46–47.
18. *Ibid.*, p. 47.
19. The antiabortionist whose human sentiments are outraged at the thought of surgical mutilation and destruction of recognizably human "unborn babies," for example, does not express indignation at what is done thereby to his *own* peace of mind. That is precisely why he is not placated by the principle "out of sight out of mind." His offended state of mind, therefore, is more typical of profound offense than of mere aversion to gross, irritating, or embarrassing sights. That is why we should say that his moral sensibility and not merely his delicacy is affronted.
20. In this respect too the offense principle is parallel to the harm principle. Just as the harm principle legitimizes coercion meant to prevent all those harms that are also wrongs to their victims, so the offense principle legitimizes prevention of all those offenses that are also wrongs to *their* victims. Both principles (and there-fore all liberal liberty-limiting principles) are right-protecting principles.
21. M. J. Durey, "Bodysnatchers and Benthamites," *London Journal* 22 (1976) as quoted in Thomas C. Grey, ed., *The Legal Enforcement of Morality* (New York: Random House, 1983), p. 111.
22. N. Wade, "The Quick, the Dead, and the Cadaver Population," *Science*, March 31, 1978, p. 1420. Reprinted in Grey (footnote 21), p. 106.
23. *Loc. cit.*
24. See *inter alia*, Philippa Foot, "The Problem of Abortion and the Doctrine of Double Effect," John Harris, "The Survival Lottery," Richard Trammel, "Sav-ing Life and Taking Life," Nancy Davis, "The Priority of Avoiding Harm," and Bruce Russell, "On the Relative Strictness of Negative and Positive Duties," all in Bonnie Steinbock, ed., *Killing and Letting Die* (Englewood Cliffs, N. J.: Prentice-Hall, 1980).
25. Paul Ramsey, *The Patient as a Person* (New Haven: Yale University Press, 1970), p. 210.
26. *Yome v. Gorman*, 242 N.Y. 395 (N.Y. Court of Appeals, 1926). For reference to this case and all the other materials mentioned in this section on dead body

problems, I am indebted to Professor Thomas C. Grey and his excellent anthology, *The Legal Enforcement of Morality* (New York: Random House, 1983).

27. Willard Gaylin, "Harvesting the Dead," *Harper's Magazine*, Sept. 1974.

28. *Ibid.*, p. 26.

29. *Ibid.*, p. 30.

30. William May, "Attitudes Toward the Newly Dead," *The Hastings Center Studies* I (1972):3–13.

31. *Ibid.*, p. 5.

32. *Loc. cit.*

33. *Loc. cit.*

34. Jesse Dukeminier, "Supplying Organs for Transplantation," *Michigan Law Review* 68 (1968):811.

35. This word for having one's organs taken for transplant without one's consent was introduced by John Harris in his "The Survival Lottery," *Philosophy 50* (1975).

36. May, *op. cit.* (footnote 29), p. 6.

37. Jesse Dukeminier, *op. cit.* (footnote 34).

38. Michael Tanner, "Sentimentality," *Proceedings of the Aristotelian Society* 77 (1976–77):135.

39. May, *op. cit.* (footnote 29), p. 6.

40. When we sympathize with the dead (i.e. with corpses), Smith wrote, "The idea of that dreary and endless melancholy which the fancy naturally ascribes to their condition [or did in an earlier age] arises altogether from our lodging . . . our own living souls in their inanimated bodies, and thence conceiving what would be our emotions in this case." Adam Smith, *The Theory of Moral Sentiments*, 6th ed. (1970). Reprinted in L.A. Selby-Bigge, *British Moralists* (New York: Bobbs-Merrill, 1964), vol. I, pp. 262–63.

41. Stanley I. Benn, "Abortion, Infanticide, and Respect for Persons" in Joel Feinberg, ed., *The Problem of Abortion*, 2d ed. (Belmont, Calif.: Wadsworth, 1983), pp. 135–44.

42. Where there is little perceived difference between the two classes, however, the strain on emotional flexibility may be intolerable. It is hard not to sympathize, for example, with the nurses mentioned by Jane English ("Abortion and the Concept of a Person" in J. Feinberg, ed., *The Problem of Abortion, op. cit.* footnote 40) who were "expected to alternate between caring for six-week premature infants and disposing of viable 24-week aborted fetuses . . ." The danger here, however, is not that the nurses will be brutalized, but that they will be severely distressed or even psychologically damaged.

43. As must be apparent to the reader by now, the concept of an *insult* (or "affront") is central to the discussion of much "profound offense." That critically important concept is subjected to detailed analysis in Chapter 14 below, where the focus is on obscene language. One of the functions of obscene words is to express insults; that is why the concept of insult is analyzed in that chapter. But not all insults involve obscene words and not all obscene words occur in insults. The concept of insulting is of much more general importance.

44. The ostensible occasion of the demonstration that became the main subject of subsequent court hearings was to protest a Skokie Park District requirement that the Nazis post a $350,000 insurance policy as a condition for a permit to use the Skokie parks. The placards and banners to be displayed contained only

such slogans as "Free Speech for the White Man" and "Free Speech for White America." The "pure insult" was conveyed through the symbolism of the swastika and the Nazi uniforms.

45. Letter to the editor, *The Nation*, May 6, 1978 from Gilbert Gordon, Senior Attorney to the Village of Skokie.

46. See especially Carl Cohen's cogent articles in *The Nation:* "Skokie—The Extreme Test of Our Faith in Free Speech," April 15, 1978; his exchanges in the letters to the editor column, May 6, 1978; and "The Case Against Group Libel," June 24, 1978.

47. *Village of Skokie v. National Socialist Party of America.* Ill. Ap. Ct., 1st Div. (July 12, 1977).

48. Zechariah Chafee, Jr., *Free Speech in the United States* (Cambridge, Mass.: Harvard University Press, 1941), pp. 152, 161, 426. A similar view is upheld in *Terminiello v. Chicago* 337 U.S. 1 (1949).

49. *Village of Skokie v. National Socialist Party of America.* (See footnote 46.)

50. The classic statement of the doctrine is in *Chaplinsky v. New Hampshire*, 315 U.S. 568 (1942). I discuss it in detail in Chapter 14, §3, *infra*.

51. This definition of "fighting words" is from *Cohen v. California* (403 U.S. 15, 20, 29 L. Ed. 2d 284, 291, 91 S. Ct. 1780, 1785.)

52. There are more possible examples in this category of the display of deliberately defaced conventional symbols of the kind held to be sacred than there are of the brandishing of conventional symbols regarded as odious. Parading a cross with a naked human figure on it wearing a leering expression on his face and showing obvious manifestations of sexual excitation would be a grotesque desecration and profoundly offensive to the pious. The distinguishing features of this category would be different from those of the category containing swastikas, but both could be distinguished presumably from the instances of symbolic advocacy and mere ugliness or unpleasantness that it is not legitimate to prohibit.

10. The Idea of the Obscene

1. Justice Potter Stewart, concurring opinion in *Jacobellis v. Ohio*, 378 U.S., 184 (1964). Speaking of "hard-core pornography," Stewart wrote: "I shall not today attempt to define [that category] and perhaps I could never succeed in intelligibly doing so. But I know it when I see it . . ."

2. Cf. Louis Henkin, "Morals and the Constitution: The Sin of Obscenity," *Columbia Law Review* 63 (1963):393.

3. Harry Kalven, Jr., "The Metaphysics of the Law of Obscenity," *The Supreme Court Review, 1960*, ed. Philip B. Kurland (Chicago: University of Chicago Press, 1969), p. 2. The development cited by Kalven starts with *U.S. v. Schenck*, 294 U.S. 47 (1919) and extends to *Yates*, 354 U.S. 298 (1958).

4. *Loc. cit.* Kalven refers especially here to Judge Curtis Bok in *Commonwealth v. Gordon*, 66 Pa. D.&C. 101 (1949) and Judge Jerome Frank in *United States v. Roth*, 237 F. 2d, 796 (2d. Cir. 1956).

5. American Law Institute, *Model Penal Code*, §251.4 (1) (1962).

6. The distinction between "aphrodisiac" and "emetic" obscenity was first put in those terms by Judge John M. Woolsey in his celebrated decision in *United States v. One Book "Ulysses,"* 5 F. Supp. 182 (S.D.N.Y., 1934).

7. Bertrand Russell says of this sort of argumentative overkill: ". . . it is a sign of

weakness to combine empirical and logical arguments, for the latter, if valid, make the former superfluous. E.g. 'I was not drunk last night. I had only had two glasses; besides, it is well known that I am a teetotaller.' " Russell's word "superfluous" surely understates the difficulty! See his *History of Western Philosophy* (London: Allen & Unwin, Ltd., 1946), p. 679.

8. *United States v. Roth*, 237 F. 2d 801, n. 2 (2d Cir., 1956).

9. Harry Kalven, Jr., *op. cit.* (footnote 3), p. 41.

10. Put in terms of a metaphor that can be useful if not taken too seriously, a person experiences sexual shame when he or she inadvertently arouses the sleeping "censor" who then inflicts (self-) punishment. A person experiences a "thrill" when he or she deliberately "teases" the censor, or risks awakening him, for the sake of the exciting sensation of danger.

11. Even disgust can be "thrilling." Barbara Tuchman reminds us in *A Distant Mirror* (New York: Knopf, 1978), pp. 587–88, that fifteenth century France, exhausted from a century of war, pillage, and plague, cultivated the morbid. "Artists dwelt on physical rot in ghoulish detail: worms wriggled through every corpse, bloated toads sat on dead eyeballs. A mocking, beckoning, gleeful Death led the parade of the Danse Macabre around innumerable frescoed walls . . . [In dramas] the rape of virgins was enacted with startling realism; in realistic dummies the body of Christ was viciously cut and hacked by the soldiers; or a child was roasted and eaten by its mother." Tuchman sums it up well: "The staging of plays and mysteries went to extremes of the horrid, as if people needed ever more excess to experience a thrill of disgust."

12. Patrick H. Nowell-Smith, *Ethics* (Harmondsworth, Middlesex: Penguin Books, 1954), p. 72.

13. *Ibid.*, p. 84.

14. *Ibid.*, pp. 85–86.

15. Cf. R.M. Hare, *The Language of Morals* (Oxford: Clarendon Press, 1952), pp. 18–19.

16. Nowell-Smith, *op. cit.*, pp. 62–65 *et passim*.

17. Aristotle, *Nicomachean Ethics* I.3.

18. Peter Glassen, " 'Charientic' Judgments," *Philosophy*, April, 1958, pp. 138–46.

19. In Glassen's words: "From χαριεντοσ, genitive of χαριειϲ. '. . . in At[tic Greek] χαριειϲ was very often used of persons, in relation to qualities of mind, *graceful, elegant, accomplished* . . . οι χαριεντεϲ *men of taste, men of education* . . . *op[posed to]* οι πολλϲι. . . .' (Liddell and Scott, *A Greek-English Lexicon*, 6th ed., 1869.)"

20. *Ibid.*, pp. 138, 139.

21. *Ibid.*, p. 142.

22. *Loc. cit.*

23. Glassen's phrase is clearly a pleonasm. The only *faux pas* are charientic. A *faux pas* is to the charientic sphere what a peccadillo is to the moral.

24. This is a point that Russell Baker has appreciated well. In an astute and witty article, reacting to the profound and dismayed attacks by "vastly civilized" writers on the depravities of Times Square, Baker shrewdly diagnoses the outrage behind their use of moral terms as essentially charientic, not moral: "It is a pity the word 'cheesy' has disappeared from American slang, because there is no other that so adequately describes the depravities of Times Square. Its

depravities are the cheesiest I have encountered." Baker's own reaction is not moral outrage so much as leaden depression: "Depression comes in the presence of depravity that makes no pretense about itself, a kind of depravity that says, 'You and I, we are base, ugly, tasteless, cruel and beastly; let's admit it and have a good wallow.' " Baker's conclusion is just right: "What used to be called 'The crossroads of the world' is now a sprawling testament to the dreariness which liberty can produce when it permits people with no taste whatever to enjoy the same right to depravity as the elegant classes. The case against Times Square, then, is not that it is depraved, but that it is so common, so low, so ugly, so vulgar, and because of all these things, so unutterably depressing. Of all the world's great centers of depravity, Times Square is the slum." From Russell Baker, "Sunday Observer: Cheesy," *New York Times Magazine*, April 18, 1976.

25. One apparent exception that is commonly called to my attention are shockingly immoral acts performed deftly, subtly, or gracefully. In these cases our moral sensibilities are shocked not because of the flagrance of the act, not because it is brazen and unapologetic and rubs our noses in what it does, but because it is such a "gross departure" from a norm of propriety, such an extreme deviation from moral norms. Consider three ways in which one can tell a lie: (1) It can be a small departure from the truth expressed by subtle innuendo or slightly misleading suggestion. An observer may disapprove, but he will not be shocked "by an outrageous obscenity." (2) It can be a small departure from the truth expressed in an outright deliberate assertion, a lie so bold, it may seem obscene to the observer. (Nothing subtle about that). (3) It can be an extreme departure from the truth—a "real whopper"—deliberately conveyed for the purpose of deceiving the listener to his disadvantage and the speaker's gain, but implanted by the subtlest suggestion in the listener's mind without blatant assertion. The third case will be a subtly produced obscene lie, but the subtlety is in the technique while the obscenity is in the extent of the violation of the norm, which was not merely disobeyed, but totally defiled.

26. H. L. A. Hart, *Law, Liberty, and Morality* (Stanford, Calif.: Stanford University Press, 1963), p. 45.

27. Robertson Davies, *Fifth Business* (Harmondsworth, Middlesex: Penguin, 1977), p. 40.

28. H. G. Well's "The Time Machine", in *Selected Short Stories* (Harmondsworth, Middlesex: Penguin Books, 1958), pp. 7–83, contains vivid descriptions of the repulsive "Morlocks," fictitious sapient creatures who live in the distant future. They are coldly repellent in appearance much in the manner of cavern fungi. It is interesting to note that Wells cannot avoid the word "obscene" in his description: "I felt a peculiar shrinking from these bodies. They were just the half-bleached color of the worms and things one sees preserved in spirit in a zoological museum. And they were filthily cold to the touch." (p. 49) "You can scarce imagine how nauseatingly inhuman they looked—those pale, chinless faces, and lidless, pinkish-grey eyes!" (p. 53) ". . . this bleached, obscene, nocturnal Thing . . ."(p. 45).

It is interesting to note further, that *mold* (a type of fungus) is likely to seem especially obscene, as indicated in our common extended uses of the words "slime" and "smut."

29. A caveat is required at this point. One can take this kind of obscenity entirely too seriously. Perhaps slugs and toads and rats and bats are "obscene" in tl. expressive and predictive uses of that word, but one should not *endorse* the response of repelled loathing as appropriate without further thought. This point is made with perfect clarity by Ruth Pitter in her poem, "The Bat"—

> Lightless, unholy, eldritch thing,
> Whose murky and erratic wing
> Swoops so sickeningly, and whose
> Aspect to the female Muse
> Is a demon's, made of stuff
> Like tattered, sooty waterproof,
> Looking dirty, clammy, cold.
>
> Wicked, poisonous, and old:
> I have maligned thee! . . . for the Cat
> Lately caught a little bat,
> Seized it softly, bore it in.
> On the carpet, dark as sin
> In the lamplight, painfully
> It limped about, and could not fly.
>
> Even fear must yield to love,
> And pity makes the depths to move.
> Though sick with horror, I must stoop,
> Grasp it gently, take it up,
> And carry it, and place it where
> It could resume the twilight air.
>
> Strange revelation! warm as milk,
> Clean as a flower, smooth as silk!
> O what a piteous face appears,
> What great fine thin translucent ears!
> What chestnut down and crapy wings,
> Finer than any lady's things—
> And O a little one that clings!
>
> Warm, clean, and lovely, though not fair,
> And burdened with a mother's care:
> Go hunt the hurtful fly, and bear
> My blessing to your kind in air.

Ruth Pitter, *Collected Poems* (New York: Macmillan, 1968). Reprinted by permission of the Hutchinson Publishing Group Ltd.

30. Desmond Morris, *The Naked Ape* (New York: McGraw-Hill, 1967), pp. 235ff.

31. *Webster's* 3d gives two general definitions of "obscene," one corresponding to my "offensiveness to the senses and/or lower order sensibilities," the other corresponding to my "offensiveness to higher order sensibilities." That dictionary also gives several more specific definitions that can be subsumed under my second heading: "grossly repugnant to generally accepted notions of what is appropriate," "offensive or revolting as countering or violating some ideal or principle," "repulsive by reason of malignance, hypocrisy, cynical irresponsibility, crass disregard of moral or ethical principles." Kurt Baier gives an example

of what some people in the 1930s called "the ultimate obscenity": ". . . when Mussolini's son raved about the beauty of Abyssinian villages exploding like stars under the impact of his bombs." See "A Liberal Approach to Pornography," 40 *U. Pitt. L. Rev.* (1979).

32. Quoted by *Webster's* 3d from *The Infantry Journal.* Further reference not provided.

33. Quoted by *Webster's* 3d from T. R. Ybarra. Further reference not provided.

34. Don Shannon, "Ball Says Kennedy Approved an Order to Overthrow Diem," *Los Angeles Times,* July 25, 1975.

35. Antony Flew, "The Principle of Euthanasia" in A. B. Downing, ed., *Euthanasia and the Right to Death* (London: Peter Owen, 1969), p. 33.

36. Quoted by *Webster's* 3d from *The New Republic.* Further reference not provided.

37. G. Gunderson, Letter to the *International Herald Tribune,* July 15, 1975.

38. Howard Moody, "Towards a New Definition of Obscenity," *Christianity in Crisis,* January 25, 1965.

39. Still another example of the obscene use of death:

AND NOW–THE ULTIMATE!

A patent has been obtained for a solar-powered talking tombstone!! A tape recorded statement can run for up to two hours. In Canada an entrepreneur proposes to build a pyramid-shaped mausoleum with crypts for 200,000 caskets and niches for 1,000,000 urns. An added feature would be a restaurant at the top of the 534 foot high structure.

From a Bulletin from the Pittsburgh Memorial Society, as quoted by *The New Yorker* under the caption "No Comment Department" (July 12, 1983).

40. Havelock Ellis, *On Life and Sex* (Garden City, N.Y.: Garden City Publishing Co., 1947), p. 175.

41. Vivian Mercier would take public beheading to be the very standard case of obscenity, but then applies that standard in a very interesting way to public sexual intercourse, emphasizing the violation of privacy and dignity as the chief point of analogy. "Watching," he insists, "makes a difference." "I would as soon witness a public beheading as a public copulation . . . If performers were counterfeiting the sexual act, I would probably feel as bored as I do during a prolonged death scene; if they weren't pretending, I would feel that I had no business to be watching. This attitude of mine is not incompatible with keen enjoyment of the visual aspects of sex in privacy. It may seem excessive to feel this uneasiness about voyeurism while watching films as well as live performances, yet I cannot help believing that many people share my squeamishness." The quotations are from Mercier's "Master Percy and/or Lady Chatterley" in *Perspective on Pornography,* ed. Douglas A. Hughes (New York: St. Martin's Press, 1970), pp. 31, 32.

42. The view expressed in this paragraph is suggested by George Santayana in *The Sense of Beauty* (New York: Scribner's, 1896), p. 23 *et passim:* ". . . aesthetic judgments are mainly positive, that is, perceptions of good; moral judgments are mainly negative, or perceptions of evil." What Santayana apparently means is that typically an action succeeds morally when it doesn't fail (e.g. fail by violating a rule or invading a right), but a work fails aesthetically when it

doesn't succeed. An act that has neither good nor bad making characteristics is morally neutral (not bad). An object that lacks both good and bad making aesthetic characteristics is aesthetically poor (bad art).

43. David A. J. Richards, "Free Speech and Obscenity Law: Toward a Moral Theory of the First Amendment," *University of Pennsylvania Law Review*, 123 (1974), pp. 45–91.

44. *Ibid.*, p. 51.

45. *Ibid.*, p. 52.

46. *Loc. cit.*

47. *Loc. cit.*

48. *Ibid.*, p. 56. Richards provides a reference in his footnote 68: "The example of coprophagy occurs in M. De Sade, *120 Days of Sodom* in vol. 2, *The Complete Marquis De Sade* (P. Gillette translation, 1966), pp. 215, 222. De Sade provides other similar examples, such as eating vomit, which someone might find obscene, even if he would not find pornography obscene. *Ibid.*, p. 215." Not finding pornography obscene, presumably, is *all* that Richards shares with De Sade.

49. ". . . the obscene is a subcategory of the objects of shame. Shame is, I believe, properly understood in terms of a fall from one's self-concept in the exercise of capacities which one desires to exercise competently." Richards, p. 51.

50. That is because most of us hold moral principles that attach a certain inviolable sanctity to human nature. Pious persons, of course, also attribute a sacred character to God, and to religious symbols, rites, and sacraments. Sacrilege and profanation of those sacred objects can thus be just as shockingly offensive to religious persons as the blatant abusing or perverting of human nature, yet the word "obscene" is not typically used of profanity and desecration. I think that is because peculiarly religious offensiveness is thought to be "obscene and then some." There is something awesome and frightening about it, as if it were to be followed necessarily by the hushed expectation of lightning bolts and cosmic retribution.

51. Mercier (*op. cit.*, pp. 31–32) cites a Frank O'Connor short story with a plot similar to this example. O'Connor's moral, however, is a more fundamental one. Mercier writes: ". . . I share the view of the narrator in Frank O'Connor's story 'The Man of the World.' Having been persuaded by his friend Jimmy to spy on a young married couple going to bed next door, he doesn't see anything salacious, but as the young wife knelt to pray, he '. . . felt someone else watching us, so that at once we ceased to be the observers and became the observed. And the observed in such a humiliating position that nothing I could imagine our victims doing would have been so degrading.' "

52. In the characteristic response of sardonic amusement lies the germ of ribald comedy—a form of art not to be confused with obscenity. *D* is struck by the incongruity between the behavior of *B* and *C*, on the one hand, and standards of propriety that he, and presumably they, would espouse, on the other. If he looks at the incongruity from the point of view of the violated standards themselves, then his cynical laughter is directed at the foibles of the flagrantly transgressive parties. But in comic ribaldry there is always some ambivalence, and insofar as *D* identifies with the violating parties, to that extent he is poking fun at the standards. That is what contributes the flavor of naughtiness to genu-

ine ribaldry, and (along with glorying in pure incongruity) distinguishes it from mere scornful derisiveness.

11. *Obscenity as Pornography*

1. High on the honor roll of those who have *not* made this pernicious error is the late Paul Goodman, who wrote in his article "Pornography, Art, and Censorship" [reprinted in D. A. Hughes, ed., *Perspectives on Pornography*, (New York: St. Martin's Press, 1970), pp. 42–60] that "The pornographic is not *ipso facto* the obscene" but, rather, simply that which is designed and used for the purpose of arousing sexual desires. But "if the stirring of desire is *defined* [emphasis added], and therefore treated, as obscene, how can a normal person's interest in sex be anything *but* shameful? This is what shame is, the blush at finding one's impulse to be unacceptable. . . . So the court [by treating pornography as *ipso facto* obscene] corrupts. It is a miserable social policy." The honor roll also includes Stanley Edgar Hyman, whose essay "In Defense of Pornography" also is reprinted in the Hughes collection; David A. J. Richards, *The Moral Criticism of Law* (Belmont, Calif.: Wadsworth, 1977); and Frederick F. Schauer, *The Law of Obscenity* (Washington, D.C.: Bureau of National Affairs, 1976).

2. *Cohen v. California*, 403 U.S. 15 (1971).

3. *Ibid.*, p. 20.

4. *Connecticut v. Anonymous*, 34 Conn. Supp. 575, 377 A. 2d 1342 (1977).

5. *Ibid.*, p. 1343.

6. Douglas A. Hughes, ed., Introduction to *Perspectives on Pornography* (New York: St. Martin's Press, 1970), p. xiv.

7. Precisely parallel questions can be raised, of course, about the characteristic features of pictorial art (painting and sculpture) and pornographic pictures.

8. There may be some strange souls, somewhere or other, at some time or other, who have found even dictionaries, cookbooks, and telephone books useful aids to masturbation. See Earl Finbar Murphy, "The Value of Pornography," *Wayne Law Review* 10 (1964):655ff. for some amazing examples. There is hardly any limit to human differences, especially sexual differences. But that fact should not hinder efforts at definition and classification.

9. Anthony Burgess, "What is Pornography?" in Hughes, *op. cit.* (footnote 6), p. 5.

10. Following E. and B. Kronhausen, *Pornography and the Law* (New York: Ballantine Books, 1959).

11. Burgess, *op. cit.* (footnote 9) p. 6.

12. *Loc. cit.*

13. George Steiner, "Night Words: High Pornography and Human Privacy," reprinted in Hughes, *op. cit.* (footnote 6), p. 47.

14. *Ibid.*, p. 98.

15. *Loc. cit.* See also Donald E. Westlake, *Adios Scheherazade* (New York: Signet, 1970), pp. 8–13, for the four basic formulae followed by rote by pornographic fiction writers . . ."practically a blueprint . . . the closest thing to carpentry you can imagine . . . I don't see at all why I couldn't write up the formula and sell it to *Popular Mechanics*" (p. 6).

16. Steiner, *op. cit.*, p. 103.
17. Kenneth Tynan, "Dirty Books Can Stay," in Hughes, *op. cit.* (footnote 6), p. 111.
18. For example, Vivian Mercier, "Master Percy and/or Lady Chatterly," in Hughes, *op. cit.* (footnote 6), p. 24.
19. Tynan, *op. cit.* (footnote 17), p. 112.
20. *Loc. cit.*
21. *Loc. cit.*
22. *Ibid.*, p. 113.
23. Bernard Drew's review in Westchester-Rockland Newspapers (the Gannett chain), November 17, 1975.
24. No doubt a genuine love poem of high literary merit like the biblical "Song of Songs" can be used pornographically, as any kind of thing can be used for a purpose other than that for which it is made and which defines the kind of thing it is. On this see E. F. Murphy, *op. cit* (footnote 8). It is more natural and less dogmatic, however, to classify artful love poems that celebrate the joy of sexual love with pornographic pictorial art that achieves genuine aesthetic merit and to attribute the relative scarcity of the former to the greater difficulty of the genre.
25. In addition, attempts to create art objects, insofar as they are forms of personal expression, have a "special position" on that ground too.
26. In particular, offended states that occur only because of the offended party's abnormal susceptibility to offense are not to count as "very serious" offenses, although they surely are genuine.
27. George P. Elliott, "Against Pornography," in Hughes, *op. cit.* (footnote 6), pp. 75–76.
28. *Ibid.*, p. 76.
29. *Ibid.*, p. 77.
30. *Loc. cit.*
31. See *infra*, chap. 12, §2, 3. Of course expressions of opinion, scientific findings, and the like are also "absolutely protected" by the first amendment. In the Court's verbal usage, genuine works of art, expressions of opinion, and the like are not called "obscene" in the first place. It might have been more natural to say that we have a constitutional right to attempt to create and exhibit works of art, *even obscene ones*, to express political opinions, *even obscenely*, and so on. When the court says that the first amendment does not protect obscenity it means that it does not protect obscene non-art, obscene non-expression, and the like. In particular it does not protect mere erotic stimulants or symbolic aphrodisiacs.
32. I do not wish to imply that there is one position about the punishability or censorship of pornography that all writers called "feminists" hold. Some, like Ann Garry in "Pornography and Respect for Women" (*Social Theory and Practice*, vol. 4, 1978) deny that pornography is necessarily by its very nature degrading to women. Others, like Wendy Kaminer in "Pornography and the First Amendment: Prior Restraints and Private Actions" in *Take Back the Night: Women on Pornography*, ed. Laura Lederer (New York: William Morrow and Co., Inc., 1980), accept the analysis of pornography that I discuss in the text, but deny that it provides a sufficient ground for censorship. The view I attribute to "feminists"

is simply one held by many leading radical feminists, and most frequently and plausibly defended by feminist writers in the 1970s and '80s.

33. Lisa Lehrman, Preface to the Colloquium on Violent Pornography: "Degradation of Women Versus Right of Free Speech," *New York University Review of Law and Social Change* 8, (1978–79), p. 181.

34. The figure estimates are from Sarah J. McCarthy, "Pornography, Rape, and the Cult of Macho," *The Humanist*, Sept./Oct. 1980, p. 11.

35. Ann Garry, *op. cit.* (footnote 32) is persuasive on this point:

> Imagine the following situation, which exists only rarely today: Two fairly conventional people who love each other enjoy playing tennis and bridge together, and having sex together. In all these activities they are free from hang-ups, guilt, and tendencies to dominate or objectify each other. These two people like to watch tennis matches and old romantic movies on TV, like to watch Julia Child cook, like to read the bridge column in the newspaper, and like to watch pornographic movies. Imagine further that this couple is not at all uncommon in society and that non-sexist pornography is as common as this kind of nonsexist relationship. The situation sounds fine and healthy to me. I see no reason to think that an interest in pornography would disappear in the circumstances. People seem to enjoy watching others experience or do (especially do well) what they enjoy experiencing, doing, or wish they could do themselves. We do not morally object to people watching tennis on TV: why would we object to these hypothetical people watching pornography? (p. 419)

I would qualify Garry's account in two ways. First, it is not essential to her point that the two people "love each other," provided only that they like and respect each other. Second, their pleasures will be possible only if the film is well done, in particular keeping at least minimal photographic distance from what is depicted. Otherwise it might arouse anti-erotic repugnance.

36. Norman Mailer, *The Prisoner of Sex* (New York: New American Library, 1971), p. 82.

37. Gloria Steinem, "Erotica and Pornography, A Clear and Present Difference," *MS*, November, 1978, p. 53.

38. *Ibid.*, p. 54. Susan Wendell proposes a similar definition according to which depictions of "unjustified physical coercion of human beings" with some exceptions will count as pornographic even if they are not in any way *sexual*. See David Copp and Susan Wendell, eds., *Pornography and Censorship, Scientific, Philosophical, and Legal Studies* (Buffalo, N.Y.: Prometheus Books, 1983), p. 167. Pornography [all pornography] is to Susan Brownmiller "the undiluted essense of anti-female propoganda"—*Against Our Will: Men, Women, and Rape* (New York: Simon and Schuster, 1975), p. 394. Lorenne Clark takes it to be essential to pornography that it portrays women "in humiliating, degrading, and violently abusive situations," adding that "it frequently depicts them willingly, even avidly, suffering and inviting such treatment." See her "Liberalism and Pornography" in the Copp-Wendell volume, *supra*.

39. Steinen, *op. cit.* (footnote 36), p. 54.

40. Lisa Lehrman, *op. cit.* (footnote 33), pp. 181–82.

41. Kathleen Barry, *Female Sexual Slavery* (New York: Avon Books, 1979), p. 206.

42. Steinem, *op. cit.* (footnote 36), p. 54.

43. The most extreme of these definitions is that of Andrea Dworkin in her "Por-

nography and Grief" in *Take Back the Night: Women on Pornography*, ed. Laura Lederer (New York: William Morrow and Co., 1980), p. 288—"The eroticization of murder is the essence of pornography . . ."

44. Fred R. Berger, "Pornography, Feminism, and Censorship," (Unpublished paper, Philosophy Department, University of California, Davis), pp. 17ff. I am greatly indebted to this scholarly and well-argued essay.

45. *Ibid.*, p. 18.

46. "Defamation [libel or slander] is an invasion of the interest in reputation and good name, by communications to others which tend to diminish the esteem in which the plaintiff is held, or to excite adverse feelings or opinions against him."—William L. Prosser, *Handbook of the Law of Torts* (St. Paul: West Publishing Co., 1955), p. 572.

47. The studies are cited by Berger, *op. cit.* (footnote 43), p. 38.

48. Aryeh Neier, "Expurgating the First Amendment," *The Nation*, June 21, 1980, p. 754.

49. *Loc. cit.*

50. The former major league baseball pitcher Ryne Duren had a brief but distinguished career despite his constant heavy drinking and rowdiness off the field. Only when he was nearing forty did he manage to reform himself with the help of a rehabilitation center. Why did he behave so irrationally—playing, for example, with a constant hangover? "The problem is the image of the macho man who defies everything," he says. "Most of the guys I played with admired anyone who could drink all night and play baseball the next afternoon." *Newsweek*, June 20, 1983, p. 13.

51. Sarah J. McCarthy, "Pornography, Rape, and the Cult of Macho," *The Humanist*, Sept./Oct., 1980, p. 15.

52. *Ibid.*, p. 17.

53. Susan Brownmiller, *Against Our Will: Men, Women, and Rape* (New York: Macmillan, 1975).

54. Quoted by McCarthy, *op. cit.* (footnote 50), p. 17.

55. Kent Greenawalt, "Speech and Crime," *American Bar Foundation Research Journal*, no. 4 (1980), p. 654.

56. Berger, *op. cit.* (footnote 44), pp. 23–24. The study cited by Berger is: Freda Adler, "The Interaction Between Women's Emancipation and Female Criminality: A Cross-cultural Perspective," *International Journal of Criminology and Penology*, 5 (1977):101–12.

57. The Supreme Court's standards of seriousness and dangerousness have been so extraordinarily high, however, that even a magazine article advocating (in a general way) rape might escape constitutionally valid punishment unless it urged *imminent* action against precise victims. In the landmark case *Brandenburg v. Ohio*, 395 U.S. 444 (1969), the court ruled that advocacy of illegal violence may be proscribed only when the advocacy amounts to *incitement* of imminent lawless action. Two conditions must be satisfied for liability. The advocacy must be (1) "directed to inciting or producing imminent lawless action," and (2) likely to succeed in inciting or producing such action.

58. Edward Coke, Second Part of the *Institutes of the Laws of England*, p. 182.

59. John Stuart Mill, *On Liberty*, chap. 3, para. 1. Mill writes: "An opinion that corn dealers are starvers of the poor, or that private property is robbery, ought

to be unmolested when simply circulated through the press, but may justly incur punishment when delivered orally to an excited mob assembled before the house of a corn dealer, or when handed about among the same mob in the form of a placard."

60. This interpretation is persuasively argued by Frederick Schauer in his article "Speech and 'Speech'—Obscenity and 'Obscenity': An Exercise in the Interpretation of Constitutional Language," *Georgia Law Review* 67 (1979).

61. Fred L. Berger, *op. cit.* (footnote 44), p. 28.

62. Sarah J. McCarthy, *op. cit.* (footnote 51), p. 11.

63. On the other hand, it is hard to know how typical is Andrea Dworkin's highly personal response to other people's pornography—". . . pornography silences me . . . pornography makes me sick every day of my life." Panel Discussion, "Effects of Violent Pornography" in "Colloquium on Violent Pornography," *op. cit.* (footnote 33), p. 239.

12. Pornography and the Constitution

1. See, e.g. *Meyer v. Nebraska*, 262 U.S. 390 (1923); *Cantwell v. Connecticut*, 310 U.S. 296 (1940); *Abington School District v. Schempp*, 374 U.S. 203, 253–58 (1963) (Brennan, J., concurring).

2. A wire service press dispatch describes a very typical occasion for interest-balancing in the application of the free exercise clause:

> OAK CREEK, WIS., OCT. 23, 1977 (AP). The folks at the Parkway Apostolic Church believe in making a joyful noise unto the Lord. Some of their neighbors think it's just noise.
>
> In fact, the neighbors were upset enough to get the Common Council in this Milwaukee suburb to make the church subject to the same ordinance that prohibits industries in residential neighborhoods from exceeding a 58-decibel limit.
>
> "We have the only church and school in Oak Creek where voices cannot be raised above 58 decibels," said the Reverend Frank Tamel, pastor of the church. "That's discriminatory."
>
> Admitting that "our people do sing loudly," the minister said, "there's a joyful noise that comes under the heading of worship—if you infringe on that noise, you infringe upon the First Amendment."
>
> The church's band includes guitars, trumpets, and saxophones. There is a 50-person choir and a sound system.
>
> Alderman Dell Nirode reported that at one nearby home it was impossible to carry on a conversation on the patio because of the noise. Most of the complaints have come during summer when windows are open.
>
> The first provision that the church keep the noise below 58 decibels came in September 1976 when the church received permission to expand its educational facilities. Earlier this month, when the church was granted approval to build a school the same limit was stipulated.
>
> Four times last summer, city building inspector George Simmons made unannounced visits to the church, carrying a decibel meter. Each time he found the noise level below 58, but he said a true reading was difficult to obtain because the church service was not a constant noise source. . . .
>
> "You have to expect some noise to come out of a church when you live next door," he said. "It's not a tomb."

While the ordinance so far has not been enforced against the church, Tamel said it might be if enough people complain about the noise level.

He also said biblical stories indicated that the gatherings held by the original Apostles weren't always quiet. "If the Apostles had met in Oak Creek, they would have been disturbing the peace," he said.

No doubt this is a close case, but it is worth noting that the only way it differs from any other public nuisance problem is that the offending practices have a special constitutional standing, a kind of constitutionally certified social value. That would seem to imply that if 58 decibels is the highest permitted noise level for commercial-industrial activities, then the permissible level ought to be somewhat higher for activities that enjoy a first amendment shelter. Apart from that, there is nothing special about the problem, and the unavoidable balancing tests must be applied. How central to the religion of the Apostolic Christian Church are trumpets and amplifiers? How great an inconvenience would it be to require neighbors to leave their homes for one hour on summertime Sundays, or to lower their windows? (Is the offense reasonably avoidable or is there a genuinely captive audience?) One can easily imagine similar tests for the dissemination or exhibition of pornographic materials that affront not the senses but the sensibilities of neighbors and passersby. If the offending materials have first amendment protection as "speech" or expression, that would be a substantial weight on the side of toleration, but if their offensiveness is extreme and not reasonably avoidable, and the like, the weight on the side of prohibition could be even greater.

3. 381 U.S. 479 (1965).
4. 405 U.S. 438 (1972).
5. 394 U.S. 557 (1969).
6. 410 U.S. 113 (1973).
7. Graham Hughes, *The Conscience of the Courts* (Garden City, N.Y.: Doubleday, 1975), p. 56.
8. *Ibid.*
9. L.R. 3 Q.B. 360 (1868).
10. Thomas I. Emerson, *The System of Freedom of Expression* (New York: Random House, 1970), p. 469.
11. See, e.g. *American Civil Liberties Union v. City of Chicago*, 3 Ill. 2d 334, 121 N.E. 2d 585 (1954); *Excelsior Pictures Corp. v. Regents of the State of New York*, 3 N.Y. 2d 237, 144 N.E. 2d 31, 165 N.Y.S. 2d 42 (1957); *People v. Doubleday & Co.*, 297 N.Y. 687, 77 N.E. 2d 6 (1947), *aff'd*, 335 U.S. 848 (1948).
12. L.R. 3 Q.B. at 371.
13. 354 U.S. 476 (1957).
14. *Ibid.* at 488–90.
15. *Commonwealth v. Friede*, 271 Mass. 318, 171 N.E. 472 (1930).
16. *Commonwealth v. Isenstadt*, 318 Mass. 543, 62 N.E. 2d 840 (1945).
17. *Attorney General v. "God's Little Acre,"* 326 Mass. 281, 93 N.E. 2d 819 (1950).
18. *United States v. One Book Called "Ulysses,"* 5 F. Supp. 182 (S.D.N.Y. 1933), *aff'd*, 72 F. 2d 705 (2d Ar. 1934).
19. Similar standards in other cases for determining the seriousness of *harms* would also minimize the seriousness of harms produced by socially useful activities only to rare individuals with unusual vulnerabilities.

20. 354 U.S. at 489.
21. *Ibid.*
22. *Ibid.*
23. *Ibid.* at 487.
24. *Ibid.*
25. Not unless the peculiar term "prurient interest" provides such a test. Some commentators might be tempted to try this approach. They could look up the word "prurient" in an etymological dictionary and learn that it derives from the Latin term that translates "to itch or long for a thing, to be lecherous." Hence, it now means "having lustful ideas or desires." But this doesn't tell us anything about the erotic states characteristically induced by pornography that we didn't already know. It hardly gives us new information that can help us identify erotic materials more accurately.
26. 378 U.S. 184, 197 (1964) (Stewart, J., concurring).
27. *Ibid.* at 197.
28. See, e.g. D. Kronhausen and P. Kronhausen, *Pornography and the Law*, rev. ed. (New York: Ballantine Books, 1964).
29. *Roth*, 354 U.S. at 489.
30. 370 U.S. 478 (1962).
31. 383 U.S. 502 (1966).
32. 370 U.S. at 482.
33. *Ibid.* at 485–86.
34. *Ibid.*
35. *Ibid.*
36. *Ibid.*
37. 383 U.S. 463 (1966).
38. 383 U.S. 502 (1966).
39. 383 U.S. 413 (1966).
40. I owe to Professor Barbara Levenbook the further point that the phrase "average person" may be useless in obscenity contexts. When it comes to prurient appeal, there may be only an "average man" and an "average woman."
41. 383 U.S. at 508.
42. 383 U.S. 463 (1966).
43. 224 F. Supp. 129 (E.D. Pa 1963), *aff'd*, 338 F. 2d 12 (3rd Cir. 1964), *aff'd*, 383 U.S. 463 (1966).
44. 383 U.S. at 468.
45. *Ibid.* at 474–75.
46. 383 U.S. at 418.
47. *Ginzburg*, 383 U.S. at 468.
48. *Ibid.* at 467, quoting *Roth*, 354 U.S. at 495–96 (Warren, C. J., concurring).
49. *Ibid.* at 470.
50. *Ibid.*
51. *Ibid.* at 475–76.
52. *Ibid.* at 470.
53. *Ibid.* at 471, quoting Schwartz, "Moral Offenses and the Model Penal Code," 63 *Columbia Law Review* 669, 677 (1963) (emphasis added).
54. *Ibid.* at 467, quoting *Roth v. United States*, 354 U.S. 476, 495–96 (1957) (Warren, C. J., concurring).

55. *Model Penal Code* §207.10 (Official Draft, 1962).
56. Louis B. Schwartz, "Morals Offenses and the Model Penal Code", 63 *Columbia Law Review*, 669, 678 (1963).
57. *Ibid.* at 677–81.
58. *A Book Named "John Cleland's Memoirs of a Woman of Pleasure" v. Attorney General*, 383 U.S. 413 (1966).
59. 349 Mass. 69, 296 N.E. 2d 403 (1965).
60. 383 U.S. at 418.
61. *Ibid.* at 564–66 (discussing *Griswold*, 381 U.S. 479 (1965).
62. *Ibid.* at 564–66 (discussing *Griswold*, 381 U.S. 479 (1965).
63. 394 U.S. at 565 (emphasis added).
64. 413 U.S. 15 (1973).
65. 413 U.S. 49 (1973).
66. *Miller*, 413 U.S. at 30–34.
67. *Paris Adult Theatre I*, 413 U.S. at 66.
68. *Ibid.* at 68–69.
69. *Miller*, 413 U.S. at 24–26.
70. *State v. Flynt*, No. B-761618 (Com. Pleas Hamilton County, Ohio 1976).
71. Willard Gaylin, "Obscenity," *Washington Post*, Feb. 20, 1977, Outlook section, at 1.
72. 413 U.S. 49, 73–74 (1973) (Brennan, J., dissenting).
73. *Ibid.* at 81.
74. *Ibid.* at 86.
75. *United States v. Harriss*, 347 U.S. 612, 617 (1954).
76. *Paris Adult Theatre I*, 413 U.S. at 88 (Brennan, J., dissenting) citing *Ginsberg v. New York*, 390 U.S. 629, 674 (1968) (Fortas, J., dissenting).
77. *Paris Adult Theatre I*, 413 U.S. at 88 (Brennan, J., dissenting).
78. *Ibid.* at 88–90.
79. *Ibid.* at 91–93.
80. *Ibid.* at 103.
81. 228 Ga. 343, 185 S.E. 2nd 768 (1971).
82. 413 U.S. at 107.
83. *Ibid.* at 108, quoting *Stanley*, 394 U.S. at 565, 566.
84. 413 U.S. 113.

13. Obscene Words and their Functions, I

1. Cf. Peter Farb, *Word Play: What Happens When People Talk* (New York: Bantam Books, 1975), chap. 4.
2. The British still enforce the old common-law offense of "blasphemous libel" for offensive materials that are regarded as obscenely profane. A recent case was the threatened prosecution in 1977 of James Kirkup for publishing in a homosexual magazine his poem "The Love that Dares to Speak its Name." The poem was described by the *London Times* as "about a Roman centurion's homosexual love for Christ at the Crucifixion." Perhaps the poem was both profane and obscene but not because (or not simply because) it used conventionally obscene or profane words and phrases, but rather because the theme of the poem itself (an "idea") is thought to be obscene-profane, quite another matter, and it would

seem, a *less* serious matter. This chapter is restricted to the use of conventionally obscene *language* for whatever purpose.

3. *Webster's New International Dictionary of the English Language*, 2d ed. unabridged (1954). Italics added.
4. *Ibid.*
5. Ernest Hemingway, *For Whom The Bell Tolls* (New York: Bantam Books, 1951), p. 338.
6. *Ibid.*, p. 396. The skeptical soldiers are anti-clerical republicans in the Spanish Civil War. The sentence that follows those quoted above is: "Then someone else said, 'The best thing is to toss a bomb down on him.' "
7. *Webster's, op. cit.* (see note 3).
8. J. G. Frazer, *The Golden Bough: A Study in Magic and Religion* (New York: Macmillan, 1958).
9. *Ibid.*, p. 230.
10. The confusion between the profanation of the sacred and contact with the polluted survives to this day in references to profane terms as "dirty words" and to uses of scatological terms as "profanity."
11. Frazer, *op. cit.* (see note 8), p. 260.
12. *Ibid.*, p. 284.
13. *Ibid.*, p. 285.
14. *Ibid.*, p. 290.
15. *Ibid.*, p. 293.
16. "That a superstition which suppresses the names of the dead must cut at the very root of historical tradition has been remarked by other workers in this field. 'The Klamath people,' observes Mr. A. S. Gatschet, 'possess no historic traditions going further back in time than a century, for the simple reason that there was a strict law prohibiting the mention of the persons or acts of a deceased individual by *using his name.* This law was rigidly observed among the Californians [Indians] no less than among the Oregonians, and on its transgression the death penalty could be inflicted. This is certainly enough to suppress all historical knowledge within a people. How can history be written without names?' " (Frazer, *op. cit.*, p. 297.)
17. *Ibid.*, p. 302.
18. Burgess Johnson, *The Lost Art of Profanity* (Indianapolis and New York: Bobbs-Merrill, 1948), p. 39.
19. *Ibid.*, p. 82.
20. *Ibid.*, p. 83.
21. Robert Graves, *Lars Porsena Or The Future of Swearing and Improper Language*, 2d ed. (London: Kegan Paul, 1927), p. 50.
22. From *The Iliad* (Smith and Miller trans.) as quoted by Johnson, *op. cit.* (see note 18), p. 101.
23. Johnson, p. 86.
24. *Ibid.*, p. 52.
25. *Loc. cit.*
26. *Ibid.*, p. 53.
27. Frederick Pollock, *Spinoza, His Life and Philosophy* (London: C. Kegan Paul & Co., 1880), p. 18.
28. Johnson, *op. cit.* (see note 18), p. 54.

29. Twice in one summer, a number of years ago, my automobile suffered a flat tire within hours of resuming a holiday trip and my hearty exclamation "We're off—like a dirty shirt!" I've never been able since to bring myself to employ that expression in an automobile, although I know, of course, that the words have no causal effect on the tires.

30. Edward Sagarin, *The Anatomy of Dirty Words* (New York: Lyle Stuart, 1962).

31. *Ibid.*, pp. 161–62.

32. *Ibid.*, p. 143.

33. Peter Farb, *op. cit.* (see note 1), p. 95.

34. Sagarin, *op. cit.* (see note 30), p. 152.

35. For a discussion of the way that male hostility toward women insinuates itself into the vulgar vocabulary see Robert Baker, " 'Pricks' and 'Chicks': A Plea for 'Persons', " in *Philosophy and Sex,* edited by Robert Baker and Frederick Elliston (Buffalo: Prometheus Books, 1975), pp. 45–64. The cult of macho, described *supra* chap. 11, §8, is an extreme exaggeration and distortion of the personal insecurity, the resentment of dependence, and sour-grape denigration of females that lies behind much compulsive use of sexual vulgarities.

36. Sagarin, *op. cit.* (see note 30) p. 47. Robert Graves tells the story of "the soldier shot through the buttocks at Loos in World War I who was asked by a visitor where he had been wounded and could only reply 'I'm so sorry, ma'am, I don't know: I never learned Latin." *op. cit.* (see note 21), p. 19.

37. Sagarin, p. 47.

38. *Ibid.*, p. 64.

39. Hemingway, *op. cit.*, p. 306.

40. When obscenities are used constantly, as in army barracks, they lose their shock value and with it the capacity to intensify and confer emphasis. A scholarly discussion of the slang of the British soldier includes a story illustrating how the deemphasizing of the word "fuck" occurs—"From being an intensive to express strong emotion it became a merely conventional excrescence. By adding *-ing* and *—ingwell* an adjective and an adverb were formed and thrown into every sentence. It became so common that an effective way for the soldier to express emotion was to omit this word. Thus, if a sergeant said "Get your fucking rifles!" it was understood as a matter of routine. But if he said "Get your rifles!" there was an immediate implication of urgency and danger." John Brophy and Eric Partridge, *Songs and Slang of the British Soldiers, 1914–1918* (London, 1930), pp. 15ff, quoted by Mencken, *The American Language,* 4th ed. (New York: Alfred A. Knopf, 1946), p. 315.

41. Mencken, p. 563.

42. Graves, *op. cit.* (see note 21), p. 32.

43. One is reminded of the practice of very orthodox Jews who never write the English word "God" but only "G-d." The practice of American publishers until recently of printing only "f---" and "s---" is reminiscent also of primitive name-taboos and the ways in which they are compromised and evaded. One sins only by violating the exact letter of the taboo.

44. Charles L. Stevenson, *Ethics and Language* (New Haven: Yale University Press, 1944), p. 39. Stevenson finds a nicely illustrative example in the "extravaganzas" of Edgar Rice Burroughs where "it is narrated that the Green Men of Mars always express their amusement (even a relaxed, kindly sort of amusement) by

piercing shrieks, and express their anger by hearty laughter." This is something that *we* cannot do given the insurmountable expectations of others based on observations of *human* behavior in all countries. If we trained ourselves to express feelings in the "Martian manner" and warned our friends in advance of our intentions, then we could express amusement by shrieks and anger by laughter *to them*, but in effect we would be speaking a special language or a private code in doing so.

45. Stevenson's general theory of meaning which conceives of meaning as a disposition of words to cause responses in hearers or readers has been widely criticized and is now largely out of favor. There is no need in this work, however, to examine the theoretical underpinnings for the useful distinction we have borrowed from Stevenson, or to endorse or reject them. Some critics, like J. O. Urmson in *The Emotive Theory of Ethics* (London: Hutchinson & Co., 1968), acknowledge that there is a non-descriptive and expressive element in language, but prefer to characterize it as a kind of "force" of language rather than a kind of meaning. We need not get involved in that technical controversy here, since our sole interest is to make, with Stevenson, the modest point that interjections are a part of language, and that conventions of language determine what we can express by means of them. I shall continue to use the phrase "emotive meaning" in the text but in a way that is noncommittal in respect to deeper controversies among philosophers.

46. Stevenson, *op. cit.* (see note 44), p. 72.

47. *Cohen v. California*, 408 U.S. 15 (1971).

48. *Ibid.*, p. 1786.

49. *Loc. cit.*

14. Obscene Words and their Functions, II

1. Burgess Johnson, *The Lost Art of Profanity* (Indianapolis and New York: Bobbs-Merrill, 1948), p. 124.

2. Christopher Fry, *The Lady's Not For Burning: A Comedy* (New York & London: Oxford University Press, 1949), p. 28.

3. *King Henry IV, Part I*, act 1, sc. 2.

4. See David Hume, *An Enquiry Concerning the Principles of Morals*, §VI, pt. I, para. 16.

5. Johnson, *op. cit.* (see note 1), p. 163.

6. *Ibid.*, p. 161.

7. Obscene expressions with *dependent emotive* meaning are the most shocking, and the most likely to lend themselves to pure insults of the fourth category. They shock more because of what they say (e.g. "Eat my shit") than because of the particular words they use to say it.

8. Carl Sagan, *The Dragons of Eden* (New York: Random House, 1977), pp. 52–54. Quoted at length by permission of the publisher.

9. J. L. Austin, "Performative Utterances," in his *Philosophical Papers* (London: Oxford University Press, 1961), pp. 220–40.

10. Similarly, there are many ways of promising that do not involve the use of the work "promise."

11. One such conventional gesture is to extend one's middle finger, an ancient form

314   NOTES

of obscene insult called "giving the finger." Nelson Rockefeller, former governor of New York, won instant notoriety when he gave the finger to a crowd of political hecklers during a campaign speech in the 1960s. In large cities, harried motorists give it to one another every day. The *Dictionary of Gestures* (Metuchen, N.J.: Scarecrow Press, 1975) states that "The extended middle finger or *digitus impudicus* is a phallic symbol. Its use as a semierotic insult is of ancient origin. Diogenes is reported to have insulted Demosthenes with it." (p. 71)

12. *Chaplinsky v. New Hampshire* 315 U.S. 568 (1942).

13. *Ibid.*, pp. 571–72.

14. Thomas I. Emerson, *The System of Freedom of Expression* (New York: Vintage Books, 1970), p. 17.

15. *Ibid.*, pp. 337–38.

16. J. L. Austin's technical term, *op. cit.* (see note 9), pp. 224ff. Austin has many more occasions to speak of infelicitous utterances than of felicitous ones.

17. Peter Farb, *Word Play: What Happens When People Talk* (New York: Bantam Books, 1975), p. 96.

18. *Loc. cit.* Farb's view is derived from that of G. Legman in *Rationale of the Dirty Joke* (New York: Grove Press, 1968), pp. 17–23.

19. Farb's point applies more obviously to *special* anxieties that are denied or "foisted off" in dirty jokes of a very special ("sick") kind. It applies hardly at all to sexually explicit jokes evoking Rabelaisian laughter from persons who do not take ordinary sexual prohibitions seriously and have little anxiety about their enjoyment of sexual pleasures. Legman, who has compiled and classified the definitive collection of dirty jokes from all cultures, seems clearly to have certain very special and very threatening themes in mind when he makes his claim that the principal function of the dirty joke is to allay anxiety: "The folktale or joke . . . represents a protective mechanism whereby the seriousness, and even the physical reality of the situation, can be denied and made light of, by telling it—or by accepting some serious original ancedote describing it—simply as a joke; as something allowing the accumulated tension of living this situation, or telling about it, or listening to it, to relieve itself in the harmless but necessary explosion of laughter. This is perhaps the principal function of the creation of humor, and certainly of the accepting of things as humorous, such as cuckoldry, impotence, homosexuality, castration, death, disease, and the Devil, which are obviously not humorous at all. Sexual humor is a sort of whistling in the dark, like Beaumarchais' Figaro, who 'laughs so that he may not cry'." *op. cit.* (see note 18), p. 18.

Perhaps in our time the best examples of jokes that fit the Legman thesis have nothing whatever to do with the erotic and the excremental, but exploit instead moral prohibitions that are firmer still, and anxieties that are very special indeed. I refer to the "dead baby jokes" currently in circulation on college campuses. For example, "Which is easier to load into a truck, dead babies or bowling balls?" Ans. "Dead babies, because you can use a pitch fork." "Why did the dead baby cross the road," Ans. "It was tied to a chicken." "How do you make a dead baby float?" Ans. "Mix a dead baby and two scoops of ice cream in an electric blender," etc.

20. Max Eastman, *Enjoyment of Laughter* (New York: Simon and Schuster, 1936), p. 49.

21. *Ibid.*, p. 39. The best jokes and witticisms contain both Aristotelian and Kantian elements. Consider the remark in a student's exam book (as recalled by Michael Walzer in *The New York Review of Books*, vol. 26, no. 15, October 11, 1979, p. 6): "Machiavelli stood with one foot in the Middle Ages, while with the other he saluted the rising star of the Renaissance." That funny remark implants a ludicrous image, but it also sets the reader up for one consummation ("and the other in . . .") then surprises him with an unexpected twist.

22. *Webster's New Collegiate Dictionary* (Springfield, Mass.: G. & C. Merriam Co., 1977), p. 1346.

23. Eastman summarizes some of these in a dismissive footnote about "vague mechanics or hydraulics of the brain specially imagined for this purpose" *op. cit.* (see note 20), p. 23: "I refer to theories like that of Herbert Spencer with his idea that laughter occurs only when our nervous energy is prepared to perceive a big thing and a little one follows; the "psychic damming theory" which the Austrian psychologist Lipps built upon Spencer's foundation; and Freud's idea, derived from Lipps, that comic pleasure is due to an 'economy of psychic expenditure.' . . . The sole reason for inventing these legendary systems for the special benefit of laughter is that the comic pleasure occurs when to a serious mind pain seems the natural thing to expect . . ."

24. Arthur Koestler, *Insight and Outlook* (New York: Macmillan, 1949) p. 3.

25. Dewitt Henry Parker, *The Principles of Aesthetics* (New York: F.S. Crofts & Co., 1947), pp. 94–102.

26. Farb, *op. cit.* (see note 17), p. 99.

27. *Loc. cit.*

28. *Ibid.*, p. 100.

29. Legend has it that so many other practical jokes were played on the noble statue in subsequent years that the authorities finally had the offending organ amputated with a hacksaw.

30. In terms of characteristic responses, the contrast between pure and nearly pure pornography, on the one hand, and obscene humor on the other, is especially sharp. The comic and erotic responses are very nearly mutually exclusive. Pornography, even in its famous guise of "comic strips," builds up erotic tension and then leaves it, presumably for a discharge that is triggered outside the work itself, whereas laughter is itself a discharge of tension achieved directly by the comic work. The only laughter characteristically produced by effective (that is, unfunny) pornography are self-conscious giggles and smirks. Cf. Robert Graves's distinction between "the humorously obscene" and "the obscenely obscene," in *Lars Porsena, Or The Future of Swearing and Improper Language*, 2d ed. (London: Kegan Paul, 1927), p. 52.

31. Eastman, *op. cit.* (see note 20), p. 267.

32. *Loc. cit.*

33. *Loc. cit.*

34. *Loc. cit.*

35. *Ibid.*, p. 274.

36. Burgess Johnson, *op. cit.* (see note 1), p. 212.

37. *Loc. cit.*

38. *Ibid.*, p. 213.

39. Peter Farb, *op. cit.* (see note 17), p. 97.

40. Edward Sagarin, *The Anatomy of Dirty Words* (New York: Lyle Stuart, 1962), p. 133.

41. A taboo can be "purely linguistic" in the sense that it applies only to uses of certain words, as opposed to behavior of other kinds (e.g. sexual behavior), but at the same time be a genuine moral rule or rule of manners in a particular community as opposed to (say) a rule of grammar or syntax. Violations of rules of grammar do not shock as infractions of taboos do. The rules they violate are "linguistic rules" of a quite different kind from the "linguistic rules" with which we have been concerned in this chapter, namely, rules of manners or morals that happen to apply to word usage. Grammatical rules tell how to speak a language correctly; word taboos, and other rules of manners, tell how to behave well (politely) when one does so.

15. Obscene Words and Social Policy

1. This point is not without its purely religious exceptions. In many primitive tribes, words normally proscribed as sacrilegiously obscene and prohibited in all ordinary circumstances, are actually required during certain sacred religious ceremonies and crisis situations. Cf. E. E. Evans-Pritchard, "Some Collective Expressions of Obscenities in Africa," *Journal of the Royal Anthropological Institute of Great Britain and Ireland*, vol. 59 (1929), pp. 311–31, and Edward Sagarin, *The Anatomy of Dirty Words* (New York: Lyle Stuart, 1962), pp. 23–25.

2. Gershon Legman, *Rationale of the Dirty Joke* (New York: Grove Press, 1968), espec. chap. 14. In contrast, Sagarin, *op. cit.* (see note 1), p. 15, prefers the more exactly antonymous Greek "cacophemism," and credits the latter term to Allen Walker Read who first used it in his *Lexical Evidence from Folk Epigraphy in Western North America: A Glossarial Study of the Low Element in the English Vocabulary* (Paris: privately published, 1935), p. 11. (This book was republished in 1977 under the somewhat less euphemistic title *Classic American Graffiti* by the Maledicta Press of Waukesha, Wisconsin.) As far as I can tell, Sagarin means the same by "cacophemism" as Legman means by "disphemism." Neither writer makes the distinction proposed above in the text which employs the two terms as contrasting.

3. Read, *op. cit.* (see note 2), p. 13.

4. William Safire, "On Language," *New York Times*, Sept. 25, 1981.

5. H. L. Mencken, *The American Language*, 4th ed. (New York: Alfred A. Knopf, 1946), espec. chap. 6.

6. This term is traced by Mencken to the slang at eastern women's colleges in the 1930s. The term for toilet used at Vassar in the 1920s was "The Fred." See also Sagarin, *op. cit.* (see note 1), p. 73.

7. When my four-year-old son in conversation with a neighboring child referred to his "penis" in the same casual straightforward way he might refer to his arm or leg, he was puzzled when the other child replied that his mother had said that "penis" is a naughty word. "What is a naughty word?," he later asked his mother.

8. H. L. Mencken, *op. cit.* (see note 5), pp. 284–89.

9. If this projection seems exaggerated, consider H. L. Mencken's chronicle of Victorian America:

When Captain Frederick Marryat . . . came to the United States in 1837, he got into trouble. . . . Gazing upon the wonders of Niagara Falls with a young woman acquaintance, he was distressed to see her slip and bark her shin. As she limped home he asked, 'Did you hurt your *leg* much?' She turned from him 'evidently much shocked or much offended', but presently recovered her composure and told him gently that a *leg* was never mentioned before ladies: the proper word was *limb*. . . . In the same way *pantaloons* became *nether-garments* or *inexpressibles;* stockings yielded to *hose;* . . . *breast* became *bosom; lady* took the place of the too frankly sexual *wife; bull* became *cow-creature* (more commonly *cow-critter*); . . . *to go to bed* became *to retire;* servant girls ceased to be *seduced* and began to be *betrayed;* and *stomach*, then under the ban in England, was transformed by some unfathomable magic, into a euphemism for the whole region from the nipples to the pelvic arch. The '30s and '40s saw the Golden Age of euphemism. *Bitch, ram, boar, stallion, buck,* and *sow* virtually disappeared from the written language, and even *mare* was looked upon as rather racy . . . and *to castrate* became *to change, to arrange,* or *to alter*, even on the farm. *Chair* was abandoned for *seat*, which presently began to be used for *backside* too, and so became obscene itself. To use the word *shirt* in the presence of a woman was 'an open insult'. The very word *woman* became a term of reproach, comparable to the German *mensch*, and the uncouth *female* took its place. But even *female*, after a while, acquired a bad name, and when Vassar was established in 1861, under the name of Vassar *Female* College, the redoubtable Mrs. Sarah Josepha Hale, editor of Godey's Lady's Book, protested loudly, and *female* was expunged. Any hint of sex, in those delicate days, was forbidden. Even the word *decent*, if applied to a woman, was indecent. [Mencken, *op. cit.* (see note 5), pp. 302–303.]

Mencken describes the climax of this development: "In 1931 the Chattanooga police, on arresting a man for picking up a streetwalker on the street, announced that he was charged with 'walking the streets accompanied by a woman', and it was so reported in the local papers." (p. 304). The word "woman" thus seems to have run an erratic course, from a neutral term to a slightly shady cacophemism for an adult female person to a euphemism for "prostitute"!

10. Sagarin, *op. cit.* (see note 1), pp. 173–74.
11. Even various "positive attitudes" toward sex can generate powerful "negative attitudes" toward sexual obscenities. Robert Graves comments that it is "difficult to determine how far this [the sexual] taboo is governed by the sense of reverence, and how far the feeling is one of disgust and puritanical self-hate." *Lars Porsena or The Future of Swearing and Improper Language*, 2d ed. (London: Kegan Paul, 1927), p. 19. A person who takes the "sacramental attitude" toward sex once advocated by Havelock Ellis [*On Life and Sex: Essays of Love and Virtue*, vol. I (Garden City, N.Y.: Garden City Publishing Co., 1947), pp. 68–69] would find the word "fuck" repugnant in precisely the same way a religious person would be offended by sacrilege, not because he thinks sex is wicked or disgusting.
12. Peter Farb explains why the elimination of the very possibility of linguistic obscenity is the goal of so many writers: "Many scholars have concluded that [having word taboos] is not a hallmark of refinement and civilization but rather a wound in the body of language. When a speech community isolates certain words and designates them as taboo, it debases natural things like sexual intercourse and the bodily functions; it spreads guilt by causing people to repress

words and even any references at all to the natural acts of the body these words
describe; it encourages the exhibitionist, who then goes out of his way to use
the taboo words; and it provides an excuse for low forms of scatological and
sexual humor." *Word Play: What Happens When People Talk* (New York: Bantam
Books, 1975), p. 92.

13. *Ibid.*, p. 105.
14. Read, *op. cit.* (see note 2), p. 14.
15. *Ibid.*, p. 10.
16. *Ibid.*, p. 12.
17. *Loc. cit.*
18. "The only way a taboo can actually be broken is to use a word unemotionally in
its simple literal sense." *Ibid.*, p. 13.
19. *Ibid.*, p. 14.
20. *Ibid.*, p. 15.
21. Bertrand Russell, *Marriage and Morals* (New York: Liveright Publishing Corpo-
ration, 1929), pp. 105–106.
22. Cf. Mencken, *op. cit.* (see note 5), p. 313: "In 1931 . . . L.W. Merryweather
observed that '*hell* fills so large a part in the American vulgate that it will
probably be worn out in a few years more', and in anticipation of this catas-
trophe he suggested that the divines of the land be invited to propose a suitable
successor to it. But it continues in daily use, and there is every reason to believe
that it will go on indefinitely."
23. Graves, *op. cit.* (see note 11), pp. 52–53.
24. Burgess Johnson, *The Lost Art of Profanity* (Indianapolis and New York: Bobbs-
Merrill, 1948), p. 167.
25. *Ibid.*, p. 190.
26. *Ibid.*, p. 212.
27. Alfred George Gardiner, as quoted by Johnson, *ibid.*, p. 168. The Dumas
character is Planchet in *The Viscount de Bragelonne.* "Malaka!" is a word he uses
"only in the direst need."
28. On this point Johnson seems to have the truth exactly upside down when he
writes that "The chief trouble in this creative business is that the art of profane
ejaculation, like the other arts, must provide emotional relief for the swearer, as
well as emotional shock to the swearee, and only the second can be gained by
meaningless terms." Johnson, *op. cit.* (see note 24), p. 172.
29. The popularity of this epithet among Americans has long been a source of
amazement to foreigners. Mencken expresses his contempt for the phrase:

> . . . we have nothing properly describable as a vocabulary of indecency. Our
> maid-of-all-work in that department is *son-of-a-bitch*, which seems as pale and ineffec-
> tual to a Slav or a Latin as *fudge* does to us. There is simply no lift in it, no shock, no
> sis-boom-bah. The dumbest policeman in Palermo thinks of a dozen better ones
> between breakfast and the noon whistle. The term, indeed, is so flat, stale, and
> unprofitable, that when uttered with a wink or a dig in the ribs, it is actually a kind
> of endearment, and has been applied with every evidence of respect by one United
> States Senator to another. Put the second person pronoun and the adjective *old* in
> front of it, and scarcely enough bounce is left in it to shake up an archdeacon.
> Worse, it is frequently toned down to *s.o.b.*, or transmogrified into the childish
> *son-of-a-gun.* The latter is so lacking in punch that the Italians among us have bor-

rowed it as a satirical name for an American: *la sanemagongna* is what they call him, and by it they indicate their contempt for his backwardness in the art that is one of their great glories. In standard Italian there are no less than forty congeners of *son-of-a-bitch*, and each and every one of them is more opprobrious, more brilliant, more effective. In the Neapolitan dialect there are thousands. [Mencken, *op. cit.* (see note 5), pp. 317–18.]

I can only reply lamely that such as it is, this phrase is one of the best we have. It would be folly to pull its last remaining teeth.

16. Obscene Words and the Law

1. Burgess Johnson, *The Lost Art of Profanity* (Indianapolis and New York: Bobbs-Merrill, 1948), p. 28.
2. A point recognized even by the Supreme Court: "Some uses of even the most offensive words are unquestionably protected." Justice Stevens in *Federal Communications Commission v. Pacifica Foundation*. (See note 10.)
3. *Cohen v. California*, 91 S. Ct. (1971) at 1784.
4. Even in its own moral terms the paternalistic argument may be self-defeating. It might well be the case that a certain amount of exposure to obscene utterance is needed in order to maximize a delicate person's sensitivity. If she almost never encounters obscene utterances, she will be more likely to respond with surprise or astonishment than with genuine shock.
5. Among others, see E. and B. Kronhausen, *Pornography and the Law* (New York: Ballantine Books, 1964), pt. III, "The Psychology of Pornography."
6. American Law Institute, *Model Penal Code*, Proposed Official Draft of May 4, 1962 (Philadelphia, 1962), pp. 224–25.
7. We can assume that this includes merely *dangerous* conduct, that is, actions that create unreasonable *risks* of harm.
8. An earlier draft of 250.4 made criminal "attempts to harass another by repeated telephone calls . . ." A comment in the final official draft explains that the earlier language was revised "to take account of criticism of the earlier draft because it proscribed only 'repeated' telephone conversations, thus failing to reach the culprit caught making a single abusive call, or one who calls several people indiscriminately but none repeatedly." *Op. cit.* (see note 6), p. 225. These are reasons of a quite different order from those given in the text. The argument in the commentary is not that a single obscene message is a much magnified offense when delivered over the phone, but rather that slight as it may be as an offense to its victim, there are strong practical reasons for making it a crime anyway: (1) that it is an unreasonable burden on law enforcement to require the police to provide evidence of two or more calls, especially when they have caught the culprit red-handed in his first call, and (2) that the guilt of a person who makes many obscene calls but no more than one to a customer is out of all direct proportion to the degree of offense caused to any one victim. The second argument implies that offense is not additive in these circumstances but that guilt is, a claim that seems very doubtful. The malicious culprit who harasses one victim with a hundred calls, other things being equal, is *more* culpable morally than the prankish culprit who pesters one hundred different victims with as many calls. One's conscience may prevent one from causing a

great lot of distress to any person, while permitting one to cause a little bit of distress to a great many persons.

9. The Texas Penal Code Art. 476 (1948) requires "vulgar, profane, obscene or indecent" language. The Virginia Code §18.1-238 (1960) outlaws calls that abuse . . . or use vulgar, profane, or indecent language." The Indiana statute at §10-1511 (1956) does not require obscene language but does require *repeated* calls "for the purpose of annoying, molesting, or harassing." The Wisconsin statute at §947.01(2) (1958) is among the toughest, requiring neither obscene language nor repeated calls, but outlawing even a single call if made "with intent to annoy another."

10. *Federal Communications Commission v. Pacifica Foundation*, 438 U.S. 726 (1978).

11. Justice Powell in his concurring opinion apparently finds the statement of such impact to be self-evident, especially when dogmatically reiterated:

> Thus, children may not be able to protect themselves from speech which, although shocking to most adults, generally may be avoided by the unwilling through the exercise of choice. At the same time, *such speech may have a deeper and more lasting effect on a child than on an adult* . . . The Commission properly held that the speech from which society may attempt to shield its children is not limited to that which appeals to the youthful prurient interest. *The language involved in this case is as potentially degrading and harmful to children as representations of many erotic acts.* (Emphasis added.)

Justice Powell offers no explanation of how mere words can have such devastating effects.

12. Justice Brennan spells this out: "The words that the Court and the commission find so unpalatable may be the stuff of everyday conversation in some, if not many, of the innumerable subcultures that comprise this nation. Academic research indicates that this is indeed the case . . . As one researcher concluded, 'words generally considered obscene like 'bullshit' and 'fuck' are considered neither obscene nor derogatory in the [black] vernacular except in particular contextual situations and when used with certain intonations.' The quotation is from C. Bins, "Toward an Ethnography of Contemporary African-American Oral Poetry," *Language and Linguistic Working Papers*, (Washington, D.C.: Georgetown University Press, 1972), no. 5, p. 82.

13. It would seem at first sight that the new phenomenon of "dial-a-porn" telephone service falls half way between the clearer examples of radio-TV and telephone communications. On the one hand, the messages enter the home via phone and would seem subject to prohibition on that ground if they are "obscene," especially since children who have learned the number may gain access to them. On the other hand, the entry into the home of these pornographic messages is entirely initiated by the receiver of the messages, and is thus even further removed from harassment than ordinary radio and TV. On balance, the case for prohibition on a nuisance theory seems weak. The availability of the phone "service" does not seem overly to tax the disciplinary capacities of parents.

14. "Note—Filthy Words, The F.C.C., and the First Amendment: Regulating Broadcast Obscenity," *Virginia Law Review*, vol. 61 (1965), p. 617.

Index